THE MODERN RESEARCHER, REVISED EDITION

THE MODERN RESEARCHER

REVISED EDITION

Jacques Barzun & Henry F. Graff

Harcourt, Brace & World, Inc.

New York   Chicago   San Francisco   Atlanta

$$\frac{D}{13}$$
$$.B34$$
$$1970$$

ISBN: 0-15-562510-1 / paperbound
0-15-161482-2 / hardbound
Library of Congress Catalog Card Number: 72-115861

Printed in the United States of America

The authors wish to thank the following copyright holders for the privilege of quoting from their works:

The Clarendon Press, Oxford—for the passage from *History of the Elizabethan Stage,* Volume 1, by E. K. Chambers, copyright 1923.

Lord Oxford—for the passage from *On Englishing the Bible* by Mgr. Ronald A. Knox, copyright 1949; published in the United States by Sheed and Ward as *Trials of a Translator,* copyright 1949.

The Macmillan Company—for the passage from *The Age of the Great Depression* by Dixon Wecter, copyright 1948 by the Macmillan Company; for the passage from the article, "Anthropology," in *The Encyclopedia of the Social Sciences,* edited by E. R. A. Seligman, copyright 1930 by the Macmillan Company.

Routledge & Kegan Paul Ltd.—for the passage from *The Letters of Saint Evremond,* edited by John Hayward, copyright 1930.

The H. W. Wilson Company—for a representative column of entries from the *Readers' Guide to Periodical Literature,* Vol. 69, No. 4 (April 10, 1969).

Every one of you gentlemen, every thinking man generally, is always searching for sources and is, in practice, an historian. There is no other way to understand the events that take place before your eyes. Every business man who handles a complicated transaction, every lawyer who studies a case, is a searcher for sources and a practicing historian.

—Theodor Mommsen
Rectorial Address at the
University of Berlin, 1874

This revised edition
is dedicated with
renewed (but unrevised) affection
to
JOHN ALLEN KROUT

Note on the Revised Edition

The reception of this book, not alone by college students and their instructors, but by readers from all walks of life, has encouraged us to prepare a new edition. We were naturally glad to undertake a piece of work which not only would extend the life and use of the book, but also would allow us to consider its contents afresh and enable us to bring our treatment up to date.

Yet we were somewhat apprehensive about the danger of spoiling previous work done right. Certainly the order and proportion of our combined purposes must not be touched, those purposes being to guide and instruct the student in the arts of research and writing. On close review we also came to think that certain of our examples from history could be replaced only at the cost of losing features important to instruction and memorableness. So those too must remain, together with such statements of truth and practical advice as we thought definitive, for the simple reason that we saw no way to enhance their logic or lucidity.

These passages once identified, we set about raising the remainder nearer to the ideal mark we had in mind. Numerous points were given new illustration or embellishment from recent events; many others were added in order to make the book helpful and persuasive to an even greater number of readers; still others were supplied to make our specimen cases more compelling. Hardly a page was left without improvement in some respect or other, as we corrected details or sharpened expression.

Our principles are unchanged, but we have given them new extension by taking up social facts and cultural tendencies that had not emerged fifteen years ago. In the light of these developments we have reexamined the aim and art of the historian; and after scanning a decade and a half of new attempts and achievements, we offer estimates of the latest methods proposed to the modern researcher: the computer, the "model," and the ancillary techniques of psychiatry, anthropology, and sociology.

Finally, we have made a selection from among the many new books and articles published since 1956 on the great variety of subjects we deal with. Reference to these publications is made at the appropriate places in the footnotes, and a further substantial group of titles is distributed throughout the bibliography. Our text has put on more bulk, but we hope and believe that it is as handy as before, and—despite the larger number of matters taken up—as fluent. All its topics and their interplay have been made more accessible by means of a fuller index.

What the general reader and professional student of this edition will find reaffirmed without change is the point of view about historical writing, whether in the form of the modest report or of the full-blown book. We continue to believe that most ordinary writing includes narrative portions that are history-writing. We continue to believe that all history is one, because the human race is one. Subject matter may differ from west to east, from recent to remote, but the retelling of what happened calls for the same procedures and judgments. Moreover, the narrative and analytic arts that we call history are open to anyone who can read, write, and think: they require application and intelligence, but, unlike the sciences, no mathematics or machinery. In short, historiography is but an extension, without change of nature, of the simple utterance: "I was there; I saw it; let me tell you about it."

We are grateful to the readers who took the trouble to write to us, whether in approval or correction, and we invite our readers new and old to continue giving us assistance and pleasure in the same way.

Jacques Barzun
Henry F. Graff

Columbia University
December 15, 1969

Acknowledgments

The authors have been greatly encouraged in the writing of this book by their colleagues in the Columbia University History Department. Some of them, and others outside the Department and the University, have been kind enough to read all or parts of the manuscript. It is an inadequate measure both of the debt incurred and of the sense of obligation felt simply to name them, for without their kind vigilance the text would be much more imperfect than it is. Our gratitude accordingly goes to:

Crane Brinton, David Donald, Peter Gay, Richard Hofstadter, Mrs. Lewis Webster Jones, Garrett Mattingly, George T. Matthews, Dwight C. Miner, Richard B. Morris, Ernest Nagel, Fritz Stern, Wendell H. Taylor, Lionel Trilling, John Neal Waddell, Robert C. Waddell, Constance M. Winchell, Henry H. Wiggins, and John H. Wuorinen.

We are happy to acknowledge a further debt to our friends and colleagues for their help in the preparation of this new edition. We owe much to Donald C. Anthony, Hubbard W. Ballou, Joseph P. Bauke, Harry Boardman, Harold L. Burstyn, David Donald, Rita G. Keckeissen, Maxwell H. Kolodny, Cecile E. Kramer, Roger H. Nye, Paul Seabury, Eugene P. Sheehy, Wayne Somers, Jerome L. Sternstein, Maurice F. Tauber, Constance M. Winchell, Herbert I. Winer, and C. Vann Woodward.

We have drawn on the expert secretarial assistance of Violet Serwin and Virginia Brown—supplemented by the special help of Ellen T. Graff—and on Virginia Xanthos Faggi for the preparation of the index.

Contents

Part III. *Writing*

List of Figures

Foreword

This book is for anyone who is or will be engaged in research and report-writing, regardless of his field of interest. The work is planned on unconventional lines because the authors have found in their experience as teachers and editors that the needs of writers and researchers—whether in college or graduate school, in business or the professions—are met neither by the usual "Introduction to Research" nor by the usual "How to Write" book. Rather, the need is for a new view of the single subject, Research-and-Report, which these conventional manuals split apart. In academic life, the fallacy of the split is expressed in the impatient outcry: "Why doesn't the English Department teach them how to write?"

The authors are historians who sympathize equally with the English Department, with the universal demand for better writing, and with all those who, soon or late in their education, try to master at once the techniques of research and the art of expression. What such persons need, clearly, is a manual of combined operations. It must be designed to give not so much a set of rules as an insight into what the mind is about when it searches for facts in library books and prepares a report on its findings for the inspection of other men.

To carry out its purpose, this book concentrates on principles of thought and the analysis of difficulties. It illustrates both theory and practice by examples from many fields, and it shows how methods of work, that is, devices of investigation and expression, follow from the characteristic features of typical problems. These devices, it need hardly be said, are the general ones of scholarship, not the particular ones of statistical and mathematical work, or the laboratory and field techniques of testing and interviewing. The present book, in short, aims at imparting the fundamentals of informed exposition.

The scheme of the work is accordingly simple. Any researcher's first question is: What kinds of aids—indexes, bibliographies, dictionaries, catalogues, monographs—are there accessible to me? And his next is: How can I make them yield just so much of their information as I want? The technique for satisfying these wants is universal and it is teachable. Its rudiments are set forth here with examples and graphic illustrations.

The digging and delving once done, the next step is to verify one's data. This soon takes one from the mechanical part of research to the intellectual. On that plane, questions arise that are too important as well as too interesting to be disregarded: What is the nature of the "story" we recover from records? How far can we trust our sources? What is the effect of bias? the mechanism of causation? the value of philosophic systems? If every researcher produces a different picture from the same sources, and if on large subjects rival interpretations continue to flourish, how can the reader of history and biography escape confusion and ultimate skepticism?

Such ideas as these may not cross the mind of the researcher as he works at a limited project for an immediate purpose—a report on the operation of a business or an army camp, a study of divorce statistics or of consumer tastes. But at some time or other the query "What is truth?" will occur to any seeker after facts or will be put to any man who reports: "This is what happened."

Well before such a writer or speaker is challenged he will have run into the problem of exposition. The facts *never* "speak for themselves." They must be selected, marshaled, linked together, and given a voice. Moreover, research is not an end in itself. The day comes when the pleasures of the detective hunt are over and the report must be written. At that point, fit expression no longer appears as a mere frill added to one's accumulation of knowledge. The expression *is* the knowledge. What is not properly presented is simply *not present*—and its purely potential existence is quite useless.

Except in the rare cases where formulas and graphs can stand alone, the sole carriers of information are words, and these, as everybody knows, are hard to handle. Not only is it difficult to make words agreeable to read and impressive enough to remember; it is also difficult to make them reveal the exact contours of the facts and thoughts one has unearthed—to make them say what one means.

This book does not profess to make good writers by rule and precept, but it does attempt to show how skillful expression is connected throughout with the technique of research and the art of thought. Understanding a text and taking notes on it require the same attention to words and meanings as preparing and polishing a report. Whoever attains skill at the one and is a good researcher can develop skill at the other and become a good report-writer. Having begun by showing how the critical mind works on sources, we conclude by detailing systematic ways in which anyone—the student, the government expert, the lawyer, the journalist, the business executive, the editorial assistant, the club secretary, the man of science, as well as the professional scholar or the scholar-in-spite-of-himself—can criticize and improve his writing and make his report come closer to the reality he has discovered by research.

J. B.
H. F. G.

PART I

First Principles

1

Research and Report
as Historian's Work

The Report: A New and Fundamental Form

In a once famous book on the Middle East, the English archeologist Layard printed a letter in which a Turkish official answered an Englishman's question. It begins:

My Illustrious Friend and Joy of My Liver!
The thing you ask of me is both difficult and useless. Although I have passed all my days in this place, I have neither counted the houses nor have I inquired into the number of the inhabitants; and as to what one person loads on his mules and the other stows away in the bottom of his ship, that is no business of mine. But, above all, as to the previous history of this city, God only knows the amount of dirt and confusion that the infidels may have eaten before the coming of the sword of Islam. It were unprofitable for us to inquire into it. O my soul! O my lamb! Seek not after the things which concern thee not. Thou camest unto us and we welcomed thee: go in peace.[1]

This unruffled public servant obviously made no annual report

[1] Austen H. Layard, *Discoveries in the Ruins of Nineveh and Babylon ...*, London, 1853, 663.

3

of any kind to anybody—those were the good old days. At the distance of a century it is interesting to note the three things that he so courteously declined to provide. They are: vital statistics, business reports, and history. Life as we know it today would stop if information of these three kinds were not readily to be had on every sort of subject. All over the globe, every moment of the day, someone is being asked to make a search and write a report on some state of fact, or else to read and analyze one, so that action may be taken. Reports are the means by which we try to substitute intelligence for routine and knowledge for guesswork.

This characteristic behavior of modern man makes "the report" fundamental in the conduct of affairs. It has become a familiar form, like the business letter or the sonnet.

Every report implies previous research, whether by the reporter or by someone else. Thousands of men not connected with academic life are thus turned into more or less able scholars. The Turkish official of today has dropped his hookah, leaped from his cushion, and is busy counting the houses for the Ministry of the Interior. The figures he gathers are then published as government statistics, which other researchers will use for still other reports—from the university student writing a paper on modern Turkey to the foreign businessman who wants to establish a branch office in that country.

Among the many useful documents that may strictly or loosely be classed as reports there is no essential difference of outlook or method. The student writing a book report for a Freshman English course is doing on a small scale and with a single source the same thing as the president of a corporation who prepares his annual report to the stockholders, or as the President of the United States when, with the aid of all his departments, he reports to the people on the state of the Union. Scope and purpose will of course differ, and this affects the worth of the report as an historical record. But the general form and the devices employed are identical in all three. The reader will readily think of other examples of the same truth.

The common element in all these tasks is that they present similar problems of investigation and exposition, which are solved in similar ways. Moreover, the writers of reports draw upon the same vast reservoir of information. Apart from the special facts that, to pursue the examples above, the treasurer of a corporation or the Secretary of State supply to their respective presidents, the written sources for the millions of words uttered in reports are the familiar ones—newspapers, learned journals, histories, statistical abstracts, law cases, state papers, and so on through the many categories of books found in great libraries. This huge accumulation is what the researcher must learn to use in order to satisfy his particular need. And as the conditions of the search are common to all researchers, it is possible to discuss research and reporting regardless of their occasion or subject.

The Historical Attitude Underlies Research *and* Report

To regard the report as a form is further justified by the fact that the attitude and technique of the report-writer are derived in a straight line from one of the great literary and academic disciplines— History. It is from historical scholarship—originating with the antiquarian—that the world has taken the apparatus of footnotes, references, bibliography, and so on, which have become commonplace devices, not to say household words. It is from the historical study of texts by philologists and historians that writers at large have learned to sift evidence, balance testimony, and demand verified assertions.

At this point someone may object that there remains a great difference between the scholar's main interest and that of the ordinary report-writer. The former seeks to know the past; the latter is concerned with the present, generally with a view to plotting the future; hence their outlooks must be quite different. This difference is more striking than significant. Whatever its purpose, a report is invariably and necessarily historical. Insofar as it reports facts it gives an account of the past. Recorded opinions obviously belong to what has gone before, to history. Suppose a study of American foreign policy designed solely to change future action. It can do so only by criticizing principles or personnel: but to do this its arguments must lean on the evidence of what has been happening—on what is past, recorded, and beyond the reach of change. What else is this but a piece of history?

The same holds true when a report is, as we say, "purely fact-finding," for example, a survey of the conditions of the public schools in a certain town. This description of "the present" is actually a description of the past—recent it may be, but nonetheless a backward glance. Only events already gone by can disclose the prevailing state of things. Even the unassuming book report is a record of the past. It records, to begin with, what the student thought and felt at 2 A.M. the day it was due. Further, it is part autobiography, part criticism, and part literary history. The book was probably read earlier and compared with still older experiences; and the words of the book, which the report may quote, refer to a yet more remote past. Whatever else it is, every report is historical and cannot avoid being so.

The way the historian goes to work and his attitude toward sources are parts of the report-writer's equipment, no matter what his subject may be—literary, economic, political, scientific, or anything else that belongs among serious recitals of fact.

Historical Writing in Daily Life

A few examples of the generality just advanced will show how frequently in ordinary life we are asked to give our attention to fragments of historical writing in the midst of other things. These fragments of course are not necessarily *good* historical writing. They and the reports in which they occur may be inaccurate, biased, fanciful, or downright fraudulent. That is not the point. The point is that the workaday world cannot do without historical materials put in historical form. "In a certain sense," said Carlyle, "all men are historians. . . . Most men . . . speak only to narrate." The following, for example, is part of a seventy-page report issued by the Columbia Broadcasting System to its stockholders in advance of a meeting at which a merger was to be approved:

CBS was incorporated in the State of New York in 1927. In its early years, CBS's major activity was radio broadcasting. In 1939, CBS entered the field of recording and marketing phonograph records. Developments in television broadcasting became commercially practicable after World War II, and led to the development and growth of CBS's television network and stations operations in the 1950's. In 1966 it entered the field of educational services and products.[2]

This terse paragraph is business history, obviously, but it is also technological and cultural history. From it, an archeologist of the future could be confident of drawing solid conclusions about mid-century America.

Now turn to the description of a college class by one of its members, in which we find a fragment of social history:

Three years and 241 days ago Fontbonne College brought forth a new class, conceived in tradition and dedicated to the proposition that traditions can be changed if you try hard enough. Now we are engaged in a great struggle to the end, testing whether these students or any students so conceived can long endure.[3] [Notice in passing the somewhat amateurish parody of a famous historical document.]

We do not usually consider the advertiser a great champion of Fact, yet he too wants to find out what's what. Here is a New York agency making known through an advertisement its philosophy of research. The heading runs: "First, Get the Facts." Then:

More business mistakes are due to faulty facts than to faulty judgment. As used by us, research takes many forms: motivation studies, copy testing, leadership surveys, consumer opinion research, store audits, consumer panel surveys, and dealer surveys. . . . In innumerable instances, research has provided a foundation for building a more efficient advertising program and taking the guesswork out of future planning.[4]

What emerges from the jargon is that advertisers have caught the habit and put on the trappings of modern historical investigation. One can imagine the endless reports arising from all these panels and surveys, the steady repetition of "It was found that . . . " and the

[2] Columbia Broadcasting System, Inc., *Notice of Special Meeting*, May 19, 1967, 17.
[3] Margie McNamee in *Fontbonne*, XIX (1969), 2.
[4] *New York Times*, July 11, 1955.

scholarly comparisons, with dates and percentages, between the devotees of tooth paste and the partisans of tooth powder.

Like advertising, journalism has adapted to its use the ways of
historical research and popularized its externals. Magazines such as
Life, Time, Look, and *Newsweek* employ whole corps of persons who
bear the title of Researcher and whose function is to verify every
statement made in the stories turned in by those whose title is Reporter.

As a final example of the varied forms that historical writing
may take—this time on the geological scale—consider these few sentences
taken from an issue of the *Scientific Monthly:*

> The element uranium changes gradually, through a series of
> transition products—the most important of which is radium—into its
> inactive end-product, the lead isotope with an atomic weight of 206.
> The transformation rate is extremely small; in any uranium mineral,
> only 1 percent of a given amount of uranium is transformed in 65
> million years. . . . Similarly, but even more slowly, thorium is trans-
> formed. . . . The older methods of geologic age determination were
> based on the determination of the lead and helium content of uranium
> and thorium minerals.[5]

History the Great Catch-All

It is evident from these examples that History is not simply an
academic subject among many others but one of the ways in which
we think. Every use of the past tense—"I was there." "He did it"—is
a bit of history. True, false, or mistaken, it expresses our historical
habit of mind. We have newspapers because we are interested in the
previous day's history. We correspond with our friends to tell them
what has happened to us since the last time we wrote and to hear
their story in return. People keep diaries to preserve their memories
clear or to impart their doings to posterity. People delve into their
genealogies because this nourishes pride and enhances the secure feeling
of "belonging." The physician buttresses his diagnosis by asking the
patient for his history—his previous illnesses and those of his parents.

[5] Otto Hahn, "Radioactive Methods for Geologic and Biologic Age Deter-
minations," *Scientific Monthly,* LXXXII (May 1956), 258.

Every institution, club, and committee keeps minutes and other records, not merely as proofs of achievement but as stores of experience: What did we do last year? How did we answer when the question first came up? Lawyers and judges also think with the aid of precedents, and their thought is our law. And our most popular form of literature, the novel, apes the form of genuine history in order to bestow an air of reality on imagined events.

All this remembering and recording is conveyed by the written word. But other kinds of signs are also historical. As a critic and museum director reminds us:

There is one point which must always be kept in mind in thinking about contemporary painting and sculpture: that a work of art is truly contemporary only to the artist while he is actually producing it. Once he lays down his brush or chisel on the completion of his work it is already history—yesterday's work.[6]

And without prearrangement a distinguished musician confirms the art critic while making a further point as to the role of history:

One of the principal tasks of musicology has always been to discover what meanings notational symbols had in their own time and to transcribe the music into symbols generally understood at the date of transcription. In this, musicology directly serves, of course, the performing, "practical" musician. . . . The two activities—performance and scholarly investigation—are aspects of the same search.[7]

Out of all that survives of these portions of history—true or imaginary, written or composed, painted or carved, intimate or public, curious or practical—the formal narratives of an age or of a man's life are fashioned. The letter that carried news or affection becomes a documentary source; the public man's diary, written for self-communing or self-protection, throws light on governmental secrets; the broken pottery or the cave painting tells of a vanished people, as the modern novel and daily paper variously reveal the temper of the age.

[6] James Johnson Sweeney, "Today Is Yesterday Already," *Phillips Exeter Bulletin,* LII (July 1956), 3.
[7] Arthur Mendel, "The Service of Musicology to the Practical Musician," Committee Report to the American Council of Learned Societies, 1955.

Hence the intertwining of "history proper" with our speech, our beliefs, our passions, and our institutions. Theoretically, everything we can think of has its history and belongs to History: not only kings and battles and economic forces, but costume and courtship,[8] railroading and the game of chess, mathematics and the meanings of words, military strategy and old silver, the crust of the earth and the invisible stars.

Nor are these subjects separate; all are part of the history of man, even the history of stars; for, as the philosopher William James pointed out, history is the great humanizer:

You can give humanistic value to almost anything by teaching it historically. Geology, economics, mechanics, are humanities when taught with reference to the successive achievements of the geniuses to which these sciences owe their being. Not taught thus, literature remains grammar, art a catalogue, history a list of dates, and natural science a sheet of formulas and weights and measures.[9]

Lacking as we do the time to study every subject in this historical way, we tend to learn the history of what most deeply interests us, to extend our experience and preserve it: the baseball fan quickly becomes an amateur historian of the game. But what enriches the individual's life is a necessity to the group. For a whole society to lose its sense of history would be tantamount to giving up its civilization. We live and are moved by historical ideas and images, and our national existence goes on by reproducing them. Congress has established the National Trust for Historic Preservation in the United States, whose object is "to halt the wanton destruction of historic buildings, homes, and sites." Like other nations, we put the faces of our great men on our coins and stamps, we make symbols of historic places and objects—Monticello, Plymouth Rock, the Liberty Bell—and we take pains every year to relive historical events and translate them into visual forms. Not many years ago an English society subtly flattered our national consciousness by sending across the Atlantic a replica of

---

[8] See E. S. Turner, *A History of Courting*, New York, 1955.
[9] "The Social Value of the College-Bred," in *Memories and Studies*, New York, 1911, 312–13.

the *Mayflower,* confident that every American, regardless of his origins, would look upon that ship as a symbol of friendship and a measure of America's progress.[10]

The spate of anniversaries noticed in the press, on television, and through local celebrations implies a sense of the past and helps to sustain it. Usually the motive is simple sentiment, as when the first issue of *Yank,* the army newspaper of the Second World War, is recalled twenty-five years later;[11] sometimes the purpose is political, as when President Nixon chooses the tenth anniversary of the opening of the St. Lawrence Seaway to visit Prime Minister Trudeau of Canada at a time of uncertain relations between the countries;[12] sometimes the purpose is commercial, as when a bank or shopkeeper notifies the world that it or he has been in business twenty years. Many firms that would scorn anniversaries nonetheless print on their stationery: "Established 1877." The suggestion is that no financial panic since then has been able to unseat them.

Consider the similar motives and memories behind much of our architecture—the restoration of part of a town at Williamsburg, or the Gateway Arch on the Mississippi at St. Louis, which symbolizes the westward movement of a whole people. Note also the embodiment of strong historical emotion, not this time in some form of building, but in a single word:

An angry group of Scottish patriots scolded Queen Elizabeth II . . . because [she] had called herself "Queen of England" and referred to the first Queen Elizabeth as her forebear. The reference . . . is "entirely inaccurate. Queen Elizabeth of England died unmarried and childless. The ancestor and forebear of our noble Queen was Scotland's contemporary monarch—Mary Queen of Scots—not Elizabeth of England. The council also urges that the words Britain, Britons, and British shall be used at all times when Britain or the British nation and peoples [i.e., England, Scotland, and Wales] are referred to."[13]

When the thought of the past can arouse so much feeling, it is not surprising that it can also satisfy mankind's insatiable curiosity,

[10] *New York Times,* Sept. 23, 1956.
[11] *Ibid.,* June 24, 1967.
[12] *Ibid.,* June 27, 1969.
[13] *Ibid.,* Jan. 3, 1954.

FIGURE 1 *History as a Language of Symbols*

"Ah, mon ami, the English just don't fit HISTORICALLY into this new Europe of ours..."

Vicky in the *Evening Standard* (London), January 21, 1963.

This cartoon appeared in a London newspaper shortly after France had kept Great Britain out of the European Common Market in 1963. The message relies on the historical symbols represented and the historical facts they evoke. No words are required to tell the reader that the setting is Paris. He recognizes President De Gaulle as Napoleon by associating the hat with the Emperor and the Cross of Lorraine with De Gaulle. The reader also sees that Chancellor Konrad Adenauer of Germany is represented as Frederick the Great, wearing the familiar tricorn hat, wig, and sunburst decoration. It does not matter that Napoleon and Frederick never met: England was a determining force in the history of France and Germany, as every literate person recalls automatically, even when he has forgotten the details.

In most countries certain historical figures have been permanently symbolized by cartoonists through the representation of two or three features (for example, Lincoln is depicted as a tall, rangy, ugly youth splitting rails). In the *Saturday Review,* the cartoon series by Burr Shafer, "History Never Told in Time," relies on such visual legends to suggest to the reader's mind the historical facts that are not set down in the caption but that are required for enjoying the anecdote.

afford readers elevated pleasure, and, by simply showing how anything came to be what it is, furnish every man a unique kind of reassurance. The excitement caused by new accounts of old stories is seemingly inexhaustible. Books about Lincoln, Caesar, Mary Queen of Scots, Captain Bligh, Marie Antoinette, Lewis and Clark, Winston Churchill, Joan of Arc, and dozens of other familiar figures are always sure of a large audience, almost irrespective of the merit of the work. The naive interest in small detail is what often carries the reader along. Thus in *The Day Lincoln Was Shot*, the author, a newspaper reporter and not a professional historian, made the search into such details his life's work. He read seven million words of contemporary testimony to glean curious scraps. He shows, in addition, our modern zeal for numerical accuracy: "I traveled the escape route of Booth in an Oldsmobile and checked it to the tenth of a mile."[14]

Making a fetish of fact goes with the notion that all records whatever are valuable. The result is overcrowding—and surreptitious disposal by subordinates. Some 500 pounds of New York State papers were caught on their way to a pulping mill in Canada, and boxes of records of the City of New York were discovered in cavities within the framework of Brooklyn Bridge. One never knows, of course, when a remote and nearly forgotten fact can be useful. Until recently students of the special problems of arid lands neglected history. But Paul B. Sears of Yale made the point that history and archeology must contribute valuable information for future planning: "We can do no better in some places than find out where the ancients had their irrigation systems." Searching among the Roman ruins is thus the prerequisite to reclamation. In Peru, it appears, farming under irrigation 2,000 years ago permitted the cultivation of 40 percent more acreage than at present.[15]

Finally, the "argument from history" is a commonplace of domestic politics. In accepting the late Adlai Stevenson as a presidential possibility for the second time, the public argued from precedent; the last word was with a writer from Pittsfield, Massachusetts, who cited

---

[14] Jim [James Alonzo] Bishop, in the *Book-of-the-Month-Club News,* January 1955, 4.

[15] *New York Times,* May 8, 1955.

Jefferson, John Quincy Adams, Andrew Jackson, William Henry Harrison, and Grover Cleveland as having lost and then won. Only four men ran twice and were never elected, and it was suggested that "even a cursory glance at a reliable reporting of history will illustrate why."[16]

So much for the excitement and the practical utility of history. The solution of mysteries is no less important for our pleasure and peace of mind. People are still bothered by such questions as: Who was the Man in the Iron Mask? Who wrote the "Letters of Junius"? How did Judge Crater disappear? Speaking of a famous modern crime and the alarm it caused, the English writer Rebecca West pointed out that:

The position of man is obviously extremely insecure unless he can find out what is happening around him. That is why historians publicly pretend that they can give an exact account of events in the past, though they privately know that all the past will let us know about events above a certain degree of importance is a bunch of alternative hypotheses.[17]

Miss West is quite right about man's insecurity without history and quite wrong about the historian's "public" versus "private views." This is a point we shall return to.[18] She goes on:

But they find such hypotheses. Here, however, was a crime that was not in the past but in the present, and was much simpler than any important historical event. But it remained a secret: a secret which was in the hands of a talkative spiv, yet was unbreakable.[19]

A parallel of even greater magnitude is found in the prolonged controversy over the assassination of President Kennedy, about which a sense of fear and mystery persists.

To return to Rebecca West's view of history, it is clear that she goes astray on one point. Though she speaks of a contemporary crime, the act and its causes were no more "in the present" than the murder

---

[16] Nancy Quirk, July 21, 1956.
[17] Rebecca West, *A Train of Powder*, New York, 1955, 226.
[18] See Chapter 7, pp. 155 ff.
[19] West, *loc. cit.*

of Caesar. They were well in the past, or she could have written no report. Nor was her subject "much simpler than any important historical event." Historical truth is always complex and always difficult to ascertain. Eyewitnesses are generally few, hard to find and question, and they often prove untrustworthy. For these very reasons the secret of a small private crime is more likely to remain hidden than the truth of a great public event.

History's Home and Foreign Relations

We have not advanced far enough to list the kinds of resources the historical researcher must be familiar with, but only to point out that the all-pervasiveness of history connects him with nearly every other branch of learning and makes him a "generalist" as well as a specialist. Take this eye-catching paragraph from the announcement of a scholarly work: "The year *The Communist Manifesto* appeared, gold was discovered in California, *Vanity Fair* was published, Metternich resigned, the new French Republic elected Louis Napoleon president, Emperor Ferdinand abdicated."[20] What these remarks are supposed to do is transport us back to 1848. In order to report intelligently about those six events (out of many more) an historian must prepare himself to write about the following subjects, among others:

For *The Communist Manifesto:* about Marx and Marxism, the history of economic thought, and Utopian Socialism.

For the discovery of gold: about Californian geology, geography, and settlement; the history of exploration and of western expansion.

For *Vanity Fair:* about Thackeray and the English and Continental novel.

For Metternich: about the Congress of Vienna, the Holy Alliance, Nationalism, and Friedrich Gentz.

For Louis Napoleon: about Napoleon Bonaparte, his empire, his

---

[20] Raymond Postgate, *The Story of a Year, 1848,* New York, 1956. Compare the still more ingenious reconstruction and "unification" of a much shorter period, *A Sultry Month,* by Alethea Hayter, London, 1965. Postgate has recently published another story of a year, *The Story of a Year: 1798,* New York, 1969.

brothers, their fate and their descendants. Also: the genesis of the Second French Republic, its constitution, parties, and problems.

For Emperor Ferdinand: about the house of Hapsburg, the Austrian Empire in the nineteenth century, its national and linguistic minorities, and the rise of Liberalism.

By this point our historian has become something of an economist, a geographer, a literary critic, a sociologist, an anthropologist, and a political theorist, as well as a student of military campaigns, diplomacy, constitutional law, and philosophical systems. Besides which, he has to be a wide-ranging biographer, hence acquainted in some measure with all the unpredictable matters that human lives contain.

It is obvious that the historian cannot be all these things in full. Life is too short to master so many extensive disciplines. But he must know how to use the results supplied him by others in their studies (called monographs) upon the related topics that he encounters while pursuing his own.

What he himself contributes is twofold. First, he contributes the results of his own search for facts as yet unknown, or possibly ill handled by a previous worker.[21] Second, he contributes the organizing principles and the conclusions or explanations (what Rebecca West calls the "hypotheses") that make of the disconnected facts "a history." In his first capacity the work of the historian may be likened to a science. In the second, it may be considered an art. Actually, these two functions are not separable except in thought; the historian is an exact reporter working in the realm where the concrete and the imponderable meet.

The Research Scholar and Writer

It is now possible to draw conclusions about the identity of the historian's techniques with those of the researcher-at-large preparing a report. Both men have recourse to the same infinite range of materials, find their way among books by the same devices, gather and test facts according to the same rules, exhibit their results in the same order

[21] See Chapter 4, and Chapter 15, pp. 347–48.

and spirit, and hope to impress other men's minds by the same literary means.

The difference is chiefly one of scale and aim. One thinks of an historian as treating in lasting fashion a large slice of the past. The maker of a report concentrates on some narrow set of facts whose interest is momentary. But this is not invariably so. Alexander Hamilton's *Report on Manufactures* was a political document by a public official, yet it is a more valuable piece of research and writing than Parson Weems's *Life of George Washington*.[22] To repeat once more, the obvious and important difference between the professional student of history and the unpretentious reporter of contemporary matters does not affect the similarity of their problems and instruments of work. Neither does the quality of the results they produce or the subject matter they take up.

Putting together two of our previous examples should clinch the point. Suppose a college student of literature reporting on *Vanity Fair* or, alternatively, a graduate student writing a master's thesis on that book. These students may think of themselves as "English majors" or literary critics, and not at all as historians, yet the bulk of their work exactly parallels that of the historian of 1848 who finds *Vanity Fair* an "event" in his path.

To be sure, other things than "straight history" will go into the "literary" thesis, but the hunting for books, the selecting of facts, the verifying of points, the shaping of chapters, the framing of sentences, the quoting of authorities, the casting of footnotes, the listing of bibliography will be the same as in the historian's work, and the parallel will hold, with modifications, for all other disciplines.

In literature, to pursue the same example, not even the discussion

[22] In this biography by the itinerant preacher Mason L. Weems appeared the original of the best-known fabrication in American history, the cherry-tree episode. It did not come into being until the fifth edition of the work (1806), half a dozen years after the first. The anecdote itself may go back to an earlier date. See Arthur H. Merritt, "Did Parson Weems Really Invent the Cherry-Tree Story?" *New-York Historical Society Quarterly*, XL (July 1956), 252–63. A judicious estimate of Weems's contribution as an historian despite his penchant for literary invention will be found in Marcus Cunliffe's introduction to the latest edition of Weems's *Washington* (The Belknap Press of Harvard University Press, Cambridge, Mass., 1962).

of artistic form, style, and words will be wholly free of historical elements. The critic and the literary historian are brothers. If the work under review is a poem, the critic will go for "close reading" of the text to the great *Oxford English Dictionary on Historical Principles* and will compare effects or influences by reference to other writers, who necessarily have an abode in history. If the work is a novel, it will probably embody social observation and historical fact. The battle of Waterloo inspires scenes in *Vanity Fair,* and the fortunes of the imaginary Crawley family form a résumé of social history.

Students in every field will accordingly profit from a conscious attention to the ways of the historian, which they may have formerly regarded as special and limited. These are (as we have seen) universal, and we now turn to them as the fundamentals of research.

2

The ABC of Technique

The Prime Difficulty: What Is My Subject?

Any account, report, or other piece of historical writing is intended to take effect on someone at some time. It must consequently meet that someone's demands. Those demands can for convenience be summed up in a pair of questions: [Is the account true, reliable, complete? Is it clear, orderly, easy to grasp and remember?] All the devices and methods that the researcher combines under the name of technique exist to satisfy these elementary demands.

[This in turn means that the researcher must first ask the questions of himself, and not only at the end, when the finished typescript is being neatly clamped in attractive folders, but at many points between the beginning and the end.] It is evident that in order to be able to answer "Yes" to each part of the two questions, the writer must be sure of what his subject is. If he does not know, how can he tell whether the treatment is complete? If he does not know, how can he expect another man to find his paper clear? If he does not know, what yardstick can he use for including and omitting, and how can he proceed in orderly fashion from opening to conclusion? If he does not know, how can he test reliability? For reliability only means: "These words fairly represent certain things outside (facts, events, ideas) that are naturally linked to form 'a subject.' "

Now a writer always starts with *some* idea of what his subject is, even if that idea is contained in a single term—Blimps or Fish or Alexander the Great. But the discovery of the true, whittled-down subject that the essay will propose to the reader and that will inevitably determine his demands is a task that begins with the first steps of research and ends only when the last word has been written and revised.

The truth of this abstract statement you will experience the moment you tackle *your* subject. Between the first notion of it and the final draft you will probably modify your conception more than once. It does not greatly matter if in doing your research you pick up a number of facts or ideas that you later discard as irrelevant. But it is obvious that if you take time to collect nearly everything that somehow clings to any part of your topic, you will have a library on your hands, and not the materials with which to work up a report on "a subject." Fortunately, as you proceed, your judgment grows more and more assured about what belongs and what does not, and soon you begin to *see your subject.* From then on you must not take your eyes off it. You must keep seeing it at every moment of fact-gathering and of composition.

The reason for this constant attention is that a subject does not let itself be carved away from neighboring subjects the way a butcher carves off one chop from the next. A subject is always trying to merge itself again into the great mass of associated facts and ideas. Take a small book (230 pp.) like Rachel Carson's *The Sea Around Us.* Before starting, the author undoubtedly had the general notion of writing for laymen about certain facts relating to the sea. She could hardly have chosen a more difficult *notion* to turn into a *subject.* The sea is immense. Its action and effects, its form, substance, and inhabitants furnish matter for thousands of monographs. Yet the writer could not choose for her book a few of these matters at random and then stop. The result would have been the same as that produced by the amateur writer who called up a publisher and asked: "How long is the average novel nowadays?"

"Oh, between seventy-five and ninety thousand words."

"Well then, I've finished!"

The anecdote illustrates by a negative example the principle that there has to be unity and completeness in the works of the human mind, whether large or small. In order to perceive what is necessary to completeness, that is, what the subject requires, you must first know the projected size of its treatment. Suppose a stranger to Western civilization asks you: "What does 'Roman Empire' mean?" You can answer him in a sentence, in a paragraph, or in a page. You can refer him to an essay, a book, or Gibbon's six volumes. All these forms determine what is and is not part of the subject, for if you have but one sentence at your disposal you will certainly not mention the geese that saved the Capitol, or even the three wars against Carthage; and if you have six volumes at your disposal you will nowhere find it necessary to give a one-sentence definition of the whole.

In other words, your subject is defined by *that group of associated facts and ideas which, when clearly presented in a prescribed amount of space, leave no questions unanswered* WITHIN *the presentation, even though many questions could be asked* OUTSIDE *it.* For example, if you defined the Roman Empire as "an ancient power which sprang from a city-state in central Italy to cover ultimately both shores of the Mediterranean, and which between 100 B.C. and A.D. 476 transmitted to the West the cultures it had conquered to the East," you would have, not indeed a *perfect* definition, but one that is complete as far as it goes. In any longer account, the added detail must sustain the impression of closeness to the central idea and of even distribution around it.

Without unity and completeness, details make, as we say, "no sense." Even a reader ignorant of your subject will notice something wrong if you give a page to the legend of Romulus and Remus suckled by a she-wolf and later on dispose of Caesar's murder in one sentence. Nor can you at the last page leave a dozen questions hanging in the air. The reader knows from experience that things written about exhibit a logical structure. Time, place, and meaning give things their connectedness, which must come out again in a report upon them. And once subjects have been made distinct by an appropriate treatment they will not readily mix again. This is the point of Dickens' joke about Mr. Pott, the journalist in *Pickwick Papers,* whose colleague had written an article about Chinese Metaphysics, though he knew nothing of the subject. He used the encyclopedia, said Mr. Pott, and "read for metaphysics under the letter M, and for China under the letter C, and combined his information."

To test the relevance of any subclass of ideas within a large subject and, so to speak, to draw a circle around whatever should be in, the researcher will find that an expanded title often helps. This is one reason why reports of factual investigation generally carry long and explicit titles. Books used to be entitled in this same descriptive fashion, for example, Malthus' *Essay on the Principle of Population, as it affects the future improvement of Society: with remarks on the Speculations of Mr. Godwin, M. Condorcet, and other writers* (1798). The title not only gives fair warning about the contents; it also sets limits. It makes a kind of contract with the reader as to what he will get, and the contract helps the writer to fulfill the bargain. In this regard such a title is at the opposite extreme from the modern style shown in *The Sea Around Us.*

Note that a seemingly clear, sharply defined subject like "The American Presidency" actually conceals a multitude of separate subjects. Would a book on the Presidents from 1789 to the present take up their private lives and their careers before election? If so, to what extent? And what about their characters, their wives, their illnesses? We can think at once of instances in which any of these topics would be immediately relevant to the central theme—if we knew what that theme was. "The American Presidency—The Conflicts Between the Executive and Congress" is a different book from "The American Presidency—A Study in Personal Power." Lengthening the title to narrow the limits has the effect of driving doubts into a corner. There your mind can grapple with them and decide the recurring issue of relevance: is this particular incident a case of personal power, Yes or No? Does it duplicate or amplify a previous instance, Yes or No? And so on until you decide In or Out.

These difficulties are inseparable from research. They illustrate the general truth that reading, writing, *and thinking* are the three activities of research. As a student naively but truthfully remarked in discussing the matter in an examination, "thinking about one's subject should be a frequent process, whether or not one is reading or writing."

Though painful, the delimiting of the subject has one advantage, and this is a thought in which the weary researcher, struggling with his notes and ideas like a man filling a featherbed, can take comfort: (a writer cannot "tell all." No one wants him to. The writer will often wonder, "Do I need to mention this?" And he can and must frequently answer: "They don't want to hear about *that!*"

To sum up, the researcher-reporter fashioning his subject may be likened to a sculptor in clay who is working from visual memory. He shapes his work by adding and by taking away until the lump resembles the image he has carried in his mind's eye. He is aided by his general knowledge of how objects look, but he must use trial and error to achieve the desired likeness. The reason why research is like sculpturing *from memory* is that in neither is there a concrete visible subject to copy directly. The subject—as sculptors themselves are fond of saying—is hidden in the block of material.

"I Have All My Material"—But Have *You?*

The "block of material" in research is the huge mass of words bearing on the innumerable topics and subtopics within the subject.[1] The obvious first step in carving out the substance of your report is to find out whether someone has already dealt with its subject in print—in an article, it may be, or in a book. At this late date in the world's history very few subjects of research can be entirely original. Even the newest experiment in science has been led up to, and the report on the new work usually gives a bibliography, which is but a record of previous findings.

The record of earlier work in any field—known as its "literature"—is accessible in many ways, of which more will be said in Chapter 4. The fact to note here is that, barring exceptional cases, leads to your material exist, probably in abundance. Discovering them is a question of skill and patience—of technique.

Technique begins with learning how to use the card catalogue of a library. Anyone will soon grasp the system, which is only an

---

[1] Field investigations and laboratory experiments are in part exceptions to this generality, though they too involve library research.

expanded form of the alphabetical order of an encyclopedia. A ready knowledge of the alphabet is therefore fundamental to all research.[2]

But it must be supplemented by alertness and imagination, for subjects frequently go by different names. A simple example is that of coin collecting, which is called Numismatics. More subtle is the step by which someone who wants information about the theory of the divine right of kings looks up "Monarchy." He might conceivably have reached the same result by looking up "Right, divine," or even possibly "Divine Right," if his library owns a book by that title or is fully cross-indexed. What is certain is that there is little chance of success if one looks up "King" and no hope at all if one looks up "Theory." In other words, one must from the very beginning *play* with the subject, take it apart and view it from various sides in order to seize on its outward connections.

Suppose that after some ingenuity and considerable tramping about the library you have found two articles and three books, all bearing clearly and largely on your topic; the temptation is now strong to consider that the search in research is pretty well over. You like to think that what remains is to read, take notes, arrange them, and write your essay. You probably announce that you "have all your material." In this error you are not far removed from the naive man who "combined his information." True, you may as well start reading, but research has not yet begun: the chances are that you have scarcely read more than a few pages in the second article when you discover between it and the first a discrepancy in date or name, which the books, when appealed to, do not resolve. You consult the nearest encyclopedia: it offers you a third variant. You are perplexed, yet you should feel a certain elation: research—as against *re*-search—is about to begin.

How far it will take you, no one can predict. By the time you have tracked down all uncertainties, followed up side lines to their

---

[2] This remark may sound obvious to the point of foolishness; it is deliberately made as a hint to those college and graduate students, more numerous than one would suppose, who are crippled in research by an inability to follow quickly and accurately the alphabetic order beyond the first or second letter of the key words. If a Bachelor or Master of Arts has not fully mastered the alphabet, he should study it and practice its use.

dead ends, filled in gaps in logical or chronological sequence, and reached solid conclusions of your own, you will have stored up a sizable amount of information, written matter, and technique. But you may still not be entitled to tell your inquiring friends, "I have all my material."

What you have done—to go back to our pair of fundamental questions—is to make sure that your report will be true and reliable, but there is one more test of completeness to be applied. Assuming that you have been working steadily with library resources and that in your single-mindedness you have perhaps neglected your ordinary routines, you must now remember that [while you were so engaged the world has been moving on, newspapers have continued to come out, people have died, other researchers' work has been published.] You must therefore make a last survey. Recent issues of periodicals will not have been indexed nor death dates recorded; you have to rely on your wits. To the very end of your work on the paper, you must keep an eye on events and publications for the latest relevant facts. At the worst, to neglect them may mean that you have overlooked something that knocks the props from under your results; at best, it may mean that you will be disconcerted in public or private when someone brings up a fact that everybody knows but you.

The Practical Imagination at Work

The nucleus of two articles and three books presumably on your subject has expanded by addition and verification into material for an essay or report possibly twenty pages long. This report of yours will be no mere précis or résumé of what was in the nucleus. It should offer something not directly or fully treated in any one source. It will be a new arrangement consisting of tested facts and fresh thought. At the moment, the new arrangement does not exist, but only the materials for it. These so-called materials are in fact scribbles you have made on pieces of paper—notes taken as you pursued the elusive dates, the missing middle name, the descriptive detail, or the clinching piece of testimony supporting a conclusion.

But it is not possible to write a report direct from the sum total of the available materials. You can *compose* only from what you deliberately select from your notes, which bulk larger than your report when done. It takes no argument to prove that this collection of notes you have taken can very soon become unmanageable. You must therefore adopt some system for creating order as you go, so that you may select intelligently later on. There is no one system to be preferred above all others, except that the system most congenial to you will probably give you the best results.

What you want to establish is a regular procedure that will enable you to turn to a given note without having to riffle through sheafs of stuff. At any time in research you may want to compare a quotation you took down a while ago with a new version you have just come across; or you may want to fill in a blank with a date that has turned up unexpectedly. Ultimately you will need to sort your notes into bunches preparatory to making your first draft.

For all these purposes, experience shows that you must take notes in a uniform manner, on paper or cards of uniform size. Some researchers favor notebooks, bound or looseleaf,[3] others prefer ruled or blank index cards—3 by 5 inches or 4 by 6 or 5 by 8—but one size only for the main materials. Those who use notebooks, large or small, copy out facts or quotations as they come, regardless of subject. They leave a wide margin straight down one side to permit a key word or phrase to be put opposite each note as a guide to the eye in finding and classifying that note. It is also possible to write in notebooks in such a way that each note will fill no more than a given amount of space on the page. Then, when the book is filled, the pages can be cut into slips of uniform size and shuffled into groups.

The same principle underlies the use of small cards. Those who favor them make a point of noting down only one thing on any one card. Room is left in an upper corner for the key word by which related cards are later assembled. Advocates of the larger cards use them as do the users of notebooks. Other variations of these fundamen-

---

[3] Many technicians throw up their hands in horror at the thought of notebooks, but great examples justify their use (Gibbon, Rhodes, A. F. Pollard, Oman), and the theorist of notetaking, E. W. Dow, wisely says that this older practice will probably continue to have its devotees. Certainly the researcher who has to travel is better off with notebooks than with stacks of cards.

tal ways will suggest themselves. A distinguished English physician of the last generation, Sir Clifford Allbutt, recommended using slips of paper the size of a check and leaving a wide left-hand margin, partly for keying, partly for gathering under a snap clip. The notes for each section being held together provide the researcher with a series of small booklets that he can leaf through thoughtfully as he is about to write.[4]

The common feature of all these devices is clear: the information is extracted from all sources as it comes and is set down on one kind of card or paper. Before the miscellaneous collection becomes unwieldy, it is roughly keyed or indexed for ready reference and later sorting. The single-fact-to-a-card system gives the most thorough index. But it has the drawback of producing very quickly a large, discouraging pile of cards, bulky to carry around and clumsy to handle when the time comes for writing. The notebook system is much less cumbrous but also less strictly organized. Which to choose? A researcher should consult his taste and find out whether his temperament makes him want to have everything just so, or whether he can stand a certain amount of extra leafing through pages for the sake of having his materials more compact and portable.

The nature of the subject may also dictate a choice. For very large statistical surveys it may prove desirable to use punched-cards and machines, which would be a nuisance, say, in writing a biography.[5] In deciding upon a notetaking method, there is no substitute for judgment. But no researcher, it goes without saying, should permit himself to amass notes higgledy-piggledy on a variety of slips or notebook pages, leave them unkeyed, and then face the task of reducing the chaos to order. If at times you are unexpectedly forced to take down a reference on the back of an envelope, you should as soon as possible transfer it in proper form to the regular file.

The only sensible irregularities are those that have a use. For example, users of notebooks often find it convenient to make out a 3-by-5 card for each book and article they encounter, alphabetizing them by author as they proceed. Similarly, users of cards may keep

---

[4] See Allbutt's lively little book, *Notes on the Composition of Scientific Papers,* 3rd ed., London, 1925.

[5] See below the discussion of computers, pp. 95–98.

a small notebook in which to list queries as they arise—points to look up later in reference works or elsewhere. It is a saving of time to do these verifications in batches, rather than interrupt the train of thought while reading and notetaking. One can set aside for days of headache or indisposition the more mechanical tracking down of dates and the like, thus reserving one's best mind for study properly so-called.

In short, if you will have an eye to the obvious, foreseeable uses to which you are going to put your notes, and also observe your own preferences or peculiarities, you can put together a system that will suit you. Once you adopt it, stick to it, for it will serve you best from the moment you no longer think about it but use it automatically. Be sure, though, that by a preference you do not mean a congenial bad habit whose effects will repeatedly cause trouble. For example, you may have carried with you from grammar school the habit of writing in pencil. This is bad, for pencil rubs off when cards are shuffled or pages pressed together; and instead of a note you have an illegible smudge.

Again, if you do not discipline yourself to the habit of always writing down author, title, and page number each time you note a fact or copy a quotation, you will lose endless hours later in an irritating search for the exact reference. The same holds for clippings from newspapers: write the date and year of the issue, for the dateline of the news story may be several days before, and the year is never given. Finally, there is in research one absolute rule that suffers no exception: NEVER WRITE ON BOTH SIDES OF ANYTHING. If you violate the rule and do it once, you will do it again; and if you do it from time to time you can never remember when you have done it; you thereby condemn yourself to a frequent frustrating hunt for "that note," which may be on the other side of some unidentifiable slip or card or page. You will go by it a dozen times without seeing it, turn over hundreds of pieces of paper to discover it.

A Note Is First a Thought

So much for the mechanical side of notetaking. The intellectual side cannot be as readily described or discussed. The advice "Don't take too many notes" is like the recipe in the cookbook that begins: "Take enough butter." How much is "enough"? Taking too many notes is tantamount to copying out your printed source in longhand. If you find yourself approaching this limit, even over the stretch of one page, halt and take stock. You might conceivably need a full page verbatim, but this is seldom true, apart from the need to reproduce letters, diary entries, and the like; in that case it is safer, because more accurate, to have photocopies made from the book.[6]

Rather than try to gauge your notetaking skill by quantity, think of it in this way: am I simply doing clerk's work or am I assimilating new knowledge and putting down my own thoughts? To put down your own thoughts you must use your own words, not the author's. Make a conscious, steady effort to do this until it becomes second nature. For example, you read in your source:

The early 1860's were the years of Garibaldi's greatest vogue and notoriety. The United States minister, Marsh, wrote home to his government in 1861 that, "though but a solitary and private individual, he is at this moment, in and of himself, one of the great Powers of the world.[7]

Out of this you may make the lazy man's note:

1860's G's greatest vogue and notoriety; Marsh, U.S. Min., wrote home (1861) G. was "one of the great Powers of the world."

The *work* you have done on that passage is minimal. It is also negative, in that you have merely cut out connectives and fullness

---

[6] Because photocopying machines are easily accessible, some students like to make them do the work of taking notes—whole pages at a time. But although the accuracy of quotations is increased thereby, the saving of time hoped for is an illusion. Putting the substance of the notes through the mind, as described in the paragraphs that follow, cannot be eliminated; it is only postponed.

[7] Denis Mack Smith, *Garibaldi*, New York, 1956, 113.

of expression. Such notetaking soon becomes absent-minded. You do it while half thinking of other things; hence what you read leaves little trace in the memory. This lack will handicap you at the writing stage and will not be compensated by the fact that your notes will be a perpetual surprise to you—stranger's work. Suppose that instead of merely making a telegram out of the two sentences above, you recast the thought and the wording as you go:

G. at peak of renown in 1860's. U. S. Min. Marsh called him in 1861 dispatch "one of the great Powers of the world."

What you have accomplished is threefold: you have made an effort of thought, which has imprinted the information on your mind; you have practiced the art of writing by making a paraphrase; and you have at the same time taken a step toward your first draft, for here and now these are *your* words, not a piece of plagiarism thinly veiled by a page reference. The principle here applied is that of précis writing. As for the blank purposely left, it is a reminder that you must look up Marsh to find out his full name and dates of service in Italy. Why dates? Because your author may just possibly have written Marsh when he meant Mason or Morris or Masham, and the dates would disclose the error.[8]

If you are good at taking notes, you will have seen that the example just given does not show great compression. Five lines are reduced to three in either version. But with a longer original you can probably do much better than that. Whole paragraphs or sections can be summed up in a couple of sentences. This may be due to the original's being diffuse or badly written, as will be illustrated later on, or it may be because the detail in the source happens to be of no

---

[8] There is of course no error in the text quoted. The philologist George Perkins Marsh was the first U.S. Minister to the new Kingdom of Italy; he served from 1861 to 1882.

importance for your purpose. Here is where the notetaker's grasp of his subject comes into play. He is aware that the book in front of him was written with a certain aim in view—say, to give the story of Garibaldi's life—whereas he, the researcher, is working on a study of American foreign policy. The two aims intersect, and only at the points of intersection does the researcher make a note. He makes it with *his* purpose in mind, leaving out what would be essential to another. He omits, for example, part of the quoted dispatch, which only elaborates the point. If the note taken shows signs of having passed through a mind, it is a good test of its relevance and adequacy.

The reader will also have noticed that in order to make the note as short as possible abbreviations were used. This is legitimate, but subject to the general caution that abbreviating must not lead to confusion. If in your notes G. stands for Garibaldi, it must not also stand for Gladstone. Words as well as names can be shortened if, once again, the notetaker is systematic. He must not only know what he is doing, but also imagine trouble ahead. At the moment it is taken down, the note speaks volumes and looks foolproof. But nothing grows colder more rapidly than notes. A week later that beautifully condensed and abbreviated statement may be an utter conundrum.

Even when the statement is clear and, at the time, pregnant with meaning, the notetaker may think it advisable to guide his later self by an additional remark—anything from "X says this, but be sure compare Z, *Hist. Italy*" to a full-fledged comment that might find a place in the finished paper. When such asides are put, quite rightly, next to the fact they refer to, it is advisable to mark off the notetaker's addition by a special sign. A pair of slashes around the remark is convenient; it means: /I, the notetaker, am saying this, not the author I am transcribing./ Once adopted, the symbols for this or any other device must be invariable.

After taking notes on a book or two, the researcher begins to discern the large natural divisions of his subject—the main heads of his report. He is now ready to begin indexing the notes that have been growing under his hand. If the report is planned to be of modest size— twenty to thirty pages—three or four divisions will suffice. If the work is to be larger, he should break the main heads down into subdivisions, giving each a provisional name or, if he likes, a number.[9] In a biography, for instance, there might be: Youth and Education; Adult Beginnings; Success as Lawyer; Politics; Early Character and Advocations; Crisis of 1889; Voluntary Exile; Last Years and Death; Estimate of Career; Bibliography.

These working titles, or their initials, or else Roman numerals corresponding to the outline on which the titles appear, form the key or index. The appropriate word or sign is written in the margin of the notebook opposite each note, reference, or quotation. If cards have been used, the key word or sign is entered in the chosen corner. Misjudgments as to where a certain fact belongs are bound to occur. For this reason, it is best not to scrawl a large key word in the available space. You may have to cross it out and substitute another. Or again, a given fact may have two or more uses and need as many key words. It is likely, for instance, that some fact under Crisis of 1889 will come up again under Estimate of Career and be anticipated in Early Character.

This grouping of notes carries as yet no hint of detailed order and sequence, but it does show how much is still lacking for a balanced treatment. The category Politics may be bulging with notes while Youth and Education is thin and anemic. Since no relevant reference to other sources goes unnoted, the Bibliography group grows as fast as any and gives promise of supplying the lack of information disclosed by the indexing.

It should be unnecessary to point out that every one of the technical hints just given is transferable. The last example has been taken from biography because the life of a man is a typical subject familiar to all. But the ways of notetaking, abstracting, indexing, and classifying are applicable to any report based on research. The sources need not even be books in the library sense. They can be manuscript letters or diaries, answers to questionnaires, a court record of testimony, or the books (in another sense) of a business firm. Wherever there is a multitude of facts and assertions to be selected, marshaled into kinds, and used as evidence of a state of affairs, the operations of the mind that guides the pen are fundamentally the same.

[9] See Chapter 11.

Knowledge for Whom?

The effort of research is so taxing and exhausting that whoever has gone through it feels a natural desire to exhibit the results. Sometimes his audience is ready-made: he may have been commissioned to undertake the investigation, and interested people are waiting for his report. At other times the research has been entirely self-propelled. In either case the report-maker never knows to a man whom he is addressing. He knows only the general category of persons. Even a college student writing "for" his instructor may find his paper being read to the whole group, or learn that it has been used as an anonymous example in another class. Similarly in the world of published research, it is impossible for the writer to foresee into whose hands his work will eventually fall.

These circumstances impose on the writer a double duty. He must *general* write so as to inform his immediate colleagues, employers, or other *educated* familiar audience, and he must also discharge his obligation to the *Public* Unknown Reader. Though he may fondly expect his intimates or fellow workers to understand him regardless of his powers of expression, he knows that he cannot hold other readers' attention unless he is clear, orderly, and, if possible, agreeable to read. In truth, the difference between the two groups is an illusion. Neither the close nor the distant readers can be expected to see through a brick wall, to strain their wits to grasp at a meaning. Those steeped in your subject may manage to catch your drift; but they will not be grateful or admiring if they do it in spite of you. A writer who has some contribution to make must so put it that any interested reader will grasp it with only a normal effort of attention. The possibility of this is what makes the report useful, what gives the measure of its value.

It follows that *the report-maker must write always as if he were addressing the whole educated community.* His yardstick is: can another trained mind, not expert in my subject, understand what I am saying?

In using this standard of self-criticism, technical terms are of course left out of account. The assumption is that they will be used correctly, and they generally are. But a good reader need not know their meaning in order to tell at a glance whether a report outside his field is intelligible. He sees at once from the ordinary words whether he could understand the report if he took the trouble to learn the technical vocabulary. The failure of all "difficult" writing without exception lies elsewhere than in the technicalities.[10] In such writing it is the common words that are misused, the sentence structure that is ramshackle, and the organization that is wild or nonexistent. And as we shall see, every one of these faults goes back to a fault in thinking. It follows that a fault in expression is a flaw in the knowledge that is supposedly being conveyed.

Let us take an example. When the Salk polio vaccine was first introduced, its merits and defects were of urgent concern to all Americans. Deaths had occurred following its use. The United States Public Health Service accordingly issued a report on the vaccine supplied by the Cutter Laboratories, which was suspected of having caused, instead of prevented, the disease. That report exactly fits our double specification: the physicians who made it had to address their colleagues on a professional matter and at the same time inform the lay public. From either point of view the report could hardly have been more clumsily framed.

The organization was logical, for scientists are trained to follow a set form,[11] but they are seldom trained to express themselves clearly

[10] This statement is confirmed by the abundant literature that attempts to correct bad technical writing by drawing attention to it with amusement or impatience. See for example: N. Vanserg, "How to Write Geologese," *Economic Geology*, XLVII (1952), 220–23; A. B. Hepler, "The Medical Paper," *Western Journal of Surgery, Obstetrics, and Gynecology*, LXI (September 1953), 553–58; E. H. McClelland, "Slips That Pass in the Night," *Journal of Chemical Education*, XX (November 1943), 546–53; Walter McQuade, "Jargon, Past and Present," *Architectural Forum*, CXXVII (September 1967), 92; L. M. Lecron, "Readable Writing," *Northwest Medicine*, LXII (April 1963), 264–65; "The Significance of Significant" (editorial), *New England Journal of Medicine*, CCLXXVIII (May 30, 1968), 1232–33.

Business and government express a like concern; see "The Lexicography of Deception," *Du Pont Stockholder*, Spring 1956; "Words—Precision Tools," *Dun's Review*, October 1952; and the handbook *Plain Letters* issued by the General Services Administration for the use of "those who write and those who sign government letters." Unfortunately, this manual is not nearly so good as the earlier one published by the Department of the Interior for the use of geological surveyors.

[11] See Sam F. Trelease, *The Scientific Paper*, 2nd ed., Baltimore, 1951.

and accurately, apart from the use of technical words.[12] Here is how the report in question dealt in paragraph eleven with a point of importance to every family:

There were ninety cases of poliomyelitis in household contacts occurring within forty-nine days after vaccination of a household associate with Cutter vaccine. In seventy-one of these cases the occurrence of the disease could be associated with specific distribution lots of vaccine.[13]

It is difficult enough, even on a second reading, to grasp this short fragment; when twenty-five paragraphs in this style follow hard on one another the effect is very likely total bewilderment. The ordinary citizen modestly concludes that here is science too abstruse for him. He skips to the summary and this what he finds:

The study produced nothing which pointed to contamination as a source of the live virus but it did produce data suggesting the combination of inadequacy of virus inactivation and failure of the safety tests as responsible for live virus remaining undetected in the finished vaccine.[14]

Now let us see what might have been said if pains had been taken to communicate with the public as was evidently intended. The first passage meant to say:

Ninety cases of poliomyelitis occurred within forty-nine days after another person in the same household had received the Cutter vaccine. In seventy-one of these cases a connection could be shown with particular lots of the vaccine.

Before going on to the "translation" of the second passage, some of the changes made in the first are worth analyzing. In the original text the ninety cases occurred not in people but in "household contacts," an ambiguous phrase, which leaves unclear whether it was the disease or the contact that occurred "within forty-nine days."

[12] Many scientific journals maintain a staff writer to rewrite the articles they accept from contributors.
[13] *New York Times,* Aug. 26, 1955.
[14] *Ibid.*

Throughout, phrases are run on in defiance of syntax, and the word "associate" is used in two senses oddly linked ("household associate with Cutter vaccine") ("associated with distribution lots"). The result is to destroy the plain connections of things: people associating with people, disease occurring in people, and investigation tracing the cause to a particular (*not* a "specific") group of substances. The report is confusing also by its continual repetition of "distribution lots," as if other lots of vaccine, undistributed, could have been involved.

In the summary the ideas presumably intended were these:

The study brought out no facts to show that the live virus came into the vaccine by contamination. But the facts did suggest two reasons why the live virus was present in the finished vaccine. One was that the means used did not make the virus sufficiently inactive. The other was that the tests for safety failed to detect this.

When the meaning is brought out of the depths in this way, it is seen to be a good deal less imposing and perhaps even a little silly: since there *was* dangerously live virus in the vaccine, it is clear that it had not been deactivated and clear also that the safety tests had failed. These two alleged reasons follow from the one important fact that the live virus had not got in by contamination. Considered as a piece of historical writing—a report on a series of events—the document in question falls far below the standards that the conscientious report-writer will set for himself.

⌈It is but fair to add that the whole tendency of our civilization is to make clarity and precision of expression rare and difficult.[15] We rely on instruments, formulas, and technical vocabularies, believing that if those are correctly handled the rest will take care of itself, the rest being common words. But the rest does not take care of itself, and it is the rest that controls public opinion, that fills and shapes our minds, that forms the stuff of our inner lives.⌋The national mistakes that we suffer from, like the private boredom and the painful struggle to understand, go back ultimately to some writer's or speaker's careless

---

[15] This tendency is not limited to the United States; it may be observed in European countries where literacy is often thought uniformly high. See the satirical sketch by Alex Atkinson, "How I Done My Research," *Punch*, CCXXIX (Oct. 12, 1955), 416.

thought and indifference to expression. This failure is of course not limited to scientists or technologists or to any other profession or class. The *rapporteur* of a university-sponsored seminar on European integration conveyed the opinion of a distinguished participant by saying:

> In summary, Mr. X noted that progress toward regional integration in the earlier period was the result of the perception of rewards from unity and the absence of divisive factors in the European system. Its later decline resulted from a decline in threat perception and the injection of divisive factors from outside the European system. He concluded by stating that of his four areas political cooperation is the most important since poor political relations in the short run can wipe out long-run gains in the other areas.[16]

And the writer of business reports, whether Chairman of the Board or outside auditor, is likely to spin out tautologies: "Our examination was made in accordance with generally accepted auditing standards, and accordingly included such tests of the accounting records and such other auditing procedures as we considered necessary in the circumstances."[17] That is: "We audited."

Hard Labor Makes Royal Roads

The point of these quotations is not to hold up the writers to ridicule or show superiority over them. Any of us might under certain conditions have written those sentences. They do no more than mirror the way the mind strings together ideas—in an endless, shapeless series. But having written such sentences, the man who is going to thrust them on someone else's attention has a duty to make them more intelligible and attractive. He must try to read them with the eyes of a stranger, see their faults, and correct them. This obligation defines one of our principles: except for those who compose slowly in their heads before setting down a word, NO ONE, HOWEVER GIFTED, CAN PRODUCE A PASSABLE FIRST DRAFT. WRITING MEANS RE-WRITING.

[16] Private communication of document dated January 7, 1969. The meaning is: when good political relations pay, they are maintained; when outsiders interfere they break down, regardless of benefits from cooperation.
[17] Union Pacific Railroad, Annual Report, 1969.

FIGURE 2 *Writing Means Re-Writing*

cap./

~~There were~~ *also* ninety cases of polio occurr~~ing~~ *ed*

within ~~of vaccination~~
∧49 days, ~~after a person in a given~~

~~household had been vaccinated~~ after

another person *in the house* ~~or one of his housemates~~
∧

~~(~~had received the Cutter vaccine.

In seventy-one of these cases ~~the~~ *it could be*

~~disease there~~ ~~appeared~~ *it* a connection∧ could be shown

~~that~~ with particular lots of the vaccine ⊙

~~had been used in the~~

A satisfactory last draft cannot be achieved without the labor of trial and error.

The question is, how to go about it? The act of rewriting implies that you are dissatisfied with what you put down in your first grapple with your idea. This dissatisfaction should take many forms and apply to many features of the work, from diction (the choice of words) to coherence (the linking of ideas). For your self-criticism to be rapid and effective, you must be alive to a great many distinct faults and master an equal number of corrective devices. The most important of them form the subject of Part III of this book.

What you must be persuaded of at this point is that care lavished on expression is not some optional embellishment added to your work; it is the means through which your work begins to exist. Your research turns up raw materials—very raw. Writing and rewriting make them into finished, usable products. Until brought out in full view by the best possible arrangement of words, your results remain incomplete, doubtful, hidden from every mind but your own. And your own, as your first draft shows, is none too clear.

The attempt earlier to rewrite a few sentences from the official report on the Cutter vaccine showed what revision uncovers: it reveals errors and absurdities of thought. This is invariably true, as every experienced report-writer knows: the analysis of expression is nothing else than the analysis of thought. You are therefore thinking hardest and most searchingly about your subject when scanning successive drafts to make your words "clear, orderly, and easy to grasp and remember."

The best position from which to do this is that of an editor—the editor of a magazine or the person in a publisher's office who goes over every word of a manuscript for sense and style before sending it to the printer. To develop for your own work the sharp eye of an editor, it is best to let some days elapse between writing and revision. You will then find that you yourself cannot make out the meaning of a sentence that seemed perfectly clear when it was fresh. You will notice repetitions, illogicalities, circular arguments, tautologies, back-trackings, and all the other causes of confusion, from the vagueness of clichés to the ambiguity of pronouns with multiple antecedents.

Students, who in general resist the idea that their writing needs to be improved, are the first to complain when they are assigned readings in poorly written books. They call them "dry" or "dull" and imagine that the fault lies in the subject. But every subject can be made interesting because every subject *is* interesting. It would never have aroused human curiosity if it were not. The trouble with the uninteresting assignment is that the interest has been blotted out. The book makes heavy going because the ideas do not flow, because the sentences are off balance, because the syntax gives false cues that compel one to go back and read again, because the words do not say what they mean. Reading in that case is like wading in a swamp.

To illustrate this point a second time, and strengthen in the report-writer the passion for the clarity and order that insure reading ease, consider how even an acceptable fragment of prose can be edited into something still more desirable, because sharper, cleaner, and swifter:

> For a book like the one before us, consisting as it does of a mass of close on to a hundred and fifty heterogeneous documents, what seemed to be needed in the way of introduction was a short historical sketch to furnish some sort of explanatory background for the persons and events with which these documents have to do. Accordingly that is what we have here, far as it is from telling the whole story. It is hoped, however, that it may make a little plainer what kind of men took part and why certain things happened as they did in the first of the great international congresses of our history.

That opening paragraph was, at a guess, the writer's Draft No. 3 or 4; that is, he reread it three times, changing some details each time. Now compare what we shall call Draft No. 6:

> A book such as this, comprising nearly a hundred and fifty documents of various kinds, needs by way of introduction a brief historical sketch of the events and persons to which the documents refer. Such a sketch cannot, of course, tell the whole story. It is hoped, however, that this account may make a little plainer both the causes of events and the character of the men who took part in the first great international congress in our history.

It is not the mere saving of nearly a third of the words (79 in place of 111) that recommends this last version, though brevity in itself is a service to the reader. What is decisive is that the order and connection of ideas is now unmistakable. The mushrooming of secondary thoughts has been cut out and the reader is guided down a straight path instead of being distracted by a series of side signals leading nowhere. It is the waste of effort in responding to them that is wearisome in certain books and makes them dry, dull, heavy. In other other words, faulty expression maims the subject—which is the point we set out to prove.

Notice, from the numbering of the drafts as well as from Figure 2, that improved expression cannot be attained at one jump. Between the acceptable Draft No. 4 and the reasonably trim No. 6 there had to be two further attempts to reach adequacy. The moral of this—the last of the First Principles before we go more deeply into the substance and technique of research—is that there is no short cut to expression.

PART II

Research

3

The Searcher: His Mind
and His Virtues

History: A Joint Product of Nature and Culture

In the opening chapter of this book we drew attention to civilized man's continual reference to the past and pointed out how many fragments of written history are thrust on our attention in the daily business of life. We did not then stop to define History or to retrace its development into a subject of formal study and a branch of literature.[1] The examples sufficiently proved how familiar to everyone the idea of History is. The ordinary person takes the reality of History for granted. He readily calls it "a force" or "a precious heritage," though he has probably never asked himself what he means by those phrases; but the researcher, who is naturally subject to the same cultural influence, should become more conscious and more critical of this force and this heritage. And anyone engaged in work of the mind should at some time take a bird's-eye view of the large field of which

[1]Our generation is seeing a return to the traditional view of history as literature and as distinct from the so-called behavioral sciences. See *History*, a symposium by John Higham with Leonard Krieger and Felix Gilbert, Englewood Cliffs, N.J., 1965.

he will cultivate a small patch. This is the journey we now invite the researcher to take.

Seeing how impossible it would be to uproot historical ideas and feelings from our lives, we are tempted to conclude that man is "by nature" an historical animal. He is a being who remembers his past, individual and collective. This observation holds true even when the memory is vague, as it was in the example of the Turkish official of a century ago. Though he had little interest and no precise information about his birthplace, he did remember having lived there all his life and he would have been sure to notice any marked change in the look or character of the town. [Without this developed sense of the self, and without words in which to record experiences, man would be doomed to live entirely from moment to moment, like a cow in a field.]

The first thing to note about History, then, is that it has its origin in man's awareness of continuity. But this idea is at once modified by that of separateness—of moments, days, years, hours, centuries. Ideas and objects find their place in Time, or more exactly in recorded Time (which is History), with the aid of Before and After. This is why dates matter so much, though for reasons different from those parroted to schoolchildren. Periods, like centuries, are arbitrary divisions for convenience, nothing more.

Yet though all men share the perception of time, the very fact that we discuss it and feel the need to define history shows that the awareness of history in the larger sense can differ in degree. Our invaluable Turkish official offers the example of a man who knew just enough history to be aware that Mohammed had existed and laid down the precepts of the true religion; and perhaps on this account our Turk was not interested in past events of merely earthly import. This outlook has been shared by whole civilizations, notably India. Almost nothing like ancient histories is to be found in India's literature, though nearby [China from early times supplied itself with historians and historical writings.]

One concludes that having an established and developed History is a cultural phenomenon. History is an invention, an art, probably due in the first instance to the thought of a genius whose novel idea others took up. In the Chinese language we find that the original form of the character for "historian" represented a hand holding a receptacle used to contain tallies at archery contests.[2] From recording this or similar matters of passionate interest, men in various civilizations came to record other things—court ceremonies, religious sacrifices, and striking events. Ultimately a day-to-day record was kept—in China it was known as the *Spring and Autumn Annals* though it covered the entire year. But this rather dull chronicle (eighth century B.C.) had been preceded by a collection of notable sayings and moral injunctions to officials that is called *The Book of Documents* or *Book of History*. This earlier record was a more poetic and attractive work than the dry calendar of facts and can be likened to a fanciful archive of state papers. The *Annals* were a sort of public diary. Both together would be, to us, materials for a true history.

In Western culture the same sequence of interests and expression is found, with two important differences. If we take Homer's account of the Trojan War as paralleling the Chinese *Book of Documents,* we find in the [Greek work a much richer, more highly organized piece of legendary history—a better work of art.] And when we look for a Greek parallel to the *Annals* in Herodotus, who lived in the fifth century B.C., we find not only superb literary art once again, but also a deep curiosity about other peoples and *their* history—the Egyptians, Medes, Persians, and so on. The seamless fabric of History is thus extended beyond local limits and domestic concerns.

The curiosity that took Herodotus on his many travels in search of information was not confined to the author himself. The Greeks, as traders and seafarers, were an active, bustling, wide-awake people who "wanted to know." Herodotus gave them what he called *historiai,* which means "researches." His book begins: "These are the researches of Herodotus of Halicarnassus"; and what follows is a series of reports for oral delivery. We know they were read by the researcher himself, in the open air, to any Athenian who cared to stop and listen. This

[2] For this and the following facts, see Burton De Witt Watson's Introduction to his translation of the *Shih-chi.* (Unpublished doctoral dissertation, Columbia University, 1956), and his life of the Grand Historian of China, *Ssu Ma Chien* [145–90? B.C.], New York, 1958.

was an added reason for making these *logoi,* or speeches, attractive little works of art. [The fact that Herodotus was the first to weave his researches into a continuous and shapely narrative, ultimately for readers, is what justifies his ancient title of "Father of History." After Herodotus written history is, in the West, an accepted art.]

This tradition having remained unbroken, [Western culture may be said to be the historical culture par excellence.] Just as Herodotus went back in time to explain to the Greeks how the Persian invader came to be where he was, so we try to grasp our own situation with the aid of innumerable historical ideas. We are doing this right here and now by tracing back our daily historicism to an ancient Greek and calling him the "father" of one of our intellectual disciplines.

We recognize historical continuity by the way we refer to the various divisions of what we possessively call *our* civilization. We ascribe one custom to the Middle Ages, another to the Renaissance, and a third to modern times, but the joint product survives in ourselves. We explain our ideas and ways of life as continuous transformations through twenty-five hundred years and more—just as we explain the form and meaning of our commonest words, including the word History itself: all but a few European languages use derivatives of the word that the Greeks had for it: Latin and Spanish *historia,* French *histoire,* English *history,* Italian *storia.*

From this same root we have also the cognate noun "story," and as we pointed out before, the West is so accustomed to conceiving life historically that in the novel, the dominant literary form today, we enjoy seeing how fiction and imagination have been subdued to the critical control of fact. In pure history, naturally, it is understood that nothing is reported but verified fact. In other words—and this shall be our first definition—[*History at its simplest is the story of past facts.*]

Four Meanings of the Word History

A moment's thought, however, shows that we commonly use the word History in two senses, and perhaps more. In one use, as in the title *History of the Second World War,* we mean the story of what happened. In another use, as in "By that decision, the President made history," we mean the notable fact itself; not the story but the substance of what happened.[3] This ambiguity is inevitable and it turns out on reflection to be very instructive. For it records our belief that what is in the book exactly corresponds to what occurred in real life. When we read, "the story" is like witnessed History. We could say that a history (with a small *h*) deserves its name when it truly represents a portion of History (with a capital *H*). The aim of written history is realized when it achieves what an ancient critic said in praise of Herodotus: "He takes you along and turns hearing into sight."[4]

Written history, then, holds its place in our civilization because we know that it reports things that actually took place. Civilized man has a passion for facts. This is so strong that a great writer of our century, when giving advice to a beginner, made his cardinal precept: "Get your facts right first: that is the foundation of all style."[5] Though the proposition is far from self-evident, we accept it because we connect factuality with honesty, honesty with sincerity, and sincerity with style.

The man who has got his facts right and is about to report on them may or may not think of himself as an historian; but if he does, the term History very likely has for him a third sense. He may say, for instance, 'History requires the most painstaking research." It is clear that he means by History something halfway between the past events and his report, as yet incomplete, namely, the *fashioning* of written history. This, he knows, requires method. The professional attitude makes certain demands and the art obeys certain rules. To refer to this disciplining of the mind it might be better to use the term Historiography, and henceforth in this book an attempt will be made to observe the distinction. Yet so close is the association in our minds between the event, the account of it, and the means by which the account is prepared that a consistent usage is difficult. The ideas overlap and prompt the speaker to use the most general term for the science, the art, and its substance: History.[6]

Modern man's position as a latecomer in Time encourages this

[3] The German word for History is *Geschichte*, which comes from the verb *geschehen*, "to happen"; and its other use—as "story"—parallels the practice of the other languages cited above.

[4] Longinus, 26.2.

[5] George Bernard Shaw, *Advice to a Young Critic*, New York, 1955, 13.

[6] In Chinese too the same ideas seem to have merged, since there is current a false etymology of the character for "historian," which is often analyzed to mean "a hand holding the correct thing." Watson, *op. cit.*

fusion of ideas. We in the West have for so long had access to abundant written sources, as well as to written histories based on these sources, that we take both for granted and think of them together as almost physically containing "our past." But in an age that lacked the printing press and was limited in literacy, oral communication was the dominant cultural form. History must then have seemed more at the mercy of chance, more an accident of individual memory than a collective possession.

This feeling left its mark on Herodotus and Thucydides—indeed on all the historians in ancient times. They wrote like orators because whatever sounded right had the special merit of being more memorable. To us this seems "unhistorical"; for Fact, we think, matters above all else. Yet we may be going to a dangerous extreme on the opposite side when we imagine that something set down on paper, no matter how, is history even if nobody reads it. Our national and other archives pile up documents by the cubic mile: in what sense are they history if no mind ever subjects them to the processes of historiography? And during those processes, what is the proper action of the reader's mind upon the substance of History? A soldier-scholar like Lawrence of Arabia scorned the squirrel-like habits of a Paper Age, and counseled a friend accordingly:

You are retired to write your book about the Empire. Good. Remember that the manner is greater than the matter, so far as modern history is concerned. One of the ominous signs of the times is that the public can no longer read history. The historian is retired into a shell to study the whole truth; which means that he learns to attach insensate importance to documents. The documents are liars. No man ever yet tried to write down the entire truth of any action in which he has been engaged. All narrative is parti-pris. And to prefer an ancient written statement to the guiding of your instinct through the maze of related facts, is to encounter either banality or unreadableness.

[7] And to the archives kept by government at every level there are now added—since Franklin Roosevelt—the libraries of "presidential papers." The precedent once set will most likely continue, until a conscientious student of American history will find that he must spend the better part of his life traveling from one presidential birthplace to the next. For the sum total of national document collections, see H. G. Jones, *The Records of a Nation*, New York, 1969.

We know too much, and use too little knowledge. Cut away the top hamper.[8]

This "cuts away" too much. Documents are not all liars. But Lawrence has a sound point about the workings of the human mind, and he has the support of some distinguished professionals. At a meeting of a British learned society in the mid-1930's, a paper by C. S. Orwin entitled "The Open Fields" was greeted by the renowned scholar R. H. Tawney with the words: "What historians need is not more documents but stronger boots."[9] The implication, as a noted economic historian puts it, is that "history, when it is written from documents alone, is dead stuff and probably more false than true."[10] Without the *experiencing mind,* the searcher after truth cannot bridge the gap between the lived occurrence and the dusty record.

If other men are to enjoy and use the knowledge gathered from records by the searcher's critical methods, the breath of life must be in the product. Otherwise, it is no more than the evidence digested and collected. It is a report, not on the events, but on the documents and the search. Or as the famous parody of history *1066 and All That* made plain by a brilliant exaggeration: "History is what you can remember. All other history defeats itself."[11] This was in fact the principle that the ancients believed in and acted on. In making up the speeches of ambassadors and generals as they *might* have been spoken, Thucydides knew that they would become what he hoped his whole history would be—lifelike and memorable: we still quote from his pages Pericles' Funeral Oration.

We thus come, by way of the gravest problem of historiography, to yet another meaning of History: the recollection of the past in the minds of a whole people. This Popular or Folk History is of course not of uniform quality. It includes legends like that of Frederick Barbarossa asleep in his cave until he wakes to found a new German Empire; the virtuous deeds of national heroes; the biased interpretations that make all national wars noble and all drawn battles victories;

---

[8] *The Letters of T. E. Lawrence,* ed. David Garnett, New York, 1939, 559.
[9] Quoted in W. K. Hancock, *Country and Calling,* London, 1954, 95.
[10] *Ibid.*
[11] W. C. Sellar and R. J. Yeatman, *1066 and All That,* New York, 1931, vii.

and a mixed lot of names and dates, images and slogans, which rouse immediate emotion and serve as triggers to action: "No Entangling Alliances," "Fifty-four Forty or Fight," "The Big Stick," the covered wagon, John Brown's body, Pearl Harbor, the New Frontier, the Great Society. Every institution, every family has such catchwords and lives by them. In these familiar forms History is the past shaping the present and future, having first shaped the minds of the historian and his audience. To sum up: History-as-Event generates (through History-as-Hard-Work) History-as-Narrative, which in turn produces History-as-Maker-of-Future-History.

The Changing Uses of a Changing Past

On the power of historical recollections rest the numerous arguments for the importance of historical studies. But each argument tends to make of history something different, and the researcher must distinguish, in himself and in others, what the authentic historical residue may be. There is the patriot's history. A nation being united by language, intermarriage, territory, and common historical traditions, its young in school study history in order to become true citizens. The adult population of democracies is told that it must read current history in order to understand the world it lives in and vote intelligently on national issues. Political leaders likewise profess to find history the best guide to action. The faith in the utility of history must be widespread indeed, or we would not find the campaign literature for President Eisenhower's first election making a point of his being "a great reader of Thucydides," or hear it reported that President Kennedy gave Prime Minister Macmillan a copy of *The Guns of August*.

History also moves minds by what it inspires. According to President Truman, the most formative book he read as a child was a compilation entitled *Great Men and Famous Women*—from Nebuchadnezzar to Sarah Bernhardt; and it is well known that Plutarch's *Lives* once exercised an incalculable influence on the minds of men. The most heroic careers of early modern times, the noblest passions of the French Revolution, followed the models in those short biographies drawn from the history of ancient Greece and Rome. The same kind of emulation permitted Lyndon B. Johnson to say of his labors for civil rights legislation: "Lincoln walks the corridors with me. The Emancipation Proclamation is being made a fact."[12]

Prophets (and politicians also) tend to agree with Lamartine, the poet who was part historian and part statesman and who said that "History teaches everything including the future." But most professional historians refuse to predict. Many of them deplore the distortions brought about by "present-mindedness," the habit of going to history with modern ideas and intentions. Yet some have not hesitated to admit their desire to influence events by "proving" the rightness or wrongness of a cause out of its historical antecedents. And the makers of great historical systems, as we shall see, set out to discover the "laws" of history so that man may foresee the shape of things to come. Such men, of whom Marx was the least deterred by doubts, believed that History itself was speaking through their mouths.

The laws, needless to say, have not yet been found, though the detailed knowledge of a particular culture or country often enables students to distinguish the constant from the fleeting, and thereby to guess intelligently at the outcome of a given situation. Thus in the middle of the Second World War nine American historians were brought together in Washington and "asked to predict, largely on the basis of what had already happened, the ability of the Nazi war machine and the German people to stand up under Allied pressure."[13] The nine men read secret documents, heard the testimony of scores of witnesses, and within three months made their report. When it was reviewed in the light of subsequent events it was found "a remarkably accurate forecast."[14]

The application of history to a purpose so sharply defined is rare. The benefit more usually expected of it is an enrichment of the imagination that promotes a quick and shrewd understanding of the actions of men in society. Hence the value of historical training to the student of any aspect of man's life and to the worker in any branch of social intelligence. Judge Learned Hand, who called history the cornerstone

[12] In conversation with Henry F. Graff at the White House, June 11, 1965.
[13] *New York Times*, June 8, 1946.
[14] *Ibid.*

of a liberal education, explained why the subject is a begetter of social wisdom.

Most of the issues that mankind sets out to settle, it never does settle. They are not solved, because . . . they are incapable of solution properly speaking, being concerned with incommensurables. . . . The dispute fades into the past unsolved, though perhaps it may be renewed as history and fought over again. It disappears because it is replaced by some compromise that, although not wholly acceptable to either side, offers a tolerable substitute for victory; and he who would find the substitute needs an endowment as rich as possible in experience, an experience which makes the heart generous and provides the mind with an understanding of the hearts of others. The great moderates of history were more often than not men of that sort, steeped, like Montaigne and Erasmus, in knowledge of the past.[15]

So many are the possibilites of history that James Harvey Robinson, theorist of historiography, was once led to remark that it "may well become the most potent instrument for human regeneration."[16] But the diversity of searchers' minds remains. Lynn Thorndike, another distinguished professional, pointed out in discussing Robinson's phrase that "for some, history is literature; for others, facts; for some, delving in archives; for others, interpretations of the sources; for some, an art; for others, a science; for some, drudgery; for others, a romance; for some, an explanation of the present; for others, a revelation and a realization of the past."[17]

No man can dictate to another the kind of historian he shall be; or can himself tell, at the outset of his career, how research and reflection will make him ultimately view his subject. It is obvious that for many researchers the interest lies in the chase. Historiography is armchair detection par excellence. But its results furnish the mind with quantities of new and unexpected ideas, which it is also a pleasure to contemplate and a challenge to fit into a communicable pattern. Then, too, such ideas permit one to generalize and to compare, until increasing familiarity with men and nations dead and gone, their words

[15] Address at the evening session of the 86th convocation of the University of the State of New York, Albany, October 24, 1952.
[16] James Harvey Robinson, quoted in Lynn Thorndike, book review of *The Human Comedy*, in *Journal of Modern History*, IX (September 1937), 369.
[17] *Ibid.*

and their deeds, their costumes and their thoughts, ends by making the student feel thoroughly at home in the varieties of human life—as if he had traveled for years in strange lands and learned many languages.

In other words, whether history is put to use in the present, or simply garnered out of curiosity, or enjoyed as an object of contemplation, we can frame its inclusive definition by saying: *History is vicarious experience.*[18] Knowledge of history is like a second life extended indefinitely into the "dark backward and abysm of time." When history is described in these terms it is usual to add that history is an art, not a science. All this means is that history communicates "incommensurables," not formulas to be applied. It acts directly from mind to mind; it affects personality rather than policy; its power to change men is subtle, not violent.

This undoubted influence answers a question that puzzles many people and to which we shall return in Chapter 7. Historians are often asked: "How can History be of any value in use when what it tells us is so uncertain? Every historian differs from every other, and all discard their predecessors' views every generation. With such instability about the past, which manifestly cannot change or be changed, History seems hardly knowledge, only a serious kind of entertainment."

Though we postpone discussing the reliability of history, we must take note here of the important fact that in its mutability history does not differ from science. Science too changes its interpretations every few years, and on its frontiers hypotheses conflict. Yet one could say of Nature as one says of the past that it is an unchanging reality that should allow no difference of opinion. The fact remains that both science and history are variable.

Some Varieties of Occidental History

One cause of the diversity in historical writing is temperament, as Lynn Thorndike suggested above. He might have gone on to say that in addition to his pairs of historians contrasted by temperament

---

[18] "Experience" here is to be taken literally as meaning the "actually lived"; it is not the imagined experience that we also make our own in reading fiction or beholding a work of art.

there were schools and periods and entire ages that cherished opposite conceptions of historiography. Until the advent of modern science, which captivated one group of historians, the two dominant conceptions of history were the moral and the political. Herodotus and Thucydides conveniently represent these two tendencies. Herodotus wants his history to give great men "their due meed of glory"; he believes that great lives and deeds have permanent value as moral teachings. He has political interests too, and zeal for knowing things simply in order to know them, but morality is his text and pretext.

Thucydides repudiates this view. He considers both the idle curiosity and the moralizing intent irrelevant to his purpose, which is the practice of politics. His manner is impersonal and austere; he will not digress and would rather not entertain. He is a general and statesman writing for his peers.

Other pagan historians fall into one or the other of these two categories. Polybius, Caesar, and Sallust belong to the tradition of Thucydides; Livy, Suetonius, Tacitus, and Plutarch to that of Herodotus. With the coming of Christianity the moral concern of historiographers overwhelms every other interest. Saint Augustine and—with far less power—Orosius narrate great events like true historians, but they interpret catastrophes as God's chastisement. Events formerly taken to be under the rule of change or natural law are now interpreted as the working out of a divine plan. The Christian historian applies to the past a rigid moral standard enforced like a retroactive law, and his curiosity is modified by revelations, prophecies, and concern about the aftermath of Judgment Day.

To this intense moralism there was added in the Middle Ages a ready belief in the occurrence of the supernatural on earth. Chronicles and lives of saints continued to show that Western man cared about keeping records and writing biography, but these activities reflected even more the spiritual and theological preoccupations of the writers, who belonged for the most part to the clergy. Consequently, the reawakening of historiography in the ancient (and present-day) sense coincides with the secularization of life in early modern times. The rise of monarchies and nation-states, the passionate scholarship of the Renaissance humanists, the widening discussion of methods and results in physical science—all contributed to the reinstatement of the historical and critical virtues. Pierre Bayle's famous *Historical and Critical Dictionary* (1695–97) summed up the results of the scholarly attitude that had been at work in Europe for two centuries: the word "critical" was a triumphant declaration of independence for research.

In the next generation Voltaire enlarged the scope of hitherto monarchical history by showing in his *Essay on the Manners and Customs of Nations* (1756) that aspects of civilized life other than battles and kings have importance and can interest the general public. Finally, in the nineteenth century, two great revolutions sealed the triumph of history as a subject of universal interest. One was the French Revolution of 1789, which set peoples on the thrones of kings and thus stimulated nations to rediscover their past all the way back to the Fall of Rome. With the same ardor, oppressed nationalities all over Europe founded their unity on the basis of their popular histories. It was this cultural nationalism that inspired Walter Scott to make Scotland as well as the Middle Ages live in his great creation, the historical novel. Thanks to the enormous popularity of his works Scott may be said to have taught Europe history.[19]

His influence was reinforced by the gradual spread of the idea of Evolution. When the debate over it grew violent after 1860, a second cultural revolution occurred. It put physical science at the top of the tree of knowledge and affected the form of all traditional subjects. From evolutionary thought in biology everyone borrowed the "genetic method." This stated that behind every phenomenon was a long chain of facts, which must be discovered before the fact in front of us could be understood. Not only individual and national life, but laws, customs, institutions, ideas, morals, religions, and even deities began to be studied genetically, which is to say historically. The modern Western mind is thus doubly historical.

Accordingly, it has seemed to many that historiography must push beyond the old purposes of morality and political practice: history must be made scientific, on a par with geology, paleontology, and biology. Accumulation and verification must take precedence over literary skill, and encyclopedic thoroughness must become a commandment. To be scientific, a monograph must tell all about a single small

[19] See G. M. Trevelyan, *Clio, A Muse,* New York, 1930, 165–66.

subject, and what the work contains must purport to be definitive. Present-day historiography has abated some of its original scientific claims, though its attitude continues to deserve the name; and researchers of all kinds are at one with the public in acknowledging the sway of the genetic interpretation. Every discourse begins with "the background"; nothing, it is thought, can be understood apart from a knowledge of what went before.

The Searcher's Virtues

Enough has been said of the nature and effect of our long historical training to enable the reader to form some idea of the ingrained tendencies a researcher will possess to start with. It remains to say something of the qualities he should develop in addition. Temperament and point of view cannot be legislated about; they are his affair; but the fundamental virtues are a prescribed *sine qua non*. Fortunately, they are capable of development by exercise and self-control. It is in fact this possibility that justifies our giving to any branch of learning the name of discipline.

In speaking of "virtues," one is of course using the word as a piece of shorthand to suggest what impulses the researcher must curb or encourage in himself. No doubt many more qualities than the half dozen about to be listed are called into play. But these are indispensable, and giving them names may not only help the student in his research, but also deepen his understanding of what this book attempts to teach him. He should, after pondering the six virtues, go over the present chapter again and, by connecting them with the topics discussed, discover how inherited ideas affect the individual's curiosity about fact and his ability to find and interpret it.

1. The first necessary virtue is ACCURACY. No argument is needed to show why. If "History is the story of past facts" (our first definition), those facts must be *ascertained*. Making certain implies being accurate—steadily, religiously. To this end, train yourself to remember names and dates and titles of books with precision. Never say to yourself or to another: "It's in that book—you know—I forget what it's called

and the man's name, but it has a green cover." [Being precise means *attending* to the object when you first examine it and noting small differences instead of skipping over them:] "Here is a volume on the Lincoln Memorial in Washington. It is edited by Edward Concklin, and the author spells his name with an added *c*." There is no profound significance in this fact, no imperative need to remember it, but if you do this kind of thing repeatedly, regularly, you will avoid a multitude of blunders. Some few blunders you are bound to make. Everybody is liable to them almost in proportion to the length of his work. But they can be kept to a minimum by the habit of unremitting attention. Do not fear that such details will clutter up your mind: they will lie dormant until needed, and often will suggest important links with other matters you would not otherwise have dreamed of.

2. Next comes the [LOVE OF ORDER.] There is in any piece of research so much to be read, noted down, compared, verified, indexed, grouped, organized, and recopied, that unless one is capable of adhering to a system the chances of error grow alarming, while the task itself turns into a perpetual panicky emergency—What did I do with those bibliographic notes? In what notebook did I list the dates I checked? Does this page belong to Draft 1 or Draft 2? And so on ad infinitum. [Some people may overdo orderliness, but most of us underdo it, usually from groundless self-confidence.] You may think you know what you are doing and have done. The fact is that as you get deeper into a subject you will know more and more about *it* and very likely less and less about your own movements and belongings. [Hence the value of the system, which keeps order for you. Sticking to it is never a loss of time, though it calls for the union of three minor virtues: calm, patience, and pertinacity]

3. It might be thought that orderliness would imply also LOGIC. In practice it seems to do so to a negligible extent; the one is mechanical, the other intellectual. [The logic considered here is not the formal art of the philosopher, but its ready and practical application to the perplexities of library research.] As will be shown in the next chapter, [the researcher must quickly learn the schemes of innumerable reference books;] if he is not adept at inference he will bog down or make mistakes. For example, in the *Thesaurus* of ancient Latin authors, which offers to the eye under each entry an unappetizing block of print,

the punctuation is faint and confusing. If you do not reason correctly from the first or last quotation in each block, you will infallibly connect the one you look for with the wrong author.

The physical arrangement of books in any given library may present the same kind of problem: if over here we are in the *G*'s and over there in the *K*'s, the intervening books (including the *H*'s, which I want) must be in some obvious but self-concealing place, such as the lower part of this large reference table, which has shelves—and here in fact they are. If you run to the librarian for the solution of every puzzle, mental or physical, trivial or important, you will be an old but *in*experienced researcher before you have finished.

4. Elsewhere HONESTY may be the best policy, but in research it is the only one. Unless you put down what you find to be true with complete candor, you are nullifying the very result you aim at, which is the discovery of the past as embedded in records. You may have a hypothesis that the new fact shatters, but that is what hypotheses are for—to be destroyed and remolded closer to the reality. The troublesome fact may go against your moral purpose or prejudice, but nothing is healthier for the mind than to have either challenged. You are a searcher after truth, which should reconcile you to every discovery. And even if you should decide to become an advocate for a cause, you had better know beforehand all the evidence your side will have to face. For if one fact is there obstructing your path, you may be fairly sure others to the same effect will be turned up, possibly by your adversary. It is the nature of reality to be mixed, and the research scholar is the man on whom we rely to chart it. His accuracy about neutral details is of little worth if we cannot trust his honesty about significant ones.

5. Some persons are honest as far as they can see, but they do not see far enough; in particular they do not see around themselves. They lack the virtue of SELF-AWARENESS. The searcher needs it first in order to make sure that he is not unwittingly dishonest; and, second, in order to lessen the influence of bias by making his standards of judgment plain to the reader. No man can be a perfectly clear reflector of what he finds. There is always some flaw in the glass, whose effect may be so uniform as not to disclose itself. The only protection against this source of constant error is for the writer to make his assumptions

clear. To invent an *outré* example, a fanatical teetotaler might in a biographical sketch of General Grant assert that here was a man of revolting and immoral habits. Given nothing else, the reader is inclined to trust the conclusions of the writer. But if the accusation reads: "Anyone who habitually drinks whiskey is a man of revolting moral character; therefore, General Grant, etc.," the reader has a chance to dissent and judge for himself.

This simplified instance bears on two important realms of reporting—the description of cultures alien in time or space, and biography. In both, it is essential for the researcher to control his emotions as he finds evidence of behavior repugnant to him or to the standards of his age. It is also essential for him to set forth (though more subtly than in the example above) what his criteria are when he passes judgment or describes by epithets. Failing this, the way is open to the meanest kind of libel and defamation of character.

6. Everybody is always urging everybody else to have IMAGINATION, and this is indeed good advice. But perhaps the hint should suggest not so much laying in a stock as releasing what we have. Convention and lazy habits often suppress the happy thought that, if let alone, would lead to the desired goal. In research this goal is double—practical and abstract. The researcher must again and again *imagine* the kind of source he would like to have before he can find it. To be sure, it may not exist; but if it does, its whereabouts must be presumed. By that ingenious balancing of wish and reason which is true imagination, the seeker can make his way from what he knows and possesses to what he must possess in order to know more. The two chapters following will give concrete instances. And the researcher must also perform these acrobatics of the mind around his abstract problems. For example, working upon a critical study of Henry James and noticing the novelist's persistent attempts in later life to become a playwright—a determination shown also in the dramatic tone and structure of the later novels—the critic begins to wonder what theatrical influences could have formed this taste. Is it possible that James as a child or youth attended the New York theaters, then famous for melodrama? The dates coincide, and behold, autobiographical evidence when sought confirms the inspired guess.

The historian's imagination has other uses that go far beyond this simple pulling of oneself up by the bootstraps. We have not said the last word on the subject. But the historical imagination of a genius cannot be asked of every modest workman. It is the modest imagination that is insisted on here as an implement that none can do without. Remember, too, that even with the lesser kind there is no law requiring it to be used in modest doses.

Let the researcher give free play to these six virtuous forms of energy and he is ready for his first foray into that *terra incognita*, the library.

4

Finding the Facts

The Detective and His Clues

What is tantalizing about the proverbial task of finding the needle in the haystack is that you are assured the needle is there. The space is restricted, the object is unique, it must be possible to find it. And no doubt, with enough care and patience, and working by system, it could be found with just a pair of eyes and a pair of hands. Of course, if the hay were to be packed in small cubes and a large magnet brought to bear as the contents of each were spread out, then the task would be greatly facilitated — it would almost turn into a game.

This fairy-tale problem has its analogue in the researcher's hunt for his facts. [The probability is great that any one fact he wants is in some printed work and the work in some library.] To find it he has to find the right cube of hay—the book or periodical—and then use his magnetic intelligence to draw out the needlelike fact.

That "the library"—as yet unspecified—is the repository of by far the largest part of our recorded knowledge needs no demonstration. The author of an article on West Africa who reports that the annual rainfall in Fernando Po is 100 inches found this information in the library—in a book. It is most unlikely that he measured the rain himself.

Aside from the direct knowledge of an event by an eyewitness, or a firsthand investigation on the scene through interviews, laboratory or field work, or the study of relics,[1] [the shortest path to the facts is library research.]

The library may be a small collection on a special subject, owned by a business firm and housed in a single room; it may be a college library designed to meet the needs of undergraduate courses; it may be a reference collection of moderate size for the researchers of a magazine such as *Life;* or it may be an "encyclopedic" library—properly a research library—that owns millions of old books and has a standing order with leading publishers for all new books of serious import. Unless the library accessible to you is rigidly specialized, the chances are that it contains something you want, if not for itself, then as a lead. If this something does not furnish positive and sufficient information, it may well prove negatively useful by enabling you to cross off what looked like a lead. [In either case, there is no choice: into the library you must go. It is the researcher's first port of call, whether or not he knows what profit to expect from it.]

It is natural enough for beginners to feel disconcerted—lost and lonely—in a strange library. You can overcome this feeling quickly by setting out to learn your library. Regardless of size, [all libraries have common features that the experienced researcher immediately looks for. After you have conquered a few of these strongholds you will realize that to master one is to master them all.] It is like having *In the U.S.* → learned to drive a car: you soon discover that knowing one make enables you to drive any other. Each dashboard looks different, but it is only the superficial arrangement that differs.

What then do you look for in a library? First, the card catalogue—where is it? How do the tiers of drawers run, perhaps from one room to the next? Is the catalogue all one, or subdivided into Books (authors and subjects) and Serials (periodicals)? The heading at the top of the cabinets will give you the answers. What is the cataloguing system in use? Open a drawer and see if the now standard Library of Congress cards (with their characteristic call numbers) are there, or some other kind.[2] Shut the drawer quickly if the cards are

---

[1] See Chapter 7.

[2] For a reproduction of a Library of Congress card with explanations of its contents, see Figure 3.

of another size and pattern, denoting an older system. You will have to study it *de novo,* perhaps with the help of the librarian.

Turn now to the shelf or section of reference books. It will tell you roughly what kind of collection the library contains—its size and its specialization if any; for in these respects the reference shelf mirrors the rest of the library. Next discover or inquire whether you have access to the stacks: if a placard of stack floors and their contents is prominently displayed to the public, this doubtless means that you may go direct to the books. Make a mental or written note of the floors where books on your subject are housed. Then turn back to the catalogue.

We will assume that the cards are the Library of Congress cards, or that you have worked out, alone or with help, the principle of some other type. All but a few systems are in the form of a continuous alphabet of cards, which give the reader at least this information: author's name, title of book, place and date of publication, indication of the spot where the book stands in the library. We will further assume that you have not stepped in merely to ascertain the annual rainfall on Fernando Po. You are looking for at least three or four books—that nucleus spoken of earlier. Fewer than this number are hardly likely to give you the materials for even a short paper or thorough book review. The catalogue holds the clue to the existence and whereabouts of those books.

Publishing has so greatly increased, the world over, that it is no longer possible simply to scan a few shelves and take down the works likely to be useful. In consequence, the researcher's task has become a good deal more intricate—to say nothing of the librarian's. The expansion of the resources of inquiry is indeed as alarming as it is gratifying. Sixty thousand new books in English are thrown annually into the sea of printed literature. The libraries of the great institutions of learning double in size every sixteen to eighteen years.[3] But there are various patterns of growth. Columbia University acquired its one-millionth volume in 1925—forty-two years after the consolidation of its separate collections. Its two-millionth volume arrived in 1946, and its three-millionth in 1960. The four-millionth was catalogued recently.

[3] Keyes D. Metcalf, *Planning Academic and Research Library Buildings,* New York, 1965, 9.

In 1968–69 alone 150,000 new books came in to swell these holdings.[4]

The rate of growth is not the only predicament. The wood-pulp paper generally used in books published since 1870 has deteriorated so badly, owing to the alum-rosin sizing with which it is prepared for printing, that "most library books printed in the first half of the 20th century will be in unusable condition in the next century."[5] [Many books, especially those from certain foreign countries, are printed on paper of such low quality that they begin to disintegrate before they can be catalogued.] If catalogues are to be prevented from becoming mere fossil records of books that once existed, something will have to be done, either through chemical preservation or through large-scale, recurrent reprinting.

The Microcard System advocated by the late Fremont Ryder for both saving space and lengthening the life of relentlessly growing periodicals has not come into being, but the latest news from the technologists is that the "ultra-microbook" is on its way. With modern methods of molecular manipulation, it is possible to reduce 3000 pages to an area a few inches wide; the slip (called a *microfiche*) is then made durable by lamination. A table- or lap-viewer enables the reader to see without strain a double page open before him. A photocopier can be linked with the viewer to reproduce a desired page readily.[6] Al-

---

[4] Richard H. Logsdon, "Source Document on the [Columbia] University Libraries," (July 7, 1966), 8; and Logsdon, "Annual Report, July 1, 1968–June 30, 1969" (June 18, 1969).

[5] W. J. Barrow, *Deterioration of Book Stock: Causes and Remedies,* ed. Randolph W. Church, Richmond, Va., 1959, 16. Microfilm, which once seemed likely to keep books "in print" forever, is no longer so regarded. Apart from inconvenience in use, microfilm is also subject to deterioration in only twenty-five to thirty years. "The Preservation of Deteriorating Books," Part I, *Library Journal* (January 1, 1966), 51–56; and Part II, *ibid.,* 189–94. (January 15, 1966). Those interested in the problem and the remedial research underway should see David G. Lowe, "The Case of the Vanishing Records," *American Heritage,* XX (August 1969), 34–35, 107–11.

[6] The *Encyclopedia Britannica* has already offered to libraries the opportunity of subscribing to a 20,000-volume set of American works and documents on microfiches, covering most fields of learning other than science. A valuable introductory manual on the preservation through various "micro" means of historical records is Albert H. Leisinger, Jr., *Microphotography for Archives,* published by the International Council on Archives (Washington, D.C., 1968).

though the microfiches should present no difficulty for ordinary reading, for consulting and comparing they may prove a little less satisfactory than books. But it often happens that a book is not to be had, on loan or in any other way, because of distance, rarity, or disintegrating state. The card will prolong the life of the book and multiply its presence. [Moreover, since the preparation and printing of the microbooks will be facilitated by the use of computers, the machine will also provide an exhaustive single topical index of all the works associated in one set or category.]

Regardless of the form of the book you seek, when you step up to a catalogue of books to begin your search, you should already have answered in your mind the question: What am I hunting down? We shall make a number of alternative suppositions to show that "knowing what you want" depends on "knowing what you don't want." Thus you are looking for Louis Napoleon's early political ideas, but not necessarily for the latest biography of him; you want a detailed explanation of the Guaranteed Annual Wage, but will not be sidetracked to a general history of labor; you want to know the origin of the use of firecrackers in patriotic celebrations, but will not need a history of the Declaration of Independence.

If by luck or cunning you already know the name of the author of a particular book on your subject, you will save time and effort. You simply go to the right alphabetical catalogue drawer, look up the name, and under it find the work you want. You obtain it and are launched on your research, for the author's citations and bibliography will carry you forward a good distance.

[If you cannot name the author, look up the title instead.] You are an unusual person—almost a professional—if you have remembered it correctly. Most often you retain the sense of the title but unconsciously change the wording. You want *The Origins of the American Revolution,* but you recall it as *The Causes of the Revolutionary War.* You must from now on make a point of remembering books by their authors. Not only does this knowledge help you to discriminate among the many books on the same subject, but it also helps to offset the fact that on some topics all the titles are bound to sound alike. Sometimes, indeed, they are identical: at least four books about New York have been called *East Side, West Side;* three other books, on different subjects, are called *East of the Sun and West of the Moon.* Moreover, a garbled title is more difficult to straighten out than a garbled name, because librarians, like others who deal daily with books, tend to remember books by their authors rather than by their titles or the color of their bindings.

If neither the "author entry" nor the "title entry" in the card catalogue brings you what you want, you have no better course to follow than to look up the subject. When you are seeking information about a public figure this is easy. The lives of Benjamin Franklin (as well as his works) are both catalogued under "Franklin, Benjamin." Sometimes you have to know the man's birth and death dates in addition to his name, because the catalogue includes a number of people with the same names, for example, Samuel Butler.[7] Their dates are the readiest means of telling them apart. To work up a biographical sketch, then, all you need know to start with is that books *by* the individual come first, followed by books *about* him (or her), these last books being in the alphabetical order of their authors' names.

To find a subject other than a person, you must bring to bear on the problem a little more knowledge and imagination. As was shown in Chapter 2 with regard to the divine right of kings, you must guess under what word or words your subject has been catalogued. If it is "flying saucers" you want, you are not likely to go astray even though books and articles will call them U.F.O.'s—Unidentified Flying Objects. But for many topics you must know how the librarian thinks when he classifies books. Not all librarians think alike, but there is reason in their ways. The researcher's puzzlement usually comes from small variations of words. If you are studying the opening of Japan, for example, you discover that some of the pertinent books are listed under "Japan Expedition of the American Squadron, 1852–1854"; others under "U.S. Japan Expedition of the American Squadron, 1852–1854"; and still others under "United States Naval Expedition to Japan, 1852–1854." Why is this so? Because books on this subject have been published for over a century now, and rules and fashions of cataloguing, like other rules and fashions, have changed with the years. Keeping

---

[7] First names are essential: there are two poets named Pope in English literature. But there are not always first names to be had: two Greek generals are named Thucydides. Here only dates help.

this example in mind, form the habit of imagining synonyms and possible permutations of terms.

Moreover, odd as it may seem, new subjects are continually being created for which the old catalogue with all its fixed subject entries must still serve. For example, until 1954 the word "desegregation" was seldom used to describe the movement to end Jim Crow. The researcher confronting the card catalogue will have to try a number of subject headings, such as "Negro," "Civil Rights," and "Afro-American(s)."[8] [Finding these "cognate headings" is the first knack the researcher acquires. He learns his way in libraries through learning the ways of librarians.]

Cross-Questioning the Book

But there is more yet to be squeezed from the catalogue cards. Study the card reproduced in Figure 3. Leaving out for a moment the numbers at the top left, which will differ in some libraries, and reading down one paragraph at a time, you will find the card telling you the following things:

1. That the author was born in 1915 and is presumably still alive.
2. That the name that appears on the book is a pseudonym (pen name). The real name is the first one on the card, and you were led to it by a cross reference when you looked up the pseudonym.
3. That the work is a translation from the German in a revised edition, published by a well-known New York firm in 1967.
4. That the work is of some magnitude and has illustrations and portraits. For other books the card will tell you of special features, such as appendices and supplements; and older cards will explicitly mention the index, which here you infer from the notation "xiv" coming after the pages for the body of the text.
5. That the book bears on the two topics listed in small type in the third line from the bottom of the card. Any possible ambiguity in the title is thereby dispelled; for instance, Perry Miller's *The Raven and the Whale* will not be a study in natural history but in literature: the raven is Poe's and the whale is Melville's.

[8] In many libraries a list of subject headings may be consulted at the reference desk.

FIGURE 3   *The Library Card*

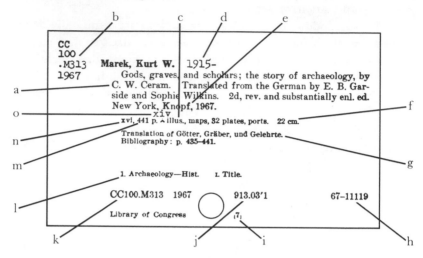

a. Author's "literary" name (pseudonym) that appears on the book; b. call number; c. statement of illustrations, portraits, and maps; d. date of author's birth; e. publisher; f. height of book; g. original title; h. Library of Congress *card* number; i. number of hundreds of cards printed; j. Dewey classification number; k. Library of Congress *call* number; l. subject heading; m. number of text pages; n. number of pages of prefatory material; o. number of pages of index (added here by the local librarian).

Taking a good look at the cards that stand for your tentatively chosen books may save you the trouble of going to the shelves or waiting at the delivery desk for a work that is of no use to you. In many large libraries the shelves are not open to the public and you ask for books sight unseen; hence the value of knowing how to size up a book by rightly interpreting the card. From the wording of the title in full—for example, its "jazziness"—you know it is not what you are after. Suppose you want an account of the military history of the Civil War. Among the titles you find James Street's *The Civil War*. The card gives you its subtitle: "An Unvarnished Account of the Late But Still Lively Hostilities." This suggests either a jocular handling of the subject or a narrative by a contemporary. But this second alternative is ruled out by the author's date of birth, which is given as 1903.

The quality of a book is sometimes indicated by the publisher's name, which you learn to look for on the catalogue card. The researcher soon comes to know that, today at any rate, a privately printed work is one that was not able to enlist the interest of any established publisher. This is often a clue to a book's reliability. Unlike the regular firms, [a private printer almost never edits, criticizes, or recommends changes in the text he sets in type.]

[The size of the book also tells the reader what he may expect of the work itself.] A history of the steel industry in 16mo size,[9] or one only sixty-four pages long, is not likely to be the volume, rich in details, that you are looking for. It is probably a publication sold in supermarkets or given away as a piece of promotional literature. In general, books published by university presses are scholarly in form and treatment; books with indexes are more likely to be serious works than those without (though exceptions keep occurring); and books imported from England or translated from a foreign language may be supposed to justify this expense and effort. But all of this is only *presumable.*

[The date of publication is a further sign that the inquirer should not overlook.] Suppose you want to read a biography of Benjamin Harrison. Your search of the catalogue turns up one by Lew Wallace published in 1888. Since you once saw the movie of Wallace's *Ben Hur* with pleasure, your first impulse may be to acquaint yourself with his writings through this work. But the fact that Harrison was elected to the Presidency in 1888 should occur to you at once and stay your hand. Obviously, Wallace's book is a "campaign biography," designed not so much to instruct and elevate your mind as to instruct the voters and elevate Harrison. In the date itself lies the hint to you that the work in question is partisan, incomplete (for Harrison was still alive), and written in haste.

[No less important than the date of publication is the edition of the book.] This information is not to be deemed important to rare-book collectors only, but to every researcher. When Charles A. Beard brought out a new edition of his famous work *The Economic Basis of Politics* in 1945, he added a chapter that put his conception of the subject

---

[9] 16mo = sextodecimo; each page is 4½″ × 6¾″.

in an entirely new light. The researcher makes it his business to know whether the book he seeks has appeared in more than one edition and whether the new edition or editions were enlargements, reductions, or some other form of revision. Depending on the problem he is studying, he will decide whether he must get all the editions for comparison or whether any one of them will do. In short, the card gives him the means of identification—the credentials—of the book. Scanning them intelligently tells him whether he wants to make a nearer acquaintance or decline it out of hand.

Once you have found the titles you want, you mark down their call numbers. These are the figures and letters that appear in the upper left- or upper right-hand corners of the card (practice varies from one library to the next). They direct you to the books themselves. The system of numbering once most commonly used was devised by the late Melvil Dewey and is known as the Dewey Decimal system. It assigns to each subject category a fixed number, each author a fixed letter (almost always the initial of his last name), and each volume a volume number. As new fields of knowledge developed, the Dewey system proved to be not sufficiently flexible. It could not, for example, provide a range of numbers for all the new subdivisions of the social sciences. [Today the system of classification most commonly used in large libraries is that of the Library of Congress.]According to this system, categories have fixed letters or letters and numbers. You will soon learn that the category of United States history runs from E to F 999 and European history from D to DR. Economics is in the range HB to HJ, books about pure science are under Q, and technology is under T.[10] You need not memorize these and other designations; they will be posted in more than one place in any library and frequent use will make them or their like as familiar to you as your own address.

Though you need not learn the techniques of a cataloguer, you can profit from knowing a fact or two more about the way librarians have coped with the flood of books since the turn of the century. The Dewey and Library of Congress systems replaced by a subject clas-

[10] In the Dewey system, American history begins with 973, European with 940, economics in the 300's, pure science in the 500's.

sification the former alphabetization by author alone. Thus if you are seeking facts about the city of Paris in the nineteenth century, the call number for the anonymous work *An Englishman in Paris* will bring you to a shelf of books on France and her history, subsection "Paris."[11] The books in that group are in one way or another related to your subject. One may be Hillaire Belloc's *Paris,* another Jules Ferry's pamphlet *Les Comptes Fantastiques d'Haussmann.* You never noticed the latter item in the card catalogue, very likely, because you were paying less attention to authors' names than to useful titles. Nevertheless, this is a book you want to look at; so in the same way that you carefully analyzed the catalogue cards before you, you now examine the shelfmates of the book you have come to find.

Cataloguers of course make mistakes like the rest of us and they may assign call numbers that cause books to appear in unexplained if not hostile company. In a large eastern library George Eliot's *Mill on the Floss* rested next to Mill *On Liberty* for many years before being sent back to "English Literature" where it belonged. Walter Bagehot's love letters were in the business school library of a great university because of the author's *Lombard Street,* which rightly suggested a banker.

These are some of the hazards with which the researcher must reckon. They are sometimes amusing, often irritating—as when the journal *Agricultural History* is filed close to periodicals dealing with soil chemistry—yet also understandable as part of the great need to organize books in such a way that people who do research can most readily organize knowledge. Since many books cross the boundary lines of any classification,[12] scanning the shelves is a great advantage. But because a book can be in only one place at a time, while duplicate cards in the catalogue can be filed in three or more places—author, title, and various subjects—the researcher must rely primarily upon

---

[11] That anonymous work, by the way, is a hoax perpetrated by the journalist Philip Vandam, but it is an excellent hoax, because he had the instincts of an historian and he made his work a fair reconstruction of a time he did not witness.

[12] Where, for example, would you put Chaddock's *The Safety Fund Banking System in New York, 1829–1866*? It could be put under works on banking, or with books on the Jackson era, or under New York State history.

the catalogue. Going to the likely shelf first and looking around casually is not the way of the professional.

The foregoing advice applies when a book on a subject is known or may reasonably be expected to exist. [You will soon develop a sense of what subjects are unlikely to have been treated in a book.] These are the subjects which embrace a multitude of facts that in their nature are only fitfully recorded; for example, the form and amount of the patronage given the arts in any century.[13] Several lifetimes of random note-gathering would not suffice for such a study, though occasionally a work of this sort *is* written—a wonder of nature. Arthur Loesser's *Men, Women, and Pianos* is one such book, and, concerning a different but similarly disunified array of facts, so is Hans Zinsser's *Rats, Lice, and History.* The first is a social history of one type of musical instrument—its makers and users and their habits. The second is a history of epidemic diseases. Both subjects are so intertwined with the petty detail of life that to have extracted their histories from books about other subjects could only have been a labor of love and long patience. The researcher can never *assume* that subjects such as these have been written about.

[At the other extreme is a type of book that one can confidently expect to find: political biography.] Almost without exception, a biography exists for every head of state in the Western world during the last three centuries. Biographers rarely overlook any significant or picturesque figure. This has been especially true in recent years, with the great rush of Ph.D. candidates toward untouched subjects. In any case, a biography is the most predictable outcome of every political career. Despite Mrs. Warren G. Harding's destruction of all the papers of her husband that she could lay her hands on, she could not delay or deter biographers from their self-appointed task.[14] The researcher

[13] Such a book exists for an interesting period of American history: Lillian B. Miller, *Patrons and Patriotism: The Encouragement of the Fine Arts in the United States, 1790–1860,* Chicago, 1966.

[14] She failed to suppress the record as she thought she had—a lesson to all who would make the attempt. The discovery in 1964 in Marion, Ohio, of a cache of love letters from Harding to Carrie Phillips, a married friend, enabled Francis Russell to write with special point his study, *The Shadow of Blooming Grove: Warren G. Harding in His Times,* New York, 1968.

who can make biography the starting point of his labors has a head start.

Professional Informers, or Reference Books

The forms and uses of the card catalogue have been dwelt on at length because the catalogue is for the researcher the fundamental type of guide to his sources. Every other aid, in whatever form, is a catalogue, *is a list*. All but a few lists follow the alphabetic order, once the broad classifications by subjects or periods have been made. Until the researcher actually lays hands on the books he wants, he is consulting catalogues, which are, once again, alphabetical lists of names and works.

The physical form a list may take varies widely. It may be: a many-volume printed catalogue, like that of the British Museum or of the Paris Bibliothèque Nationale;[15] a variation on this, like the *National Union Catalog,* the successor to the catalogue of the Library of Congress; a single-volume handbook, such as Burke and Howe's *American Authors and Books: 1640 to the Present Day;* or a bibliography of a few pages appearing in one issue of a periodical or in an annual publication like the *Index Translationum,* the international bibliography of translations. In essence they are all one.

Nor does the subject pursued greatly affect the form of the listing. The researcher may be tracking down someone's portrait through the catalogue of paintings and engravings of the American Library Association,[16] or hoping to find an autograph letter by going through the annual issues of British and American *Book Prices Current.* In all of these and a thousand more books of reference, the principles of organization are the same. Only the type and layout, the abbreviations, the symbols, the length and detail of each entry differ.

These different schemes themselves are codified, usually at the beginning, under a heading that signifies "How to Use This Book."

[15] Completed to the name "Uleyn, Le P. Arnold" by 1967.
[16] *A.L.A. Portrait Index,* ed. W. C. Lane and N. E. Browne, Washington, D.C., 1906.

Do not, then, open the book at random and merely follow the alphabet: you may fall in the section covering A.D. 1500–1800 instead of the one you want, earlier or later. [Turn, rather, to the explanatory note or preface and master its instructions, using any nearby entry to follow what is being said.]Do not let the seeming intricacy drain away your energy or scatter your attention. Remember the motto that a famous mathematician prefixed to his book on calculus: "What one fool can do, another can."[17] Some reference books are better designed than others, but all are meant for people of ordinary intelligence, not clairvoyants: the sale of reference books is small enough as it is.

It follows from all this that the reference shelves of the library are the real training ground of the researcher. If he happens to be working in a library of limited scope, the card catalogue may yield little or nothing to his purpose. In that case, instead of struggling with the cards, his best move is to consult a bibliography that covers or includes his subject and to draw from this his first list of books and articles. He then obtains these works by purchase, borrowing, or, if remote and out of copyright, by microfilming. Most bibliographies will not give the researcher the same broad survey as the large library catalogues, but the first few titles will enable him to break into his subject, and the bibliographies appended to these books will lead him to others.

It is again to the reference shelves that he repairs, in any library, when he has to find a book whose existence he only suspects, when he requires information found only in periodicals,[18] or when he has no notion whatever of the existing literature. It is in the course of worming answers out of dumb books that he acquires the experience, the judgment, the facility that will shorten and make more assured the same operation the next time. Even then this part of research calls for the instinct of the gold prospector and the skill of the detective. Fortunately, both are abilities that develop in proportion to the attention one pays to detail. It lies with the researcher whether he soon knows his way around or remains a permanent babe in the woods.

The questions that come up in research are never all of one kind.

[17] Sylvanus Thompson, *Calculus Made Easy*, 2nd ed., New York, 1914.
[18] In the physical sciences especially, long monographs go quickly out of date and the literature of value is mainly periodical.

The historian, as we said, specializes in being a generalist; he is at the mercy of his subject or his author. Only reference books can tell him quickly where to read about Bismarck's religious opinions as a young man; where to find a specimen of Martin Van Buren's signature to compare with an A.L.S.;[19] what was in the *Lusitania's* hold—gold or munitions or both—when she was sunk; and who was the judge who sentenced Martin Luther King's assassin.

Of course, the answer to these questions might be more quickly and easily found by applying to the reference librarian. But you cannot ask him or her to do your work on the hundreds, the thousands, of questions that will arise in the writing of your book or essay. You must be self-reliant. You must come to know automatically in what *kind* of book a *kind* of fact is recorded.

This obviously means knowing the scope of a great many types of books. But it also means knowing the scope of a particular work within each type. For example: if you are a student of Western culture, the biographical facts you need will be best found in biographical dictionaries of the national sort, *not* in encyclopedias. But to know that is not enough. If you are looking for, say, a nineteenth-century French figure, you must first recall whether he flourished in the first or the second half of the century. The big work by Michaud, like that by Hoefer, hardly goes beyond the halfway mark. For later figures you must consult Larousse, Vapereau, or some other, each of which has characteristics that you take into account before you pull it off the shelf. In short, familiarity with your instruments is the great time-saver. You do not want to spend half-hours poring over an atlas when the fact you seek lies in a gazetteer, or riffling through a dictionary of dead authors when your subject is still alive.

For the beginner's convenience reference books can be grouped into the nine types that are listed with comments in Figure 4. If you are a student in any field, including history, you may begin with the most general bibliography of bibliographies, namely the indispensable *Guide to Reference Books* by Constance M. Winchell.[20] If you are a student of any portion of history, the first work to consult is the general historical bibliography in English, which the American Historical

[19]The standard abbreviation for "autograph letter signed."
[20]8th ed., Chicago, 1967.

FIGURE 4 *Types of Reference Books*

---

1. Encyclopedias (national, religious, and topical, e.g., the *International Encyclopedia of the Social Sciences*).

2. Biographical Dictionaries (national, in one or many volumes; regional; professional; topical, e.g., musical; contemporary, e.g., *Who's Who;* and current, e.g., *Contemporary Authors*).

3. Indexes to Periodicals (retrospective and current, e.g., *Poole's* and the *Readers' Guide;* also devoted to special literary forms, e.g., the *Book Review Digest;* to special subjects, e.g., *Chemical Abstracts,* which, as the name suggests, furnishes more than an index; and to single publications, such as newspapers, e.g., the *New York Times Index,* and journals, whose indexes are published annually in one of their issues and are sometimes cumulated every five or ten years).

4. Dictionaries of Quotations, and Concordances (e.g., of the Bible and of famous authors).

5. Atlases and Gazetteers. (Some atlases are historical, e.g., Shepherd's, whose latest edition appeared in 1964, or refer to particular matters such as languages, treaties, etc.)

6. Chronologies or Books of Dates (many kinds).

7. Language Dictionaries (many kinds).

8. Handbooks and Source Books (dictionaries, manuals, and anthologies, e.g., the *Oxford Classical Dictionary* and Commager's *Documents of American History*).

9. Bibliographies (national, topical, current, i.e., the books of the month or year; and individual, e.g., Bengesco, *Bibliographie des Oeuvres de Voltaire* in four volumes).

Association published under the learned editorship of a board headed by George Frederick Howe, although it is already considerably out of date.[21]

The nine groups of books described in Figure 4 give only a rough idea of the vast territory they cover. The sciences, and more lately

[21] *American Historical Association Guide to Historical Literature,* New York, 1961.

business and industry, have spawned a large number of specialized works of reference.[22] Still other works swell the list of reference aids and serve very special concerns—for instance the several "Dickens Dictionaries," in which the author's multitudinous characters are treated biographically. Those in Balzac's *Comédie Humaine* have been similarly traced through the many stories in which they pursue their fictional lives. Such books, which are immensely useful for the rapid verification of allusions and quotations, are but a few of the works around which in any large library are to be found the eager neophyte and the seasoned professional.

Which Do I Want?—A Series of Examples

So important is it for the neophyte to acquire seasoning that he should make mental and written notes of his discoveries among reference works. The particulars he will want to be quickly reminded of by a look at his own private "research manual" can be indicated by examples that will suggest others in the reader's own field.

Suppose that you are describing the emergence of new institutional forms in modern American life, and you want to know by what date the supermarket had become a common phenomenon. The work entitled *Editor and Publisher's Market Guide* is a key to the economic life of almost every community in the United States. From it you learn how many drugstores there are in Atlanta, the resources of the banks in Spokane, and the quality of the tap water in Cheyenne. Having once consulted this annual, you will know how helpful back issues can be for social history, long after they have ceased to interest the advertisers and salesmen for whom they are compiled.

Suppose again that you are working on the postwar history of the French franc. Experience has taught you that unlike ourselves the French seldom thoroughly index their periodicals. But the Germans are diligent and they publish an excellent index to foreign periodicals—including the French—called *Bibliographie der fremdsprachigen*

---

[22] For a selection, see the reading list on pp. 401–07.

Zeitschriftenliteratur. Your needs are met—except that for the years before 1963 you have to know the name of your subject in German!

[For handy use, the researcher will want to remember that the men and women whose lives are recorded in the *Dictionary of American Biography* are dead] This simple fact is the first that one notes about the *D.A.B.* The same rule applies to the *D.N.B.*, the *Dictionary of National Biography*, that great British compilation, which was said to add a new terror to death, and upon which the American was modeled. But the user of the *D.A.B.* should know further that not all of the twenty volumes were published at the same time. Volume I appeared in 1928 and Volume XIX in 1936. Any important figure named, let us say, Adams, and who died in 1929, would be missing because the *A*'s were already done, but a notable Williams who died in 1934 would be included.

Encyclopedias should similarly be "learned" and not blindly used. The childhood faith in *the* encyclopedia that happened to be the one large book of knowledge in the house should be replaced by a discriminating acquaintance with others. Many Americans who were reared on the *Britannica* are not yet aware that it is now owned and published by Americans in Chicago. The fourteenth edition was the first to cater to the Anglo-American audience, and of the previous ones the ninth and eleventh have special virtues. A new edition on an entirely new plan is in preparation. At present the chief English encyclopedia is the venerable *Chambers's,* which was entirely recast by 1950 and whose latest edition appeared in 1967.

Encyclopedias are useful for quick reference and confirmation of minor points—dates, titles, place-names—but on main subjects their deliverances must be verified in detail, for several reasons: (1) scholarship is always ahead of any but a newly published encyclopedia; (2) the size and scope of an encyclopedia make error or ambiguity more likely than in a book; and (3) revisions and additions introduce discrepancies.

Here again it must be pointed out that latest does not automatically mean best;[23] your purpose—and your knowledge of the composition of the work—can make any edition the best. The *Century Dictionary and Cyclopedia,* last republished in 1913, defines "Communist" without

---

[23] The word "latest" must take into account the fact that encyclopedia makers now keep their works up-to-date by "continuous revision," that is, by making certain indispensable changes every time they reprint the volumes.

reference to the Russian Revolution—naturally—but for that very reason it yields the researcher important historical information; on other subjects it will never be out-of-date, notably in its comprehensive dictionary of names. In many ways, the *Century* remains the finest work of its kind ever published in the United States. Among other encyclopedias latterly brought up-to-date and worth consulting are *Collier's*, the *Americana*, and the *New Catholic Encyclopedia*.

You also know that in recent times some of the national encyclopedias have become the voice of the party in power rather than of disinterested scholarship. If you are studying cultural bias, that latest edition is for you the best; if that is not your subject, an older edition should take its place. On points of dogma, a religious encyclopedia is the best; on church history it may not be. Out of the many works bearing in English or foreign tongues the name "encyclopedia" ("circle of all teachings") there is ideally the best for every particular purpose.[24]

[Sooner or later the researcher will have to turn to a dictionary and may require one that gives the histories of words.] In English, Murray's *New English Dictionary*, commonly known as the *Oxford English Dictionary* (hence as the *O.E.D.* for short), is the most complete. Craigie and Hulbert's *Dictionary of American English on Historical Principles*, coupled with Mitford Mathews' *Dictionary of Americanisms*, corresponds to the great English model. For the slang and vulgarisms of all English-speaking peoples, Partridge's *Dictionary of Slang and Unconventional English* (and supplement) is standard.

Consider a moment the uses of these works for the writer of history: anyone studying the era of the American and French revolutions will frame a correct conception of that time only after he has learned how the late eighteenth century used such words as "liberty" and "authority." An historical dictionary will describe the shifts in meaning. Amer-

[24] The researcher should not be abashed at finding that the appropriate reference work for him is in a language he does not know. Let him turn to the article he needs and see what he can make out. If he can read French, he should be able, with a dictionary at hand and a little patience, to muster enough "encyclopedia Spanish" or "encyclopedia Italian" to read what he requires. Similarly, on the basis of German, one can make use of Dutch, Danish, and Swedish reference works. The reading is usually for the sake of a single point that, when found, is copied out verbatim for verified translation by a colleague. For lack of this venturesomeness, scholars working on Jefferson may miss the article on Mazzei, the great Virginian's friend, in the *Enciclopedia Italiana*.

ican historians a decade or so ago were concerned with the question of whether Andrew Jackson was really the friend of labor, or perhaps rather a spokesman for the small entrepreneur. This again is a dispute about words. It hinges on the meaning of "workingman," which some have argued meant "proletarian" while others have insisted it meant the owner of an independent business. The studies of Jacksonianism would be improved by an inquiry to settle that point, the first step being toward the historical dictionary.

Popular quotations, catch phrases, and allusions are also signs of the times, and hence worthy of attention. What is the connection of "twenty-three, skidoo!" with the spirit of the 1890's? What is a "tandem" in the history of locomotion? What are "routs," "crushes," "kettledrums," in the context of sociability? Who, exactly, belongs to the *demi-monde*, and when was the phrase first used? Finding origins and contexts is often as necessary as defining the single word.

A late edition of the *Oxford Dictionary of Quotations* reports the dropping of 250 quotations that no longer seemed familiar. What does this signify about literary culture? The change of interest, which is not at all unusual, points once more to the utility of earlier editions of the book. Good librarians keep old issues, and the researcher seeks them out for "period work."

The Fruits of Experience

After these representative examples of the researcher in action, it does not seem necessary to repeat that imagination, seconded by patience, is indispensable to success. Developing these two qualities among the half-dozen mentioned earlier depends on the acquisition of a steadily increasing stock of information. The more you know, the easier it is to imagine how and where to learn still more, and self-confidence carries you over the frequent stoppages of baffled ingenuity.

Some researchers seem to have an equivalent of the gardener's "green thumb." It is perhaps nothing more than a "well-read thumb," the researcher having his references at his fingertips. The most common kind of research problem can be the most hopeless if you do not begin by knowing enough of the small points. How, for instance, do you deal with the many-sided question posed by the common phrase ["Who's Who"? Some persons are not important enough to have had a biographer.]Others have not been dead long enough. Still others became prominent a few months or weeks ago. Many are notable only in certain circles. Others *were* notables but are not so any longer. Some owe their place in history to mere position, inherited or acquired. Still others have multiple namesakes. How to begin?

First the researcher knows that most countries have: (1) a general *Who's Who* of the living[25] and (2) a biographical dictionary of dead notables. Not so many countries, but some, have (3) a "current" biography or its equivalent for newcomers to renown; (4) classified lists of authors, physicians, scholars, actors, journalists, clergymen, etc.; and (5) directories of various kinds—the peerage and other social registers, city and parliamentary directories, and the like. There are in addition a few international lists, and an indefinite number of "vanity" lists, designed chiefly to be sold to those listed in them. Seldom reliable by themselves, they may give clues to a better source, even when they are as narrowly conceived as the *Who's Who Among Americans of Italian Descent in Connecticut* or as unlikely as *Who's Who in CIA* (Berlin, Julius Mader, 1968, 592 pp.).

The researcher starts, then, with set categories within one or more of which his Unknown fits. A few points are worth keeping in mind:

1. The title of the general *Who's Who* in each country is usually that same phrase in the given language, followed by the name of the country. The exception is the British *Who's Who,* which stops short with those two words, seemingly on the assumption that anybody who is anybody is a British subject, but which actually includes a number of Americans and other foreigners.
2. *Who's Who in America* is published every two years, but certain biographies of the living are not reprinted in full in each issue. A reference is given to the year of the full listing. (The publishers of the British *Who's Who* and of *Who's Who in America* also select from among the recent dead certain names for their respective *Who Was Who*'s.)
3. Remember such peculiarities of foreign biographical dictionaries in many volumes as were mentioned above (p. 80), and bear in mind that a French-looking name may be Belgian or Swiss; a

[25] A number of current foreign *Who's Who*'s are being issued in English by the Intercontinental Book and Publishing Company of Montreal.

German one, Austrian; and so on. Different nationals will be found in different works.

4. Some of these works have supplements (e.g., the *D.A.B.*) and also concise editions (e.g., the *D.N.B.* in one volume). The first *D.A.B.* supplement contained biographies of people who died not later than the end of 1934. The second goes as far as December 31, 1940; the third, covering 1941–45, is in preparation.

5. Newspaper indexes, such as that of the *New York Times,* give clues to much biographical information. The semimonthly issues are made into a volume for each year, available some time after its close. A rich source of biographical data not readily obtainable elsewhere is the *New York Times Obituaries Index,* containing over 350,000 listings of deaths that have appeared in the *New York Times* since 1858. *Biography Index* refers you to printed sources in English that contain biographical data, without restriction of subject, time or nationality.

6. For newcomers to renown, of whatever nationality, try *Current Biography,* issued monthly, which provides sketches and portraits of figures that have suddenly attained prominence—a new movie star, dictator, or Olympic champion.

Occasionally, one of these reference works will unwittingly mislead, as when *Who's Who in America* printed in good faith the "facts" (complete with a Heidelberg medical degree) about a drug manufacturer who was an ex-convict living under a false name.[26] Again, the nineteenth-century *Appleton's Cyclopaedia of American Biography* contained at least forty-seven sketches of persons invented by one or more unscrupulous contributors.[27] In this way an explorer named Bernhard Hühne came into existence, credited with discovering part of the California coast, and a French epidemiologist was battling cholera in South America fifty years before the disease appeared there.

Because the data in most *Who's Who*'s is supplied by the subject himself, the sketches can sometimes be puzzling or revealing. The entry for Richard M. Nixon does not record his service with the Office of Price Administration during the Second World War, though it was an important phase of his development. Theodore Roosevelt omitted

---

[26] Trusting researchers and editors were not the only people he fooled. For a full account see Charles Keats, *Magnificent Masquerade: The Strange Case of Dr. Coster and Mr. Musica,* New York, 1964.

[27] See Margaret Castle Schindler, "Fictitious Biography," *American Historical Review,* XLII (July 1937), 680–90.

to state that he ran unsuccessfully for the presidency in 1912; and William Howard Taft unwittingly validated that omission by reporting that he had been defeated by Woodrow Wilson in that year, as if no other candidate had run against him or received more votes.[28] But imposture and suppression are exceptional, and researchers will not be alone in their embarrassment if they are led astray.

In seeking identities, it is well to remember that persons' names follow certain conventions. Knowing the conventions may shorten the search, and observing them in narrative distinguishes the trained writer from the amateur. To begin with, names should be given as the bearers themselves used them. It is H. L. Mencken, A. P. Herbert, Calvin Coolidge, H. G. Wells—not Henry L., Alan Patrick, John Calvin, or Herbert George. Giving the full spread only confuses the reader who, in the case of Wells, will imagine a person different from the familiar H. G. With French names this distinction is essential, because it is usual for parents to give their children two or more first names, often including their own in permutation. The bearers of these names usually choose to be known by only one: the full name of Chateaubriand, the historian and statesman, is François-René de Chateaubriand (all first names are hyphened into a single group). In life he used René; yet in a useful American anthology on Romanticism he appears as François Chateaubriand. Knowing the conventions would have prevented this error, as well as that of omitting the *de*.[29]

[28] See Cedric A. Larson, *Who: Sixty Years of American Eminence. The Story of 'Who's Who in America,'* New York, 1958.

[29] French usage about *de* only seems to be complicated. The most succinct account of it occurs in Follett's *Modern American Usage*, New York, 1966, 329:

De is invariably used when it is attached: *Robert Delattre* gives by itself *Delattre*; it never appears in any other form. All other names with *de* separate, fall into three classes: names of one syllable, names of more than one syllable, names of more than one syllable that begin with a vowel. All the names of one syllable must always have *de* before them: *De Thou, De Retz, De Mun.* All the longer names, unless they begin with a vowel, *must* drop the *de: Tocqueville* says . . . ; *Vigny's poems are austere; Gobineau was no racist*—and hence: *Maupassant* (not *de*) *wrote innumerable short stories.* But names longer than one syllable that begin with a vowel break the rule for long names and require *D': D'Argenson, D'Artagnan.* The simple aid to memory is: *De Gaulle, Tocqueville, D'Artagnan.* A further comfort: all the foregoing applies exclusively to *de. Du* and *des* are invariably used with the last name, short or long, voweled or not: *Des Brosses, Du Guesclin.* And when the first name is given there is again no problem: *Alexis de Tocqueville.*

A different usage applies to pseudonyms: they are not separable into first and last names. *Mark Twain* is one unit, alphabetized under *M.* Nor do these made-up names admit of titles. One does not write Dr. Mark Twain (after he got an Oxford degree) nor should the French cartoonist Caran d'Ache (Karandash, which is Russian for "pencil") be referred to as M. D'Ache.

Finally, there is a sort of tact applicable to persons whose names or titles changed during their lifetime.[30] Thus in writing about biographical matters, one might put down "Sir Arthur Conan Doyle," whereas it is more natural to refer to "Conan Doyle's Sherlock Holmes stories." The shorter form is more historical, too, since most of the tales were written before his knighthood; but the point is: the more famous, the less fuss about details. We say Homer and Caesar and Shakespeare, disregarding any other nomenclature.

All this is common knowledge, yet certain errors of naming are embedded in the common tongue, which it would be pedantic and impossible to correct, even if one were to give full time to the task. For example, "Joan of Arc" is a misnomer. Her name was not D'Arc, but Darc, which does not mean "from Arc." She was from Domremy. But whereas no one will waste breath to point this out to playwrights who dramatize her life as Joan of Arc, any historical account of her should make use of her right name. Familiarity with such points will obviously direct—and shorten—the practical reader's search for names.

Chronology to the Rescue

No advance information saves more time for the researcher than the dates of certain guidebooks. He knows these dates by heart and he acquires more as he goes along. Each man makes up a list tailored to his needs. For example 1802–1906—the years included in *Poole's Index to Periodical Literature.* Knowing this, you know that you cannot

---

[30] A useful book of modest size, *Titles and Modes of Address* (London, A. and C. Black, various editions), will assist the American student who may be confused about English titles. It also gives the (unexpected) pronunciations of certain English names, many of which have importance for the historian.

find listed there any contemporary magazine articles on either the guillotining of Marie Antoinette (1793) or the sinking of the *Titanic* (1912). Again: 1876–1909, and also 1913. The first pair are the inclusive dates of the *New York Daily Tribune Index;* the date 1913 standing alone marks the year when the *New York Times Index* first appeared in its present form.[31] Hence there is no printed index to articles in those newspapers about the death of Edward VII (1910) or the three-cornered presidential campaign of 1912, although work is under way to fill the gaps in the *New York Times* indexes. One more date for good measure: 1873—the year when the *Congressional Record* begins; but remember that verbatim reporting begins in the *Congressional Globe* in 1851.

Speaking of Congress, it is convenient to have a ready way of computing when, let us say, the Forty-third Congress was elected. The facts of our history suggest the formula: double the number of the Congress, add this sum to 1788, and subtract 2. The worker in European history will similarly want to know by heart how to translate "the year VIII" of the French Republic or the dates of New Style and Old Style as they affected the Germanies until 1700, England and the colonies until 1752, and Russia until 1918.

In making these changes in dating, it must be kept in mind that working out the correct date of an event that occurred in England when the Julian (Old Style) calendar was in force is not without pitfalls, as is shown by the arguments over the date of Newton's death. The inscription in Westminster Abbey gives the date as "20 March 1726." The year should be 1727 (as it is given in most handbooks and encyclopedias); but the day of the month should also be changed to March 31, because in the shift to the Gregorian calendar in 1752, the date of September 2 was immediately followed by September 14.[32]

[31] Indexes for earlier years (1851–58, 1860) may be had on microfilm from the *New York Times.* Indexes for the years 1863 to 1906 have been published in seven volumes. The current *New York Times Index* is naturally a work of increasing complexity, almost as difficult to find one's way in as the world that it mirrors. When the subject sought is steadily in the news ("Vietnam," "Medicare") patience and ingenuity are needed to find the article one has previously read or is sure must have appeared. The subheads are themselves overflowed by the substance.

[32] In other words, the gap is eleven *days,* though subtracting the first *date* gives the answer 12. In the Russian changeover during our own century the gap was thirteen *days.*

A good example of how these niggling details affect important statements is the frequent mention of the supposed coincidence between Galileo's death and Newton's birth: "both in the same year." The fact is that this conjunction holds only if one reckons in both calendars at once. For Galileo died on January 8, 1642 N.S. and Newton was born on December 25 O.S. If one makes the adjustment of putting Newton on the same calendar as his great predecessor, he turns out to have been born on January 4, 1643. Think of the annoyance of those who celebrate centenaries![33]

Long before the researcher has assimilated some of these tricks of the trade he will have lost the bewildered feeling that assailed him when he first entered the library and faced the row upon row of tired volumes in well-thumbed buckram. Instead of being somewhat on the defensive, as if the catalogue and the books were in league to defeat him, he will have taken the offensive and be challenging them to show cause why they should not help him. More than that, he will have grown into habits of noting and collecting which, though as automatic as reflex action, nonetheless imply foresight and prudence.

For instance he will always carry a few 3-by-5 cards for jotting down facts and ideas casually encountered. He will clip articles, large or small, from newspapers or book catalogues; for the telling modern instance or the unusual remark in an unpublished manuscript in private hands cannot be sought for, it comes of its own accord; to be useful it must come ahead of the need for it. Cards and clippings are classified "on arrival" in suitably marked folders.

It goes without saying that the student will miss no chance to add the name of a reference volume to his panoply, even if he sees no immediate use for it—for instance, the *Weekly Compilation of Presidential Documents,* which contains statements, messages, and other matters issued by the White House up to 5 P.M. of each Friday. Another such source turns up as you read for another purpose an old issue of the *Mississippi Valley Historical Review* (now the *Journal of American History*), the chief periodical devoting itself exclusively to American history. The list in question is Herbert O. Brayer's "Preliminary Guide to Indexed

[33] The careful reader will note that whereas the gap for Newton's death (in the eighteenth century) was eleven days, that for his birth in the seventeenth was only ten.

Newspapers of the United States, 1850–1900," the value of which is self-evident. Another suggestion may strike the eye in a newspaper advertisement, or may come to you in the mail—perhaps a notice from the R. R. Bowker Company announcing a new directory: *Who's Who in American Politics.*

Thanks to relatively cheap methods of combined photography and printing (photo-offset), many scholarly books that no one would dream of reissuing in the usual way, by setting type, are now being brought back into print by publishers that specialize in the library and scholar's market. Entire runs of newspapers and periodicals are likewise to be had on this plan, at high prices no doubt, for the sale of such works is small, but for some purposes worth having at any price. One by-product of this trade is the emergence of reference works that relatively few persons have ever heard about—to take an example at random, the French list of books and drawings suppressed or prosecuted between 1814 and 1877, including such authors as Rabelais, Villon, Gautier, and Flaubert. This list, *Catalogue des ouvrages, écrits et dessins de toute nature poursuivis supprimés ou condamnés depuis le 21 octobre 1814 jusqu'au 31 juillet 1877* (published in Paris, 1879, and reprinted in 1968 in Bruxelles by Gabriel Lebon in his series *Éditions Culture et Civilisation*), gives summaries of the legal proceedings and the names of participants following the titles and dates, and constitutes a useful compendium for the historian of nineteenth-century culture.

Books Beyond Reach and the Lonely Fact

With an exact idea of what he wants, no researcher should feel constricted by the limitations of the library or libraries he works in: it is now possible to borrow by interlibrary loan from other institutions. Your librarian will tell you how to make the arrangements. If the books themselves cannot be borrowed, the relevant portions can be microfilmed or photocopied, subject to the rules of copyright.[34] The same is true of newspapers and journals, whose whereabouts are de-

[34] See Ralph R. Shaw, "Copyright in Relationship to Copying for Scholarly Materials," in Lowell H. Hattery and George P. Bush, eds., *Reprography and Copyright Law*, Washington, D.C., 1965.

tailed in the invaluable "Union Lists" of American newspapers and of "serials." Microfilming is now so commonplace, convenient, and cheap that all but the most penurious library can obtain for you a replica of the Gutenberg Bible or a file of the *Emporia Gazette*. Moreover, in *Newspapers on Microfilm* you can find out what is available and where.

The Library of Congress is of course the great American repository of printed and manuscript materials that the researcher will first think of for his remote sources. A Library of Congress card is prepared for every book copyrighted in this country. Since 1956 these cards have been reproduced and published (together with cards for the holdings of 700 other libraries) as the *National Union Catalog*.[35] For other kinds of materials, the searcher will have to explore in the series of bibliographies that span our publishing history.[36]

It is evident that the only hopeless task is to look for a book that never existed. Yet the modern student who wants to be sure of the date, edition, and contents of a particular work unquestionably faces a harder task than his predecessor of twenty-five years ago. The reason lies in the proliferation of reprints, paperback and other, which seldom disclose their true or their full natures, and which often escape systematic listing in catalogues and bibliographies. More is said on this subject in the note that precedes the bibliography of this book.

As for nonexistent books, their birthplace—or at least their cradle—is someone's listing from which you copied the title. A volume

[35] The *National Union Catalog* is now being extended backward in time to cover the years up to 1956. When completed this undertaking will consist of over 600 volumes of 700 pages each in "the largest single publication since the invention of printing." It is expected to be finished by 1980.

[36] For books, pamphlets, and periodicals published in the United States through the year 1800, consult Charles Evans' *American Bibliography*. Overlapping this in part, but extending in coverage to the latter half of the nineteenth century, is Joseph Sabin's *Dictionary of Books Relating to America*, which, like Evans' volume, usually indicates where copies of the items it lists may be found. (The period 1801–71 is covered further, though somewhat unevenly, by R. R. Shaw and R. H. Shoemaker's *American Bibliography*, by O. A. Roorbach's *Bibliotheca Americana*, and by James Kelly's *American Catalogue*.) For the years since 1876 the field is well covered by two series, the *American Catalogue* (1876–1910) and the *United States Catalog* with its supplement, the *Cumulative Book Index*, which has been published regularly since 1899.

of *Who Was Who in America* ascribes a biography of James Wilson, a signer of the Declaration of Independence, to Burton Alva Konkle, thus implying that the published book exists. The truth is that the book never appeared; it is a "ghost book." Such "books" are rare and not likely to turn up in your path any more often than forged documents, but you should be prepared for all contingencies.[37]

Your adventures as a researcher in the library result, ordinarily, from your wanting to "get the facts." Very different is the task of finding "the fact," in the singular. If "the fact" is incidental or recondite, do not let it hold you up. You can write about the Republican campaign of 1860 now and postpone until later trying to find where Lincoln stayed during the convention, just as you can follow the career of Lord Byron without knowing which of his legs was deformed. If, however, you must prepare for a newsmagazine a complete list of the Presidents of the United States who have left the country during their terms of office, and give details of their trips, you obviously have nothing to postpone.

This kind of search can be anguishing beyond belief, and success correspondingly enthralling. Since "the fact" may turn up almost anywhere, you must be ready to spring in any direction. For American "facts" other than quotations, you can try James Truslow Adams' *Dictionary of American History* or Thomas H. Johnson's *Oxford Companion to American History*. For European facts, the compendium is William L. Langer's *Encyclopedia of World History* (an *n*th revision of the German original by Ploetz), supplemented by Alfred Mayer's *Annals of European Civilization: 1501–1900*. An amazingly large number of facts, together with interpretation, are organized chronologically and topically in Richard B. Morris' *Encyclopedia of American History*. If "the fact" is a name, past or present, a thing or person or place, fictional or legendary or mythological, begin with the three volumes of Barnhart's *New Century*

[37] How a ghost book may arise is shown by what happened to one of the authors of the present work. In 1939 he published a book called *Of Human Freedom*. Before publication, the editor of a periodical to which the writer was contributing an article announced in the "Personal Column" that Mr. Barzun's next book would deal with Culture in a Democracy. The capital letters led to the words' being copied here and there as a title and to this day there come inquiries about the way to obtain a copy of *Culture in a Democracy*.

Cyclopedia of Names (100,000 entries), or the earlier edition mentioned above.[38]

If "the fact" appeared in an article, or if the fact *is* an article, go to the various guides to periodicals we have listed. With *Poole's Index* you must be prepared for a blow: it contains a subject index only and follows canons of indexing that are obsolete.[39] For all manner of numerical data, you should learn to use the *Historical Statistics of the United States* and the latest *Statistical Abstract of the United States.* For electoral data you should at once and confidently turn to Richard M. Scammon's *America at the Polls.*

[38] If the fact is known to be American and historical and has been the subject of an article or book since 1902 (a safe guess is that it has been), consult *Writings on American History* (1902–03; 1906–40; 1948–59), compiled by Grace Gardner Griffin and others. Each volume is exhaustively indexed, but all diggers should be aware that a meticulous cumulative index covering the years 1902 to 1940 has been issued (American Historical Association, 1957), making the series very convenient to use. This series is scheduled to be discontinued with the volume for 1961. For a much briefer bibliography on a subject in American history, the reader can turn to the *Harvard Guide to American History* (1954).

Every seeker after facts should know where to find those contained in United States government publications. Access seems at first complicated, but a little practice removes the difficulties. The collected edition of documents comprising House and Senate Journals, Documents, and Reports is known as the Serial Set, amounting now to about 13,000 "volumes." The puzzle is to find the serial number of the volume you need. For the years 1789–1909, use the *Checklist of United States Public Documents, 1789–1909,* if you know the number of the document or report you want. If you do not, turn to the chronological listing: B. P. Poore, *A Descriptive Catalogue of the Government Publications of the United States, September 5, 1774 to March 4, 1881.* This is followed by J. G. Ames, *Comprehensive Index to the Publications of the United States Government, 1881–1893,* which is arranged alphabetically by subject and contains also an index to proper names. For the years 1893 to 1940, use the "Document Catalog," a short title for the *Catalog of the Public Documents of the —— Congress and of All Departments of the Government of the United States.* This is a dictionary catalogue listing documents in one alphabet under author, subject, and sometimes title. If you are delving for government publications issued since 1940, you must turn to the *Monthly Catalog of United States Government Publications.* Unfortunately, this does not list serial numbers, for which you must rely on *Numerical Lists and Schedule of Volumes of the Reports and Documents of the —— Congress.*

[39] Entries from *Poole's Index* and the modern *Readers' Guide* are reproduced in Figure 5.

FIGURE 5   *The Chief Indexes to Periodicals*

HORSE

Horse, The, Fossil, from the Tertiary of Nebraska. (O. C. Marsh) Am. J. Sci. **96**: 374.
— Sir Francis Head on. Chamb. J. **35**: 19.
— How he is cheated and abused. (E. I. Sears) Nat. Q. **27**: 346.
— in Geology. Pop. Sci. Mo. **16**: 258.
— in the Malayan Archipelago. Penny M. **7**: 312.
— in modern Society. (E. L. Godkin) Nation, **15**: 277.
— in Motion. (T. A. Dodge) Dial (Ch.), **2**: 288.
— Locomotion of. Pop. Sci. Mo. **6**: 129.
— Necessary Food for. (M. Bixio) Ecl. Engin. **19**: 245.
— Question of Ribs in. (T. M. Müller) Pop. Sci. Mo. **7**: 214.
— Rarey's Method of taming. Chamb. J. **29**: 261.
— Saddle-. (G. E. Waring, jr.) Scrib. **15**: 84.
— Something about. (T. B. Thorpe) Harper, **13**: 751.
— Thoroughbred. (G. E. Waring, jr.) Scrib, **15**: 157.
— — English and Arabian. (W. S. Blunt) 19th Cent. **8**: 411.
— Tractive Power of. (E. Morris) J. Frankl. Inst. **28**: 79.
— Wild, Species of. Penny M. **14**: 414.
Horses. (C. J. Lever) Blackw. **98**: 679. — Chamb. J. **42**: 502.
— American, Anecdotes of. Penny M. **9**: 19.
— and Horse-Copers. (A. Wynter) Once a Week, **11**: 453.
— and Horse-Dealing. Tinsley, **8**: 277.
— and Horsiness. Temp. Bar, **14**: 443.
— and Riding, Nevile on. (G. E. Waring, jr.) Nation, **26**: 420.
— and their Feet. (Sir G. W. Cox) Fraser, **102**: 784. Same art. Pop. Sci. Mo. **18**: 468.
— and Treatment of. (M Chambers) Chamb. J. **52**: 289.
— Anecdotes of. Bentley, **31**: 225. Same art. Ecl. M. **26**: 20. Same art. Liv. Age, **33**: 249.
— Arabian. (Abd-el Kader) House. Words, **7**: 190. — (R. D. Upton) Fraser, **94**: 375. — Chamb. J. **41**: 84. Same art. Ecl. M. **62**: 291.
— Bits and Bearing-Reins. Blackw. **117**: 742.
— Bitting of. Penny M. **5**: 159.
— Breeding of. Ed. R. **138**: 426.
— Breeds and Races of. All the Year, **11**: 319.
— British. Penny M. **10**: 225.
— Classes and Breeds of. (D. Low) Ed. New Philos. J. **40**: 179.
— English. Ed. R. **120**: 114.
— — and Eastern. (Sir F. H. Doyle) Fortn. **35**: 572, 704.

SPACE rescue work
  Rescue techniques tested on Soyuz 4, 5 missions. Aviation W 90:26 Mr 17 '69
SPACE research
  Capturing a moon and other diversions; proposals of S. F. Singer. il Time 93:66-7 F 21 '69
    History
Ten years in deep space. W. Cloud. il Pop Mech 131:128-31+ Mr '69
    Russia
Progress in science and cosmonautics. A. A. Blagonravov and IU. Zaitsev. Space World F-2-62:4-5 F '69
Soviet space schedule may include large booster test. D. C. Winston. il Aviation W 90:132-4 Mr 10 '69
    United States
Apollo: how the United States decided to go to the moon. L. Mandelbaum. bibliog Science 163:649-54 F 14 '69
New space policy may stress earth uses. W. C. Wetmore. il Aviation W 90:113-14+ Mr 10 '69
Next objective in space. W. O. Roberts. Science 163:521 F 7 '69
Nixon goal is balanced space effort. il Aviation W 90:99 Mr 10 '69
Pace of post-Apollo planning rises. W. J. Normyle. Aviation W 90:16 F 3 '69
Space sciences. Sci N 95:283 Mr 22 '69
What's up in space? fourth International symposium on bioastronautics and the exploration of space. il Space World F-2-62:40-3 F '69
SPACE stations
Apollo applications shrinks to evaluation of orbital workshop. il Aviation W 90:109-10 Mr 10 '69
Large station may emerge as unwritten U.S. goal. W. J. Normyle. il Aviation W 90:103+ Mr 10 '69
NASA aims at 100-man station. W. J. Normyle. Aviation W 90:16-17 F 24 '69
Putting comfort in orbit. R. R. Gilruth. il Space World F-2-62:42 F '69
SPACE suits. See Astronauts—Clothing
SPACE technology
Technology: father of human welfare. E. C. Welsh. Space World F-2-62:41 F '69
SPACE vehicles
    Crews
    See Astronauts
    Design
Special report, Apollo lunar module. il Aviation W 90:40-1+ F 17 '69
    Landing systems
Flexible-wing recovery system set for unmanned trials. C. M. Plattner. il Aviation W 90:56-8 F 10 '69
Lifting body interest gaining. Aviation W 90:51 F 3 '69
    Moon
Apollo 9 maneuvering sequence planned for first manned flight of lunar module. il Aviation W 90:64-7 F 24 '69
Apollo 9 readied to test lunar module. il Aviation W 90:17-19 F 3 '69

To the left, part of a column from *Poole's Index;* to the right, a sample from the *Readers' Guide.* Notice the simpler but less informative citation in the older work: *Poole* gives the title of the magazine, the volume number, and page. *The Readers' Guide* gives the title of the magazine, the volume number, and page; adds the month and year, and the date if appropriate. It also puts in "il" if the article is illustrated (specifying "por" for portrait, "diag" for diagram, and so on), and it states "play" or "story" to distinguish those forms from expository prose.

But unquestionably the most baffling quarries are quotations and anecdotes. Try to find, for example, the circumstances in which Hamilton is supposed to have said, "Your people, sir, are a great beast." Or where Gouverneur Morris told how he greeted George Washington by a slap on the back and got in return for his exuberance a cold stare that he remembered for the rest of his days?

"Bartlett" is almost synonymous with ["Quotations,"] but note that unlike the first eleven editions, which offered "classic" and famous quotations, the twelfth edition and the fourteenth (1968) introduce much contemporary prose and give representation to foreign authors hitherto neglected. Other compilations include those by Burton E. Stevenson, H. L. Mencken, J. K. Hoyt, Rudolf Flesch, J. M. and M. J. Cohen (Penguin series), James B. Simpson, P. H. Dalbiac, and the editors of the Oxford Press. Foreign quotations are to be found at the back of Hoyt's *Cyclopedia* or in separate volumes by H. F. W. King, H. P. Jones, G. Büchmann, O. Guerlac, E. Genest, and many others. If the quotation is not in any of these books, your little problem has suddenly become a big one. If you do not believe this, wait until it happens to you, or else ask a friend who has been looking through all of Matthew Arnold's writings page by page for a sentence he knew must be there, but now thinks may be by Walter Pater after all.

To mention other "fact" books here would be futile, they are so numerous. Until you set out on your search you will not credit how many patient people have toiled weary hours to enable you to find in half a minute some isolated name, date, or utterance. The sum total of such books in all languages, no one knows; but the most prominent and promising you will find listed in Constance M. Winchell's *Guide to Reference Books* already cited. It describes most books in great detail and presents them in groups. On American politics, for example, you find three timesaving compendiums: Kirk H. Porter's *National Party Platforms, 1840–1960;* Thomas H. McKee's *National Conventions and Platforms, 1789–1905;* and Richard C. Bain's *Convention Decisions and Voting Records.* Winchell's *Guide* will also assist those interested in "firsts" by referring them to such curious works as Joseph N. Kane's *Famous First Facts* (3rd ed., 1964), which tells when the first safety razor appeared and who is the mother of Father's Day.

To be sure, running the eye down somebody's alphabetical list and pawing over pages till column 978a comes into view, or tossing thick tomes from hand to shelf and back again, is not the be-all and end-all of research. Far from it. But it is the inescapable prerequisite, and the demands that these activities make upon the mind are close kin to those that occur at the later and higher stages. The difference between a good researcher and a poor one is not decisively shown by their respective skill in using the library, but that skill is certainly a main ingredient of excellence. The writing of a report for a class assignment or the creation of a masterpiece of history both depend in the first instance on the ability to summon up the past that reposes in library books—forcing them, as it were, to yield their secrets.

The Computer: Ally or Distant Friend?

It was inevitable that the advent of the computer in the science laboratory, the registrar's office, and the library should put ideas in the heads of scholars in neighboring buildings. The reputed feats of the machine, its speed and accuracy, its superficial comparability with the mind of man, and its taste for a fast life (obsolescence of each "generation" in ten years or less)—all excited a natural wonder and desire to gain access to the controls, in hopes of lifting from scholarly shoulders the heavy burdens of drudgery and thought. Articles in the press soon gave encouragement to the hopeful by reporting that one researcher was studying Hawthorne's ideas with computer aid; another was determining the date and context of the Dead Sea scrolls by measuring the probability of the recurrence of phrases; still others were making a huge index of the works of Aquinas or were carrying on stylistic studies in medieval music or determining definitively the authorship of *The Federalist*—all this by punching cards and receiving voluminous print-outs in return.[40]

[40] In the *Newsletter* of the American Council of Learned Societies for May 1965 (XVI, No. 5, 7–31) are listed several dozen projects of computerized research, arranged by subject matter and giving names and places as well as brief descriptions of purpose. A valuable source of information on trends in computerized research is the journal *Computers and the Humanities*, which began in 1966.

At the present time, the enthusiasm for computers among historians and other humanists is variable. At one end is the dean of a West Coast liberal arts college, who says that soon all knowledge will be at the fingertips of any student able to sit at a console and watch a screen behind it. No more books, for they bind up disparate information in rigid covers instead of loosing each fact into the blue like a pigeon, to be retrieved and combined with others of its kind by the seeker. At the other end of the range of opinion is the skeptic, who says that facts do not keep well when out of context; that it would take much knowledge to acquire other knowledge console-fashion, whereas books inform you of questions as well as of answers; and that, finally, the cost of putting "all knowledge" on punched cards and giving every student a free run of the resulting "bank" is out of all proportion to the quality of the use that would be made of it.

What is unquestionable is that for all systematic marshalings of bare facts—indexes, checklists, concordances, frequency tables, and even bibliographies, the computer is a powerful helper.[41] It does not tire, lose its eyesight, or make more mistakes at the end of the day than at the beginning—proof enough that it is not human. But the users still are, and so are the programmers, card punchers, and proofreaders; hence the computer may well lighten the drudgery without producing perfect or conveniently arranged reference books, even of the simplest sort.

Nevertheless, the thought lingers that by a judicious mixture of "storing" in the machine and thinking in the mind a fuller survey of what is known, a richer substance for analysis, and therefore a greater gain of truth would be possible. On this point we have the results of the computing center that was set up in Pittsburgh to assist research in the law. It was designed to supply extracts from decisions in which a given subject is mentioned. First, a list of key words related to the topic under review is drawn up. If, say, the topic is *eminent domain,*

---

[41] One of the most successful systems for the retrieval of bibliographical information is MEDLARS (Medical Literature Analysis and Retrieval System) of the National Library of Medicine at Bethesda, Maryland. MEDLARS is about to be replaced by a still further improved system. It is clear that the extension of such systems to all categories of source materials would be of immense benefit to all researchers and their librarian-helpers.

the key words might be *condemn, expropriate, appropriate,* among others. The computer will print out from each decision in which any one of those words occurs the few lines that surround it. The legal expert then looks up the full decision in those cases that seem to him closest to his concern.

The evident benefits of this "expanded index" (as it might be called) did not come up to expectations. To begin with, the materials turned up were often discouragingly voluminous, partly as a result of ambiguity. It would be enormously expensive and elaborate to distinguish between *appropriate* (verb) and *appropriate* (adjective). Besides, the five or six lines from each decision frequently misled or tantalized the mind of the researcher, who felt obliged to go to the source as he would have done without the computer. A conclusion widely held by observers was that: "the less likely you were to do research as part of your practical daily labors, the more likely you were to like the computer's cases."[42] In other words, the more experienced scholars were the least satisfied. And this says something important about the so-far unsurpassed complexity and power of the human mind.

There is another aspect of this much-debated topic that the modern researcher will want to bear in mind as he pursues his patient effort of fact-finding. The notion of "computer-aided research"—or indeed the very word computer—has led some workers in one or other of the historical disciplines to suppose that theirs was becoming a science because, via the machine, it was approaching measurement. And such workers are likely to quote the words attributed to the great French scholar Georges Lefebvre, "To write history, one must know how to count." Lefebvre made his name with painstaking studies of agrarian and other economic conditions before the French Revolution, and these studies required counting, that is, quantitative findings or estimates about social reality.

But it is a great mistake to suppose that counting and measurement are interchangeable terms. Modern physical science is characterized by measurement, not counting. And measurement implies several features that historical research does not show: a standard unit, a closed "system" within which the chosen factors act without intrusion

[42] Martin Mayer, *The Lawyers,* New York, 1967, 450.

from others, and the correlation of the observed action with another, also expressed in standard units. What is obtained is then a "rate" uniting mathematically a cause and an effect. The rate is the measurement of the chosen phenomenon—it predicts with the required accuracy the amount of change of whatever kind—velocity, acceleration, expansion, radiation, and so on.

How very different the *counting* of small landholders in the district or the number of Jacobins in the town![43] This is not to say that counting is not important to the historian, or that he may not attempt to find correlations and percentages. In fact he cannot avoid them, for he deals in election returns, party memberships, suicide rates, publication figures, imports and exports, and many other numerable things. But such figures do not measure anything in the scientific sense and lead to no laws of nature akin to those of science.

[43] See below, p. 246, and for further discussion of measurement in social affairs, p. 248.

5

Verification

How the Mind Seeks Truth

⌐ Every thinking person is continually brought face to face with the need to discriminate between what is true and what is false, what is probable and what is doubtful or impossible. These decisions rest on a combination of knowledge, skepticism, faith, common sense, and intelligent guessing.⌐In one way or another, we decide whether the road to town is too icy for going by car, whether the child is telling the truth about seeing a burglar upstairs, whether the threatened layoff at the local plant will take place after all. ⌐Any adult has acquired techniques for verifying rumors and reports so that he can take appropriate action.⌐He supplements his experience and learning by recourse to special sources or items of information—the broadcast weather report on the state of the road; the child's known habit of fantasy; or the word of the plant manager who has access to firsthand knowledge.

Few of those who run their lives in this way stop to think that in the first case they trusted a technical report which, though not infallible, is the only authority on the subject; that in the second case, the ground for judgment was prior observation and inference; and that

99

the third resort was to a competent witness. It is sometimes possible to use all three kinds of aids to judgment, and others besides, such as the opinions of neighbors and friends, to say nothing of trial and error. All but the most thoughtless and impulsive will, in short, use their minds before giving credence to others' say-so, and try to collect evidence before trusting their own surmises. [The world is too full of error and falsehood to make any other course mentally or physically safe.]

The intelligent newspaper reader, for example, daily encounters "incredible" stories and tries automatically to "verify" them, first by "reading between the lines" and drawing what seems at the moment an acceptable conclusion, and later by looking for further reports. Limited as this effort is, one cannot always make it from an armchair.

Take the once shocking news story that appeared under the headline: "Clare Luce's Illness Is Traced To Arsenic Dust in Rome Villa."[1] According to the article, Mrs. Luce, at that time United States Ambassador to Italy, had in the summer of 1954 begun to experience symptoms of anemia and fatigue that disappeared when she was absent from her post in Rome, but recurred as soon as she returned to it. Hospital tests, it was said, disclosed that she was the victim of arsenic poisoning. Who was administering the poison? Investigation had brought out that "arsenic paint" on the roses adorning her bedroom ceiling was the source of the poison. Minute flakes of the paint were dislodged by people walking in the laundry above and drifted down, to be inhaled by the Ambassador or swallowed with her morning coffee. Skillful detection by the Central Intelligence Agency was credited with finding the cause of the trouble; and it was announced that steps had been taken to remove it.

The critical reader's immediate response to the story is amazement verging on incredulity—emotions which impel the mind toward the work of truth-seeking or verification. To begin with, one can think of no reason why the report should have been fabricated. Second, one notes that the events were first made known in a newsmagazine published by Mrs. Luce's husband: he had a double reason to protect his reputation for accuracy. Third, one reflects that since the announcement was made by Mrs. Luce just before returning to her post,

[1] *New York Times,* July 17, 1956.

the incident is almost certainly true. What patriotic person would want to embroil Italian-American relations by raising even the possibility of a plot to poison the American Ambassador?

But offsetting these probabilities, the critical reader notes, is the absence of any corroborative statement from either the Department of State or the Central Intelligence Agency—or from any Italian source. It is difficult, moreover, to imagine the United States Ambassador living in a house where the paint is so old as to flake off, and where the washing is done on a floor above the bedrooms. If the reader has a smattering of medical knowledge, he is even more puzzled. Is the poison arsenic, which produces a particular set of bodily symptoms, or arsenate of lead, formerly a common ingredient of house paints, which produces different symptoms, those of lead poisoning? If it was arsenic, what was it doing in the paint? If arsenate of lead, why are people with scientific training miscalling it? When the ordinary reader encounters a story of this kind and carries his speculation as far as we have supposed, he ends by doing one of several things: (1) he accepts it because it appeared in a newspaper he trusts; (2) he rejects it because it does not square with what he thinks likely; (3) he suspends judgment until more information appears; or (4) he ignores the difficulty altogether.

A judicious reader will adopt (3), though there is nothing downright foolish about the other choices. But the researcher and historical reporter has a greater responsibility, which denies him the right to any of the four solutions. He may indeed come to rest on (3), but not until he has done a great deal of work; and except under certain conditions, (1), (2), and (4) go against his professional training and obligations. As the student of past events tries to answer the question What *did* happen? he confronts the same uncertainties as the newspaper

[2] Subsequent reports confused the original story beyond hope of armchair unraveling: first, the Ambassador herself cast doubt on the chronology by putting the poisoning back one year; and then the American physician who had been consulted at that time asserted that no tests for arsenic had been made. (*New York Times,* July 22 and Nov. 20, 1956.) The episode continues to be mystifying. Mrs. Luce has stated that she plans to write her account of it (letter to Henry F. Graff, Aug. 10, 1967); her secretary in Rome, Letitia Baldridge, has written about it in *Of Diamonds and Diplomats,* Boston, 1968, 75–80.

reader, but with this important difference: ⌈*the historian must try to reach a decision and make it rationally convincing, not only to himself, but to others. The steps by which he performs this task constitute Verification*⌋

Verification is required of the researcher on a multitude of points—from getting an author's first name correct to proving that a document is both genuine and authentic.[3] Verification is accordingly conducted on many planes, and its technique is not fixed. It relies on attention to detail, on common-sense reasoning, on a developed "feel" for history and chronology, on familiarity with human behavior, and on ever enlarging stores of information. Many a "catch question" current among schoolboys calls forth these powers in rudimentary form—for instance the tale about the beautiful Greek coin just discovered and bearing the date "500 B.C." Here a second's historical reflection and reasoning are enough for verification: the "fact" is speedily rejected.

The first sort of verification consists in clearing up the simple obscurities that arise from one's own or somebody else's carelessness. A good example is found in the following account of a copyeditor's search, as reported by the publishing house where she worked:

In the bibliography of a manuscript there appeared this item: "Landsborous, A., and Thompson, H. F. G., *Problems of Bird Migration.*" In the line of duty, the editor queried the spelling of Landsborous, but it was returned by the author without change or comment. Not satisfied, she searched in various bibliographies and in two library catalogues for the name. She could find neither it nor the title of the book. Then she began to look for "Thompson, H. F. G.," but without success. Under the subject "Birds—Migration" she was referred to "Aves—Migration." There she found that an A. L. Thomson (without the "p") had written *Bird-Migration* (2nd ed.). Further research in the subject index of the British Museum Catalogue revealed that the first edition had indeed been entitled *Problems of Bird-Migration.* The proper entry then proved to be: "Thomson, Arthur Landsborough. *Problems*

---

[3] The two adjectives may seem synonymous but they are not: that is genuine which is not forged; and that is authentic which truthfully reports on its ostensible subject. Thus an art critic might write an account of an exhibition he had never visited; his manuscript would be genuine but not authentic. Conversely, an authentic report of an event by X might be copied by a forger and passed off as the original. It would then be authentic but not genuine.

of Bird-Migration." The initials following the name "Thompson" in the original version continued to puzzle the editor until someone suggested that they might indicate an Honorary Fellowship in Geography. . . .[4]

Not all uncertainties are so thoroughly grappled with and disposed of. Some are like prickly fruit: one does not know how to take hold of them. Others are plain enough but require enormous patience and tireless legwork. No interesting or important question, it is fair to say, can be settled without detailed knowledge, solid judgment, lively imagination, and the ability to think straight. What to do and how to go about it comes with practice; to enumerate rules would be endless and of little use. The best way to show in what the practice consists is to describe in some detail a variety of typical operations that were gone through in actual research.

Collation, or Matching Copies with Sources

One of the fundamental ways of verifying complex facts is known as collation. This simply means "bringing together." Thus when a scholar has found a manuscript and is about to print it, he must collate the successive proofsheets with the original before he passes them for publication. Collating is best done with help: one person—the "copyholder"—reads the text, punctuation included, while the scholar—who is known in this role as the "editor"—follows the printed version.

Many rules govern the form in which this kind of transfer from manuscript to type is to be made. They need not concern us here. But the principle of collation should be noted as being what, on a small scale and apart from work with manuscripts, is called comparison. It is by rapid single-handed collation that you discover small discrepancies or oddities and are able to stop error. But you must be ready to tackle the many problems of verification.

Among examples of the persistence of error through endless repetition in print, none could be more striking than the presence of a certain

[4] Columbia University Press, *The Pleasures of Publishing,* XIV (June 30, 1947), 2.

proper name in one of Edgar Allan Poe's best-known stories. The name is La Bougive and it occurs in "The Purloined Letter," side by side with those of Machiavelli, La Rochefoucauld, and Campanella, all of whom are scorned for their shallow and specious notions of the human mind. La Bougive never existed; there is no use looking for him in any dictionaries or pseudonyma.[5] He is simply a misprint for La Bruyère, the French moralist and writer of maxims, who lived in the seventeenth century. Poe was fond of reading him, and in other stories and essays Poe spells the name correctly. But he missed the "typo" both in proof and in his own annotated copy of the *Tales* (1845). In the 1890's the editors of the Chicago edition made the proper guess and put in La Bruyère, but still in the late 1960's new anthologies, both the cheap paperback and the would-be scholarly, go on faithfully reproducing the error.[6]

The basis of the necessary correction here is a full knowledge of French literature and a sense of language in relation to proper names. Usually, discrepancies disclose themselves more simply by a conflict that anyone would notice. Suppose that you are reading the interesting letter dated July 6, 1776, in which the composer Joseph Haydn gives a young lady a brief account of his life and career. The article contains not only the text of the letter but a facsimile reproduction of part of the document. Near the beginning of the letter Haydn says: "I was born on the last day of March, 1733." You have no reason to doubt so plain a statement; in that year the Continent used the modern calendar and there is no problem of "Old Style."[7] But you note that the magazine has merely printed the letter, without any signs of scholarly editing. Your inclination is of course to take Haydn's word for such facts as his birth date, the names of his birthplace and of his early patrons and teachers, and so on. But the titles of some unfamiliar works, as well as allusions to other composers, lead you to seek verification of these allusions.

[5] See below, p. 127.
[6] One of the authors of the present book made a survey of all English and American editions available in print or on library shelves and found fewer than one in four with the correct reading. See Jacques Barzun, "A Note on the Inadequacy of Poe as a Proofreader and of His Editors as French Scholars," *Romanic Review,* LXI (February 1970), 23–26.
[7] See above, p. 87.

You begin by looking up Haydn in some reliable work of reference, such as *Grove's Dictionary of Music and Musicians*. You pull down Volume II of the Third Edition, flip the pages, and your eye falls on the running head "Haydn," page 590. You can see that you have hit on the end of the article, so you turn back a page, only to find "Haydn, Johann Michael," born 1737. This obviously is the wrong Haydn. You move forward again, since Joseph comes after Johann—or should, for he doesn't. Instead, you have landed in the middle of the article "Hayes." It is impossible that Joseph Haydn should not be in *Grove*. Back you go to Johann, in front of whose name you notice the figure (2). There must be a (1), who turns out to be *"Franz* Joseph, born in the night of March 31, 1732."

This is puzzling in two ways: whose is the misprint as to the year, and what is the meaning of "the night of March 31"? It may mean either the night from March 30 to 31 (which would accord with Haydn's phrase "the last *day* of March"); or it might mean the night of March 31 to April 1st. As it happens, you have brought your "original" with you to the library, including, as we have mentioned, a fragment in facsimile. As you recall it, this was either the beginning or the end of the letter, to show off the salutation or the signature. By good luck it is the beginning, and you read plainly in Haydn's neat script: 1733.

Now there is no question but that a man is an eyewitness to his own birth. Yet it is an event about which he has to take other people's word for the rest of his life. He *may* therefore have erred about the date—or again he may have had reason to falsify it. Napoleon and two of his brothers did just that on the occasion of their marriages, with the result that records show all three to have been born within the same year.

You are still suspended in doubt about Haydn's dates. You turn to the end of the article in *Grove* for the Haydn bibliography, and incidentally to see who wrote the sketch you have been reading. "C.F.P." leads you to the key, which says: C. Ferdinand Pohl. This German name wakes an echo in your mind—perhaps you remember the writings of Richard Pohl about his contemporaries, Wagner and Berlioz. Ferdinand Pohl doubtless belongs to the next generation. The certainty comes over you that this article in *Grove's* third edition (1927, 1935) is an old one reproduced or recast from the original edition

(1879, 1896). And from experience you know that the original tended to be more garrulous and thereby often more informative. It is at any rate worth a try. The library keeps both editions side by side on the reference shelf, the first having an invaluable index not repeated in the later one.

You confidently turn to "Haydn, J." only to find that he has again revolved around his brother Johann Michael, being listed here as plain Joseph. And the very first words solve most of your perplexities: "Haydn, Joseph, or, according to the baptismal register, Franz Joseph, the father of the symphony and the quartet, was born in the night between March 31 and April 1, 1732." Blessed garrulity! Here at last is a reporter—it is, you note, your same friend Pohl before he was cut down for the next edition—here is a reporter who professes to speak from the baptismal register, a better source than a middle-aged man's autobiographical letter to a Mademoiselle.

For ordinary purposes you could stop right there in your "collation." But if you want to make assurance double sure, go to any standard work on Haydn, such as Geiringer's,[8] or consult the massive *Die Musik in Geschichte und Gegenwart,* which by 1968 had reached completion with Volume 14.

Skepticism, or Sifting Out the Probable from the False

It may seem more difficult to start questioning small details in genuine documents than to doubt a legend or anecdote that sounds too pat to be true, but Verification may be as laborious in the one case as in the other.

The doubtful anecdote you recognize immediately; it bears a family likeness common to the many that you know to be apocryphal. One such famous story has for its hero Stephen A. Douglas, the Illinois Senator contemporary with Lincoln. Tradition has it that on September 1, 1854, a few months after reopening the slavery question by introducing the Kansas-Nebraska Bill, the "Little Giant" stood

[8] Karl Geiringer, *Haydn: A Creative Life in Music,* New York, 1946, 21 and n. The latest *Grove* (3rd ed.) reprinting gives: "born 31 March or 1 April, 1732."

before a hostile crowd in Chicago and attempted to justify his action. Booed, jeered, and hissed, Douglas held his ground for over two hours, determined that he would be listened to. Finally, so the story goes, he pulled out his watch, which showed a quarter after twelve, and shouted: "It is now Sunday morning—I'll go to church and you may go to Hell."

How does an historian verify his doubts of a "good story" of this kind? The steps taken by one scholar[9] to establish or destroy this legend were as follows: First, he searched through the Chicago newspapers of late August and early September, 1854, for some account of Douglas' return from Washington. This, he found, had been regarded as a great event, impatiently awaited by the public and fully covered in the press. Next, he scanned the accounts of the meeting itself, looking for any reference to the scornful remark. He found none. Neither the newspapers nor the first biography of the Senator, which was published in 1860, reported the incident. So far the results of a good deal of work, being negative, seemed to justify the doubt.

Yet on the main issue the search turned up some positive though indirect evidence. Two papers, one in Chicago and one in Detroit, stated that Douglas had left the platform at ten-thirty. Moreover, the meeting had taken place on a Friday, not a Saturday night! In the absence of a dated newspaper, a perpetual calendar (every researcher should own one) will quickly establish the day of the week on which a date fell or will fall in any year of the Christian era. This is a fixed point: no doubt is possible about it, September 1, 1854, was a Friday.

But considering the simple ways of press reporting at the time, another possibility remains: perhaps in the uproar no newspaperman heard Douglas' emphatic remark. Of course, if we suppose this in order to support the story, we must also assume that Douglas was so rattled by the heckling of the crowd that he could neither read his watch correctly nor remember what day of the week it was. When the researcher finds himself multiplying hypotheses in order to cling to a belief, he had better heed the signal and drop the belief.

[9] Granville D. Davis, "Douglas and the Chicago Mob," *American Historical Review,* LIV (April 1949), 553–56.

By now our scholar's curiosity was aroused and he wanted to know the full history of the anecdote. Where had it first appeared? Perhaps Douglas himself had uttered or recorded the statement after the incident. If this were so, his biographers would surely have discovered the starting point and noted it. What do they in fact quote from when they repeat the tale? From a volume written by Douglas' father-in-law, James Madison Cutts, and published in 1866, five years after Douglas' death. The work is entitled *A Brief Treatise upon Constitutional and Party Questions;* it contains so many half-truths and outright fabrications that it may be deemed generally untrustworthy. Only one small chance remains: that on this single matter, the book is accurate. True or made up after the event, the tale may have been told by Douglas to Cutts himself.

Beyond this the scholar cannot go. What certainty has he garnered for his pains? Enough to reward his labors. He now knows—as *we* know, thanks to him—that Douglas spoke on a Friday night, that he was not reduced to complete silence by the crowd, and that the meeting did not go on past midnight. The probability is great that Douglas would not have mistaken the day and announced his intention of going to church on a Saturday morning. If he told his audience to "go to Hell," no contemporary seems to have noticed the words. The remark seems a trifle intemperate for a calculating politician who had his eye on the Presidency. Combining certainties with probabilities, the verifier reaches the inescapable judgment that the famous remark was never made. At best, it is what Douglas might have wanted to throw in the teeth of his hecklers but never did.

Myths and "good stories" will of course persist despite the efforts of historians.[10] What fits a situation or a character develops a life of its own and is immortal. Verifiers must therefore be attentive to the work of dispelling done by their fellows and thereby avoid embarrassment. The most recent biography of Douglas, for example, still

---

[10] For example, Captain Kidd stands in the popular imagination as the pirate par excellence, whereas it is quite likely that he did not commit the acts for which he was tried and which gave him his reputation. Likewise with Dr. Crippen "the murderer," who was a physician but not a doctor, and who probably poisoned his wife accidentally with the then unfamiliar drug hyoscine.

offers the Douglas taunt as if no contrary evidence had ever been assembled.[11] Since it is patently impossible to verify every "fact," it behooves the researcher to scan the steady flow of books and articles that correct and reinterpret what is "well known," and, in what bears on his interest, to remember the discredited "facts." Later on, at the right moment, that recollection will help establish the new-found truth at the expense of the old error.

A celebrated piece of historical mischief illustrates the kind of fact that a researcher must make his own long before he needs to know it. In 1917 H. L. Mencken published in the *New York Evening Mail* what purported to be a history of the bathtub. Along with other sprightly and persuasive details, Mencken recounted how Millard Fillmore, on becoming President of the United States in 1850, "instructed his secretary of war, Gen. Charles M. Conrad, to invite tenders for the construction of a bathtub in the White House." This satirical vision—with its absurd suggestion that the bathtub did not appear in America until the 1840's—soon made its way into respectable reference books. Mencken finally confessed in 1926 that his article was only "a piece of spoofing to relieve the strain of the war days." But by that time his "facts" were "accepted as gospel everywhere on earth. To question them becomes as hazardous as to question the Norman invasion."[12]

Attribution, or Putting a Name to a Source

The historian, we conclude, arrives at truth through probability. As we shall see in a later discussion,[13] this does not mean "a doubtful kind of truth" but a firm reliance on the likelihood that evidence

[11] Gerald M. Capers, *Stephen A. Douglas: Defender of the Union,* ed. Oscar Handlin, Boston, 1959, 120.

[12] H. L. Mencken, *The Bathtub Hoax and Other Blasts and Bravos from the Chicago Tribune,* ed. with an introduction and notes by Robert McHugh, New York, 1958, 3–15. Fillmore's connection with the bathtub seems now perdurable. The author of the first authoritative work on Fillmore adopts it: Robert J. Rayback, *Millard Fillmore: Biography of a President,* Buffalo, 1959, 373. And a guidebook sold at the White House is giving the notion fresh currency: Lonnelle Aikman, *The Living White House,* Washington, D.C., 1966, 120.

[13] See Chapter 7, pp. 159–69.

which has been examined and found solid is veracious. If you receive a letter from a relative that bears what looks like his signature, that refers to family matters you and he commonly discuss, and that was postmarked in the city where he lives, the probability is very great that he wrote it. The contrary hypothesis would need at least as many opposing signs in order to take root in your mind—though the possibility of forgery, tampering, and substitution is always there.

As everybody knows, the number of signs that point to genuineness reinforce one another and vastly increase the total probability. If their force could be measured, it would amount not to their sum but to their product. In other words, with each added particle of truthfulness, it becomes far less likely that deception or forgery has been practiced. Hence in cases where no direct sign is available, a concurrence of indirect signs will establish proof. The "circumstantial evidence" of the law courts is a familiar example of this type of mute testimony. It must always be received with caution and tested bit by bit, though sometimes it is convincing at first sight, as when—to use Thoreau's example—you find a trout in the milk.

One type of difficulty that the researcher overcomes by looking for cumulative indirect proof is that of identifying the unsigned contributions in periodicals. The problem is a frequent one, for until about a century ago nearly all journalism was anonymous. Sometimes an account book survives to tell us who was paid for writing what.[14] But usually nothing remains except the researcher's sharp wits. Here is how such a researcher arrived at an important identification some years ago.[15] In the early 1830's, the young writer John Stuart Mill was greatly interested in the work of the Saint-Simonians, a French socialist group. He met some of their emissaries in England and studied their ideas. So much is clear. Now on April 18, 1832, there appeared in Le Globe, which was the newspaper of the French society, a long letter signed "J." that purported to give an Englishman's opinion of

[14] This was the method used by Daniel C. Haskell in producing Volume Two of his Indexes of Titles and Contributors of The Nation . . . 1865–1917, 2 vols., New York, 1951–53.
[15] Hill Shine, "J. S. Mill and an Open Letter to the Saint-Simonian Society in 1832," Journal of the History of Ideas, VI (January 1945), 102–08.

the Saint-Simonian doctrines. The mind naturally jumps to the possibility that this letter was a translation of something written by Mill. But jumping is not proving. How do we make sure?

First, research discloses two earlier allusions by one of the editors of the paper to the effect that "one of the most powerful young thinkers in London" intended to write a series of open letters on the new ideas.

Second, there exists a letter to that same editor announcing the visit of a third party who would bring him, among other things, "the work of your young friend M." With the published "J." the "M." makes out a *prima facie* case for identifying the writer as John Mill; yet it needs strengthening.

Third, it was within three days of receiving the piece of news just recorded that the newspaper published the open letter of "an Englishman" who signed himself "J."

At this point the scholar whose researches we have followed remarks that "a cautious reader will still properly feel some reservations" about attributing the letter to Mill.[16] He therefore continues the chase. "Two further bits of circumstantial evidence," he tells us, "seem decisive." They are, to pursue the enumeration:

Fourth, a letter of May 30 from Mill to his Saint-Simonian friends referring to "my letter which appeared in *Le Globe*"; and

Fifth, a footnote added to that private letter by the editor of Mill's correspondence, stating that Mill's public letter appeared on April 18, 1832.

At this point no further doubt is possible and the researcher can exclaim, like Euclid at the end of a theorem: "Q.E.D."

Explication, or Worming Secrets Out of Manuscripts

Young researchers who want to obtain their professional license by earning the Ph.D. often believe that the greatest proof of merit is to find a packet of letters in an attic. The implication is that historians

[16] *Ibid.*, 106.

value a new find of primary sources[17] above any other achievement of the human intelligence. This is not so. But new evidence is always interesting; and it may be extremely valuable. If it consists of manuscripts, it creates special problems for the verifier. Manuscripts often come to him in huge unsorted masses—the "papers" of a man or a family, which are the bulky leftovers of busy lives. Of such papers, letters are perhaps the most difficult to subdue: they must be forced, in spite of slips of the pen, bad handwriting, or allusions to unidentified persons, to tell the exact story that the author intended and that the recipient probably understood.

In this kind of decoding and classifying no librarian can go very far in supplying help. It is an expert's job, and no one is an expert until he has made himself one. You learn your letter-writer's quirks and foibles from what he wrote and said; you date and interpret the documents by internal and external clues. To do these things, you go back and forth between clear and obscure, dated and undated pieces, acquiring information by which to pull yourself forward until gaps are filled and contradictions become intelligible. Dumas Malone, for instance, learned from long familiarity with Jefferson's papers that his subject's vocabulary grew more "radical" in writing to younger men. This was a sign not so much of Jefferson's eagerness for a new revolution as of his desire to awaken the coming generation to its responsibility for progress. This fact, once observed, becomes a test for the literalness of some of Jefferson's most advanced proposals. The point of this example is that only an expert—one might even say: only *the* expert—is in a position to make sound inferences from a given letter.

Dealing with letters, then, is not a sinecure. It requires an agile mind, or one made such by repeated bafflement and discovery. Consider the simplest of questions: When was this written and to whom? Unless the writer was a regular "dater," or the post office stamped the letter itself, or the envelope has been kept, or the recipient was a methodical

---

[17] In historiography, a primary source is distinguished from a secondary by the fact that the former gives the words of the witnesses or first recorders of an event—for example, the diaries of Count Ciano written under Mussolini's regime. The historian, using a number of such primary sources, produces a secondary source. See Chapter 7, pp. 146–51.

person who endorsed each letter with the particulars of its date and bearing, the precious piece of paper may raise more questions than it answers.

For a pair of representative puzzles we may turn to the letters of the composer Hector Berlioz (1803–69). These letters keep appearing on the market as the plans for publishing his full correspondence are under way in the centenary year 1969. It becomes the scholar's task to fit the new items among the hundreds already known or published. Before he can do this he must supply deficiencies of place, date, or addressee's name. Two forms that this operation can take may be briefly illustrated. The A.L.S. says, in French:

19 rue de Boursault,
Thursday June 23

DEAR SIR:
Here is the Table of Contents of the book about which I had the honor of speaking to you. If you will kindly look it over, you will have a rough idea of the subjects dealt with and the general tone of the work. Till next Monday.

Yours faithfully,
HECTOR BERLIOZ

Now the address with which the note starts is in Paris, and it is one at which Berlioz resided from July 1849 till April 1856. (This knowledge comes from a table that the researcher has prepared for himself from a survey of all the letters extant.[18]) So the piece to be identified falls within those seven years. The next step is to the perpetual calendar, which gives Thursday, June 23, as falling in 1853. This seems to settle the matter, except that the only book Berlioz had in hand during those years was ready by May 1852 and was published the same December. We are forced to conclude that despite the "Thursday June 23" the note was written not in 1853, but in 1852. This is at once confirmed by the table of domiciles, which shows that in June 1853 Berlioz was in London, not Paris. We know from other

---

[18] For this table and examples of the dating technique, see Jacques Barzun, *New Letters of Berlioz*, New York, 1954, 304–05 and 273 ff. Letters subsequently found require two changes in this table (see the revised edition of *New Letters of Berlioz*, New York, 1970).

instances that he frequently mistook the day of the week. Moreover, in June 1852 the twenty-third falls on a Wednesday; so that, assuming a mistake, his dating would be only one day off. Combining these likelihoods, and knowing also who accepted the book when presented, we conclude that the note was sent to Michel Lévy, a well-known publisher. An inquiry at the present offices of the firm showed that no records of the period were preserved. Internal evidence is therefore our only guide.

The subject of the note just examined was of small moment, but sometimes the identification and collation[19] of an original will rectify a universally held opinion. Witness our second example. In 1846, when Central Europe was seething with nationalistic passion, Berlioz was giving concerts in Hungary and Bohemia and performing there for the first time his rousing *Rákóczy March.* Soon after the premiere, a German periodical got hold of one of his letters to a young Czech musicologist, who was also a patriot, and printed a piece of it as if it were the whole, garbling it in such a way as to turn the message into something of a political document. As late as 1940, when a Hungarian scholar quoted it again in the New York *Musical Quarterly,* no one questioned the letter, and its editor commented on the politico-musical passion it displayed.

Ten years later, in tracking down Berlioz letters in private collections, one of the authors of this book was given an opportunity to copy a long letter dated one day before the published one. Suddenly, in the midst of it, familiar words appeared: they were part of the famous "political" letter, which the German paper had garbled and reduced to one paragraph out of eight. In the full text, all but half a dozen lines have to do with music, and these few lines show that the newspaper resorted to grave distortion, while also misdating the letter for reasons no longer ascertainable.[20]

Each such correction may be small in itself, but the cumulative effect over a series filling several volumes may be very great. Moreover, the editor of a famous man's complete letters never knows when the rectification of a single date or name, unimportant from his point

[19] For further reference to the technique, see Chapter 16, p. 363.
[20] Barzun, *New Letters of Berlioz,* 308.

of view, may not resolve the difficulty of a worker upon another subject who is searching for the verification of *his* uncertain data.

Disentanglement, or Unraveling the Tangle of Facts

Not every problem of textual verification is found in rare manuscript letters. Most researchers never use anything but printed sources. Yet these too are full of contradictions that have to be resolved, as are also the inferences from artifacts. Imagine, for instance, an observant student who has noticed that the words "In God We Trust" appear on some of our old coins but not on others, nor on old paper money. Imagine him further as writing a textbook on American history, for which he wants to verify his reasonable guess that the four words in question form the official, yet seemingly optional, motto of the United States.

His first step might be to find out how early in our history the slogan was used on our coins. Thumbing through *The Standard Catalogue of United States Coins,* he would learn that the phrase is not to be found before 1864. It first appeared on the bronze two-cent pieces, and two years later on all gold and silver coins. The verifier would also observe that it disappeared from the five-cent pieces in 1883 and did not return till 1938. What is more, it appeared on some of the gold coins struck in 1908 and not on others. Clearly, this alternation of "now-you-see-it, now-you-don't" suggests either fickleness or the probability that inscriptions on American money are not ruled by settled official policy.

Noticing that the picture of Secretary of the Treasury Salmon P. Chase adorns the greenbacks, or paper money, issued during the Civil War, when the motto was first used, the historian might conclude that Chase had a special interest in the design of our money. The obvious course would be to seek more light in a biography of Chase. The surmise about Chase would be wrong but the upshot would carry the researcher one step forward. He would find that although Chase took no interest in the numismatic art, he was a religious man. He put "In God We Trust" on the coins to satisfy a crusading clergyman who thought it imperative. Next, from the issuance of coins both with and without the motto in 1908, our scholar would correctly conclude that the choice lay within the discretion of the Secretary of the Treasury.

No sooner would he be confident that the motto had no official standing than he would discover in his research a newspaper account about the decision of Congress—ninety-two years after Chase's—to make the words official and inscribe them on all our currency, both metal and paper.[21]

Note by way of summary that this verifier had to consult a coin catalogue, one or more books about Chase, one or more about Theodore Roosevelt for the events of 1908, and a newspaper file before he could solve his puzzle.

Clarification, or Destroying Legends

The amount of verifying a researcher does depends not only on his own curiosity but also on the grasp of his subject that he possesses at the start. The more he understands at the beginning, the more he finds to question and ascertain. [It is expected, of course, that the researcher into any subject will approach it with a well-developed sense of time—whether the time be the few weeks or months of a particular crisis or the centuries separating St. Augustine from St. Thomas. Thus the narrator of the French Revolution or the First World War proceeds by days in those fateful summer and autumn months, whereas the historian of Rome must without stumbling move across a span of twenty generations.]

But the investigator's original fund of knowledge must embrace even more than a well-populated chronology; it must include an understanding of how men in other eras lived and behaved, what they believed, and how they managed their institutions. This kind of mastery fills the mind with images and also with questions, which, when answered and discussed, make for what we term depth. Meanwhile the funded information suggests the means for conducting the research.

Consider the sort of inquiry that leads to the exploding of a legend.

[21]Bill signed by President Eisenhower, July 30, 1956. The President offered no public comment on the occasion.

Legends, we know, abound and flourish despite the verifiers. But this does not lessen the importance of truth, for important new ideas are often made to rest upon pseudo-truths that "every schoolboy knows." Some years ago, for example, a reputable psychiatrist published a volume embodying his clinical researches into the states of mind of dying patients.[22] In this work he draws conclusions affecting our present culture and he buttresses them with historical statements. Unfortunately one of these happens to be a myth:

> When the first millennium after the birth of Christ approached its end, Occidental man was seized by the fear of and hope for the Lord's return. The end of the world was envisaged, which meant man's final end [sic] had arrived. With the approach of the second millennium, the conviction again has spread that the days of man are counted. . . .[23]

That this parallel is false in every respect will be clear if we retrace the path of the scholar who well over half a century ago disposed of the legend about the end of the world coming in the year 1000.[24]

His first step was to discover when the tale originally came out in print. He found that this was in a 1690 edition of a late-fifteenth-century chronicle. Thus the first public record of the story is found about seven hundred years after the supposed date of doom. Seven hundred years is a long time—twice the span since Shakespeare's death, four times that since Cornwallis' surrender at Yorktown. By the eighteenth century, a period when the Middle Ages were in disrepute and instances of their superstition were gladly seized on, the published tale of 1690 referring to an event seven centuries earlier was first widely circulated. Indeed, it became usual to ascribe the launching of the Crusades to the relief felt by the Christians when the end of the world did not come in A.D. 1000. This emotion was also said to account for the remarkable increase in church building. Although these several explanations were discredited by nineteenth-century historians, at the turn of the new century educated people still believed the myth—they

---

[22] K. R. Eissler, *The Psychiatrist and the Dying Patient,* New York, 1955.
[23] *Ibid.,* 108.
[24] George L. Burr, "The Year 1000 and the Antecedents of the Crusades," *American Historical Review,* VI (April 1901), 429–39.

still do, as our modern example shows. The terror of the year 1000 was the core of many a piece of moralizing. Said one confident writer of the 1880's about the men of A.D. 999:

Some squandered their substance in riotous living, others bestowed it for the salvation of their souls on churches and convents, bewailing multitudes lay by day and by night about the altars, many looked with terror, yet most with secret hope, for the conflagration of the earth and the falling of the heavens.[25]

In the face of such vivid, though belated, reports, what could make a thoughtful scholar suspect the truth of the whole episode? The answer is: his intimate knowledge of the Middle Ages.

He knew to begin with that the end of the world had been foretold so often that only the ignorant in the year 1000 would seriously believe a new rumor. Moreover, long before that year, it had become orthodox belief and teaching that if the end of the world were really to come no man would know the time in advance.

Third, he knew that however impressive round numbers based on the decimal system are to us, they had no such hold on the imagination of medieval man. The numerals of that era were the Roman I's, V's, X's, L's, C's, D's, and M's. For the Middle Ages no magic property would attach to "The Year M." Rather, mystery and significance would have been connected with 3's, 7's, 12's, and their multiples. For these were the sacred numbers of the Jews, and the Christians had repeatedly used them for prophecy.

Fourth, our scholar knew that the Christian calendar did not come into general use until after 1000. And even then there was no agreement on dating. Nor was this the only difficulty arising from the calendar. When did the year 1000 begin? At Christmas, at Annunciation, at Easter, on the first of March (as in Venice), at the vernal equinox (as in Russia), on the first of September (as in the Greek Empire), or on the first of January (as in Spain)? In such a state of things the world could obviously not end everywhere on schedule.

Fifth, our accomplished medievalist knew that bare numerical dates meant little or nothing to the ordinary medieval man. He guided

[25] H. v. Sybel, *Geschichte des ersten Kreuzzugs*, 2nd and revised ed., Leipzig, 1881, 150; quoted in Burr, *op. cit.*, 429.

his life by the feast- and fast-days of the Church, not, as we do, by engagement books in which not merely the days, months, and year are marked, but the hours and half-hours, A.M. and P.M. We carry watches and consult them every few minutes. Medieval time, differently divided, was of a different texture.

In short, it is profoundly unhistorical to read back our habits and behavior into an age many centuries past, and the conclusion is plain: taking the lack of any contemporaneous evidence of panic together with the facts of daily life and thought in the Middle Ages, the scholar demolishes a legend whose effects, potent as they are, would be still more benighting if his work had not enlightened at least a part of the educated public.

The dissemination of historical knowledge tends to be slow in proportion as the error is dramatic and "fitting." Like the year 1000, the capture of Constantinople by the Turks in 1453 has struck the general imagination and provided a convenient "cause" for Columbus' discovery of America: European traders could no longer go East; they sought a westward passage. As late as 1967, this notion was used to introduce the visitor to a superb exhibition of the Dutch in Manhattan at the Museum of the City of New York. Professor A. H. Lybyer, who conclusively disproved the connection between the Turks and westward voyages, had published his study exactly fifty-two years earlier.[26]

Identification, or Ascertaining Value Through Authorship

Sometimes a problem of verification is solved by reaching behind your desk and taking down the single reference book that contains the fact you need.[27] Sometimes a day or two in the library is required. More often the task becomes for a time one's central occupation.

[26] "The Ottoman Turks and the Routes of Oriental Trade," *English Historical Review*, CXX (October 1915), 577–88.

[27] The researcher will soon discover that reference books frequently disagree. This does not always mean that all are wrong except one; what happens is that one book in giving, say, the date of a treaty will give the year of its signing, and another book the date of its ratification, months later. Similar disparities can and do occur about most events, private and public, so that the "right" date is frequently a conventional choice among several possibilities.

This is almost sure to be true when the problem is to trace the unnamed or disputed authorship of a large and important source. If there is no chance of examining and comparing handwritings because the document exists only in print, the undertaking can be laborious indeed. Even with a manuscript original, such as that of a government document, one may be foiled by the fact that it is the work of an amanuensis.

One does not set out to discover authorship as a pastime, but because important consequences follow: knowing who the author is will help establish responsibility for acts or words; it will identify persons, explain meanings, and clear up allusions throughout the text as well as in other places; and it may relieve other historical figures of malicious charges, false rumors, and silent imputations of error. The fact that John C. Calhoun, not James Monroe, was the author of the War Report of 1812[28] is a minor matter in our history, but it serves to strengthen the view that the "War Hawks," of whom Calhoun was one, helped precipitate the war, rather than Secretary of State Monroe, to whom the warlike document was originally ascribed.

Of all the problems of authorship in American history, that of finding out who wrote "The Diary of a Public Man" has been the most gigantic. Indeed, the odyssey on which it took the chief investigator is unparalleled. The document first appeared in 1879 in four installments published by the influential *North American Review*. Covering the winter of Secession, 1860–61, the diary consists of entries for twenty-one days between December 28, 1860, and March 15, 1861. A fact of great importance to the user of the diary and, as we shall see, to the verifier, is that on twenty of these days the author was in Washington; on one, February 20, 1861, he was in New York City.

The value of the document may be gauged from the fact that it is the only source for a number of incidents about Lincoln's acts during the crisis of the Union. Among its more picturesque revelations is the account of Douglas' conduct at Lincoln's inauguration, which schoolchildren have learned ever since: "A miserable little rickety table

[28] Charles M. Wiltse, "The Authorship of the War Report of 1812," *American Historical Review*, XLIV (January 1944), 253–59.

had been provided for the President, on which he could hardly find room for his hat, and Senator Douglas, reaching forward, took it with a smile and held it during the delivery of the address. It was a trifling act, but a symbolic one, and not to be forgotten, and it attracted much attention all around me."

Who then was "me"? Professor Frank Maloy Anderson spent nearly thirty-five years trying to find the answer.[29] His undeviating persistence seems in retrospect to have been as single-minded and tireless as any in the history of verification. The fact that the question is still in dispute does not lessen the utility of his labors or their exemplary value for the researcher. Every attempt at verification advances knowledge, whether or not luck rewards his efforts.

Anderson's earliest move—in 1897, only eighteen years after the "Diary" appeared—was to try to identify the document by external means. He wanted to find out how the *North American Review* had received it in the first place. The editor of the *Review,* he discovered, had refused to discuss the question at the time of publication and his papers had disappeared after his death. The publisher, D. Appleton and Company, had acted as printer and distributor only and therefore had no record of payments to the contributor. Mr. Anderson then took a different course involving a number of separate steps:

1. He tried to discover if persons mentioned in the "Diary" had been interviewed in 1879 by journalists who had attempted to identify the author.

2. He examined the files of fifty important newspapers and magazines to find out if they had discussed the likely authorship of the document when it first appeared.

3. He investigated the qualifications for authorship of a number of persons previously suggested.

When these three efforts yielded nothing, Mr. Anderson tackled the question: What *kind* of person was the writer? A Senator? He found in the *Congressional Globe* the names of the Senators absent from their places on February 20, 1861, but none of them fulfilled the Diarist's

[29]Frank Maloy Anderson, *The Mystery of "A Public Man": A Historical Detective Story,* Minneapolis, 1948.

description of himself as a man of "long experience in Washington." A member of the House of Representatives? He eliminated for various reasons each of the fifty-four Representatives who were absent on that day. It seemed highly suggestive that the Diarist nowhere refers to the proceedings of the House. What were his politics? Whig? Republican? Democrat? Was he a Southerner? A New Englander? The text provided no conclusive evidence that the man had been one of these things more than another.

Mr. Anderson now decided to list the characteristics of the man that he thought he could discern in the "Diary." The most important were:

1. He was a man of weight in Washington: the entries show that his advice and prestige were enlisted by important people who had to deal with Lincoln.

2. He was a tall man. (Lincoln, he reports, asked him if he had ever matched backs with Charles Sumner, who was a tall man.)[30]

3. He was an experienced writer, who knew the French language.

4. He was a sophisticated man of the world, amused that Lincoln had worn *black* gloves to the opera.

5. He had many well-placed friends, and he himself had long resided in Washington.

6. He was devoted to the cause of the Union, but knew the South well.

7. He had met Lincoln in 1848 and again in 1861, but the Diarist had no recollection of the earlier meeting. ("I can not place him even with the help of all the pictures I have seen of such an extraordinary looking mortal.")

8. He was interested in business conditions and especially in tariff, patent, and postal problems.

9. He frequently attended the sessions of the Senate.

10. He was an intimate of William H. Seward and Stephen A. Douglas.

[30]According to the New York *Herald* for December 28, 1871, Sumner was "six feet three inches high," though on Sumner's passport his height is indicated as six feet two. David Donald, *Charles Sumner and the Coming of the Civil War*, New York, 1960, 27.

11. He was familiar with New York City and on easy terms with its leading citizens.

12. He was in New York on February 20, 1861, and in Washington on twenty other days between December 28, 1860, and March 15, 1861.

Mr. Anderson's search was correspondingly detailed and thorough. A long list of possibilities was methodically reduced, one by one, until the name of Amos Kendall[31] emerged as the best candidate. Imagine the researcher's excitement as point after point of Kendall's life and personality met the requirements: he was tall; he had traveled extensively in the South; he had for fifteen years been involved in patent litigation, as a result of his association with S. F. B. Morse in his telegraph enterprises; he was a former postmaster-general. Would such a man have spent a great deal of time in the Senate galleries? Of course—the Senate in the Secession Winter had before it a bill to renew the Morse telegraph patent.

Every requirement Mr. Anderson had established for the Diarist, Amos Kendall met—all except one, which would now require the closest investigation. Was Kendall in New York on February 20, 1861? The evidence showed that Morse had left New York to visit Washington on February 19. It seems certain that he stayed with the Kendalls in the capital. Only the most urgent business, therefore, could have brought Amos Kendall to New York during Morse's visit.

Mr. Anderson studied the lists of hotel arrivals that were published in the New York newspapers, in vain. Next he learned that Kendall, whenever he came to New York, stayed at the Astor House. If only Mr. Anderson could put his hands on the hotel register! His heart must have skipped a beat when he heard that the brother of a lady working at the Morgan Library in New York had been the last manager of the old Astor. Maybe he knew where the registers were deposited. Alas, he did not.

Now Mr. Anderson recalled that as a boy in Minneapolis he had distributed a newspaper called the *Hotel Gazette,* which listed hotel arrivals, and he remembered hearing at the time that all big cities

---

[31] Amos Kendall (1789–1869) is best known for his important role in Andrew Jackson's "Kitchen Cabinet."

had such a paper. He set out to find the name of the one in New York. After much effort he discovered a reference to *The Transcript*. Now to find a file of it. There was one at Yale, but to his dismay it lacked the issues he needed. Back from New Haven, he went to the New-York Historical Society. The catalogue showed no *Transcript*, but Mr. Anderson, running his eye down the list of newspaper headings, noticed *The Daily Transcript*. The file proved to be complete for the desired period. With mixed doubt and delight, the researcher found that the issue for February 19, 1861, contained an entry for a "J. Kendall" at the Astor House. Was this a misprint for "A. Kendall"? Or was this Amos' nephew "J. E. Kendall," or perhaps Amos' son John, who had recently moved to New York?

Whoever it was, Amos Kendall's presence in New York could not yet be established beyond a doubt. Mr. Anderson now turned to establishing his man's presence in Washington on the stated twenty days. The evidence conclusively proved that Kendall could *not* be the Diarist, for on at least two of the critical days he had certainly not been in Washington. No one, perhaps, can adequately describe Professor Anderson's feelings as he struck Kendall's name off the list.

Because no other figure had come so close as Kendall to matching the requirements, Mr. Anderson now tried another line of investigation. Was the document authentic? A number of points had already given the scholar pause:

1. Virtually all the persons mentioned in the document were dead by the time of its publication in 1879.

2. The dashes that replaced the names of persons appeared to stand for fictitious characters, because few could be identified from the context.

3. The "Diary" was usually vague on points about which a diarist could be expected to be precise.

4. There was a suspiciously large number of quotable remarks ascribed to Lincoln.

5. A good many excellent anecdotes and striking incidents were recorded in what is after all a brief span.

6. The Diarist's uncanny penetration in judging men and events was unusual for a contemporaneous reporter.

7. The amount of important data contained in the "Diary" that could not be confirmed by any other source was abnormal.

8. The polished style of the "Diary" contrasted with the expectable carelessness of diary-keepers.

Mr. Anderson's examination of the Diarist's account of his interviews with Lincoln now raised many questions about their truthfulness; and among the anecdotes, that of Douglas' holding Lincoln's hat seemed diagnostic. After exhausting research Mr. Anderson found only one contemporaneous account of this incident and in a dubious source—poor evidence indeed for such a striking fact, especially considering all that had been written by eyewitnesses about the inauguration. Mr. Anderson, moreover, showed convincingly that the Diarist's portraits of Douglas and Seward reflected the historical estimate of those men rather than the contemporary one of 1860–61.

Mr. Anderson decided that he could now entertain two hypotheses: (1) the "Diary" was a work of fiction; or (2) it was a combination of fiction and truth.

Mr. Anderson accepted the second alternative because he could not find a single instance of what is common in complete fabrications—the Diarist's having slipped up and referred to something provably false.

At long last, then, the original question, "Who was the Diarist?" had become "Who was the fabricator?" An inspiration came to him while he was engaged on a quite different project. He suddenly thought of a man who had been in Washington in the Secession Winter and who was a friend of Seward's. This was Samuel Ward, brother of Julia Ward Howe, who wrote "The Battle Hymn of the Republic."

Indefatigably again, Mr. Anderson went in pursuit of his quarry. For fifteen years he tracked down Ward's relatives and descendants to find the private letters from which he could learn enough about the man to confirm his new hypothesis. The facts of Ward's life fitted the image given in the "Diary." Known as "King of the Lobby," Ward was a familiar figure in Washington; he was in that city during the Secession Winter; his acquaintance was extensive; he was said to have kept a diary; he was a man of the world who unquestionably knew French; he was a strong Unionist; he was interested in business, especially in the tariff, coastwise trade, patents, and postal matters; he was a New Yorker, on close terms with his leading fellow citizens; he disliked Sumner and would have ridiculed him with pleasure as the Diarist obviously did; he was an admiring intimate of Seward's and an acquaintance of Douglas'.

At last Mr. Anderson was able to answer a number of important questions. First, why the "Diary" stopped abruptly with the entry for March 15, 1861. This was obviously because Ward left Washington to accompany on a tour of the Confederate States the London journalist William H. Russell, who had landed in New York on March 16. Second, who the people were who appeared in the "Diary" by dashes or initials. They were Ward's close friends, and their remarks formed the fictitious parts of the document.

The search for the "Public Man" had apparently ended. As Mr. Anderson left the question, Sam Ward had spun his fiction around a core of genuine diary. Blessed with an uncanny memory and considerable literary gifts, Ward was the kind of man who would have delighted in perpetrating a hoax. The editor of the *North American Review* was no doubt a party to the fabrication, which would account for his silence. The "Diary" survived and fooled many researchers because its foundation was genuine. Thanks to this grounding in fact, no discrepancies can be shown. Yet for the historian—except the one who writes Sam Ward's biography—the document is worthless.[32]

Not all historians accept Mr. Anderson's findings.[33] Some advance objections to the verifier's reasoning from the text and propose other

[32] Consult Lately Thomas, *Sam Ward: "King of the Lobby,"* Boston, 1965. Thomas calls "unwarranted" the attribution of the "Diary" to Ward. But Thomas includes it in his Bibliography, describing it as a valuable "source reference for the world of Washington in Sam Ward's time."

[33] See, for example, Evelyn Page, "The Diary and the Public Man," *New England Quarterly*, XXII (June 1949), 147–72; Roy N. Lokken, "Has the Mystery of 'A Public Man' Been Solved?" *Mississippi Valley Historical Review*, XL (December 1953), 419–35; Anderson's reply and Lokken's rejoinder, *ibid.*, XLII (June 1955), 101–09; and Benjamin M. Price, "That Baffling Diary," *South Atlantic Quarterly*, LIV (January 1955), 56–64. Professor Jerome L. Sternstein of Columbia University in the course of research on the Civil War era recently found a manuscript letter dated 1909 from Edgar T. Welles, the son of Lincoln's Secretary of the Navy. In it Welles says that he has finally decided that the authorship of the "Diary" "belongs to Sam Ward." Thus, we have a contemporary's opinion that Ward was the man—a piece of testimony that Anderson had vainly sought.

candidates for the honor of authorship. But almost every disputant agrees with the conclusion that the work itself is a hybrid of fact and fiction, which leaves its documentary value precisely what Professor Anderson showed it to be—nil. This result of his scholarship thus justifies the time, labor, and ingenuity it cost.

Few researchers will choose, or be confronted with, a problem of the magnitude of Mr. Anderson's, but occasions arise when the contents of an otherwise acceptable book raise doubts in the reader which, whether or not he is just then "researching," he feels he wants to settle. For example, many books of the seventeenth and eighteenth centuries are attributed falsely to famous authors. And there is the matter of sequels: four were written after the great success of Voltaire's *Candide*, none of them by Voltaire.[34] The practice of using pseudonyms only heightens the confusion, and it is not generated only by forgers and imitators. Voltaire himself is said to have published under 160 pseudonyms and Franklin under 57. In the early nineteenth century, one L. A. C. Bombet published a book called *Lives of Haydn, Mozart, and Metastasio;* it had had some currency in France and was translated into English. Copies of it occasionally appear in modern catalogues of second-hand books under that author's name. But you will not find Bombet in any French biographical dictionary; for he is in fact Henri Beyle, otherwise Stendhal, the great novelist of *The Red and the Black* and *The Charterhouse of Parma.* To top it all, his *Lives* are largely plagiarized from Carpani, Baretti, Sismondi, Winckler, Cramer, and Schlichtegroll—a scandalous mosaic of other people's writings even if done with verve and genius.

How does one find one's way through such mazes of deliberate or accidental misdirection? For an author as famous as Voltaire, consult the critical bibliography that has undoubtedly been compiled about him. It turns out to be by Georges Bengesco and it occupies four volumes. For lesser and earlier writers, go to *The Bibliographical History of Anonyma and Pseudonyma* by Archer Taylor and Fredric J. Mosher,[35] which lists many dictionaries and other reference works likely to afford help. Their discussion of the problems will by itself spur the imagination to find the path of discovery. For recent or contemporary authors,

[34] Until recently, one of these sequels was regularly reprinted as Part II of *Candide* in a popular series of classic texts.
[35] Chicago, 1951.

the national dictionaries of authors (or sometimes, as in England, *The Authors and Writers' Who's Who*) will give lists of pseudonyms. But watch! These are not all accurate and must be cross-checked, either by consulting a list in a solider-looking work, or more simply by looking up the catalogue of the national library—British Museum, Library of Congress, etc. Finally, the authenticity or genuineness of a text will prove relatively easy if there is a large, scholarly, so-called definitive biography of the (real) author, for these questions are bound to be taken up as part of the story of his life.

Going through a search of this kind incidentally suggests that for scholarly work (as against recreation) it is important to get hold of an author's best text. This usually, but not invariably, means the latest. The preface will tell you what the editor has done or not done, and the "apparatus"—footnotes and appendices—will show what kind of information has been gathered as a help to understanding. Judging the thing itself is the only guarantee, for even reputable publishers and "series" make mistakes. *Candide* is one example. The Mermaid Series' former reprint of Marlowe's plays is another. Until the recent revised reissue of that series in paper covers, a very corrupt text of Marlowe was offered in good faith as his work.

No historian can hope to unravel every mystery and contradiction or uncover every untruth, half-truth, or downright deception that lurks in the raw materials with which he must deal. But his unceasing demand for accuracy must make him put to the test all the materials he uses. There is no substitute for well-placed skepticism.

6

Handling Ideas

Facts and Ideas, Married and Divorced

Daily speech encourages the belief that "a fact is a fact" and that it is useless to argue about it. And indeed it would be idle to dispute about pure fact. Yet we know that argument continues—in politics, science, the arts, family life, casual conversation, and the insides of books. A library is a sort of ammunition dump of unexploded arguments ready to burst forth the moment a live reader opens a book. Why should this be, if we assume that most books—aside from fiction— honestly attempt to deal with verified facts?

The answer is that facts seldom occur pure, free from interpretation or ideas. We all make the familiar distinction between "gathering facts" and "expressing ideas," but in reality most of the facts we gather come dripping with ideas. We may or may not be aware of these ideas as we move the facts about from the printed page to our minds, our notes, and our reports, but there they are, clinging together nevertheless. The only pure facts in historical reporting are those statements that express a conventional relation in conventional terms:

Thomas Jefferson was born on April 2, 1743.[1]
The Monroe Doctrine was promulgated on December 2, 1823.
President Garfield was shot by Charles J. Guiteau.

Through conventional words like "born" and "was shot," conventional names like "Monroe Doctrine,"[and conventional forms of day and year are expressed fixed relations of time, things, and persons. These relations may be said to be strictly factual because every term is clear and distinct and remains so by tacit agreement. No one disputes the calendar, not even the Mohammedan for whom the Christian year 1743 is the year 1156. Both calendars are conventions and their numbers are convertible.[2]

But if in the Garfield example we add to the phrase "shot by Charles J. Guiteau," the words "a disappointed office-seeker," we immediately pass from conventional fact into a different realm of discourse. True, it is a fact that Guiteau had sought a government post and had failed to get it[But putting these events into a phrase next to the statement of Garfield's assassination generates an idea. The effect is to say: "Guiteau's disappointment was the motive for the assassination." This is an inference, a hypothesis, an idea. No law of nature declares that all disgruntled placemen shoot their President. A psychoanalyst might maintain that the cause alleged was not sufficient; that Garfield was shot because he had a beard that reminded the killer of his stepfather; that, in any case, all human acts result from more than one motive.[3]

Historians, it is true, do not dispute the simple idea of disappointment as the motive for Garfield's murder. This may be because no great issue hangs upon it. But historians go on to say that, owing to this motive, the shooting of the President swung public opinion in favor of Civil Service reform—a further idea for which there is good

[1] Or April 13 according to the New Style calendar, which came into effect in 1752. See Chapter 4, p. 87.
[2] The Moslem year is computed from the Hejira, or Flight of Mohammed, in A.D. 622. Since it is a lunar year, it is shorter than ours, and this accounts for the fact that 622 plus 1156 equals more than 1743.
[3] The complexity of Guiteau's motives as they are now understood is examined by a medical historian, Charles E. Rosenberg, in *The Trial of the Assassin Guiteau: Psychiatry and the Law in the Gilded Age,* Chicago, 1968.

evidence, but which, once again, is not a mere fact of convention.]

What then is an idea? In a large dictionary you may find upwards of forty definitions, which shows how indistinct the term is. Nor is this to be regretted, because ideas correspond to the substance of our inner life, which is also fluid, indefinite, and changeable, besides being (as we know) very powerful and (as we say) "very real." For our purposes as reporters of the past we may put it that an [idea is *an image, inference, or suggestion that goes beyond the bare data*]

This definition is merely a convenient one to keep in mind at this stage of our work in historiography; it may not be applicable elsewhere. In historiography the statement of a fact gives the impression of ending with itself, whereas an idea leads us on. Once you have ascertained that the Monroe Doctrine was promulgated in a presidential message to Congress on December 2, 1823, what then? Any question that arises must be supplied from outside the fact—was the doctrine really the work of one man or the joint product of Monroe's, Canning's, and Adams' efforts? Is the doctrine of 1823 precisely the same as the one referred to under the same name since? Did the United States have the right to make such a declaration? Did it have the power to enforce it? These questions are ideas. They suggest doubts and possibilities. We know in a rough way what they involve, but before they can be answered they have to be further narrowed down and studied in relation to "facts," as well as compared with other "ideas" in the minds of hundreds of men, living and dead. As a result, the authoritative work on the Monroe Doctrine by Dexter Perkins is in three volumes totaling over 1,300 pages.

[It is obvious that History-as-Event is not made up of facts alone, but of facts merged in ideas.]The Monroe Doctrine's influence on the course of hemisphere history derived from its being a powerful idea. From time to time this idea was reinforced by such facts as:

A gunboat is in the harbor.
The Marines have landed in the Dominican Republic.
Secretary Rusk has made a speech.

[Fact and idea in ceaseless interplay constitute the stuff of experience;] or rather, in the seamless stuff of experience that we ponder within ourselves or report to others, we learn to make a distinction between the agreed-upon element of fact and the variable element of idea. [This does not mean that ideas are less certain.] It does mean that the historian, in order to be accurate, goes to work differently on each. There is a technique to be learned for the handling of ideas.

With facts, as we saw in the last chapter, the reporter's effort is to be exact about the conventional terms—names, dates, titles, and other technical details. [With ideas he must be no less exacting, though he cannot ever receive the same assurance of accuracy in return for his pains.] Yet his main role is to manage those more difficult matters with deftness and judgment; he is of use to others only insofar as he reports ideas intelligibly and precisely, for the "bare facts" generally do not *interest*, in the sense of engaging attention. Even the chronicler and the statistician hazard comments and conclusions, and these are ideas.

But before we take up the means by which special care about ideas is to be exercised, we have to consider still another aspect of ideas in history.

Large Ideas as Facts of History

By defining ideas as projections beyond conventional fact, we separated into two parts what most people rightly treat as one unit of thought: "Jefferson was a great President." We now know how to analyze this into the conventional part: "Jefferson was a President"; and the debatable part: "his greatness." But this leaves out of account "ideas" in the large, notable, historic sense—the idea of Evolution, the ideas in the Declaration of Independence, Nietzsche's ideas: these and a million more have the property of being facts as well: they *occurred.* Like any other event they have a place and a date. But their history is not easily reducible to conventional terms. For example, how would you date the idea of Evolution? Some textbooks say: "By his publication of *The Origin of Species* in 1859, Darwin established the idea of Evolution in Western thought." But research shows that similar ideas had made a stir in Western thought for a whole century before 1859. The contradiction would seem to hinge on the meaning of "established"—except that *The Origin of Species* did not immediately persuade mankind, but set off a violent controversy that lasted twenty years. Faced with this predicament we wonder what we mean by "a great idea" and its destiny.

Obviously, when we speak of ideas on this scale we are not talking about a *single* entity. Evolution is not one and the same idea from the beginning; nor was it after it came to be recognized and accepted with the passage of years. Darwin himself was not putting forward Evolution but what he believed to be a means (not *the* means) of evolution, namely Natural Selection. Ideas, in short, are neither single things nor simple things. To illustrate this truth by another example, what are the so-called ideas of the Declaration of Independence? We know they were clear and great ideas to Lincoln and presumably to his American contemporaries, but in his speeches he had to demonstrate their meaning and validity again and again. In his time and ours, those same ideas have been called "glittering generalities" (in blame, though without showing what is wrong with generalities or why they should not glitter). As for the theory of natural rights underlying the Declaration, it is almost everywhere disputed by people who in practice uphold the principles of the Declaration.

It is evident that the domain of ideas is full of unexpected turns, misleading appearances, pitfalls of every kind. And since ideas cling to every important fact, since ideas are what make the fact important and interesting, the reporter of events will fall into one trap after another if he is not adept at handling ideas. He must not only infer correct ideas from the evidence he has marshaled; he must also be critical about all the minds through which the facts have passed, not least his own. In other words, the management of ideas is the part of historiography in which the virtue of self-awareness must be acute, vigilant, and sustained. Perceptiveness about ideas is the duty of every moment, to exactly the same degree that in factual verification a sharp eye for dates, page numbers, and other minutiae is essential to success.

Technical Terms: All or None

The many different difficulties about ideas have one thing in common: they occur in the medium of words. Unlike figures or other fixed symbols, words possess connotations, overtones, and hence the power of suggesting more than they say. / Their arrangement, too, automatically conveys qualities and degrees of emphasis, which strike the reader's mind and affect meaning in very subtle ways. We saw above how the mere putting of two statements about President Garfield side by side irresistibly suggested an idea contained in neither of them. This happened because the reader brings something with him to every act of reading. He brings his own experience of life and a variable amount of knowledge gathered from previous reading. The result is that unless the vocabulary of a new piece of reading matter is visibly technical and strange to him, he will almost always think he understands it. This will take place even when what is said is badly put, repeatedly misleading, or adroitly tendentious. [The whole power of propaganda lies in this human propensity to catch the drift, to make out a meaning, to believe what is in print, with no thought of resistance by analysis and criticism. This being so, the writer of history must from the start turn himself into a professional critic of words and wording.]

Since History is for all men to read, and since it embraces every conceivable activity of man, it has no technical terms. You may say that "revolution," "hegemony," "entente cordiale" are technical terms. They are in fact borrowings from other subjects that history has occasion to discuss in its inclusive sweep. In a history of chemistry you would hear about oxygen and phlogiston; in a history of war, about howitzers and demilunes, and so on. To repeat, history has no technical terms of its own. But the difficulties we have been pointing out, and the reporter's determination to be accurate in more than details, cause the historian to attach such importance to words that he ends by inverting the generalization and says that for him [*every ordinary word becomes a technical term.*]

Compare three kinds of statements:

1. $(a + b)(a + b) = a^2 + 2ab + b^2$ *most precise*
2. Two molecules of common salt react with one of sulfuric acid to *very precise* give one molecule of sodium sulfate plus two of hydrogen chloride.
3. "It is a just though trite observation that victorious Rome was itself subdued by the arts of Greece."

In 1, we have a statement in the most general terms used by

man. The statement gives no particulars. For any *a* or *b* the relation expressed by the equal sign will hold; you can make *a* or *b* stand for anything you like, provided the ultimate things are units that are identical and hence can be added and multiplied.

In 2, particular substances enter into the same relation of equivalence, and a change in their form is described. This brings us closer to the tangible reality than No. 1 did. But the chemical statement is still general enough to permit any amounts of sodium chloride (salt) and sulfuric acid to be used, with identical results, provided the correct proportions are kept. The idea is broad and timeless so that, as everyone knows, it too can be expressed in formulas made up of unvarying symbols.

Number 3, which is a sentence taken at random from Gibbon, is also a broad generality and as exact as the other two. But in it none of the symbols is fixed. [Each word is used with precision in a unique way,] but the reader has to bring his own understanding and knowledge of particulars to fill out the "equation." In some later sentence, perhaps, the same words "observation," "victorious," "subdued," and "arts" would have to be filled with different meanings, and "Greece" and "Rome" themselves might not indicate the same realities.

All this may be hard to believe, though everybody goes through these shifting operations all day long. Consider: in Gibbon's statement the word "observation" means simply "a remark." It does not mean the same thing as it would in: "The patient was kept under observation." Again, "victorious" in Gibbon does not refer to any particular war or battle but to the general domination of the Roman Empire over the Mediterranean world, time unspecified. As for "subdued," it has in this sentence no connection whatever with war. The arts subdue a people only when that people—or some of them—develop a liking for art and go out of their way to acquire books, statues, and the like. We somehow knew that this is what "arts" meant in that context, but how different from a reference to "the arts by which Cleopatra captivated Mark Antony"—no statues there.

Lastly, "Greece" and "Rome" are also shifting terms, because at different times the names do not cover the same territory, power, form of government, or degree of civilization. Rome is first a city under kings, then a nation under a republic, then an empire under emperors—and so on. Each word in its present place has a special meaning; it fulfills for Gibbon the role of a technical word if, as happened here, it says just what he intended, no more and no less.

But could not Gibbon have used other words and kept the same idea? We tend to think that he could. Suppose he had said: "It is an old story that when the Roman conquerors had seized all the wealth and power of the ancient world into their hands, their henchmen began buying up Greek ornaments and works of art and sank into self-indulgent luxury." The "general idea," as we loosely say, remains the same—but does it really? The same three facts do rattle around somewhere in the bottom of each remark: (1) Rome conquered the ancient world. (2) Romans came to enjoy the products of Greek art. (3) This is well known. But the idea, the precise, particular, all-important idea, is utterly different in Gibbon and in the rewording. In each we are told many things between the lines, and the things differ in the two versions. Let us compare:

⤶ Gibbon reminds us (a) that in his century educated people knew some ancient history; (b) that the cliché he is about to repeat is correct; (c) that Greece and Rome exemplify the connection between conquest and civilization, the conquerors being usually the "newer" people, who acquire a higher culture from contact with the "older" and defeated nation; (d) that Roman art was largely borrowed; (e) that Greece maintained her artistic supremacy after defeat; (f) that Gibbon regards the whole process as admirable and majestic.

As against this, the rewritten version thrusts on the reader the conviction that (a) the remark to follow is only another sordid fact from the past; (b) the Roman Empire was the handiwork of a collection of greedy gangsters; (c) the upper class in Rome were merely the hangers-on of the conquerors; (d) these fellow brigands were philistines who bought Greek *objets d'art* mostly for show; (e) the cultivation of the arts is softening to the moral fiber; and (f) the writer considers History a tale of violence, ignorance, and turpitude.

The Technique of Self-Criticism

We are not now concerned with who is right—Gibbon or the Pseudo-Gibbon. We are concerned with the profound difference of effect produced by different words purporting to relate the same facts. Now it is bad enough when a willful or unconscious bias distorts in the written report what the researcher has discovered. It is obviously far worse when verbal incompetence distorts without the writer's being guilty of bias[The unfortunate truth is that the reader is always more sensitive to a man's *expressed meaning* than the writer himself. It is not hard to see why: the writer has his *intended meaning* at the forefront of his mind, and it too often comes between him and the actual words he writes down.]

The remedy is simple but arduous: to scan every word, not once but many times, until you are assured that it is *the* word corresponding to what you know and want to say. Apply the rule that in history every word is a technical word. For example, you as a writer would feel ashamed to call a general a captain or to write that X was "executed" when he was only convicted and imprisoned. These distinctions are so well established that to fail to observe them is a blunder that your readers and reviewers will note and you will not forgive yourself for. But less glaring mistakes are often far more important. In handling ideas, once again, you must consider every defining word in exactly the same way as you do conventional technical terms. Here are illustrations to enforce the lesson and suggest the way to practice. The examples were not made up to be easily shown wrong, but are taken from students' work—advanced students and good ones at that. The first has to do with Shelley's marital difficulties with his first wife, Harriet, who ultimately drowned herself:

> Had Shelley bided his time and talked over his problems, perhaps, the couple might have found themselves incompatible and might have been legally and justly separated. Had Shelley acted in this way he would not be the Shelley we know.

The trouble here begins with an unexpressed antihistorical idea, which comes out in the last sentence and vitiates the language in between. "Talked over his problems" is obviously a piece of modern jargon. Vague enough now, it would have meant little or nothing in the early nineteenth century. In the passage under review its only effect is to suggest, falsely, that Shelley refused to talk to his wife about their mismating. The very word "problem" is wrong here, for it is a recent idea to regard all the accidents of life as "problems." The opening should perhaps read: "Had Shelley been more patient and let his wife see his character more clearly . . ."

The next remark as it stands is nonsense: "The couple might have found themselves incompatible . . ." That is just what they did find; they had no need to wait to make this discovery. What the writer really meant appears in the sentence following: "They might have been legally and justly separated." But they *were* separated! One dimly gathers the notion hovering in the writer's mind: had the couple proved their incompatibility before a court, they might have been divorced and Harriet might not have committed suicide. This is, once again, to flout historical probability and to misunderstand human emotions. Divorce was not and is not granted for incompatibility in England, nor is there any reason to suppose that Harriet would have been made happier by a divorce. The suspicion that all these loose remarks are contrary to fact and to good sense comes out in the writer's last sentence declaring that if all these "ideas" had been carried out Shelley would "not be the Shelley we know." When a writer of history reaches such a conclusion, he should cross out and start again.

This example clearly shows two things: first, that a passage that "anybody can understand" may very well contain not one iota of sense; second, that the way to test one's writing for sense is to take each word or phrase, shake out its contents, and look at them with skepticism—almost with hostility: what in heaven's name *does* this mean? If the answer is satisfactory, let the phrase stand provisionally. How does it square with the next one? Use each to test the rest until every part is acceptable. When you have done this, reconsider the order of your words and sentences until you are sure that the ideas they evoke in the reader's mind are *your* ideas at their most exact.

Language being metaphorical to start with, the close scrutiny of words just recommended should include a testing of images, figures of speech, and set expressions. This will not only disclose mixed metaphors, which are often ridiculous, but more important it will show you where you are [missing the idea altogether as a result of loose coupling between images.] Take for example: "This set of documents emphasizes the legal aspect of the League of Nations." Can anything "emphasize an aspect"? An aspect is what one looks at. Besides, is it the documents that emphasize, or is it the editor who chose some documents and not others? The reader is in doubt, as he would not be if the reviewer had said simply: "Most of these documents (or: "The most important of these documents") have to do with the legal history of the League of Nations."

One more example, to suggest that, even in an acceptable statement, refining the thought adds strength at the same time as it sharpens the critical faculty. "We must not," says an author, "neglect the place of the individual in history." Good, but not quite good enough, for on reflection the remark raises a doubt, owing to the inevitable ambiguity of the word "history." The author may mean: "In writing history we must not neglect to make a place for the individual," that is, we must not write only about forces and factors. Or he may mean: "We must not neglect the *role* of the individual in *making* history," which is an entirely different idea. A remark two paragraphs away from the sentence in question showed which was the right interpretation, but suppose the sentence were lifted out of that context and quoted. The author would be misrepresented and might have to defend or explain himself, which is to say, do at the last what he should have done at first.

Historians' Fallacies: How to Avoid Them

[So much for words, which are both the cause of our trouble and the means to repair it.]In the handling of ideas in historiography we must also be on the watch for fallacies that words mask or make attractive. There is no room in this book to illustrate and discuss more than a few kinds of fallacy, even among those to which historical writers are especially liable. Doing the exercises in an elementary textbook on logic might help detect the fundamental forms of bad reasoning, such as begging the question, *non sequitur,* denying the antecedent, and the like. But the reporter of events seldom encounters or produces fallacies in their pure form. He is apt, rather, to generalize beyond his facts.[Bad generalizations]are often the result of careless language: the author says "all" or "every" or "never" when the evidence goes but a little way toward such a universal proposition.[Modifiers must be brought into play: "almost," "nearly," "by and large," "in a manner of speaking," "hardly," and the ubiquitous "perhaps."⌋

And yet the reporter must avoid giving the impression of perpetual timidity and indecision. He will infallibly do so if every sentence he writes hedges with "often" and "almost." History must be as precise as close research and guarded statement can make it, but it must not lose vividness and impetus. An irritated reviewer was right to complain of a book in which "every sentence reads as if it would have to be defended in court."

⌈When overextended generalization does not come from the careless use of universals, it comes from the failure to think of negative instances.⌋If after searching into the lives of Keats, Chopin, and Musset you are tempted to write one of those dubious generalities couched in the singular such as: "The Romantic artist is tubercular and dies young," you must at once test it by negative instances: Wordsworth, Landor, Goethe are there to prove you wrong with their eighty years or more apiece. Three cases are thrice enough to ruin your description of a type that is largely imaginary. The corollary caution is to beware of what is new and striking in your research. It may be new only to you; and even if generally new, its effect must not overwhelm other impressions. Remember the old anecdote about the English traveler who saw three red-headed girls at the inn where he stopped and who wrote in his diary: "All the woman in this county have red hair."

Only the quite inexperienced researcher will generalize from a single instance or from too few. The danger that besets the more practiced is rather the opposite, called the Reductive Fallacy. As its name suggests, ⌈it reduces diversity to one thing: All this is nothing but *That*.⌉Beware of the phrase itself; "nothing but" can be used only when you are absolutely sure of your ground and when that ground is limited in scope. For example, to make an event as vast as the French Revolution (no single event, really, but a group of related events) result from a conspiracy is reductive in the extreme. So is ascribing war exclusively to "economics" or to the wirepulling of munitions makers. The valuable lesson of history teaches the exact contrary of simple-minded reduction. ⌈History throws light on the complexity of events by trying to show each in its parts and in its place. Let the newspaper, which lacks time and room, enjoy the monopoly of reductionism.[4]

Between reduction and overexpansion lurks [hidden repetition, or Tautology.]It is a frequent error in histories, business reports, statistical analyses, and the like. Here is an example, again from student work: "English aggressiveness spurred the nation to stimulate commerce on the seas and win the supremacy of trade routes." Here a thing called English aggressiveness works upon the nation (England), and England works upon English commerce in a stimulating manner. The three things are in fact one, as the writer would have seen if he had stepped out of his abstractions and visualized something concrete—not commerce but a merchant, a shipowner. *He* is English aggressiveness, and he is the nation, and he is the trader who wins the trade routes. Perhaps the writer's mind was visited by a flitting idea of the English *government* acting independently of the trader, but this thought was unexpressed and it left three wordings of one thing acting on one another like separate powers.[5]

An historian's fallacy less easily discovered by the reader is [Misplaced Literalism.] It has many forms, and it is particularly insidious because the reporter must always *begin* by being literal. He must ascertain with all possible precision what his original text tells him. Lord Acton does *not* say, "Power corrupts and absolute power corrupts absolutely"; he says, "Power tends to corrupt and absolute power corrupts

---

[4] A distinguished newspaper editor, critical of his profession's shortcomings, writes of a frequent experience: "No week passes without someone prominent in politics, industry, labor or civic affairs complaining to me, always in virtually identical terms: 'Whenever I read a story about something in which I really know what's going on, I'm astonished at how little of what's important gets into the papers—and how often even that little is wrong.' The most upsetting thing about these complaints is the frequency with which they come from scientists, economists and other academicians temporarily involved in government policy but without any proprietary concern about who runs the White House or City Hall." A. H. Raskin, "What's Wrong with American Newspapers?" *New York Times Magazine*, June 11, 1967, 77.

[5] In a textbook fortunately long out of use, one found listed among the causes that brought one or another party to power: (1) the strength of the party; (2) the weakness of the opposition. This is a truly convenient way to double the number of reasons for the result of any election.

absolutely."[6] A slight but consequential difference, for it allows the possibility that a statesman, or even a mere politician, will not be corrupted by wielding power.

Having secured the author's very words, the reporter scans them for what they say, scans the neighboring words, the author's other works on the same subject, and gradually acquires familiarity with the natural movement of the man's thought. It is at this point that Literalism would be misplaced if it reentered. Its most obvious form would be to quote a remark such as Lord Acton's as if its being in print automatically gave it the same weight as every other by the same author. It may have more or less, depending on place and circumstance. Is the idea expressed the conclusion of a piece of reasoning in, say, an essay? Or is it a notion struck off in a letter to a friend? Or, conversely, is it an improvised retort to an opponent? It is the critic's duty to *judge* importance and value in the light of his wider knowledge. If he remains baldly literal and contents himself with quoting extracts, he invariably ends by showing his human subject to have been a mass of contradictions.

The Historian and the Great Ideas

Important words, then, require interpretation, and most writers are likely to use certain words in peculiar senses. The historian is in the best position to do this interpreting, because he is professionally interested in circumstances and origins. That these are bound to throw light on meanings and intentions is shown by the practice of the courts in interpreting a statute: they go back to the debates in the legislature and the known opinions of the proponents. The historian is likewise used to analyzing documents, and in case of need he knows where to turn for sources that will tell him what meanings words bore in earlier times and remote places.

The various ideas clustering around predestination, for example— justification by faith, consubstantiation, theodicy, and so on—impelled

[6] Letter to Bishop Creighton in Acton, *Historical Essays and Studies*, London, 1907, 504.

men in the sixteenth century to kill others who disbelieved in their creed, or defined it differently from themselves. Since this idea no longer has such a hold on us, we can scarcely understand its force until it is resurrected for us, turned inside-out, so that we begin to reconceive it and feel its lost power. To put this differently, the *quality of belief* that goes into the ideas of an age or a man is as great a concern of the historian as the genuineness of the document that brings it to his notice. He cannot be literal about ideas without losing his expertness as an interpreter; and by the same token, he cannot be a simple summarizer or "rewrite man" without forfeiting his claim to our confidence.

We rely on him particularly in the study of great ideas—religious beliefs or political and philosophical systems, about which we shall have more to say. Here it is enough to point out that a statement such as "Nietzsche believed in the idea of Eternal Recurrence" is by itself inadequate, even if Eternal Recurrence is explained as the doctrine that after an unspecified number of events have taken place in History, the world goes through the identical sequence again from the beginning, and so on in an infinite cycle. What we have to know at once is whether Nietzsche arrived at this notion by intuition or by reasoning, whether he adopted it as the completion or as the starting point of his system, how vivid or abstract were his imaginings about it, whether he spoke more of its scientific or of its moral consequences— all questions to which the answers may bring us to understand the *quality of his belief.*

It is for lack of such comments and interpretations that many textbooks and encyclopedia articles give such a starved and false image of the ideas that have moved great men or inspired great movements. The student who does not care about History memorizes the tags to pass his examination, but quite literally he does not know what he is talking about. What live meaning can he attach to the statement that Rousseau "wanted to go back to Nature"? It is a false statement anyway, but suppose it were true: Where *is* Nature and when did we leave it behind? What has it been doing all this time and how do we return to it? The so-called idea that the student thinks he has learned is but an empty form of words, which he fills with his own imperfect notions and gratuitously ascribes to a thinker.

This common situation defines for the writer what he must do whenever he raises the ghost of a great idea. He must avoid the ultimate [fallacy of Vulgarity,] that is to say, avoid falling into the cheap and easy ways of thought that are so fatally congenial to the uninformed. This temptation—Vulgarity being only a convenient name for it—was exemplified earlier in our warnings against the reductive fallacy: the historian should not help things lose their distinctive characters by saying they are "nothing but" something else. Similarly, the historian should not rival the gossip in assigning crude motives at sight. If Jonathan Swift satirized mankind in *Gulliver's Travels* it was not "because he wanted to be a bishop and had been thwarted in this ambition." At that rate he should have shot Queen Anne as Guiteau shot Garfield.

The historian, finally, must not assume an intellectual pose or mood that gives every diverse event the same coloring. In recent times the tendency has been for reporters of events to affect cynicism—as in the example we made up for our Pseudo-Gibbon. In this way History is vulgarly debunked. Some cast the blame for this tendency on mankind's earlier mood of general optimism and respectability. On the scale of exact ideas, automatic skepticism is as bad as automatic belief. In sound reporting there is no need of bunking, debunking, or rebunking, because historiography lays down the rules for presenting all things *in their diversity.*

[The English historian Collingwood (like the German Dilthey) arrived at the conviction that the writing of history was nothing more nor less than a rethinking of the past—recapturing in consciousness bygone events and thoughts. To these writers all history was the history of ideas in the sense that the researchers' findings without exception must once upon a time have occupied somebody's mind.]Jefferson probably said or wrote down his birth date: April 2, 1743. If he did not his parents did, or the town clerk and recorder. In rediscovering or restating a "fact" we are rethinking a previous thought, someone's idea. Similarly with every event, from the "invasion" of Rome by Greek art to the "disappointment" of Guiteau and the shooting of Garfield: every item of fact or feeling or idea that we have any inkling of must have occurred as somebody's mental state—a perception, a memory, or an imagining.

Whether this account is the final truth about the nature of History does not matter for the moment. It contains this much truth, that in dealing with everything beyond the bare conventional facts, the reporter must make himself and his works a mirror of the utmost smoothness and reflecting power. Every distortion due to wrong expression, fallacious thought, or irrelevant mood is a grievous error—an error far worse than the easily detected kind, such as a mistake in a name or date. We blush more for the latter, but we should in truth be more ashamed of distortion, and we should toil equally to avoid both.

7

Truth and Causation

The Evidences of Historical Truth

The previous chapter has perhaps left the reader wondering how much or how little of history he can trust. If the only indisputable facts are those we have called conventional and if they are generally of little interest in themselves, then the veracity or truth-value of history seems slight indeed. The thoughtful man's question to the historian, which we quoted in Chapter 3,[1] contrasts the shifting uncertainty of history with the mathematical rigor of science and concludes that truth is absent from history because it lacks the form—and the formulas—of science.

This conclusion is plausible but false. In order to see why it rests on a fallacy, one must take up several distinct problems. The first is: What kinds of evidence are available on which to base assertions?

These kinds are variously described and grouped for convenience and clarity. One may divide them first into Verbal and Mute—the mute consisting of objects such as buildings, drawings, tools, fragments of pottery, any physical object bearing no words. A coin may belong to both kinds if it has an inscription on it. Verbal, or speaking, evidence

[1]See p. 55.

146

need not, of course, be written: an oral tradition has validity under certain circumstances and with the growing use of plastic and tape recordings, oral testimony may once more regain its prehistoriographic prominence.[2] But as everyone knows, the great bulk of what is commonly handled and offered as historical evidence is in written form.

Written evidence again falls into several subgroups: manuscript and printed, private and public, intentional and unpremeditated. The last distinction has diagnostic importance for arriving at truth. Intentional pieces of written evidence are such things as affidavits, court testimony, secret or published memoirs. The author of any of these meant his words to record a sequence of events for future perusal. He presumably had an interest in furthering his view of the facts. But a receipt for the sale of a slave, jotted down in the second century on a bit of papyrus, is no premeditated piece of historical writing. Its sole intended use was commercial, and it is only as "unconscious evidence" that it becomes part of an historical narrative. The laws of states, ordinances of cities, charters of corporations, and the like are similarly unpremeditated evidence—as are the account books of a modern corporation or of a Florentine banker of the fifteenth century.

Yet, important as this difference is, the assumption that unconscious evidence is always sounder is by no means warranted; for with the widespread consciousness of history to which we drew attention earlier, there has been a general tendency to inject purposeful "historicity" into apparently unpremeditated documents. State papers nowadays frequently attempt to say more than is required by their ostensible purpose. They subtly or crudely address the world and posterity.[3] And even business documents, such as reports to stockholders, contain inter-

---

[2] In the Oral History Center at Columbia University (as well as at other institutions) the remarks of important persons who might not write memoirs are recorded on tape. The written word is still so compelling, however, that these recordings are transcribed and the typescripts filed like books. Catalogues of the available materials are published periodically.

[3] Consider the publication *Polish Acts of Atrocity against the German Minority in Poland,* published by the German Library of Information, New York, 1940, 259 pp. Its internal terminology and arrangement are those of an historical monograph, but its apparent record of fact is but disguised argument. More deceptive because more roundabout are the carefully "planted" documents left by public men; for instance, the so-called posterity letters that Theodore Roosevelt wrote to various correspondents. For examples see Elting E. Morison, ed., *The Letters of Theodore Roosevelt,* 8 vols., Cambridge, Mass., 1951–54.

FIGURE 6   *The Evidences of History**

RECORDS
(intentional transmitters of facts)

Written
1. Chronicles, annals, biographies, genealogies
2. Memoirs, diaries
3. Certain kinds of inscriptions

Oral
4. Ballads, anecdotes, tales, sagas
5. Phonograph and tape recordings

Works of Art
6. Portraits, historical paintings, scenic sculpture, coins, and medals
7. Certain kinds of films, kinescope, etc.

RELICS
(unpremeditated transmitters of facts)

8. Human remains, letters, literature, public documents, business records, and certain kinds of inscriptions
9. Language, customs, and institutions
10. Tools and other artifacts

---

*Adapted from John Martin Vincent's *Historical Research,* New York, 1911 (1929).

pretations of business that may amount to deliberate propaganda. In other words, we have become so accustomed to the idea of "the record" that we are continually tempted to tamper with it. When we mean to be candid, we are careful to specify that our words must be "off the record."

This very brief account of several kinds of historical evidence is enough to suggest the many problems it presents. The table in Figure 6 shows how the namable kinds of evidence can be grouped, somewhat differently, for a bird's-eye view. Obviously not all kinds of evidence are available for every historical report; and their classification is certainly not to be thought of as marking fixed boundaries. Where, for example, would you place a film clip of a student riot? It is stretching terms to answer, as the table would imply, "Works of Art."

⌈ No matter how it is described, *no piece of evidence can be used for historiography in the state in which it is found.* It is invariably and necessarily subjected to the action of the researcher's mind. When that action is methodical and apt, what is being applied is known as the critical method.⌋ Faced with a piece of evidence, the critical mind of the searcher for truth asks the fundamental questions:

> Is this object or piece of writing genuine?
> Is its message trustworthy?
> How do I know?

This leads to an unfolding series of subordinate questions:

1. Who is its author or maker?
2. What does it state?
3. What is the relation in time and space between the author and the statement, overt or implied, that is conveyed by the object?
4. How does the statement compare with other statements on the same point?
5. What do we know independently about the author and his credibility?

The point of these questions is easily grasped:

1. If the document or the coin is forged, it has no value as the thing it purports to be. Gauging the truth of any statement is obviously assisted by a knowledge of who made it.[4]
2. Similarly, it is essential to ascertain with more than ordinary care what the document states and what may be inferred from it. As in law, false conclusions are ruled out by the good judge.
3. The value of a piece of testimony usually increases in proportion to the nearness in time and space between the witness and the events about which he testifies.[5] An eyewitness has a good chance of knowing what happened; a reporter distant from the event by only

---

[4] The truthfulness of the presentment may also have value as evidence to convict the forger, or as evidence of his skill—witness the Van Meegeren forgeries of Vermeer paintings. (The best general account of this gripping case is Maurice Moiseiwitsch, *The Van Meegeren Mystery,* London, 1964.)

[5] This rule was doubtless hovering in the mind of the student who wrote in a comparison of Herodotus and Thucydides that Thucydides had "the advantage of being alive at the time he was writing."

a few years has a better chance than one separated by a century. (Recall the story of the year 1000 in Chapter 5.)

4 A single witness may be quite accurate, but two witnesses, if independent, increase the chances of eliminating human fallibility. If a dozen reports already exist, a thirteenth just discovered is compared point for point with the others in an effort to resolve puzzling allusions or contradictions, to strengthen or destroy an interpretation.

5 What can be learned about the author's life and character helps make up our judgment on several of the previous points. If we know his life we can answer the queries: Was he there? Had he the expertness to appreciate the facts? Was he biased by partisan interest? Did he habitually tell the truth? (Recall the clues to the "Public Man" who wrote a diary, Chapter 5.)

The principles contained in all these questions and assertions guide the researcher's mind at all times and develop in him the habit of criticism. Its operation becomes automatic, whether he is reading a President's inaugural, a new-found diary of the Mexican War,[6] or a rabid editorial in a tabloid. Every reader or writer of reports should train himself in this form of criticism. Yet it is unlikely that the ordinary researcher will encounter any problems in the science of Diplomatics, which teaches the technique of testing and dating documents, chiefly medieval. This takes special study and much practice, as does the reading of Greek papyri or the assessment of archeological finds. If a point requiring such knowledge arises in your "book research," consult an expert, just as you would if you came across a suspicious document.[7] But on ordinary printed matter no one can be critical

[6] Samuel Chamberlain, *My Confession,* New York, 1956. This volume, purporting to be the memoirs of a veteran of the Mexican campaign, did not pass the scrutiny of at least one historian: Professor Walter P. Webb maintained that although the work may not be a literary hoax it is a well-embroidered story composed long after the events it describes. See his review, "The Memories of a Rogue," *Saturday Review of Literature,* XXXIX (Nov. 3, 1956), 36.

[7] Reading the Osborns' *Questioned Document Problems* and Weller's *Die falschen und fingierten Druckorte* (on pretended publishing places) is, however, an instructive and entertaining use of spare time. And persons of a scientific turn of mind will want to look up the latest methods of dating and testing by technical means—carbon 14 or other radiation, infrared and reflected light rays, and the like.

and historical-minded for you. If you are so by nature, it can be guaranteed that this mental faculty will find much scope even when its exercise is limited to print.

Probability the Great Guide

⌈The historical method ascertains the truth by means of common sense. When that sense is systematically applied, ⌉it becomes a stronger and sharper instrument than is usually found at work in daily life. It shows a closer attention to detail and a stouter hold on consecutiveness and order. By the very exercise of these capacities it turns into a new power which acquires new intellectual possessions. In short, the historian's common sense must be understood to mean more than common knowledge and the clichés of ordinary thought. Methodical common sense takes in both what is usually known by the well-educated and any special information relevant to the historical question being studied.

⌈This point about *informed* common sense is most obvious in the writing of biography.⌉ The historian of a man's life is bound to familiarize himself with all his subject's activities and concerns, some of which may be special; and the common sense of these matters is not simply the knowledge we have of them today, but also the state of knowledge in the subject's lifetime. A life of Caesar presupposes a knowledge of Roman roads and Roman weapons in the first century B.C.

All these distinctions need only to be stated to be understood, and no one disputes them. What is often ill understood and easily misconstrued is the meaning of common sense in matters that seem quite ordinary but are not so, matters that the plain man finds often enough in the newspaper and the educated citizen may come across in his casual reading of books. For example, after the Warren Commission Report on the assassination of President Kennedy, many persons attacked its conclusions, some in very elaborate works based on the published testimony. In a critique of several of these books, Mr. John Sparrow, an English scholar who was also trained as a lawyer, makes the point that concerns us here. It has no bearing on one's opinion about the Warren Report; its bearing is on common notions of evidence that unfortunately do not constitute common sense. Mr. Sparrow shows what the denouncers of the Report all expect before they will accord belief: they trust only consistent and congruent witnesses. Yet, as he reminds us:

Every lawyer knows that a witness . . . while wrong on a number of points may yet be right on others, perhaps including the essential one. Every lawyer knows that honest and truthful witnesses may contradict themselves, particularly on questions concerning their own and others' motives and states of mind, without thereby forfeiting credibility. . . . Finally, every lawyer knows that in a big and complicated case there is always, at the end of it all, a residue of improbable, inexplicable fact. You do not invalidate a hypothesis by showing that the chances were against the occurrence of some of the events that it presupposes: many things that happen are actuarially improbable, but they happen.[8]

Such is the common sense about evidence when evidence comes from ordinary testimony, that is, the declarations of persons, not experts, who are by chance witnesses of some important event or part of an event. And Mr. Sparrow takes us even further along the road that historian and lawyer tread together when he says: "To make up its mind, if it can, what *must* have happened, in spite of incidental improbabilities—that is the task of a Commission of Inquiry."[9] The historian is in himself such a Commission, and when he has done his work it is no refutation of it to say that he has selected his facts to suit his case. Mr. Sparrow gives us the right view of that tiresome cliché: "What else should an investigator do? It is for the critics to show that they themselves have evaluated all the evidence, and can make a selection from it as reliable as [the other], and base upon that selection conclusions that compel acceptance. . . . "[10]

So much for the lawyer's wisdom, which an intelligent man might have worked out for himself. There is a further step that the historian must often take, which brings him into possession of technical knowl-

[8] John Sparrow, *After the Assassination*, New York, 1968, 13–14.
[9] *Ibid*, 14.
[10] *Ibid.*, 15.

edge strictly so-called. Here no amount of intelligence will serve: experience certified by experts is the only source of help. In the same attacks on the official view of the murder of President Kennedy, inferences are freely made from the bullet wounds as to the number of assassins and the places where they stood. The fact seems to be that rifle bullets do the most unexpected things, contrary to "common sense." Thus "if a high-velocity bullet is fired into soft clay it does not, as one might expect, pass through it. After tunneling in for a few inches it suddenly produces a cavity many times its own diameter, and quite frequently the bullet itself is smashed into fragments." The writer, long a medico-legal expert in Egypt and Scotland, goes on to give an account of the shooting of an official by a nervous sentry. The bullet passed through a car window and struck the victim on the chin, causing facial wounds of which he subsequently died. And when the car was examined,

not one but a number of bullet marks were found. There were two holes in the license holder and the wind-screen under it, each of which looked as if it had been caused by a separate bullet. The upper part of the left traffic-indicator had also been pierced, and there were several other marks apparently produced by the passage of projectiles. . . . On the back seat a portion of a .303 bullet was found, consisting of the aluminium tip and the cupro-nickel jacket. . . . It was thought that a number of shots had been fired. From the holes in the wind-screen alone, it seemed that two or three bullets must have struck the car. However, all the eye-witnesses spoke of only one shot being fired, and one cartridge case only was found on the scene; out of a clip of five bullets, the remaining four were still in the rifle. . . . Finally, a reconstruction of the affair . . . showed pretty conclusively that not more than one bullet had struck the car.[11]

It is in such cases that the ordinary man is likely to display his ignorant skepticism. He knows better; he "uses his common sense": bullets fly in straight lines and make neat round holes. During every war and every murder trial the public entertains strong convictions that a certain person is a spy or, alternatively, the guilty man. They decide from hearsay or partisan evidence, or from no evidence at all,

[11] Sir Sydney Smith, *Mostly Murder,* London, 1959, 272–74.

that the complicated events taking place or being delved into happened according to some simple scheme of their own devising. They will tell you the answer to any puzzling doubt without a moment's hesitation.

Such improvisers would make poor historians. To be sure, even good scholars will at times take a holiday from method and speak or write irresponsibly. They will repeat campus gossip that they would scorn to accept as evidence in one of their monographs. This very fact shows the importance of method: it is a discipline, and anyone's failure to apply it is quickly rebuked by his professionally critical fellows.

For a good example, we may instance a book published in England a few years ago, which undertook to reinterpret Wordsworth, partly in the light of psychoanalysis. The author, an Oxford scholar, studied the appropriate sources—especially the Journal written by Wordsworth's sister Dorothy—and arrived at the conclusion that the poet married because he had found in himself and his sister the beginnings of a guilty attachment: "Wordsworth's object in making straight for Sockburn [where his future wife lived] . . . is clear enough. . . . By the time they reached Sockburn William was undoubtedly fully aware of the nature of his feelings for Dorothy."[12]

Neither in this passage nor elsewhere in the book is any evidence presented except that of the well-known close companionship of brother and sister and some ambiguous allusions in poems and letters. The new "truth" about the attachment rests solely on the author's repeated "it is clear enough," "undoubtedly," and the like. Upon this a scholarly critic wrote a definitive paragraph:

If Mr. Bateson suggested that there was a morbid strain in her attachment to her brother, we would perhaps agree—with the proviso that she was probably in love with Coleridge. If Mr. Bateson fancied that she and her brother might have been consciously alarmed by mutual and illicit desires, he would be entitled to air his suspicion, wildly improbable as we might think it. To present their alarm not as a hypothesis but as an undoubted fact strikes me as inexcusable.[13]

[12] F. W. Bateson, *Wordsworth: A Re-interpretation,* London, 1954, 156.
[13] Raymond Mortimer, *Sunday Times* (London), Oct. 17, 1954.

Inexcusable it is, because the rule of "Give evidence" is not to be violated with impunity. No matter how possible or plausible the author's conjecture, it cannot be accepted as historical truth if he has only his hunch to support it. What would be more than adequate for village gossip does not begin to be enough for history.

The particular error we have been examining is worth a word more, because it enshrines a common slippage from one use of evidence to another: the writer on Wordsworth found his hypothesis consistent with the facts he had gathered, and from this consistency he inferred confirmation. He may be imagined as saying: "Since there is nothing against my view; since, on the contrary, certain facts can be made to support my view, therefore my view is proved." But proof demands *decisive* evidence; this means *evidence that confirms one view and denies its rivals.* Mr. Bateson's facts will fit his view *and* his critic's *and* several other possible views as well. To say this is to say that they support none of them in such a way as to discriminate between truth and conjecture. In short, mere consistency is not enough, nor mere plausibility, for both can apply to a wide variety of hypotheses.

The commandment about furnishing evidence that is decisive leads us, therefore, to a second fundamental rule: in history, as in life critically considered, *truth rests not on possibility nor on plausibility but on Probability.*

Probability is used here in a strict sense. It means the balance of chances that, given such and such evidence, the event it records happened in a certain way; or, in other cases, that a supposed event did not in fact take place. This balance is not computable in figures as it is in mathematical probability; but it is no less attentively *weighed and judged.* Judgment is the historian's form of genius, and he himself is judged by the amount of it he can muster. The grounds on which he passes judgment are, again, the common grounds derived from life: general truths, personal and vicarious experience (which includes a knowledge of previous history), and any other kind of special or particular knowledge that proves relevant.

At many points the estimate of probability made by the student will coincide with that of an ordinary man; but there is this difference, that the scholar will not have reached it offhand—it will not be a correct snap judgment, but a correct *critical* judgment.

An historian would say, for example, that under the conditions prevailing in this country today it is not probable that a public official, such as the governor of a state, could be entirely misrepresented to posterity as regards his appearance, actions, and character. Too many devices of publicity are continually playing on public figures; whereas the probability of successful misrepresentation was far greater in fifteenth-century England. This judgment is what has enabled a number of scholars to believe that Richard III was not the murderer of his nephews, not crooked-backed, not the villain depicted in Shakespeare's play. They cannot fully prove their contention, for conclusive evidence is lacking, but they win a hearing for it because it is not against probability that the Tudor kings could blacken Richard's character and sustain the "big lie."[14]

The point here is not the pros and cons of this particular question. The point is that the carefully assessed probabilities of a known situation govern every part of the historian's judgment. What applies to a large situation like Richard III's applies to each document or relic that is put in evidence, for each document or relic is in fact the center of a "situation." We defined that situation in asking our five questions. The answer to each always rests on a balance of probabilities.

This is true even when a scientific test is applied, say to the paper on which a suspected document is written or printed. The reasoning goes: This paper is made from esparto grass. It purports to have been written in 1850. But in 1850 esparto paper was not made, it having been introduced by Thomas Routledge in 1857. Therefore the document is forged.[15] This seems conclusive, yet it is only highly probable. It is just possible that some other, unsung papermaker introduced grass into one batch before Routledge; or—to be more subtle—the tests applied may not be exact enough to differentiate between similar fibers that might have been in the paper at the earlier date.

[14] For the latest review of the evidence, see Paul Murray Kendall, *Richard III*, New York, 1956; and for a condensed account, V. B. Lamb, *The Betrayal of Richard III*, London, 1965. An entertaining piece of fiction on the subject is Josephine Tey's "detective story" *The Daughter of Time*, New York, 1952.

[15] See Richard D. Altick, "The Scholar and the Scientist," Chapter 7 of *The Scholar Adventurers*, New York, 1951, and Altick's *The Art of Literary Research*, New York, 1963.

Even after the best technical knowledge and trained common sense have been used in an inquiry, there may still be—as John Sparrow reminded us—a residue of inexplicable or contradictory evidence. Figures in the limelight are no more exempt from this uncertainty than obscure persons; obviously important facts may remain forever in dispute. To take the kind of question that historians are fond of asking, How did President Truman and his Secretary of State, James F. Byrnes, part company in 1947? In that year Byrnes published a book with the telling title *Speaking Frankly,* in which he discussed current issues in American foreign policy. That is the obvious place to start for dealing with his dimissal.

Byrnes explains in his book how he returned late in December 1945 from a meeting of the Council of Foreign Ministers in Moscow. Though physically exhausted, he sent word to the President, who was cruising aboard his yacht on the Potomac, that he "would like to report to him, at his convenience," and that he "expected to make a radio speech the following evening about the work of the conference." Soon afterward, says Byrnes, word came from the President inviting him to join the cruise. The ensuing meeting was apparently very cordial, and as Byrnes presented his report "[f]rom time to time the President interrupted to express his approval."

A few days later, Byrnes continues, certain newspaper columnists were circulating rumors that the President had in fact summoned Byrnes to the yacht and there expressed strong disapproval of the agreements entered into at Moscow. Byrnes denies this flatly: neither at the shipboard meeting nor at any other time did the President disapprove.[16]

The following April (1946) Byrnes submitted his resignation as Secretary of State, citing reasons of health; the President did not accept it until the January following, when he sent the usual letter of regret and appreciation.

Five years later, in a collection of excerpts from President Truman's diaries and private correspondence, a "memorandum-letter" from Truman to Byrnes was published—part of it reproduced in facsimile—preceded by a note signed "H. S. T." The note read: "I wrote this

---

[16] James F. Byrnes, *Speaking Frankly,* New York, 1947, 237–38.

memo and read it to my Secretary of State. So urgent were its contents I neither had it typed nor mailed but preferred to read it in order to give emphasis to the points I wanted to make." In the document Truman first scolds Byrnes for not keeping him fully informed about his negotiations with the Russians; then he criticizes in detail the policies Byrnes has been pursuing, and concludes: "I'm tired of babying the Soviets."[17]

After Truman left office he produced two volumes of *Memoirs,* which are uncommonly reliable in detail, and in which he describes his annoyance with Byrnes's failure to keep him sufficiently informed from Moscow.[18] On Byrnes's return to the United States, the Secretary asked the White House to arrange for a radio address to the American people on the work of the Conference, before—says Truman in a tone of outrage—reporting to the President on the results of his trip.

In the face-to-face interview that Truman says he insisted on, the President affirms that he told Byrnes he "would not tolerate a repetition of such conduct." Truman goes on: "I knew that it was time to make things perfectly clear between the Secretary of State and myself. I wanted to do it without delay, without publicity and in writing." So he shortly afterward wrote a longhand letter to Byrnes, which he read aloud to the addressee from the presidential desk in the White House. There follows in the *Memoirs* the text of the memo-letter previously published.

According to Truman, Byrnes accepted the criticism of his performance and agreed to comply. He

did not ask to be relieved or express a desire to quit. It was not until some months later that he came to me and suggested that his health would not allow him to stay on. He agreed to remain through the negotiations of the peace treaties that were to grow out of his Moscow commitments.[19]

[17] William Hillman, *Mr. President,* New York, 1952, 21–22.

[18] It came out afterward that Byrnes had said to Averell Harriman, then the United States Ambassador at Moscow: "I'm not going to send any daily reports. I don't trust the White House. It leaks. And I don't want any of this coming out in the papers until I get home." Cabell Phillips, *The Truman Presidency: The History of a Triumphant Succession,* New York, 1966, 148.

[19] Harry S. Truman, *Memoirs,* Vol. 1, *Year of Decisions,* New York, 1955, 550–53.

Byrnes took up the Truman "memo-letter" in his autobiography, which appeared in 1958.[20] He denied ever hearing of the document until its first publication in 1952. Pointing out that if the President had ever spoken to him so critically and caustically, he would have resigned on the spot, Byrnes found "the only explanation" of the mystery in a sentence that occurs in another part of the book that first revealed the "memorandum-letter": ". . . the President said that sometimes he wrote letters which he never sent but wished he had sent."[21]

For the historian who wants to know, and prove, what really happened, the task is in this case impossible—barring the emergence of an unsuspected eyewitness. The candid historian recognizes here that precision must often remain an ideal and finality a dream.[22]

It will have been noted that the sequence of events in the preceding uncertainty is in itself simple and familiar—an interview, a reprimand, a resignation. There are other kinds of puzzles in which unlikelihood is added to the elements that create an "undecidable" situation. Yet the historian is not thrown off his stride by this further burden; for the plausible and the implausible form no part of the historian's standards of judgment. In this too he differs from the layman, whose snap judgment ordinarily negatives the implausible. To the historian, a chain of probabilities is worth all the plausibility in the world. For example, the following series of events is not plausible, and we have not enough diverse evidence to call it true, yet the traditional report is reinforced by the written account of one eyewitness who in other respects is trustworthy. Provisionally, it is to be taken as true. In 1867, a princess of the Royal House of Italy was married. These were the incidents that surrounded the event: the bride's wardrobe mistress hanged herself; the colonel who was to lead the procession to the church fell off his horse with sunstroke; the palace gates failed to open for the procession, because the gatekeeper lay dead in a pool of blood.

---

[20] *All in One Lifetime,* New York, 1958.

[21] Hillman, *op. cit.,* 46.

[22] A persistent historian may draw conclusions (albeit tentative) from the fact that Truman, though he said he had read extracts from Byrnes's first book, refused to comment on them when asked to do so at a news conference. *Public Papers of the Presidents, Harry S. Truman, 1947,* Washington, D.C., 1963, 467.

Though the ceremony itself was not marred by accident, just afterward the best man fired a pistol at his own head. The wedding party then went to the railway station, where the official who had drawn up the marriage contract succumbed to apoplexy. Next, from excess zeal, the stationmaster fell under the wheels of the approaching train. At that point the king refused to allow anyone to board it and the party returned to the palace. The Count of Castiglione, who rode alongside the carriage, was suddenly thrown and the wheels passed over him, injuring him fatally.[23] The occasion being royal, its ill-fated incidents were kept dark.[24]

Facing the Doubtfulness of All Reports

The tale of woe just related would not do in an historical novel, but it is tenable in history, for History produced it. If we lend our minds to such a probability, even though noting it as low in the scale, how much more confident we feel when a set of events is public from the start and attested to by dozens of independent witnesses. In such instances we *know*. Let us recapitulate the two reasons why: (1) we have abundant documentary evidence, and (2) a critical examination of it discloses the high probability of its truth.

"But," says the skeptic, "you were not there. All you know is what others choose to tell you—in memoirs, newspapers, and your other vaunted evidences. How can you be sure? Most people are notoriously bad observers; some are deliberate or unconscious liars; there is no such thing as a perfect witness. And yet you naively trust any casual passerby, and on his say-so you proclaim: 'This is what happened.' "

Except for the words "naively trust," everything said above is true. But in its effort to discredit history it proves too much. The

---

[23] See Frédéric Loliée, *The Romance of a Favourite*, London, 1912, 69–72. Here is a contemporary improbability which is nevertheless true, being attested to by trustworthy reportage and a legislative investigation: "Thirty-six inmates of Rock Quarry State Prison [Georgia] broke their legs with ten-pound sledge hammers today in protest against working conditions." *New York Times*, July 31, 1956. Or see the list of a dozen coincidences linking the Lincoln and Kennedy assassinations (*Forbes*, XCIV [Aug. 15, 1964] 12).

[24] Compare the episode discussed under Verification, p. 107.

key sentences are: "You were not there" and "There is no such thing as a perfect witness." Granting the force of these two statements, what follows? It is that if any of us had been there, there would simply have been one more imperfect witness on the scene. We might be convinced that our vision, our recollection, our interpretation was *the* right one, but other witnesses would still feel equally certain about theirs.

To put it differently, every observer's knowledge of the event doubtless contains some exact and some erroneous knowledge, and these two parts, multiplied by as many observers as may be, are all the knowledge there can be. Only a divine being would have perfect and complete knowledge of the event—the event "as it really happened." Outside our imperfect knowledge, the event has no independent existence; it is not hidden in a repository of the real where we can find it. This is important to grasp and remember; it makes one both humble and grateful about the known and knowable past.

In trying to discredit this second-hand knowledge, the skeptic about historical truth unconsciously assumes that because he is alive and observant he knows the actuality of his own time, which future reporters will garble in their accounts. Or he compares the doubts honestly expressed about some event by historians themselves with an absolute record which he imagines as existing somewhere, like the standard yard in the government Bureau of Standards. He speaks of "the real past" as of a solid entity hidden from us like a mountain hidden by a mist. But this is a figment of his imagination. The only past there is is the past we have—a thing of opinions and reports.

Indeed, a famous American historian of the Civil War and Reconstruction, William A. Dunning, was convinced that in history what the contemporaries of an event believed it to be is truer—more genuinely "the past"—than anything discovered by later research and which the contemporaries did not know. Their views had consequences, whereas ours about their times played no part in the web of thought and action.[25]

In any case, comparisons with an absolute knowledge or substitu-

---

[25] William A. Dunning, "Truth in History," in the volume of that name, New York, 1937, 3–20.

tions of a divine mind for the human ones that remember the past and write history are irrelevant to historiography. Far from disproving the truth of history, they lead to the conclusion that a capable researcher can know more about the past than did those contemporary with it, which is one reason why under the historian's hand the known past changes and grows.

A simple illustration will make this clear. In the memoirs of James A. Farley, written some fifteen years after the first Franklin Roosevelt administration, the writer tells us that "the second Cabinet meeting was more interesting, because the new President again turned to the possibility of war with Japan. . . . There was much discussion of Japan's attitude in the Orient, Japan's clashes with China and other possible avenues of Japanese activity."[26] He goes on about this subject for another twenty lines, and it is plain that this is his frank and unclouded recollection of what took place at this, the first really important meeting of the administration in which he was the Postmaster-General.

Yet if we turn to the diaries of Harold Ickes, another member of the same cabinet, whose notes were made at the time, we read a rather different tale: "Most of our time was spent discussing the banking situation and the international situation, particularly the attitude this country should adopt with reference to being represented at the coming conference in Geneva. *There was also some discussion of our relations with Japan.*"[27](Italics added.)

To confuse things further, the two cabinet members disagree about the date of this meeting, Farley assigning it to Tuesday, March 7, 1933, and Ickes to Friday, March 10. Ickes is undoubtedly right and the context explains how Farley made the error: he remembered it correctly as the *second* cabinet meeting, but started counting from the first informal gathering at the White House on Sunday, March 5; whereas Ickes, also calling it the second meeting, counts Tuesday's meeting as the first formal meeting and Friday's as the second. Between a memoir writer and a diarist, the latter—unless dishonest—is clearly the authority on such points.

But the date is easily set straight compared with the disagreement

[26] *Jim Farley's Story: The Roosevelt Years,* New York, 1948, 39.
[27] *Secret Diary: The First Thousand Days,* New York, 1953, 5.

concerning what the meeting was mainly about. We can see that each reporter remembered most vividly what interested him most. But was Japan or Geneva the chief issue? We should like to have Roosevelt's view and Frances Perkins' and half a dozen more; but whose would be right? Even a tape recording would not settle that question, for supposing the time unevenly divided between the topics, it would always be open to someone to say, "Yes, we talked for an hour about Geneva, but in the five minutes devoted to Japan, everyone could feel the menace of a world war." To which the answer is: "No, not everyone—not Mr. Ickes." And we are left, not with the uncertainty of *history*—the facts here are plain enough; we are left with the variety of human judgments, which are not above but within the fabric of History. The "real" burden of that meeting, the one and only significance of that certain and dated event, no student or expert can assign with finality, because, once again, no one has access to the mind of the ruler of the universe.

We must be content, therefore, with the vast amount of imperfect knowledge that critical history discusses and delivers to us.[28] Since all human knowledge is imperfect, we should take from each discipline its characteristic truths and accept the imperfections inherent in the purpose to which the discipline addresses itself. If historical knowledge sometimes seems more imperfect than other kinds, this is due to the vividness with which it reembodies and makes articulate what is gone. It arouses interests as passionate as those of the present, and it moves people because its literary embodiment requires no initiation—"any number can play." Those who read and study history most closely do not disdain to give it credence: that too is an attested fact, whereas thoroughgoing skepticism is often a pose.[29] To the justly skeptical and comparing mind, history at its best is no more uncertain than the

[28]The reader who likes historical enigmas and their resolutions should read H. R. Trevor-Roper's inquiry into the authorship of *"Eikon Basilike,* The King's Book,"* in *Men and Events,* New York, 1957, Chapter XXXI.

[29]It has, we believe, never been noted that Voltaire, supposedly the professional doubter par excellence, did not doubt history and was on the contrary an indefatigable historian. In 1769 he published a long essay in rejoinder to Horace Walpole in which he rejected equally "an extreme skepticism and a ridiculous credulity." *Le Pyrrhonisme de l'histoire,* in *Oeuvres,* Kehl, 1785, XXVII, 9–10.

descriptive earth sciences whose assertions most people seem willing to take on faith.[30] Large parts of man's history are thoroughly well known and beyond dispute. True, the interpretations and the meanings attached to the parts, clear or obscure, are and will continue open to debate. But who has settled the interpretation or meaning of human life? Taken all in all, history is genuine knowledge, and we should be lost without it.

Subjective and Objective: The Right Usage

Our cumulative reasons for trusting history are now four: we have documents; they are critically tested; the rule governing judgment is Probability; and the notion of an absolute past, which we might know if only men did not produce faulty copies, is a delusion. Within the history we possess we can, of course, distinguish good and bad witnesses, good and bad judges of events. An historian might conceivably decide, on the evidence of the man's habitual inattention, that a cabinet member was a bad judge of what went on at meetings, and that his diary or memoirs were of no use to history.

Such a conclusion may then tempt the devil's advocate to bring up the idea of the "subjective" and point out that since, on our own showing, all history rests on "subjective impressions," therefore all accounts are equally biased and worthless. History would then be like a distorting mirror—a real reflection but all askew.

This is another misunderstanding to clear up. The words "subjective" and "biased" are in the first place not synonyms. Reserving the treatment of bias to the next chapter, let us here try to halt in the reader the unfortunate misuse of "subjective." Originally a technical term in a special brand of philosophy, the word has come into the marketplace, where it disturbs not only discussions of history but also ordinary conversation. It is always a danger to borrow technical terms without observing their definitions or without redefining them. In loose

---

[30]The public is also docile about accepting radical revisions in the huge spans of time that geologists assign to the periods of prehistory. For an account of a major alteration in the dating of the history of the earth, see J. Laurence Kulp, "Geologic Time Scale," *Science*, CXXXIII (April 14, 1961), 1105–14.

speech "subjective" has come to mean "one person's opinion," usually odd or false; whereas "objective" is taken to mean "what everybody agrees on," or correct opinion. According to this, if James Farley's memory of the cabinet meeting was disputed in the same way by six other people he would automatically be thought "subjective" and wrong. They would be thought "objective" and right. This common belief is quite mistaken.[31]

"Subjective" and "objective" properly apply not to persons and opinions but to sensations and judgments. Every person, that is, every living subject, is necessarily subjective in *all* his sensations. But some of his subjective sensations are *of* objects, others of himself, or "subject." Your toothache is said to be subjective because it occurs within you as a feeling subject. It is not an object in the world for all to see; it is yours alone. The tooth that the dentist extracts *is* an object and with its removal goes your subjective ache. While the pain lasted, both tooth and ache were real. Now only the tooth is real—hence the tendency to believe that an object is somehow "more real." It is not thought more real than a subjective impression, since all impressions are admittedly subjective, but more lasting, more public, than a *purely* subjective impression. If this reasoning strains the ordinary faculties, get rid of the whole matter by dropping the jargon use of "objective" and "subjective" as synonyms for "true" and "false."

All objects being known only to "subjects" (that is, persons), differentiating between subjective and objective in the work of research comes down to asking oneself: "Is this an object in the outer world?" If after careful scrutiny you decide Yes, then that judgment is an objective judgment. You may be partly or wholly wrong, but you are not dreaming or describing hallucinations.[32]

And here is where the idea of seeking others' backing properly

---

[31] In colleges and universities the misusage has probably been encouraged by the term "objective examinations," which is a misnomer to describe multiple-choice questions. See Banesh Hoffmann, *The Tyranny of Testing*, New York, 1962.

[32] Another example for good measure: if you see spots before your eyes, they may be objective—a piece of material with polka dots—or subjective, a diseased condition of the body. Take quinine and you may hear a ringing in your ears—purely subjective, though real. But you have no difficulty ascertaining the absence of an objective bell that could account for the sensation.

comes in. The first man who had a toothache may have asked his friends "Do you feel this?" On seeing their surprised shake of the head, he decided that his quite real feeling was purely private—subjective. But when one night he looked up and saw the northern lights and compared notes with his fellows, he discovered that he was not "seeing things" but adding to his store of knowledge about objects. To sum up, *an objective judgment is one made by testing in all ways possible one's subjective impressions, so as to arrive at a knowledge of objects.*

The researcher naturally strives for objective judgments. His "objects"—the events of history—are known to him indirectly through the testimony of witnesses, whose competence is in turn judged as we showed earlier. Comparison with other objects and other judgments is the researcher's endless task. To put it differently, in history-writing objective judgments are made every time a capable mind attends to the evidence before it. Such a mind may reach a wrong conclusion, an error may later be proved upon him, new evidence may modify his hitherto sound report, but the judgment when made was objective.

Very well, you may say, but what about individual aberration? A color-blind person makes the objective judgment that everything in the world is gray, while the rest of us say that things are blue, red, green, yellow, and so on. This difficulty is neither new nor perplexing to the historical researcher, for he is himself always raising the question of the competence of the witness. We believe that objects are red, blue, and so on, not solely because there is a vast majority that concur in the judgment, but because these colored appearances are regularly observed by people bending their whole "objective attention" on the phenomena. *Their* verified subjective sensations of objects reveal more of reality than the sensations of color-blind subjects, and this is because they are natively endowed with a greater competence in seeing. Competence, and not majority opinion, is decisive: there have been collective hallucinations that deceived large majorities.

Now translate this into a researcher's typical situation. From noted literary figures who knew Henry James we have many reports on the novelist's appearance, manners, and speech. Most of them refer to him as either stuttering or hemming and hawing. One and only one entranced listener, herself trained in speech, has written down, with the aid of tempo marks, a characteristic sentence as James spoke it. From this it clearly appears that James was not stammering or fumbling for words at all, but repeating himself in various emphatic ways as he went along, or—to quote his interpreter—"instinctively bringing out the perfect sentence the first time; repeating it [in bits] more deliberately to test every word the second time; accepting it as satisfactory the third time, and triumphantly sending it forth as produced by Henry James."[33] This extraordinary mode of speech needed an extraordinary witness to record it for posterity. Against her objective judgment and manifest competence no amount of careless reporting can avail.

In relation to his documents the historian is of course in the position of "the single competent witness." It is he who is being objective as he reviews the evidence, not the thousands of heedless persons who reason ignorantly on inadequate information. In the Henry James instance it would be plausible but uncritical to argue that people who knew James well—H. G. Wells, Hugh Walpole, Ford Madox Ford, and a dozen others—would be better judges of his mannerisms than a comparative stranger meeting him casually at dinner. The opposite is true—provided, once again, that the stranger had competence and enough subjective interest in James to wish to make an objective judgment.

The researcher is accordingly quick to seize upon the single witness' account, which, though telling, has for one reason or another not become common knowledge. Facts like these throw light on well-known events from such unexpected corners that the mere recital gives a sense of the "thickness" of History. General Eisenhower furnished a particularly striking instance of this sudden illumination when he wrote of the nerve-wracking decision he had to make during the war about seizing Pantelleria, a small island off Sicily. He related the incident in *Crusade in Europe;*[34] the memory still haunted him years later: ". . . the decision was so difficult that had the predictions of the pessimists been carried out or been realized I certainly would have been relieved [of my command]. So you can never tell at the moment, is history going

[33]Elizabeth Jordan, quoted in S. Nowell-Smith, *The Legend of the Master,* New York, 1948, 16.
[34]New York, 1948, 164 ff.

to say this was right or this was wrong."[35] The only thing that "history" in the popular sense has to say about this turning point and the emotion it aroused in one man is that very few have ever heard of it. Yet in the narrative of the great struggle, the leap across from Africa to Pantelleria was equivalent to crossing the Rubicon, about which everyone *has* heard, thanks to historians.

Knowledge of Fact and Knowledge of Causes

The vast consequences of such pivotal moves inevitably pose the problem of causation. Though we have steadily strengthened our defenses against the skeptic and shown how documentary evidence and its handling—the balancing of probabilities, the making of objective judgment, and the seeking out of competent testimony—successively raise our certitude about the past higher than any imaginable certitude about the present, this favorable comparison itself spurs the skeptic to his last effort: "Granted that you may know enough to tell a reliable story, full of significant detail, you really know nothing unless at every point you also know the causes."

The challenge takes one into deep waters. Whole books have been written about Causation. Their contents could not be reviewed in a few pages even if all the questions were finally settled in the minds of men. Only a sketch of the question can be given. The chief difficulty lies in what is meant by Cause. Neither philosophers nor scientists agree on what causation is or does. In the mid-eighteenth century, the philosopher David Hume showed that the conception of Cause as a compelling push that produces an effect is an illusion. Man has no immediate sense of the necessity that makes one billiard ball propel another after striking it; he has only an expectation of the event, an expectation that has been bred in him by habitual experience. Ever since Hume, theories of causation have been numerous but none has proved universally acceptable. All that is agreed upon is that where Cause is, there is Regularity.

[35] *New York Times,* March 24, 1955.

TRUTH AND CAUSATION | 169

Everyone nevertheless continues to believe in causes that compel. We say: "The manager's behavior caused X to resign," and we think we know what we mean. But as soon as we try to say precisely what we mean our confidence breaks down. A psychologist will show how inadequate is our grasp of the cause: the alleged cause was a mere pretext; the manager's offensive behavior was imaginary—a "projection" on the subordinate's part. Or again, the latter's behavior may have provoked the other's—hence the man himself was the cause of his own resignation. Or possibly his wife caused it, unknown to herself and to him.

These speculations are meant only to show that when we speak of causes in human affairs we are usually dealing with a variety of elements that stand at different degrees of depth from the observed event and that are not easily touched or separated. Judge Hand called them incommensurables[36] because they cannot be measured and sometimes cannot even be discerned. If a man kills himself sixteen days, five hours, and twenty-three minutes after receiving a piece of bad news, what is the cause of his suicide? In ordinary speech we say either "Things became too much for him," or "A man's vitality is lowest in the early morning," or "A man of John's tradition and character could not face bankruptcy." In other words we ascribe his death either to an unfathomable psychological state, or to a physiological fact, or to a recognizable idea born in response to a situation. We are not likely to ascribe it to the bullet and the gun, because that cause does not interest us: it interests only the coroner.

Generalizing from this we infer that what history reveals to mankind about its past does not uncover *the* cause (one or more indispensable antecedents) of any event, large or small, but only the *conditions* (some of the prerequisites) attending its emergence. Not only can we not isolate the cause, but we cannot properly define of what sort it would be. When Pascal said that if Cleopatra's nose had been shorter this would have changed the face of the world (to say nothing of her own), he was pointing out that personality plays a role in History. He did not mean that Cleopatra's nose was *the* cause of Mark Antony's

[36]See Chapter 3, pp. 53–54.

defeat at Actium: it was at best one of the antecedent conditions. In short, when we give an account of human events we fasten upon those points that seem to us suitable to connect believably with our present concerns and previous experience. If these connections are duly brought out we say we "understand."[37]

The thought occurs that we might come closer to a real cause, and obtain results akin to those of physical science, if we could only deal with well-defined kinds of events, such as, say, automobile accidents. We do in fact classify these and learn that mechanical failure caused so many percent, speeding so many, and intoxication so many. Can this possibility of classification and statistical measurement be extended throughout the realm of History so as to conquer and annex it to science? Some argue that this is impossible because the facts of History are unique and its personages also; they do not recur, or as the popular saying has it: History never repeats.

To this it is answered that *all* events are unique, even the "same" experiment done twice in a laboratory. All the individuals of the brute creation are distinct also, even the sheep in a field. This suggests that in both realms

there are facts that have nothing in common with other facts—for example, the geological formation of the earth—and of these facts we say that they do not recur; and there are facts which more or less resemble other facts—a lion that resembles other lions, a person who goes to school like millions of other persons—and of these facts we say that they *repeat themselves.*[38]

From this the writer goes on to argue that a large part of history is scientific in the sense of being based on description and classification of similar instances, just like zoology. In deciphering ancient inscriptions or studying Roman law, "the historical sources present the same sign for the same idea;" hence comparison and definition and exact analysis are possible.[39]

---

[37] For a subtle and authoritative account of causation as it is conceived in physical science today (and as it must be conceived in the "historical" realm which includes all that is not science), see Henry Margenau, *Open Vistas,* New Haven, 1961, esp. 191–214.

[38] Gaetano Salvemini, *Historian and Scientist.* Cambridge, Mass., 1939, 91.

[39] *Ibid.,* 94.

There is another sense in which history is a part of the realm of science, and which should prevent us from thinking of the two as opposed or widely removed from each other: the events of history occur in the same universe and follow the same material "laws" as the objects of science. Men are subject to gravitation and decay, states-men in transit are no different from other moving bodies, and what is most important, men's minds work upon historical data with the same perceptions and logical rules as they do in science.

A difference remains, of course, which most observers feel intui-tively even when they find it difficult to assess. History cannot, like physical science, pare down events and reproduce them at will in the simple forms and favoring conditions that we call experiment. Nor, as we saw above, can the historian sort out his materials into indepen-dent units that will stay put long enough for him to measure and relate them as constants and variables.[40] Even when we count automo-bile accidents we pursue our practical interest at the expense of strict causal analysis. The *immediate* error that caused the drunken driver's accident interests us no more than the remote cause that led him to drink.[41]

On Cause and Measurement

Every attempt in historical writing to formalize causal description or make a show of exactitude by assigning one "paramount" cause and several "contributory" causes ends in self-stultification. Any such distinction implies a measurement that we cannot in fact make; it foolishly apes the chemical formula by which a compound requires

[40]We can of course achieve this relation intuitively through historical *judgment,* as Garrett Mattingly has pointed out: "Conscious that every human situation contains certain elements of uniformity and certain elements of uniqueness, we scrutinize each new one and compare it with everything we can find out about similar situations in the past, seeking to assign values to constants and to isolate the variables, to decide which factors are significant, what choices are actually present, and what the probable consequences are of choosing course A and rejecting B." ("The Teaching of History," Princeton University Bicentennial Conference [unpublished], Feb. 20, 1947, 5).

[41]For an admirable discussion of the logic of historical analysis, see an article under that title by Ernest Nagel in *Scientific Monthly,* LXXIV (March 1952), 162–69.

several elements in stated proportions. For if, as Edward Lucas White once contended,[42] it took malaria-bearing mosquitoes and the spread of Christianity to undo the Roman Empire, the mosquitoes were as necessary as the Christians and neither is paramount to the other.[43]

The historical researcher is thus led to adopt a practical distinction about causality that has already commended itself to workers in physical science. They draw attention to the difference between causation that occurs in a long chain of events of various kinds and causation within a closed system. An example of the first is: the forming of a cloud, the darkening of the sun to earth dwellers, the lowering of temperature, people putting on coats, a thunderstorm bursting, a person taking refuge under a tree and being struck by lightning and killed. This chain of "causes" is miscellaneous and each event in it unpredictable, not because it is not determined, but because it occurs outside any controlled or controllable limits. As against this, in the physics laboratory, an elastic body of known stresses and strains goes through a series of evolving states; at any moment a single definite distribution of measured stresses and strains is the effect of the previous moment, which may therefore be regarded as its complete cause, as *the* cause.[44]

The distinctive feature of the first kind of causality is that there is no restriction on the events that may be related. It is open to the observer's insight to select, not causes in sense number 2, but conditions that belong to the chain and have the merit of interesting him and his audience. It is for them to judge whether the resulting narrative is intelligible, consonant with the experience of the race, and useful in orienting the mind amid the welter of facts.

This view, which may be described as pragmatic,[45] is peculiarly suited to historiography because of the impossibility of separating man into independent portions and units. Suppose—contrary to our view, but as some people do believe—that through the study of history, a

[42] In *Why Rome Fell,* New York, 1927.
[43] See a recent archeological hypothesis of the same simplicity: "Downfall of Indus Civilization Is Traced to Mud" (*New York Times,* May 23, 1966).
[44] For the illustrations used in this passage see Henry Margenau, "Causality in Quantum Electrodynamics," *Diogenes,* VI (Spring 1954), 74–84.
[45] "Pragmatic" is here used in its technical, Jamesian sense; it does not mean "convenient" or "practical," but "tested by consequences rather than antecedents"—the pragmatic test.

case were made out for thinking that *the* cause of war was trade, or sexual passion, or diplomacy. Clearly, this result would be untestable as long as it was impossible to isolate and uproot any of these components of our nature and civilization and abolish war. Indeed, war would probably break out over the issue of abolition, for war is also "caused" by ideas.

It is enough to state the supposition to see its absurdity. As a noted historian said many years ago:

Nothing could be more artificial than the scientific separation of man's religious, aesthetic, economic, political, intellectual and bellicose properties. These may be studied, each by itself, with advantage, but specialization would lead to the most absurd results if there were not someone to study the process as a whole; and that someone is the historian.[46]

On the view we have called pragmatic, and which attends not to causes but to variously relevant conditions, certain of the old puzzles and objections fall away. The objection that the historian selects his facts to suit himself is seen to be no objection but a helpful necessity. He is meant to think and to choose, and he is judged by the intelligence and honesty with which he does both. Again, the objection that history cannot be true because it has to be rewritten every thirty years appears as a sign of the usefulness of history: it not only should respond to the demands made upon it but it *can* respond. The successive revisions of the past do not cancel each other out, they are additive: we know more and more about the past through history, as we know more and more about nature through physical science. Finally, the need to choose among conditions in order to delineate events points to the truth that history, like all narrative, must present a pattern to the mind, must have form. Without a form, the accumulation of names and events is unintelligible and useless. It is the organization of the past that makes the past valuable, just as it is the organization of phenomena in scientific formulas that makes the study of nature valuable.

The ultimate question for the historian therefore is: What pattern?

[46] James Harvey Robinson, *The New History*, New York, 1913, 66.

8

Pattern, Bias, and the Great Systems

The Reason of Historical Periods and Labels

Some years ago a well-known publishing firm planned to issue a book that would "illustrate the 100 greatest moments of history." To make certain which *were* the 100 greatest, the publishers inquired of "distinguished historians and journalists," asking them to choose among a list of 150 those "events that capture the imagination with their drama and form a part of every man's sense of the past." These ranged from "Hammurabi's Code promulgated" to "Tobacco introduced into Europe" and "Breaking the sound barrier."

It is to be hoped that most historians declined to fill out the questionnaire and took pains to explain to the publisher that although the answers might be of some interest, the inquiry was based on a misapprehension. The book could conceivably be justified if it adequately described and illustrated a hundred striking events in Western history. Creasy's *Fifteen Decisive Battles of the World*[1] comes to mind as a model in the genre. But to try to determine for oneself or others

[1] Originally published in 1851.

174

the greatest moments in history, whether fifteen or one hundred, is an intellectual impossibility. To understand why this is so calls for an understanding of the related subjects of Pattern, Period, Bias, and System.

The last chapter concluded with the statement that the writing of history requires a pattern, the reason being that the human mind cannot fix its attention on anything that does not present or suggest form. The mind will impose a form if one is not supplied. Throw down a dozen paper clips on a table and look at them for a few seconds: they are scattered at random, yet you will find yourself "seeing" a triangle of three in one corner, a sort of cross in the middle, and a little mound at the left. The constellations in the sky are the product of this inevitable penchant for grouping-in-order-to-grasp.

Similarly in story and in history. We expect them to offer us incidents in clusters that follow upon one another. We may keep reading straight ahead uncritically, but on looking back we like to feel that the whole somehow possesses dramatic form. This does not necessarily mean emotional excitement; it means an acceptable progression from a clear beginning to an intelligible end. This is why Macaulay, proposing to give a vast panorama of the events that filled the "momentous" years from 1685 to 1701, was so concerned with his arrangement. When his *History* was done he kept scrutinizing the form and comparing it with that of his favorite, Thucydides: "I admire him more than ever. He is the great historian. The others one may hope to match: him never . . . [but] . . . his arrangement is bad. . . . How much better is my order than that of Thucydides."[2]

Some few historians have at times repudiated this interest in "order" and declared that for history to be scientifically true the facts should arrange themselves. This is a misconception of both history and science. In the study of nature the facts do not arrange themselves either. A formula, or little form, implies the selection of certain phenomena that experiment has related, first, to a scale of measurement, and then to other facts in fixed or variable connections. The choice of facts and of relations is dictated by human interest as well as by nature. It is curiosity that moves man to ascertain the relation between

[2] G. O. Trevelyan, *Life and Letters of Lord Macaulay* (first published 1876), Diary entries for Nov. 25 and Dec. 4, 1848.

the behavior of a gas and the phenomena of heat and pressure. The facts, moreover, are seen through ideas (for example, the idea of a molecule) that are not immediately visible and ready to be noted down. They are searched for with a purpose in mind. The facts once ascertained, a mind has to frame a hypothesis to arrive at what is properly called *theory:* a total view of related events.

The historian works under the same necessity of giving shape to the events that he has found and verified. Only, he has no scale with which to measure the facts, and few symbols other than words with which to express their relations. His purpose being to portray intelligibly, he must "relate" in the ordinary sense of *recount* lifelike sequences. He presents human affairs as in a story, describing conditions and complications, and reaching climaxes and conclusions to aid understanding.

He can of course measure time, and chronology supplies a natural order among his facts. But, as we shall see, chronology is long and its contents are a mixed bag. For both these reasons it too needs a pattern before it can be thought and felt.[3] This leads the historian to carve out manageable periods—reigns, centuries, eras. He also finds readymade for him certain other patterns or "constellations" created by the laity, contemporary or not, out of *their* need to group things: these groupings go by names such as Gothic and Baroque, Renaissance and Romantic. These the historian must accept as having meaning, even if the meaning has to be explained at length, and even if it remains less clear-cut than that of molecule; for the historical labels refer to the thoughts and acts of once living men, who were precisely *not* molecules.

Groups and their names usually arise in the course of intellectual or artistic debate. Thus the name "Hudson River School," now used in scholarly writing to describe a notable group of American painters, was first used by a critic in scorn of certain artists and their works.[4] It was not an exact label, as one might guess, for the men attacked did not invariably paint the Hudson River or live on its banks. But the name is now indispensable, in the first place because it is an

---

[3] For the relation of the chronological and topical treatments, see Chapter 11, pp. 259–60.
[4] See *The Brooklyn Museum Journal,* 1942, 54.

historical datum; and in the second, because it links fact and idea in the true manner of history. The ideas consist of certain pictorial principles and poetic intentions; the facts make up the biography of certain men, their dates, works, careers.

To object to labels or periods and say that "historians invent them, hence they are false" is a cliché that is itself false to the way things happen, besides amounting to a failure of imagination. Without divisions of time, groupings of men, aggregates of ideas, the historian would be reduced to unreadable, unrememberable chronicling. He would write: "There was a painter named A and he lived from 1800 to 1850, painting many works. And in those same years lived a painter named B, also very productive, but he lived a little longer. A third painter at that time was C, who liked many of the same subjects as A and B; and his youngest pupil, D, resembles the other three, except that toward the end of his life D began to do something that critics said was different."

For the reader of history the value of the historic term "Hudson River School" is that it denotes a number of great painters that share some important characteristics. It is of course not enough to learn the tag; learning history means learning its details, so one begins with "the facts"—the names of the artists, their purposes and performance. To *know* history means to have thought about it. One concludes about the Hudson River painters that they were not merely local and aquatic, but America's first and many-sided national school. Superficially misleading, the tag "Hudson River" is nonetheless the proper History-incrusted symbol of events, expressing a combination of facts in a pattern.

The Conditions of Pattern-Making

Having accepted historic groupings as given, we still remain critical of patterns at large and we ask: What elements of thought and observation go into the making of any "constellation" that unites the loose particles of fact? Not all periods, patterns, and labels are equally apt and useful; but we may for the moment leave in abeyance the question of value and merit. The first element in an historical pattern is obviously a comparison of some sort, natural or artificial. We decide that X is more like Y than like M. The difference between the natural and the arbitrary groupings of this kind is always difficult to state. As in the example of the scattered paper clips, we can argue that once scattered some of them naturally *are* in the form of a cross, or again that we *choose to see them as* a cross. Trying to settle the debate would lead us back to the philosophy of perception, which is too large a subject to be summarized here. The researcher will profit more from another distinction: between random (or historic) grouping and systematic grouping (or classification).

The first kind is given to the researcher ready-made, as in the Hudson River School. The hostile critic who made this pattern to impress the readers of the New York *Tribune* with his own sense of scorn did not conduct a thorough survey of contemporary American painters and select a certain number on the basis of features verifiably present. He was simply hurling an epithet at random—and it stuck.[5] We may assume that it did so because it corresponded to some vague kinship that needed to be named; but as we saw, in order to extract the value of this naming we have to go back to the facts themselves and make them modify the oversimple idea that the bare term raises in our minds.

A systematic grouping, on the other hand, is usually the work of a researcher who stands farther away from the living reality than the contemporary critic, and who wishes to study a genuine set or class of facts. Thus when the late Crane Brinton prepared his book *The Jacobins*,[6] he did not take merely the first half dozen whose names he happened to know, or content himself with the membership of the Paris group; he systematically sampled the membership of that historic party by examining the records of chosen Jacobin Clubs all over France. Such a study resembles what we know as sociology, but its principle is fundamental to all descriptive disciplines: generalization

---

[5] Compare the various origins of: "Quakers," "Muckrakers," "Sea Beggars," "Diggers," "Fauves," "Cubists," "Rosicrucians," "The Bloomsbury Group," "Girondists," "Jacobins," "Jacobites," "Whigs," "Tories," "Spartacists," "Huguenots," "Know-Nothings," "Irreconcilables," "Hawks and Doves," "Neo-Isolationists," "New Leftists."

[6] New York, 1930.

depends on adequate enumeration. If you want to make an assertion about the views of the board of directors, you must look up in the minutes the votes and opinions of all the members. In other words, your classification must cover the facts. Definition determines the limits of the class, even though you are still grouping together men who differ in appearance and opinion from one another.

The next condition of pattern-making grows out of this human diversity, which makes it either impossible or fruitless to report on human affairs in cut-and-dried fashion. In looking for "the views of the board of directors," it would not be enough to give a tabulation of their votes on various issues. To conceive the situation of the company accurately, we must know the words, the personalities, the intrigues, the emotions represented. And since the historian cannot and should not "tell all," he must select. We thus arrive at our first rule of pattern-making: *To be successful and right, a selection must face two ways: it must fairly correspond to the mass of evidence, and it must offer a graspable design to the beholder.*

Now the researcher never sees the facts fully displayed before him like someone selecting jewelry laid out on a counter. The researcher has begun with but little knowledge of the subject and has gradually acquired a mass of information beyond the capacity of both the mind's eye and the memory. When he selects, therefore, he is to be compared not to the customer with the synoptic view, but to the traveler exploring new country. The explorer forms his opinions as he progresses, and they change with increasing knowledge. Yet they are always conditioned by two things—the observer's temperament, including his preconceptions, and the motive or purpose of his search.

The Sources of Bias and Its Correctives

The researcher, it is clear, looks for his facts even more actively than the traveler. He must piece together the "scenery" of the past from fragments that lie scattered in many places. All this means that the researcher soon develops a guiding idea to propel him along his route, a hypothesis ahead of the facts, which steadily reminds him of what to look for.

"Ideas," says one thoughtful observer,

are themes of historical research—though not of all historical research. The clearer we are about the theme of our own research, the clearer we become about our own bias. And the clearer we are about our own bias, the more honest and efficient we are likely to be in our own research. Many of the rules laid down about the correct methods of historical research are in fact disguised declarations of the purposes of the research itself.[7]

To which he might have added: in research as in life one is far more likely to find what one looks for than what one neglects.

Since guiding ideas affect both search and selection, let us call the researcher's temperament (that is, the whole tendency of his mind) and his present intentions and hypotheses his total *interest*. We may then say without implying any blame that his interest will determine his discoveries, his selection, his pattern-making, and his exposition. This is unavoidable in all products of the mind. Mathematicians themselves recognize in the work of their colleagues the individuality that produces solutions of certain kinds or arrives at them in certain ways. In research and writing there are of course many kinds and qualities of "interest," ranging from the downright dishonest to that which in Thucydides elicited Macaulay's breathless admiration. Apart from degrees of talent, the dividing line between the good and bad kinds of interest is usually drawn through the point where interest begins to spoil the product altogether. It is then called Bias.

Bias is an uncontrolled form of interest; it is easily detected, but its presence does not tell us all we need to know about an historical report. Gibbon, for example, was biased in favor of pagan Rome and against Christianity, so much so that he devoted two long chapters to an ironic castigation of the early Church. As a result, one does not go to Gibbon for a sympathetic understanding of primitive Christianity. But the remainder of his history—the larger part—stands firm. And that valuable part, as far as we can tell, could not have been produced apart from the rest. The work as a whole would never have been undertaken and carried through without Gibbon's animus, his bias.

[7] Arnaldo Momigliano, "A Hundred Years After Ranke," *Diogenes,* VI (Summer 1954), 57–58.

Again, Macaulay is sometimes dismissed with the phrase "the Whig historian." The description is not wrong, but the implication usually is. Macaulay's sympathies were with the Whigs in the Revolution of 1688 and with their descendants, the Liberals of his own day. Yet his *History* also stands. For what he wrote is neither a party pamphlet, nor a whitewashing, nor anything less than a great history. One of his later opponents in politics, Lord Acton, who was deeply repelled by Macaulay's faults, nevertheless called him "one of the greatest of all writers and masters."[8]

Because "bias" is used pejoratively, it is assumed that some workers are biased, others not. This is to think in black and white. Gaetamo Salvemini put the situation better when he told his students: "Impartiality is a dream and honesty a duty. We cannot be impartial, but we can be intellectually honest." The student of history responds to the need for pattern and wants a strong motive to propel research—hence he cannot be neutral. Without interest on his part, his work will lack interest too.

In assessing bias, the researcher must bring to bear a certain sophistication of mind. As a thoughtful scholar he recognizes the double condition of the search for truth—it must in the end produce a form, and at any point it answers some implied or expressed interest. And as a critical judge tracing the way in which the historian's interest has contributed to the form, he asks:

1. Was the writer fastidious or crude in selecting and marshaling his facts? That is, was he hard upon his own hypotheses, fair-minded to his opponents, committed to the truth first and foremost?
2. Was he self-aware enough to recognize—perhaps to acknowledge—the assumptions connected with his interest?

[8] James W. Thompson, *A History of Historical Writing*, New York, 1942, II, 300. On one occasion, Acton told the Trinity College Society at Cambridge: " 'I was once with two eminent men, the late Bishop of Oxford [William Stubbs] and the present Bishop of London [Mandell Creighton]. On another occasion I was with two far more eminent men, the two most learned men in the world. I need hardly tell you their names—they were Mommsen and Harnack. On each occasion the question arose: who was the greatest historian the world had ever produced. On each occasion the name first mentioned and on each occasion the name finally agreed upon, was that of Macaulay.' " (*Ibid.*)

3. Does the work as a whole exhibit the indispensable scholarly virtues, however noticeable the bias?

In answering these questions, the researcher will of course try to be as fair as he would like all his witnesses to be. For whoever judges another's interest is also moved by an interest of his own—an interest that is often heightened by the fact that many others share it unquestioningly. For example, an American who lived at the time of the Cold War could more easily accept the following "historical" statement than a critical reader a century hence:

The challenge which today stems from Soviet Russia is uniquely formidable. But it is, in modern garb, similar to what our nation faced during its early years. Then Czar Alexander was the world's most powerful ruler and he and his allied despots of Europe extended their power throughout much of the world—in Europe, Asia, South America, and North America. Along our West Coast the Russians both held Alaska and infiltrated south as far as the San Francisco area. It was this menace, primarily as it stemmed from Russia, which led to the pronouncement of the Monroe Doctrine.[9]

Judged according to our question 1, this paragraph is from beginning to end pseudo-history. Each sentence purports to inform, but the speaker's interest is not embodied in a manner sufficiently careful of the truth to rank as an historical statement. In order to pass muster, the same "facts" would have to be much qualified, and their relations better conceived. To say nothing of the untenable view of Alexander and the supposition of a Russian "menace" behind the Monroe Doctrine,[10] the parallel between 1823 and 1953 has the effect of brushing aside Marxist Communism as if it were no new or important factor in world history. And in leaving the old monarchical imperialism as

[9] John Foster Dulles, Speech to the Annual Convention of the CIO, November 18, 1953. (State Department release, 2.)
[10] The careful student Thomas A. Bailey, in his *Diplomatic History of the American People,* 8th ed., New York, 1969, 183–84, says of the allusion to Russia in the message of 1823: Monroe's "failure to make more of [the noncolonization principle] was probably a result of his knowledge that the so-called Russian menace in the Northwest was not threatening, and that negotiations were proceeding smoothly . . . ."

the threat "in modern garb," it virtually denies the reality of 130 years of Western history.

Measuring self-awareness—the burden of question 2—most often means being alive to implications; for there is no law requiring a writer to say in so many words: "These are my assumptions, how do you like them?" He may content himself with statements of principle that he hopes you will accept as true, or at least as working hypotheses. For example, when Macaulay remarks that

> During more than a hundred years . . . every [English] man has felt entire confidence that the state would protect him in the possession of what had been earned by his diligence and hoarded by his self-de-nial. Under the benignant influence of peace and liberty, science has flourished and has been applied to practical purposes on a scale never before known. The consequence is that a change to which the history of the old world furnishes no parallel has taken place in our country,[11]

we easily infer that the writer favors peace, liberty, property, applied science, and the Industrial Revolution. He is also a Little Englander, patriotic but not imperialistic, an advocate of laissez-faire and of the moral traits that go with that philosophy: self-reliance, rationalism, and a respect for worldly achievements.

The value of knowing all this as one reads an account of the past is that it affords a basis for judging the writer's own judgments. The reader proceeds by a sort of triangulation: here I stand; there, to left or right, stands Macaulay; and beyond are the events that he reports. Knowing his position in relation to mine, I can work out a perspective upon events as I could not if I saw them exclusively through his eyes—or mine.

Practicing this triangulation is not the same as dismissing an author after having "doped out" that he is a Whig, a Catholic, a Dutchman, a Mohammedan, an alcoholic, or a divorced man. Dismissal or systematic discounting of what a person says because of his nationality, religion, or personal history is only the crude and dull form of the delicate judgment here called for. One might as well spare oneself the effort of reading at all if one is going to make the text

[11] *History of England from the Accession of James Second,* New York, 1899, I, Chapter 3, 261.

a mere peg for a gloating distrust. The aim should be rather to obtain a large return in knowledge, some of it held under caution until two, three, or four other accounts have modified or strengthened its solid parts.

In short, reader's suspiciousness is no answer to the problem of writer's bias. On the contrary, sympathy is prerequisite to understanding, for history presents people and their feelings, which can be understood in no other way. Woodrow Wilson, an accomplished historian, went even further:

> The historian needs something more than sympathy, for sympathy may be condescending, pitying, contemptuous. . . . Sympathy there must be . . . but it must be the sympathy of the man who stands in the midst and sees like one within, not like one without, like a native, not like an alien. He must not sit like a judge exercising extraterritorial jurisdiction.[12]

Here, surely, is our old friend Imagination under another name. The fact that it is a dangerous quality does not mean that it can be dispensed with. Imagination that suggests what facts we want and where they may be found also tells us what they mean. Our contemporary, Sir Keith Hancock, has told how in writing his first book on the Risorgimento in Tuscany he identified himself with each party, one after the other: "I was zealous in turn for the House of Austria, the House of Savoy, the Papacy, the Mazzinian People, and half a dozen brands of liberalism or democracy."[13] An imaginative sympathy with all the participants sets up in the researcher's mind that internal debate which re-creates the actuality, and out of this comes right judgment. Juxtaposing his successive enthusiasms, the Australian historian formed a total view that none of the actors themselves had had, and his intellect apportioned to each element its due. In his own words, "Getting inside the situation is the opening movement, getting outside it is the concluding one."[14]

The impossibility and undesirability of eliminating interest and

---

[12] "The Variety and Unity of History," *Congress of Arts and Science, Universal Exposition, St. Louis, 1904,* Boston, 1906, II, 17.

[13] *Country and Calling,* London, 1954, 220.

[14] *Ibid.,* 221.

the effort to detect and allow for bias compensate for the lack of unanimity in historical writing. Successive views of one event may contradict one another, as when B says that A "entirely misunderstood." This is B's interest clashing with A's at short range. But later, when C revises B's interpretation, he probably restores some of the merits of A while adding new strokes to the composite portrait. The picture is never finished, because no large subject is ever fully encompassed.

A large subject is like a mountain, which no beholder ever sees entire: if he climbs it he discovers only selected aspects; if he stands off, he sees but an outline and from one side only; if he flies over it, he flattens it out. Similarly, an early historian of the Protestant Reformation would treat his subject as mainly a theological and military event; a man of the eighteenth century would view it as a reshaping of the map of Europe, a strengthening of emergent states, and a furthering of intellectual freedom. In the nineteenth century, the Reformation would appear as a religious movement with political and social implications; in the twentieth, it would rather seem a social and economic revolution with religious and political side effects. To the thorough researcher, the Reformation is all of these things, having the size and the shapes of a mountain.

The cliché that history must be rewritten every generation should therefore run somewhat differently: the past cannot help being reconceived by every generation, but the earlier reports upon it are in the main as good and true as they ever were. He who would know the full history of any period will do well to read its successive treatments, just as the ordinary researcher who would know the truth of a single incident seeks out all its witnesses. The revisionism of historians, rightly considered, does not substitute; it subtracts a little and adds more.

A further advantage of trying to harmonize the views of different periods into a larger but still coherent pattern is that in so doing one learns a great deal about the mind of each period. Pierre Bayle, the critical historian previously cited, put this with some exaggeration when he reviewed, as it happens, a contemporary history of Calvinism: "I almost never read historians with a view to learning what occurred, but only in order to know what is said in each nation about what occurred."[15] A modern researcher into Bayle's own century expressed the nub of this more exactly when she said:

The major changes in historical interpretation do not, as the layman often imagines, arise from the discovery of new evidence—the chest full of unsuspected documents . . . what is most likely to happen is that the historian will find what he is looking for, namely, the documents which will explain and illustrate his own point of view. But what *is* he looking for? Surely he is looking for the truth—for what really happened. It is his job as a scholar to form as exact an idea of past events as he can from the surviving evidence. But the instrument with which he looks at the past is modern. It was made, and shaped, and it operates, in the present. It is his own mind. And however much he bends his thoughts toward the past, his own way of thinking, his outlook, his opinions are the products of the time in which he lives. So that all written history . . . [is] a compound of past and present.[16]

The Philosophy and the Laws of History

We shall see in the next chapter how patterns, traditions, biases, and cultural and other controlling assumptions have affected the writing of European and American history in modern times. The circumstances of Europe and the New World having been different, the tenable views of the past have also differed, without on that account playing false to the zeal for truth, much less nullifying the results of copious research.

But before glancing at these important effects of interest or bias, we must look briefly at a special kind of interest that continues to furnish a motive to certain historians—the interest in discovering "the laws" of history. This interest goes by various names—it purports to give the "philosophy of history," or it establishes an historical "system," or it lays down "the law of historical evolution" as in Marx's "materialist conception of history."

[15] "Critique générale de *l'Histoire du Calvinisme* de M. Maimbourg," *Oeuvres Diverses,* The Hague, 1727, II, 10.

[16] C. V. Wedgwood, "The Present in the Past," *Listener,* LIII (Feb. 10, 1955), 235.

The latest of these systems, Arnold Toynbee's *A Study of History*,[17] is the most inductive, at least in the beginning, but it too winds up with a pattern, in which regularity is disclosed amid the "apparent" disorder of events. Wars or tyrants or revolutions or decadence follow in ordered succession on one another or upon some stated condition. One might say that just as Bias is the extreme of Interest, so System is the extreme of Pattern.

What validates any pattern, as we saw, is that it permits *a* meaning to be attached to a group of otherwise dumb, disconnected facts. What prompts the systematic historian is the desire to find *the* meaning of *all* the facts—the meaning of History. He starts from the assumption that nothing in the chaos of events known to have happened on earth for the last 10,000 years can be pointless. His faith is strong that somewhere and at some time the good and evil, the successes and failures, the pluses and minuses, must produce a kind of total that, when read off, will have significance to all men. In other words, universal history to him is not what it seems to us: a vast network of incomplete stories, upon which patterns slightly clearer than life's confusion are imposed for convenience only; rather it is *one* story, with a beginning, a middle, and an end.

When an absolute system is believed to be discoverable, the believer offers a demonstration: he shows that despite surface differences, there is unity underneath. He is then forced to explain how the governing force "underneath" produces the welter above, and he is thus brought to the view that some one powerful force, acting by necessity, has woven the great web of History. Systematic historians, in short, are committed to the doctrine of the Single Cause.

In Christendom from St. Augustine in the fifth century to Bossuet in the seventeenth, the Single Cause is God, and His law is reflected in Christian ethics. In the *New Science* of Vico, published in the early eighteenth century, the universal law is the cyclical development of the human mind through the divine, heroic, and purely human stages. (The division of history into three stages is a pattern congenial to many systematists.) A century after Vico, Saint-Simon was but the first of a group of philosophers who saw in history the maturing of mankind. He

[17] 12 vols., London, 1934–61.

traced this evolution from childhood (Egyptian civilization) through youth (the Greek and Roman world) to maturity (the medieval and modern.).

Soon after the death of Saint-Simon and the first theorizings of his part-disciple Comte[18] appeared Hegel's *Philosophy of History* (1831), which justly deserves its commanding place among modern systems. Hegel's powerful mind saw the chief defect of previous systems and tried to remedy it. That defect lay in the fact that History does not ever tend all one way. As a philosopher Hegel wanted to reduce the chaos to simple principles, but he was enough of an historian to recognize the helter-skelter of life. History is a perpetual, incoherent struggle, a mess. Yet systems interpret it to mean "fundamentally" one thing; the mess becomes a pageant.

To do this, the Christian systematists had had to say that history was a moral tale: when right triumphed it was Providence rewarding the good; when disaster befell it was again Providence punishing the wicked; when seeming injustice prevailed it was a trial of the worthy that would be made up to them hereafter. But until Hegel the philosophers of history who kept on the earthly plane had no means of fitting conflict into their systems. He solved the difficulty by pointing to the "dialectical process" at work in history.

Dialectic means dialoguelike, and Hegel applies this image to the bloody frays of History because conflicts to him are always conflicts of ideas. The Reformation is the struggle of the idea of a universal church with the idea of religious individualism. The men who fight one another in armies, or the men who fight one another in books, are alike manifestations, embodiments of an idea. The new idea is the antithesis of the old (or "thesis"), and fierce passions pit one against the other. But no antithesis triumphs completely and no old thesis survives completely. What happens at length is a mingling, sealed in blood, known as the synthesis. It contains survivals of both thesis and antithesis while differing from either. In History, Hegel rightly observed, no individual or group ever accomplishes what it aims at. The product of their effort, which is History, is therefore the realization

---

[18] For the relation of Saint-Simon and Comte to the doctrine of biological evolution, see Chapter 10, pp. 224–27.

of something other than their desires. It is, says Hegel, the realization of Spirit (*Geist*), which is free, unpredicted and unpredictable, but also invisible until men reveal it through their combined and conflicting acts. The Spirit or Idea of a period is shown when the period is over; or to put it differently, mankind makes its History partly consciously, partly unconsciously, and in so doing it develops the potentialities of Universal Reason or *Geist*.

This takes care of the visible chaos in History and it makes the single cause (*Geist*) indefinite enough to allow men's passions a role in "realizing" (that is, making real) the unseen Spirit. To bring down this high abstraction to the plane of historical experience, Hegel makes room for what he calls the World-Historical character—the great man who, like Alexander, Caesar, Luther, or Napoleon, seems superhuman in his ability to move masses of men toward a new goal. In Hegel's scheme, such men are explained as being so exactly in tune with men's brooding wills, and with the step that Spirit is about to take, that the single man's natural endowments are magnified to the size we behold.

Despite its rigidity, Hegel's system thus leaves scope for men at large and for great men in particular. After him, the great-man theory of history could be defended against the fatalists. They held that the course of History was absolutely determined, either because men had no free will or because mass movements were the real "forces" in History, and these were so mighty that any man's thought or effort had the weight of a feather in comparison. Carlyle disputed the fatalists in theory and by example. He wrote an unforgettable history of the French Revolution, which showed individuals making History; and he rehabilitated Cromwell and attempted a glorification of Frederick the Great, all the while deploring the absence of such great men in contemporary England:

> This ... is an age that as it were denies the existence of great men, denies the desirableness of great men. Show our critics a great man, a Luther for example, they begin to what they call "account" for him ... and bring him out to be a little kind of man! He was the "creature of the Time," they say; the Time called him forth, the Time did everything, he nothing—but what we the little critic could have done too! This seems to me but melancholy work. The Time

call forth? Alas, we have known Times *call* loudly enough for their great man; but not find him when they called! He was not there ... the Time, *calling* its loudest, had to go down to confusion and wreck because he would not come when called.[19]

The great-man theory need not, of course, imply that great men do all the work; it implies that their presence and their individual characters make a tangible difference. And not only do great men have this power, but so do men of small or middling stature when occupying the seat of authority. It can further be shown that such a view is not incompatible with a systematic determinism derived from the assumptions of physical science.[20]

The continuing argument whether men or "forces" are the ultimate cause of events is itself affected by changing circumstances and what they inspire in the minds of the living. The impact of the factory system, the doubling of the population, and the increase in material production and human misery worked upon the minds of Friedrich Engels and Karl Marx in such a way that they combined the system of Hegel and the social and economic criticism of Saint-Simon and others with their sense of present realities into a new theory of History that, they were confident, solved the great riddle of "what makes History go."

According to Marx, Hegel was standing on his head when he supposed that the war in society was one of ideas. He should have stood on his feet and recognized that the war is for bread, hence that the fundamental cause of historical events is economic. In great changes, men have neither free will nor clear consciousness of the outcome. They are determined to the performance of their social roles by the existing form of the means of production. Their relation to these means defines the class they belong to, and the struggle between classes for the possession of economic strength is the motive power of History.

Everything else in society—laws, customs, morality, religion, art—is

[19] Thomas Carlyle, *On Heroes, Hero-Worship, and the Heroic in History* (1840), Everyman edition, 249–50.

[20] See Sidney Hook's excellent book, *The Hero in History*, New York, 1943, reprinted 1955.

a "superstructure" without force or meaning except as energized by the real cause and force below. In turning Marxist, the Hegelian dialectic stirs mankind through the class war, itself generated automatically by economic fact. Marx elaborated his system while the ideas of biological evolution were gaining ground, and his materialism parallels Charles Darwin's without being influenced by any biological considerations. Nor is Marx's system neutral, but optimistic and progressive, its prophecy serving as a premium to adherents.

It was left to another systematic historian, Count Arthur de Gobineau, to rewrite Western history as a prophecy of doom, on the biological-cultural principle that race is the prime mover and that its "law" is downward motion.[21] According to Gobineau each of the three major races—white, yellow, and black—enjoys special inherited characteristics. When any two meet and mix, their differences of custom and outlook stimulate invention, and a new civilization is born. Overdo the mixture and decadence follows.

Though race theories sprouted by the dozen during the second half of the nineteenth century and were applied in Germany and elsewhere during the twentieth, Gobineau's system was meant neither to destroy nor to humiliate nations but to enlighten them about their inevitable fate. Disillusioned about Europe after the revolutions of 1848, Gobineau thought he could see his contemporaries falling into decadence. Only a strong infusion of vigorous "white blood" could restore the balance that was first disturbed by many centuries of hybridization along the Mediterranean shores and finally upset by Europe's colonizing the world and further mingling the races.

Since Gobineau, all but a few systematists have like him been prophets of doom. The best known of them, Oswald Spengler, entitled his book *The Decline of the West.* Not many years earlier, in 1911, Sir Flinders Petrie, an Egyptologist of note, who was more historian than philosopher and therefore did not produce the slogans that appeal to a wide public, brought out his *Revolutions of Civilization,* in which he likened the symptoms of decay in our most advanced institutions to

---

[21] On the antecedents of the gloomy historians, see K. F. Helleiner, "An Essay on the Rise of Historical Pessimism in the Nineteenth Century," *Canadian Journal of Economics and Political Science,* VIII (November 1942), 514–36.

FIGURE 7 *Famous Philosophies of History*

Cyclical Progression

PLATO (388–68 B.C.)

1. Egyptian (?) fable of periodic destruction by fire
2. Tale of the lost Atlantis

LUCRETIUS (c. 55 B.C.)

Atoms form worlds and revert to atoms

VICO (1725)

Progress of nations through divine, heroic, human stages and return to primitive

VOLTAIRE (1750)

Irregular recurrences of high civilizations: four ages in 2000 years

MALTHUS (1798)

The perpetual action of want, war, and disease keeps mankind from ever "perfecting" itself as hoped by the *philosophes*

GOBINEAU (1853–55)

Race mixture brings about and then destroys civilizations

NIETZSCHE (1885–89)

Necessity working through all things without interference from (nonexistent) spirit brings about the return of all events in exact sequence forever

FLINDERS PETRIE (1911)

Civilizations rise and die from the effects of size and complexity

SPENGLER (1918–22)

Forms (morphology) determine cultural growth and breed decay, causing the death of the societies based upon them

TOYNBEE (1934–55)

The organic response of civilizations to inner or outer threats propels them until the spirit (psychological and religious) leaves them

---

Among the "cyclical historians" one can distinguish those who posit a periodic destruction followed by rebuilding; those who believe in an "organic" law of rise and fall; and those who infer "eternal recurrence" from laws of material necessity. As to this recurrence, Shakespeare wrote a trenchant quatrain in Sonnet 59:

> If there be nothing new, but that which is
> Hath been before, how are our brains beguiled
> Which, laboring for invention, bear amiss
> The second burden of a former child.

Linear Progress

The BIBLE (c. 8th century B.C.; 2nd century of our era)

1. Partial destructions but hope of messiah
2. End of the world and day of judgment

VIRGIL (c. 20 B.C.)

Golden age not in past but in future

ST. AUGUSTINE (A.D. 413–26)

Human history a part of eternal destiny of man; hence greatness and fall of Rome intelligible as moral and religious lesson

BOSSUET (1681)

The progress of revelation from the Jews to the Romans and to Western Europe demonstrates the presence of God in history

CONDORCET (1793)

The progress already made by reason through eight stages opens the prospect of a world that will be ruled entirely by knowledge, reason, and brotherly love

SAINT-SIMON (1825)

Three stages of intellectual development usher in harmony and Christian technocracy

COMTE (1830–1842)

Three stages of intellectual development usher in positivist thought, and the triumph of science and rationalist religion of humanity

HEGEL (1820–1830)

A dialectical interplay moves all history, whose three stages of freedom usher in the freedom of all under a strong but just state

SPENCER (1850)

Natural forces move all things from the simple and alike to the complex and unlike, which in human affairs means moral and mechanical progress

BUCKLE (1857)

Intellect working under freedom achieves increasing order and power

MARX (1848–1867)

The dialectical movement is rooted in matter taking the form of economic production. Successive class struggles usher in freedom and justice under anarchy

DARWIN (1871)

Natural struggle and sexual selection produce higher societies that recognize civil and moral law similar signs of decline in the ancient world. Spengler's work, written during the First World War, came out in 1918, and fifteen years later Toynbee began publishing his long survey of twenty-one civilizations. Petrie, Spengler, and Toynbee are all "cyclical historians" in the sense that they believe human groups fated to rise, flourish, and fall. But Spengler is the most rigid and abstract among them, more rigid and abstract than Hegel himself, as a sample will show:

> Because the key to the master pattern of culture is the idea of space, a deep identity unites the awakening of the soul, its birth into clear existence in the name of a culture, with the sudden realization of distance and time, the birth of its outer world through the symbol of extension; and thenceforth this symbol is and remains the prime symbol of that life, imparting to it its specific style and the historical form in which it progressively actualizes its inward possibilities.[22]

We see here the extreme of abstraction in the use of "historical" patterns. Instead of trying to master the rich confusion of facts, our systematist empties out all but a handful of them and coordinates pure patterns. This does not mean that Spengler must be denied the title of historian; it means that in his pursuit of laws and forms he could not stay close to his data. He is often illuminating, usually at the point where some well-known event first suggests to him an inference or a relation; but when he reaches the goal of his peculiar undertaking, he has left the student of history baffled that so much intelligence should fail to see how the facts overthrow the scaffolding of generalizations.

Of what use, then, are these systems? Apart from the pleasure given by the display of human ingenuity, systems have served, historically, two useful purposes. The great systems, at least, have afforded a thorough review of large periods and have led to a breaking up and recasting of old patterns. In so doing, the philosophers of history have drawn attention to the importance of neglected classes of facts. Vico's revision of ancient history influenced legal and linguistic studies, and in the nineteenth century helped establish the idea of social evolu-

---

[22] Oswald Spengler, *The Decline of the West*, New York, 1926 (authorized English translation), I, 174.

tion. Hegel's dialectic reinforced the vision that regimes and nations are small things compared to the sweep of civilization, and that the unfathomable agitation of men conceals the potency of new ideas and great movements. Marx led historians to study economic conditions in as much detail as political and military. Gobineau dwelt on the significance of culture and custom and the anthropological method. Petrie showed what phenomena were common to advanced civilizations—feminism, for example, and the urban life of the "mass man"—and helped destroy the faith in unending progress. Spengler gave sharper contour to the meaning of certain historical terms, such as "classic" and "Faustian," and drew seductive projections of certain ages, such as that of Louis XIV. And Toynbee, besides strengthening the notion of a civilization as an historical unit, has shown that the breakdown of civilizations comes not alone from external attacks but also from inner failures of nerve and brain.[23]

No philosopher has demonstrated "the laws" of history, and every one—Toynbee as much as Spengler, though differently—has violated the elementary canon of historiography by neglecting contrary evidence. They have forced facts into arbitrary classifications; given credence to the Single Cause; called into play the reductive fallacy— "this is nothing but—"; lost, in short, the imagination of the real because of an overmastering desire for the one principle that will explain the career of mankind.

To explain it by such means would of course be to explain it away. The final formula would reduce the story to its outline, the edifice to its blueprint; and with this reduction would go the implication that story and edifice would henceforth duplicate endlessly, with minor alterations not worth notice. Systems, the researcher will conclude, are of incidental use; not what they bring but only what they suggest can be converted to the legitimate uses of reporting on the past.

[23] In a closely argued thesis on the same vast subject, William H. McNeill takes issue with the Spengler-Toynbee view that cultures "fall" as the result of internal defects or failures. He offers the counterproposition that the cultures of mankind have always been interrelated and that changes in their relative strengths are owing to periodic cultural "explosions" or "disturbances" that upset the established cultural balance in the world. *The Rise of the West: A History of the Human Community*, Chicago, 1963.

9

Historians in Europe and America

Likeness in Difference

It is a commonplace that the events comprised under the head of American History are the continuation of those known as European History, an extension into the New World of the ancient European civilization. But if we use a small letter for history and mean historiography—the writing of History—we observe that the continuity in the facts is not matched by a corresponding likeness in the styles and forms of historical narrative.

The differences between American and European historians are numerous, though they need not be deemed fundamental. Rather, they mark, through emotional tendencies and habits of mind, the obvious differences in the social and cultural circumstances of the old and the new continents. History, as we saw in the last chapter, is written under the sway of interest, as well as of bias and system. This means that it is written with an eye on one's contemporaries and one's past. And almost from the beginning the American scene diverged from the European—hence the differences in historiography that we are about to discuss. They do not put the two sets of historians in antithesis each to each. Both groups continue to belong to the same civilization, to imitate and borrow from one another, and to present "anomalies" from the point of view of any rigid contrast. But lines of separation can be traced if one will admit exceptions and take comments as suggestive rather than flatly descriptive.

The utility of lending one's mind to this differentiation is most apparent in the reading of sources: the researcher should be aware of subtle signals, if only to avoid misinterpreting what Europe addresses to us in the way of historical narrative, whether professional or propagandistic. Moreover, European customs of library research are also worth glancing at by way of warning against possible disappointments.

The first striking feature of European history is that it is national in a different sense from ours. With us the meaning of "national" is primarily geographic; it is contrasted with "local," "state," or "regional." In Europe "national" calls up not so much *nation* as *nationality* —a unique set of political and cultural facts that stand over against a corresponding set in every other country. This feature of European historical thought is an outgrowth of the conditions that tended to isolate social groups during the Middle Ages and to promote differences among languages, cultures, and political states. When the western nations began to achieve unity, about the year 1500, the unifying force was the monarchy. Histories were written about the rising dynasties and their deeds. Soon the type of history known as "battle-and-king" history became the established genre. Kings appointed "historiographers" whose writings were national in that they glorified the ruling house. This was true despite the intermarriages between dynasties and despite the sovereign claims and campaigns that reached beyond the national frontiers.

At a later time, and notably after the French Revolution, the liberal or democratic peoples inherited the mantle of kings and became the object of self-worship. Nationalism became a common faith divided into many sects, equally aggressive and especially potent in the writing of history. Exceptions to these generalities are themselves signs of Europe's deep sense of national selfhood. Whenever the nation is not the organizing principle of European history, that principle is found in partisanship, and the party is represented as incarnating the "true nation." For example, the Reformation cut across national lines and scrambled frontiers, but the histories referring to the struggle take sides. They are Catholic or Calvinist or Lutheran or Socinian. In like manner, liberals and reactionaries, royalists and republicans, believers and freethinkers, racialists and socialists, form large "sects" that rewrite the national history from their point of view.

In the cosmopolitan eighteenth century, while the monarchical and diplomatic histories continued to appear, Voltaire made a great effort to enlarge what was then called "universal history." It did not embrace the universe, but it went beyond the single nation to what was deemed the whole of the civilized world, usually Christendom. Voltaire's *Essay on the Customs and Manners of Nations* was a sketch of a new type of history, cultural in substance and global in character; it freely roamed beyond the boundaries of Europe. But Voltaire was a pioneer with few imitators. His readers were used to the more familiar arrangement by nations, whose role was still concentrated in a king. Thus his *Age of Louis XIV,* though cosmopolitan in outlook, also appealed to patriotic pride and continued to make attractive the idea of a single power's predominance in Europe. That idea may be dying in our century, but we have not as yet the makings of a truly European (that is, Continental) history.

In Voltaire's day the cosmopolitan outlook held national egotism in check; a philosopher like Hume could say, with faulty historical feeling, that anyone who wanted to know the character of the French and the English had only to consult the history of the Greeks and the Romans. Yet when Hume himself undertook history-writing, his partisan feelings came out and he produced a strongly royalist history of England that remained "standard" for three quarters of a century.

However cosmopolitan, the feeling of nationhood favored the militant ideas that prepared the French Revolution of 1789. With kings dethroned after decades of ideological warfare, national spirit grew, and hence required the writing of new histories in which the people was the hero. This meant reaching back for national beginnings to late Roman times. The uniqueness of each nation was shown at every point by an endless contrast with the neighboring nations, the "traditional enemy" or the "nefarious foreign influence."

The materials for this expanding historiography were abundant and accessible. Already in the eighteenth century the members of certain monastic orders had begun to make great collections of medieval documents with a view to showing the civilizing role of the Church. These efforts, notably those of the French Benedictines at St. Maur, were scholarship of the finest sort, a model of technique and industry. In the next century the search for documents spread from the cloister to the public place and began to serve not one but all the conceivable interests of that polemical age. As was said in Chapter 3, since the nineteenth century, history explains everything and argues or proves everything.

The first large-scale collections of national documents were begun in the 1820's at the instigation of the national governments. Every European state vied with the rest in building up and publishing what we now take for granted as national archives. England began to bring out its "Rolls Series" and "Calendars of State Papers." Germany undertook a vast issue of *Monumenta Germaniae Historica*. The French *Société d'Histoire de France,* animated by the young politician and historian Guizot, brought out dozens of volumes of hitherto hidden sources. Old châteaux were ransacked, government bureaus became research centers, and private papers emerged from cellars and attics to be classified and published with zealous care. Universities everywhere started or multiplied courses in history, with the national interest strongly in mind. This often took the form of demonstrating the antiquity and continuity of the national culture. And English literature, which had formerly been thought to begin with Chaucer in the fourteenth century, now began with *Beowulf* in the eighth. Angles, Saxons, Danes, and Jutes became the historic fathers of modern England. By the same reasoning the British parliament was believed to descend from the Anglo-Saxon witenagemot. Anglo-Saxonism was born, with important racialist consequences, of which the "Celtic" reaction and renaissance was one.[1]

This nation-and-party interest manifested itself all over Europe in startling parallels and combinations. For example, Hegel's lectures on the *Philosophy of History*, which had been delivered in the late 1820's

---

[1] Another was the form and purpose of the Rhodes Scholarships established at Oxford in 1904: they were to prepare young Germans and Americans to take part with Englishmen in governing the world.

at the newly founded University of Berlin, propounded the view that all of history could be divided into three stages: the Oriental, in which one man, the despot, was free; the Classical (Greek and Roman), in which some were free; and the Germanic (Late Medieval and Modern), in which all were free. Hegel saw the developing state as the guarantor of this universal freedom, and since he called the modern period Germanic, he has been taken for an apostle of Prussian domination. This is a misunderstanding of his revolutionary and liberal intentions—intentions that made him suspect to the Prussian government and incurred censorship for his last writings.

About the same time Guizot, whom no one can accuse of having supported Prussian hegemony, was using much the same language to explain the *History of Civilization in Europe* (1828–32). Guizot saw three shaping influences: the Roman Empire and its rigid hierarchical tendency; Christianity and its moral influence; and the Germanic ideas brought into the Roman Empire by the barbarians. It was they who had injected the idea of freedom into the legal and moral system built up by the other two institutions. When the scholarly Leopold Ranke published his *History of the Latin and Teutonic Nations* (1824), or when the journalist Armand Carrel published a hasty account of the Glorious English Revolution of 1688 just before Paris rose up against the Bourbons in 1830, the recurrent "interests" of European historians were being shown and exploited. No American reader of European history can afford to be unaware of these permanent concerns, which begin as motives for research and often end as bias, "revisionism," or great system.

Since this book cannot retrace in detail the work of the European historians in the great age of history-writing that followed the French Revolution, it may be convenient to indicate here the broad tendencies of their thought.

1. There is first the purely *national*, which ranges all the way from the cultural nationalism of a writer like Michelet to the state imposition of crudely patriotic textbooks such as the one that used to make the boys and girls of the former French Equatorial Africa speak of "our ancestors the Gauls." Moreover, the old idea of conquering all Europe lives on, even when it is only an organizing principle for the mass of facts. In recent times the large cooperative

histories of Europe produced in France have continued to cut up that history into periods of national predominance—Spain's, France's, England's, and so on.

As a subclass under the national "form" must be listed all the histories written on behalf of would-be nations seeking independence from foreign oppressors—Italy and Germany before unification; the Balkan and Baltic states in endless profusion and confusion. We have witnessed in our day a new wave of this national "irredentism" in many parts of the globe, notably in Africa and Asia — a product of many forces, among which must be counted a partisan knowledge of history. As soon as literacy spreads in those regions we may expect to see a rash of national histories of varying quality. These will be another legacy of Western culture as potent as machinery.

2. A second series of alignments follows the issues bequeathed to the nineteenth century by the French Revolution. The numerous parties are reducible to two pairs of contending groups, the one political, the other religious. The egalitarian liberals combat all forms of aristocratic or monarchical rule; or in political jargon, they constitute the Left, battling the Right. Often allied with the liberals are the anticlerical secular forces that fight the established church, Catholic or other. In England these parties bear slightly different names: Whig or Liberal *versus* Tory or Conservative, and Dissenters or Nonconformists *versus* the Church of England. In general, the Left is freethinking, republican, and egalitarian; the Right is clerical, monarchical, and in favor of the class system.

3. Since political ideas cross frontiers and split nations, European historians have often felt a need to substitute for the national unit a new homogeneous bloc of peoples supposedly sharing some great idea. The notion of the Protestant North and the Catholic South has been tried. It is a poor fit, but it is lent passing plausibility by the doctrine mentioned earlier, of Roman domination breached by Germanic freedom. The marked Anglo-Saxon "bias" of English historians before 1914 was not limited to so-called Anglo-Saxon countries. Throughout the Continent one can find "Romanists" and "Germanists," with a few "Celticists" thrown in for good measure.

4. The fourth and last dividing idea whose influence may be detected in certain European historians dates from the middle of the last century and generates two familiar types of history-writing. One is the racialist interpretation of history; the other is the Marxist. Both are materialist in principle, but the one finds the "single cause" of history in biological fact; the other in economic. The first is

particularly "reductive" in histories of the arts and thought generally; the second is particularly insidious in histories of social life and in the interpretation of great political events such as the French Revolution or America's entry into the First World War.

Peculiarities and Research Problems

So much for the fundamental features of European history-writing. Certain surface characteristics also deserve notice. European History is plentifully supplied with great figures, and of these a large number are villains. Baldly stated, this generality seems either obvious or unimportant, or both; but a moment's thought will show that its truth helps explain the form and tone of written history and confirms the antagonisms we have been describing. Great figures are more frequent in European History than in American, because the European cultural tradition is mainly a feudal, monarchical, and aristocratic tradition. As such it has provided a well-lit stage for individual action, putting a premium on boldness, violence, and risk, which often end in tragedy. A democratic society, and even more one that is also a *business* society, seldom provides such a stage for heroes; the leader is, or tries to look as if he were, part of a team. Being highly organized, moreover, trade and industry give less opportunity for the public display of strength, talent, or ruthlessness. A "respectable" democratic nation would not let King Edward VIII marry a divorced woman, whereas his predecessor Henry VIII married six wives, divorced two, and variously disposed of all but the last.

Many European villains may thus be said to have been encouraged by political and social conditions, including small populations, the acceptance of economic scarcity, and the precariousness of human life. But there are also in European history villains-by-definition, that is, figures that are permanently villains to one party and heroes to another. Cromwell, for example, who was execrated by all but a few Englishmen until his rehabilitation in the 1840's, is no hero to the Irish, nor to the influential body of English Jacobites and Catholics. Similarly, Luther cannot be expected to be a hero to the Papacy and its millions of faithful. Bismarck is suspect to German liberals and a villain to

French patriots; Karl Marx is the great prophet or the great enemy to opposing groups in Italy, Germany, France, Belgium, Holland, and Sweden, while in the Soviet Union he is the supreme prophet.

In keeping with partisanship and prophecy, European historians tend to make their writings the vehicle of something more than mere opinions. They propound theses and formulate systems. These are favored by their upbringing and that of their audience. Both writer and reader are products of a highly selective school system. Within each nation, education is remarkably uniform, so that the writer can expect from his readers a common preparation as well as a certain skill in following, detecting, and resisting ideology. The members of the history-reading public not only have an intellectual position of their own, but they want one from the writer. No doubt he must be a "good" German or Austrian or Italian, but he must also belong to an identifiable party or school of thought.

As against this, American history appears almost unintellectual. It is full of views, to be sure, but these follow no traditional patterns to which names could be given. Rather, the public love of Americana is scenic or regional, narrowly geographical or antiquarian. The nearest thing to a great divide has been the antagonism of North and South, but this was never ideological. Next in intensity is the feeling of rivalry existing between East and West, the crowded Atlantic coast and the great open spaces. But this is on the whole a tolerant feeling, which has cost no academic historian his post and no popular one his laurels.

In Europe, the "positions" are much more closely guarded and the encounters do draw blood. The state being (at least on the Continent) dispenser of favors and director of the educational system, the opportunity to write and teach history depends sooner or later on alliance with a recognized party. Throughout the nineteenth century the Continental universities were political arenas for both students and teachers—as they are today in virtually all parts of the world. Ostracism, dismissals, and retaliation in print were common events reflected in historical writings. One has only to study the successive French histories of the French Revolution to unfold the story of a hundred-and-eighty years' war. In most of these same party-ridden countries, however, freedom of research is achieved by the operation of give-and-take. Academic historians are government employees, but their tenure is generally assured by the balance of opposite forces: when a "rightist" historian retires from a faculty, he must be replaced by one of his kind lest the equilibrium be disrupted.[2]

This autonomy has permitted historiography since about 1860 to branch out into specialties at the will of the individual. The choice is perhaps less influenced by fashion than it is in America. Diplomatic, military, intellectual, and institutional history have continued to flourish in Europe side by side with the newer genres: social, economic, artistic, and musicological. The work of the demographers and "opinion researchers" has received greater attention in European historical circles than here, where these and other numerical techniques are only now being tried out.[3]

Finally, one must point out that the materials of European history are less highly organized mechanically than those of American history. The libraries abroad are rich and great and induplicable, but their catalogues, shelving systems, delivery methods, hours of access, modes of lighting, and stores of human helpfulness are generally inferior to ours. There are fewer microfilms and fewer machines to read them by, no interlibrary loans, no "union lists" of newspapers, and no possibility, at this late date, of the standardization that so greatly facilitates research. The United States enjoys the accidental advantage of having started late and the credit of having made the most of it.

Although every researcher who has been abroad will remember notable exceptions, the tendency of European intellectuals is to be somewhat more suspicious, jealous, and reticent than their American counterparts. They see no reason to help a competitor in the race for honors, and they scent competition in almost every undertaking that is likely to succeed. Even in tight little England, for all its fair play and friendliness, one must not expect the American open-door policy. Europeans generally cherish privacy more than do Americans, and family feeling has a touch of the dynastic. Hence they will not so readily put their letters at the disposal of strangers. Anything like

---

[2] Times of trouble, of course, bring on the old bloodshed and proscriptions, as witness the fate of such historians as Salvemini under Mussolini, Bernard Faÿ and Marc Bloch under opposing regimes in France, and the mass exodus of European scholars under Hitler and Stalin.

[3] See Chapter 10, pp. 217–51.

the opening of the Ford and Rockefeller papers so soon after the death of the head of the family is very rare, if not unexampled. But this same closeness works in reverse once the researcher has been "properly introduced." Then he enjoys an unrestricted monopoly; he is trusted, with an unquestioning faith in his honor and discretion.[4]

All this is but to say in different words that European intellectual society is more individualistic than ours in tone and temper; and this in turn reminds us of its origins, which are mainly feudal and monarchical, with but a recent addition of industrial democracy to modify those powerful traditions.

American Opposites and Counterparts

The United States, reared on a different political tradition, has written its history in a different mood and with different aims. The circumstances of America's settlement were apparent in our historiography from the beginning—the physical distance from Europe, the experimental, exploratory outlook, the uniqueness of the enterprise in modern times. The influence of these facts has continued to play upon American writing and has marked it off from Europe's. It may be for the same reasons that until recently our history has been of interest chiefly to ourselves. Already in the seventeenth century, the Puritan divine Cotton Mather recognized this when he wrote: "If a war between us and a handful of Indians do appear no more than a Batrachomyomachie [the mock epic of the war between frogs and mice] to the world abroad, yet unto us at home it hath been considerable enough to make a history."[5]

Many of the early colonial histories were little more than chronicles; for instance, John Smith's *A True Relation*, which was a brief account of the settlement of Virginia; or *Mourt's Relation* by William

---

[4] Regarding access to the official records of the countries of Europe—and of the rest of the world—the rules vary widely and one should try to learn them in advance of one's research trip. A good source of information is the mimeographed publication "Public Availability of Diplomatic Archives" of the Historical Office of the Department of State (May 1968).

[5] *Magnalia Christi Americana*, Hartford, 1853, II, 581.

Bradford and Edward Winslow, which was a description of the Plymouth Plantation. The first self-consciously and artistically prepared history in America was William Bradford's *History of Plimoth Plantation*, which this distinguished colonial governor wrote between 1630 and 1650. We can infer something about earlier tastes in American history when we learn that Bradford's work, although used by scholars in manuscript form for over two centuries, was not published in full until 1856. Until the Revolution, Americans, when they had time to read history, read Europe's. In addition to church histories, they read Gibbon, Voltaire, Rollin, Hume, and Robertson. Of the secular historians Voltaire enjoyed wide popularity and exercised marked influence on readers and writers in America.[6] He was an intellectual force well before the Americans began to awaken to a sense of nationhood. European events and cosmopolitan ideas conspired to enlarge the Americans' historical panorama; they could "universalize" history by transcending state or sectional boundaries; so that in the New World "universal" history paradoxically became national history, thus giving rise to a new meaning of nation: far from being unitary, self-centered, and defensive, the national outlook in the United States was inclusive, variegated, federal.

Besides, owing to the early diversity of the immigration, the national origins were many rather than one. "The past" was not altogether plain, not being a common past. As a result, American historians had in a sense to manufacture a unified American heritage, and before the thrilling events of the Revolutionary period they lacked the raw materials. One of the first and most learned exploiters of the nascent history was Jared Sparks, whose biographies of the Founding Fathers created some indelible portraits that the passage of time has not significantly altered. He was soon followed by George Bancroft, the

[6] Michael Kraus, *The Writing of American History*, Norman, Okla., 1953, 61. According to Joseph Towne Wheeler, if we except Le Sage's novel *Gil Blas*, Voltaire's historical works were the most-read foreign books in pre-Revolutionary Maryland. ("Books Owned by Marylanders, 1700–1776," *Maryland Historical Magazine*, XXXV [December 1940], 350.) But see also Bernard Faÿ, *The Revolutionary Spirit in France and America*, New York, 1927, 40, in which it appears that Montesquieu was the foreign writer most often reprinted in colonial newspapers.

most famous American historian of his time, whose ten-volume *History of the United States* (1834–74) was acclaimed as the best ever written from the democratic viewpoint. Bancroft, it was said, "voted for Jackson on every page"; despite and because of this partisanship, he celebrated at every turn the unique merits of his country's achievement. His fellow Americans, he said in his conclusion, were "more sincerely religious, better educated, of serener minds and of purer morals than the men of any former republic."[7] Here nationalism of the European brand is perhaps perceptible, yet it includes without distinction all the European nationalities represented on this continent. Fighting alien principles rather than hostile neighbors, American nationalism lacks the clannish and apprehensive tone of its European counterparts.

After Bancroft, the writing of American history came under the influence of the German style of scholarship that took root in the new American graduate schools of the 1880's. The great works now came out of the history seminar. Historians learned method from the followers of Ranke and, somewhat distorting the meaning of his maxim, sought to write of the past "as it really happened"; they conceived of themselves as writing "scientific history." They analyzed sources, criticized authorities, compared parallel documents, and when they had finished, they were ready to maintain that they knew what had happened in History. Inescapably, they worked on stubborn preconceptions that, though hidden from themselves and their readers, we can now readily discern. In an age of faith in political methods, for example, they accepted without question the dictum that "History is past politics,"[8] and thus neglected or made subservient all other elements in the record.

A by-product of the "scientific" method was that historians were writing for one another rather than for the large public. Like other

---

[7] In 1879 the Senate voted Bancroft the privileges of the Senate floor—the only unelected citizen to whom this honor has ever been accorded. When he died in 1891 the flag was flown at half-mast in Washington and in all cities through which his remains passed on the way to their resting place in Massachusetts. His funeral was attended by the President, Vice President, and Chief Justice.

[8] Edward A. Freeman, *The Methods of Historical Study*, London, 1886, 44.

masters of a special field and its literature, the historian became a "professional." He rarely aimed at broad cultural attainments like some of his European counterparts, but rather took pride in his devotion to a narrow segment of History. He was working to produce a treatment of it that should be definitive. Although he had isolated himself from contact with the American people about whom he wrote, the "scientific historian" had not been able to escape, as he believed he had, the strait jacket of contemporary culture. He was as much a product of the age as were his predecessors, though far less popular and influential.

Though more recent than Europe's, the traditions that have shaped the writing of our history have been as tenacious. The physical distance of America from Europe has given us an exaggerated sense of our isolation from Old World history. Our faith that here all immigrants could make a new start in life, could indeed remake themselves, has shaped our ideal image of ourselves. Though historians no longer share Bancroft's belief that the history of the United States is the history of the wonder-working hand of God, the conviction has been replaced by such other notions as the special nature of American genius (McMaster) or the equalizing influence of the American frontier (Turner) or the compelling character of the physical setting (Webb). With a few important exceptions our history has been written whenever possible without reference to domestic events on the other side of the Atlantic. We have studied Jacksonian democracy, for example, without relating it to the contemporaneous reform movements that culminated in revolutions in Belgium and France, and in the Reform Bill of 1832 in England. Despite all that has been written about the Civil War it is never studied as an aspect of national unification that had its counterparts in Germany and Italy in the same decade. Similarly, the so-called Progressive Era is yet to be examined in the context of changes throughout the world occurring in the same decade, including the convening of the first Duma in Russia, the Young Turk movement, the Mexican Revolution, and the creation of the Republic of China.

The perennially astonishing success of the United States in political and business innovation has also left its mark on our history-writing. The successful artist or scientist or philosopher among us has usually had to wait before becoming the subject of a biography. Far more attractive have been the figures who "got elected" or "made a million."[9] Until recently it has been hard to avoid the conclusion that our national self-conceit has depended on our ability to measure success quantitatively. The writing of American history (and much of the teaching of it) still draws inspiration and design from a far more rural period than the present. Jefferson, the spokesman for agriculture, still receives more affection than Hamilton, the spokesman for industry. Urban political machines, like Tammany Hall, are denounced for their corruptness, but rarely praised for providing moderately effective "Americanization" and antipoverty programs. The "farmer's revolt" of the late nineteenth century continues to absorb an inordinate amount of scholarly time and energy. The urban man is not yet a hero and "the urban frontier" not yet as noble as Daniel Boone's.

Again, the development of technology and the economic growth of the United States are clearly intertwined. Yet historians of the United States have been slow to deal with changing technology as a force in American life. Even today young people who will live much of their lives in the twenty-first century seem confined to learning about Samuel F. B. Morse, Alexander Graham Bell, Thomas A. Edison, and the Wright brothers. And the digging of canals and the building of the transcontinental railroads continue to engross attention, rather than airline routes and broadcast networks, which have been comparably influential in recent American history.

What is also important to the researcher (and striking to the foreign student) is that no European nation affords its historians such abundant written records as does the United States.[10] The effect of this stockpile of raw data upon our historiography is incalculable.

[9] Herbert Heaton once suggested that the Industrial Revolution could be usefully reconsidered—and perhaps better understood—if written from the point of view of those who failed. The records of the New York Court of Bankruptcy, which have been preserved since the beginning of the republic, have yet to be exploited by historians. Richard B. Morris has elaborated this idea in a number of articles. See, for example, *American Historical Review*, XLII (January 1937), 268.

[10] The zeal with which the federal government protects its historical records is nowhere better illustrated than in its relentless efforts to recover possession of certain documents pertaining to the Lewis and Clark expedition. See Calvin Tompkins, "Annals of Law: The Lewis and Clark Case," *New Yorker*, XLII (Oct. 29, 1966), 105–48.

Almost everything the American historian might choose to deal with is capable of lavish documentation. In the rare instances when the necessary proofs are missing we know precisely when they were destroyed: in the Chicago fire or the Battle of Atlanta or the San Francisco earthquake. With our love of record-keeping—doubtless a mark of our business society—the origin of almost everything is known or easily discoverable. We may dispute about the source of the nickname "Hoosier" or the word "okay," but there are at least rival etymologies to choose from; and no matter how small our home town, we know exactly when it was founded and why it was named as it is, who its first mayor was, and what was his business and his pedigree.

A side effect of this specificity is that encyclopedic fullness of detail has tended to absorb the energies of our historians; they hesitate to advance broad syntheses, preferring to establish masses of related facts rather than venture views of their philosophic significance. No fact seems too small to deserve recording, even in works for the general public. The editors of the supplements to the *Dictionary of American Biography* now ask contributors to provide, among other things, the cause of death and place of burial of their subjects—apparently a serious omission from previous volumes. It is theoretically possible to locate every will ever filed for probate in every county in the United States. We can instantaneously find out how many articles on Ulysses S. Grant were published in the magazines of the 1890's and lay our hands on all of them. The service records of every soldier and sailor are available to the historian—many of them stored today in the same drawers that they occupied when they were "current."

American historiography, thriving on abundance, has acquired a degree of particularization, a minute tangibleness found in no other nation's. For us there is no mystery of origin on which to build national myths, no Romulus and Remus suckled by a she-wolf and surviving to found Rome. We sing the ballad about Casey Jones, but we know when and why he died and a photograph shows us how he looked. His heroism is part of the files of the Interstate Commerce Commission. In other words, American History is entirely in the age of history. Our few folk heroes—such as Davy Crockett and Johnny Appleseed—turn out to have been distressingly real persons about whom fairly full records are extant, ready to be studied, and—if necessary—measured in cubic feet. Ambrose Bierce had to die abroad for the event to remain a mystery. For us, then, there is no major figure like Shakespeare, the details of whose life will forever be few and uncertain.

This plethora of written materials has put a tremendous burden on the American historian. He of all researchers must be indefatigable, and yet he can never feel secure against the charge of incompleteness. In a land where apparently nobody ever throws away the written word, unpublished records and private letters threaten him on every side. These in turn have inspired the writing of "histories" on every conceivable subject from municipal sewage disposal and the making of sod houses on the Great Plains to George Washington's experiments in breeding donkeys. The availability of documents and our indiscriminate interest in every part of our lives encourage the writing of books on subjects seldom treated in European history. This does not mean that much of this history-writing is not valuable; it does suggest that since the great masters—Parkman, Prescott, and Motley—historians in America have been content to rely on empirical data, leaving speculation to their less burdened brethren, the philosophers, and literary narrative to their first cousins, the novelists.

The Harvest of Facts

The documentary abundance and continuity in the United States reflects the smoothness of the stream of history it records. This introduces still another characteristic of American historiography: its even-temperedness. Unlike Europe's, our history has been remarkably ordered and placid. This is not to say that we have not been a violent people at times, but it is to say that violence has not been a central ingredient of our political life, and that we recognize as one of the controlling ideals of American history the bridling of human passion and the judicious exercise of the art of compromise.

It remains so far a fact that no vendettas have scored our history, leaving permanent divisions in their wake and "schools" of historians to keep up the fight from generation to generation. We have had no investiture struggle, no wars of religion, no political exiles and massacres, no periodic revolutions. We have therefore produced no Pretenders, no Robespierres, no Lenins and Hitlers, no saints and devils to divide the nation. The New Deal, which temporarily divided us, might have formed an exception, but it was soon absorbed and ratified by the Republicans; so that only the Civil War remains as a true exception to our historical unity. Yet the continued interest taken in it by the whole nation shows our predominant feeling: Americans are still finding it almost unbelievable that such a catastrophe could have happened to *us*. And we do not cherish the old feud: both Lincoln and Lee have been accepted as heroes by the whole nation.

This one seeming break in our common history, the Civil War, has in a hundred years taken on for our historians the characteristics of a second starting point. It is far from forgotten, and its remote effects are making us see that until now our history has concerned itself exclusively with white men.[11] Recent events confirm the national feeling that Reconstruction is After the Flood. New issues, interests, and ideals are dated from this point, which virtually marks a rededication to a unified destiny. The war also allows us to see ourselves as the "before" and "after" of the advertisements, and it has thereby simplified our understanding of the past. We tend to think of the earlier time as wholly different, indeed, as almost disconnected from the industrial and democratic present, which we date from 1865.

Finally, the Civil War is the only war we have fought that is exclusively "ours," the only one that has not been a "foreign" war. Its uniqueness, its threat to our great political experiment, its magnitude and the scars it has left—all have combined to make the Civil War a profound experience. Our emotional links to the war are semireligious and out of that struggle emerged some of our most revered and tragic heroes. It would therefore go against the grain to deny the "twice-born" feeling so widely shared and to deny that the coming of industrialization, or even modern internationalism, or the rise of the modern city began in the era of the great struggle.

Well before the Civil War, our historians felt the need to create a continental outlook that they called national. They wrote from an

[11] See, however, the three volumes of essays and documents, *The Negro in American History,* Chicago, 1969. Nothing comparable is as yet available for the American Indians' contribution to our national life.

American point of view that until recently was very much their own artificial handiwork. The reasons for this are not far to seek. The histories that nineteenth-century Americans read were by and large written by New Englanders, and New England had greater economic need of a well-knit nation than any other section. In their histories New Englanders projected their local interest. Daniel Webster, their greatest spokesman, provided the political rhetoric for the special American nationalism that was adopted by the whole country. Uncle Sam himself came to look like a New Englander, his rolled-up sleeves suggesting his habits of hard work just as his facial expression suggests his Calvinist origins. The word "Yankee," which was once used to refer only to the settlers of Connecticut, was enlarged to include all New Englanders; gradually it was made to mean any Northerner, and today it is used everywhere (the South excepted) to refer to every American. The writing of American history, which owes so much to the New England historians, continues even in the present to suggest a misleading idea of the homogeneity of the United States.

It may well be that the tendency to extrapolate from sectional history is in itself a characteristic of American historiography. We naturally think of groups rather than individuals, of collective action rather than single-handed accomplishment. Once the New England outlook had been writ large as "American," it was not challenged until near the end of the nineteenth century, when Frederick Jackson Turner espoused a frontier hypothesis which asserted that a steadily westward-moving line of settlements had left an indelible impress on the American nation, and especially on the growth of American democratic institutions. Critics soon saw that Turner was wresting our history-writing from New England and resettling it in his native region, the upper Mississippi Valley. From the history of that section he was now building an image for the entire country.

In similar fashion, American historians have tended to study the unique and then to make the findings representative of social groups. From the lives of unusual women like Susan B. Anthony or Elizabeth Cady Stanton we are prone to derive our conception of how the nineteenth-century woman lived in America. From a few plantations big enough and efficient enough to have kept careful business records still extant we are apt to form our idea of slavery in the ante-bellum South. From a few literate and articulate frontiersmen we have drawn our pictures of frontier life. This is a natural temptation to thinking minds anywhere. What is paradoxical in our case is that we have fallen into these errors by reason of the strong persuasive power of the written record. This does not mean that our original studies of uncommon subjects have not been reliable history; it only means that a generous "democratizing" of the uncommon is as likely to distort as bad research. Thus we have written on Andrew Carnegie, the immigrant lad who made good, and have drawn inferences about economic opportunities for all immigrants. We study Buchanan's weakness as Chief Executive and dogmatize about the requirements for successful presidents; we examine Woodrow Wilson's mistakes as a peacemaker and apply the "lesson" to terminating the Second World War.

The large amount of fundamental agreement in American life has given our historiography another important characteristic: artificial debate. The Federalists, for example, have been set so starkly against the anti-Federalists that it shocks our dramatic sense to have Burr rather than, say, Jefferson fight a duel with Hamilton. The Signers of the Declaration of Independence are contrasted with the Framers of the Constitution, as if they were two different breeds of men. In fact, the Declaration Signers who survived to 1787 were ardent supporters of the Constitution and almost to a man became Federalists. In the same search for lines of demarcation historians have made much of the struggles over the tariff, of the debate between "sound money" men and the silver party, of the conflict between the New Freedom and the New Nationalism.

A further feature of American historiography that tends to dwarf its issues, and thus inspires the desire to make them artificially prominent, is the great size of the canvas. This is in part the result of the quantity of materials. But more than that, it is the scale deliberately adopted by the historians. They deal with successive presidential administrations as if they were of nearly equal importance. The meaning of this becomes clear when we reflect on what our school histories will be like two centuries hence, when the list of presidents approaches in number the present size of the list of popes. To the layman, the two great popes Gregory—the one of the chant and the other of the calendar—have merged into a single misty figure although they lived a thousand years apart; and ten others are unremembered. Will the two Roosevelts similarly merge into one for the greater comfort of schoolboys? We may hope not. But the prospect of seventy-five presidential administrations to learn is equally dismaying.

For the immediate future the likelihood is that our history will continue to be perforated along the dotted lines of our presidential administrations. In Europe, the state itself is the repository of national prestige, and premiers are only passing figures in its history. In America, the presidency is the center of honor and attention and its temporary occupant is assured a permanent place in our pantheon. Consequently, even though every president is vilified by the opposition press and party, he is glorified in our history-writing when his service is over. No president has become a permanent villain in our books—even our bad books. This is a comforting thought, of course. But the unanimous emphasis on the purity of the presidency symbolizes the esteem in which the office is held, rather than the penetration of our political judgments; it explains the role of the presidency in our writing and thinking about American history, rather than justifies this mode of organizing the facts.

No less than in Europe, then, the history written in America reflects the culture that produces it. Our historians have chosen subjects that, like our party system and our social life, leave small room for ideas. For good or ill, American historiography has generated but few strong theses. The works of Turner, Charles A. Beard, Vernon L. Parrington, and Richard Hofstadter are the chief exceptions that come to mind. Perhaps the avidity with which they were seized upon by their contemporaries testifies to a great hunger that it is a mistake to leave unsatisfied. But the subjects that historians choose are a cause as well as an offshoot of the culture in which they work. In any case, it is as impossible for the historian as for anybody else to decide: "I will now have a great idea." Even the modest Ph.D. candidate who thinks of himself as digging a small unregarded well of truth finds out that background, inclination, and training make him do with his materials what broader assumptions than his own have determined. A lifetime of effort is not too great a price for the courageous and intelligent to pay if they mean to change a single facet of the national consciousness.

In any case, history to be influential must be read. It will be read only when both its contents and its form persuade the public that it is correct and apposite. And this, after all, means the perpetually open door for new departures.

10

The Sister Disciplines

Clio's Offspring, the Ologies

We discussed toward the end of the last chapter the temptation of generalizing from a striking instance, however deeply studied, and earlier we spoke of the goal of many nineteenth-century historians, which was to go beyond single instances and make their work a branch of science. Ever since that time the question has remained open whether Man and his activities can become the subject matter of an exact science. We know that Man and his works have long since formed the subject matter of history; and if "science" is taken to mean "knowledge," as it was until a century or two ago, then there is a science of Man and its name is history. But if the word "science" is used with the model and method of the physical sciences in mind, then we should expect from the science of Man such features as measurement, experiment, classification, and the enunciation of "laws," which together permit prediction.

In our century several important bodies of knowledge dealing with man and society have been restudied and recast in numerical forms, in an effort to arrive at laws and at prediction. These aspects of the general subject Man have taken the name of social sciences. Anthropology, Economics, and Sociology are usually referred to under that name. Other disciplines, such as Psychology, Psychiatry, and Linguistics, are equally often thought of by their practitioners as pure sciences, though their subject matter undoubtedly falls within the social sphere. The study of government was called Political Science long before the general scramble to appropriate the tag of science, and nowadays it usually elects to join the other social sciences. To group together all these sciences having to do with man in society, the term "behavioral sciences" has latterly been coined. Its use sometimes suggests a desperate conviction that man does *not* behave and should be made to with the help of science. Governments, foundations, corporations pin their hopes and their dollars to sanguine investigations along this path.

By the side of this cluster of would-be predictive and manipulative social sciences are three other descriptives ones—Paleontology (the study of fossil relics), which is linked on one side with geology and physics, and on the other with botany and zoology, and which includes the prehistory of man; Demography, which studies the composition and movements of populations; and Archeology (the study of ancient artifacts), which is an extension of history.

All these vast collections of facts, principles, and conclusions have mingled with one another and with the stream of common knowledge, so that the historical researcher, as well as the ordinary man of affairs, repeatedly encounters their elements in his work. The historian, with pardonable pride, calls these subjects "sister disciplines." They are in fact *daughter* disciplines, for they arose, each of them, out of historical investigation, having long formed part of avowed historical writing. For example, Herodotus was a comprehensive researcher in whose historical narrative one finds elements of anthropology, archeology, biology, sociology, economics, political science, psychology, and linguistics.[1]

To be sure, these elements are found in him like veins in ore; they did not become distinct entities until they had been extracted and refined. But the story of this double process only confirms the parentage of the relatively new social sciences. And since the modern

---

[1] See, for example, the study of "Herodotus on Biology," by L. P. Coonen, *Scientific Monthly*, LXXVI (February 1953), 63–70.

researcher is likely to cross and recross their boundary lines, a sketch of their origins may help to make him feel, as he should, that far from being forbidden territory they are part of his boundless preserve. Their results are so many ancillas—handmaidens—at his service. The changed form and language of their findings cannot obliterate the fact that every one of their reports is or implies a piece of history and therefore belongs to history at large.

The rise of the social sciences as distinct ologies follows, parallels, or imitates that of the mathematical and natural sciences. The movement may for convenience be divided into three periods. The first is that of the intellectual revolution that swept over Europe after the work of Galileo, Descartes, and Newton had been assimilated—from 1725 to the end of the century. This was the age that sought to apply the mathematical physicist's exact and deductive methods to man and society. The endeavor bred a belief in the possibility of finding a few simple laws governing the actions of men as they governed the movements of the heavenly bodies. The connecting link was Matter, of which man was made and which held the clue to phenomena. From this assumption the social sciences, like the physical, have not departed, even though Matter has been variously redefined.

Among the earliest fruits of the material and mechanical assumption was the system of psychology called "associationist." Founded by Hobbes and developed by Locke and others, it explained the differences among men by each man's different environment and experience: his ideas had come to him more or less haphazard from outside and were thus associated differently from his neighbor's. This "law" inspired theories of education that are still with us: control the child's environment and you shape his mind. Similar principles were extended from the individual to the group by the French lawyer and historian Montesquieu, who thus accounted for the constitution of states. In *The Spirit of Laws* (1748) he ascribes to climate and other physical conditions the constitution and laws of the great peoples from the ancient Greeks to contemporary England and France. He also discusses the "behavioral" aspect of laws by showing which motives are called forth by the three kinds of government—monarchy, republic, and despotism. His famous work, full of "sociology" as well as of political science, could also be called a first attempt at an anthropology of Western man.

By the end of the eighteenth century, the zeal for the systematic collecting and comparing of physical facts had gone so far that "anthropological" studies like Montesquieu's were beyond the power of one man. The broad subject of man in society was breaking up under the weight of new knowledge, and especially in the biological sciences the "research team" was becoming usual. Enlightened governments sent explorers all over the globe to bring back information about primitive tribes in remote places, while at home the effort to organize the data had led Buffon and his helpers to hazard as early as 1750 the elements of a theory of evolution embracing geological and biological phenomena.[2] Evolution is history going back to the beginning of things and explaining every stage of being through the operation of constant forces still active in the present. Taken up by Lamarck and Erasmus Darwin at the turn of the eighteenth century, the Theory of Development (as it was then called) implicitly denied that man was a special creation of the Deity's, and by this denial delivered him to whatever social sciences might arise: he was henceforth an object of study like any other natural phenomenon.

Although in this first period the main effort was to collect and classify, by 1790 enough materials had been gathered by physicians and explorers to encourage the hope of generalization and permit the founding of a separate science of man under the name of Anthropology. In that year, the German J. F. Blumenbach began publishing his anthropological "decades," while scientific amateurs and professionals throughout Europe were inspired to write monographs about the Hottentot Venus or to measure and tell "Of Six Tall Grenadiers."[3] Physicians were frequently research scientists and philosophers as well, and a group of such men, known in France as Idéologues, ventured for the first time into abnormal psychology. Perhaps the best symbol of the eighteenth-century effort in science is the fact that when Bonaparte went out to conquer Egypt in 1798, he took with his army more than a hundred men of science for the sake of research in new fields, especially the study of ancient cultures.

[2] See *Evolution Old and New* by Samuel Butler (first published 1879) for an account, with long extracts, of the rise of evolutionary thought in modern Europe.
[3] By Dr. Charles White in his *Account of the Regular Gradation in Man and in Different Animals and Vegetables*, Manchester, 1799.

For Archeology is also a daughter of the eighteenth century and its passion for antiquity. The rediscovery before 1740 of the cities of Pompeii and Herculaneum, buried in A.D. 79 by the eruption of Vesuvius, was the start of a new science. The English Society of Dilettanti (1732) issued to its members a manual enjoining the practice of measurement and the duty of accurately reporting finds. Thus ultimately was organized the mass of coins, fragments, inscriptions, and ruins that had formerly been but curiosities for the connoisseur of art. By the end of the century Winckelmann had sought further to found a worthy science on the relics and medals he had collected, and for one of which, incidentally, he was murdered by his servant.

In the next century the poor German grocery clerk Schliemann dreamed of the buried city of Troy as he pored over his Homer; and fired with the zeal to "verify him," he set out in the 1880's, after many trials, for Asia Minor, there to discover seven cities in place of one and to institute the archeology of that region. The Englishman Layard, whom we quoted on the first page of this book, had pushed farther east to Nineveh and Babylon; and it was left for the twentieth century to rediscover a whole pre-Greek civilization in Crete (Evans) and the remotest Egyptian antiquity (Petrie and Howard Carter).[4]

Paralleling psychology, and beginning somewhat earlier than anthropology and evolutionary thought, investigations into the economic behavior of men had by the 1700's also produced systems and "laws." As early as 1691, an English observer had launched a *Political Arithmetick*[5] and Continental writers were debating the effects of trade regulations. By 1750, the French Physiocrats, led by Quesnay (though his colleague Du Pont de Nemours, founder of the American Du Pont family, is today better known), had systematically studied the consequences of the Mercantilist system and propounded in its place a "universal" theory of economics with a view to simplifying taxation and increasing food production. Their work inspired many researchers,

---

[4] An instance of the value to historiography of quite independent archeological work is the decision taken by Salo W. Baron to rewrite the published opening volumes of his monumental *Social and Religious History of the Jews* after the discovery of lost cities in Biblical lands.

[5] By Sir William Petty (1623–87), physician, anatomist, surveyor, statistician, and precursor of the English classical economists. He labored to establish for political economy, which interested him most, a fixed unit to measure by. He hoped that this unit might be the labor of one man in one day.

whose findings enabled Adam Smith to publish in 1776 his treatise on *The Wealth of Nations*. This is an historical survey of Europe's production, price history, and commercial customs, designed to prove that economic activity, being grounded in nature, will thrive best under freedom. After this, the "laws" of economic life were not long in being formulated with exactitude and temporary "finality." Soon after Waterloo and the postwar depression, the English banker David Ricardo founded what we know as "classical" political economy by defining the "immutable" relations of Capital, Rent, Profit, and Interest, and enunciating the Iron Law of Wages.

The High Period of Mechanist Science

With the first quarter of the nineteenth century we enter the second stage of development in the social sciences. It is a period during which gains are consolidated and further subdivision is required by the accumulation of data. The evolutionary theorizing of the preceding fifty years had furnished a pattern for organizing facts: the idea of slow, steady, inevitable change by small causes. Many energetic minds made this the explanatory principle of their histories. They examined "The Origins of . . .," "The Roots of . . .," "The Development of . . .," "The Evolution of . . ." Thus the German Savigny studied the role of law in national life and its evolution with the national history, just as the Englishman Lyell studied the history or evolution of the earth. The one thereby founded modern Jurisprudence, the other modern Geology.

In that same first quarter of the nineteenth century, philology, or the study of languages, broke off from "universal grammar" and established itself as a separate discipline. For many years it deemed itself synonymous with learning, since it held sway over the classics then at the heart of liberal education. Spurred on by many discoveries (including the deciphering of Egyptian hieroglyphics by one of Bonaparte's lieutenants), philology embraced all the Indo-European languages, from Sanskrit to the modern vernaculars, and sought the laws of their development. It found at least some regularities, which it expressed in such formulas as Grimm's Law of vowel change.

Language is of course closely related to the study of cultures and of the human mind, so that philologists (and Egyptologists) found themselves flanked by other researchers who studied types, races, and peoples under the various names of Ethnology, Anthropology, Ideology, and Phrenology. This last ology later acquired a bad name as a fraudulent science, but in its day it attracted the attention of reputable anatomists, physicians, and other educated men. In supposing that bumps on the skull disclosed character, Phrenology took the materialist assumption very literally. But its system was only one step removed from that of the new physical anthropologists who were beginning to measure the "facial angle" of men in order to determine their "race" and their degree of remoteness from the apes. Until the end of the nineteenth century and a little beyond, the measurement and classification of human types through the measurement of the skull, hair, and other parts of the body continued. These findings, combined with more or less sound history and philology, produced the numerous doctrines of race that flourished in the period 1860–1914 as respectable scientific work. Tall, blond, blue-eyed, dolichocephalic (longheaded) men were Aryan, aristocratic, self-reliant, and adventurous. Short, brown-eyed brachycephalics (round heads) were a Mediterranean type of former slaves and serfs who tended toward socialism. Thus ran one of the prevailing dogmas. What Hitler picked up for his special brand of active racism was the confused dregs of this notable movement of ideas, which near the end of its sway was known as Anthroposociology.

For the "sociology" part of this compound we must again shuttle back to the early nineteenth century, when the consciousness of new powers led philosophic minds to review the entire course of History and the entire domain of knowledge. The German philosopher Hegel, as we saw in Chapter 8, gave an account of historical progression that explained the function of human struggles and promised increasing freedom and order as their outcome. And this formulation of a law and logic of change later inspired Karl Marx to erect a system of his own, which possessed the same chassis and motor as Hegel's under a different body of facts. He called his work science[6] and modern investigators still attribute to it a stimulant effect on the development of the modern social sciences. The continuity from Hegel through Marx

---

[6]It is still classified as such by the publishers of the Everyman edition of *Capital,* Vol. I.

to the present has been provided by the vision of society as something all of a piece, determined by its history and determining the actions of its members.

But this vision was not the exclusive property of the two German philosophers. While Hegel was giving his lectures on history and when Marx was still an infant, two French thinkers were setting forth corresponding ideas that influenced Marx and his progeny. First, Count Henri de Saint-Simon propounded a doctrine that makes us think at once of Christian socialism and technocracy. He called it the "New Christianity," and in order to give it authority, he reviewed all of Western history as a development that he regarded as having by his day attained maturity. This and other Saint-Simonian ideas permeated Europe—we saw incidentally in Chapter 5 how they engaged the mind of the young John Stuart Mill—and prepared the way for all later socialisms and sociologies.

Saint-Simon was interested in reform—in behavioral results, as we might say. But by the early 1820's his secretary, a young mathematician named Auguste Comte, had broken with the master and begun to elaborate still another philosophy of past and present. He called it Positivism and in it is found the theoretical basis of modern social thought: "There can be no scientific study of society either in its conditions or its movements, if it is separated into portions, and its divisions are studied apart." According to Comte, scientific knowledge alone is positive because it avoids all preconceived ideas and rests solely on the observation of phenomena. By applying the positive method to the whole universe, man generates a hierarchy of sciences, each based on the previous one and wider in its scope. The ladder starts with Physics, rises through Chemistry and Biology to reach the science of individual man or Psychology, which in turn is capped by the study of society or Sociology. Comte coined the name and foretold its supremacy when mathematics, the fundamental science of method, was joined to social observation: ". . . Social Science, which is the final result of our researches, gives them that systematic character in which they had hitherto been wanting, by supplying the only connecting link of which they all admit."[7] He sometimes spoke of "Social Physics"

---

[7] "General View of Positivism," in *System of Positive Polity*, Vol. I (1848), trans. by J. H. Bridges, London, 1875, 9.

and was convinced that patient, dispassionate investigation would solve the riddle of human life by permitting prediction and control. His motto was: *Voir pour prévoir.*[8]

What gave Comte and his followers so much confidence was the discovery that statistics, invented much earlier but new in use,[9] disclosed interesting regularities. It appeared, for instance, that suicides did not occur haphazardly but kept to certain numerical proportions depending on sex, age, occupation, and the like. Similarly, it was discovered after the establishment of the modern postal service that the number of letters mailed without stamp or address did not vary at random but in relation to the time of day, the total number of letters sent, and so on. A study of jury trials and convictions by the Belgian Quételet in the 1830's suggested even more complex regularities. It seemed likely that the notion of accident in individual or social behavior was simply a cloak for our ignorance of the hidden "laws."

Between Comte's beginnings and Marx's later works, the march of the Industrial Revolution had brought forth a greatly increased supply of statistics. Marx fashioned his elaborate attack on the capitalist system out of the famous "blue books" published by the British government on every phase of life, from the sanitation of factories and the accidents in coal mines to the incidence of alcoholism and infant diseases. A new image of society began to emerge from these serried ranks of figures. As researchers and thinkers used these abstractions more and more to gain a sense of the reality in which mankind

---

[8] "Insight brings Foresight."

[9] As the form of the word suggests, Statistics was at first intended to mean all those topics of interest to the statesman. It gained currency after Sir John Sinclair published his twenty-one-volume *Statistical Account of Scotland* (Edinburgh, 1791–97) and used the term because he hoped "a new word might attract more public attention." The origins of the science are usually traced to John Graunt, who in 1662 published a small book called *Natural and Political Observations.* . . . These were an attempt to interpret the London death figures of the earlier part of the century.

Vital statistics, collected and published by governments, arose from the idea that population is a source of national strength and that national prosperity would be increased by data on economic opportunities. The first reliable statistics on a large scale published in the United States were Timothy Pitkin's *Statistical View of the Commerce of the United States* (1816), in which he aimed at proving that the country was entitled to its rank as the second commercial power in the world. Today, *The Statistical Abstract of the United States* (89th ed., 1,034 pp.) is a repository of fact for workers in nearly every walk of life.

lives, the older conception of the social order as a group of individuals endowed with free will and moved by ideas, customs, and creeds, appeared less and less believable. For one thing, population was doubling rapidly and gathering in huge cities where individuality dwindled. Hence it seemed appropriate to believe in the existence of undifferentiated units who married or committed suicide or misaddressed letters, not by choice or personal quirk, but according to irresistible laws. These laws being hidden in numbers, the "quantification" of social observation must go on.

Well before Marx's work was even noticed, three exceptional English thinkers had begun to study society in this "collective" way, with or without the aid of statistics. Herbert Spencer wanted to ascertain the law of progress, and starting in 1850 he produced book after book to build up a complete theory of social evolution, which the liberal minds of Europe took as better than gospel truth, namely, as scientific philosophy. The titles of Spencer's chief works indicate the atmosphere to which his ideas contributed: *Progress: Its Law and Cause, Social Statics, The Data of Ethics.* An early follower of Lamarck's evolutionary views, Spencer was the man who, ten years before Charles Darwin's *Origin of Species,* coined the phrase "Survival of the Fittest" and made every "advanced" person a "Struggler for Life."

The second of these three English thinkers was Henry Thomas Buckle, whose *Introduction to the History of Civilization in England* (1857) was based on the premise that intellect in society—or civilization—follows laws as rigorous as those of astronomy. Buckle's history, unjustly neglected today, is a learned and impressive witness to the force of this assumption. As for the third thinker, Walter Bagehot, his contributions to evolutionary sociology, though implicit in his early work, came to public notice a decade after the appearance of Darwin's *Origin of Species* in 1859; they are therefore best understood in relation to the notable fate of that book. It was in 1869 that Bagehot published *Physics and Politics,* where Darwinian principles are used against Darwinian commonplaces. Bagehot destroyed moral pretenses and fatuous hopes of automatic progress by showing that the acts of nations and cultures parallel those of the beasts in the jungle much more closely than do the acts of men within a society. Bagehot was sometimes taken for a crude Social Darwinist, but he never said: "Here is a natural law, hands off!" On the contrary, he showed that acknowledging

unpalatable facts was prerequisite to conscious amelioration. By pointing to the difficulty, he meant to advance social and international
morality.

The close bond uniting the ideas of biological evolution, positivist
and statistical sociology, and the reforming arguments based on historical studies is evident in the great upheaval that followed the appearance
of Darwin's *Origin* in 1859. Few were competent to read or criticize
it and perhaps few read it, but all who took part in the battle of
ideas had been sufficiently saturated with evolutionary thought before
the book's appearance to grasp the fact that its success clinched the
main contentions of the scientific-positivist-sociological party: (1) Man
is an animal and, as such, a proper subject for study on materialist
principles. (2) Society, being made up of materially conditioned units
of life, obeys the general laws of nature—struggle, survival, change,
evolution. (3) All other such laws are expressible in numbers; in no
other form will social truths take their place as laws. (4) Until then,
even evolutionists perforce remain descriptive historians, for a living
being, an idea, an institution, a nation, or a species is but the residue
of its past. We must study its genesis and development pending the
discovery of the "law" of its being.

Though not a professional historian or anthropologist, Darwin
was tempted to give his own answer to one such problem of genesis—
how man came to be the social animal we now see. In *The Descent
of Man* (1871) he brought together a mass of facts derived from older
and contemporary research and sought, unsuccessfully, to fit them into
his theory of natural selection, supplemented by a new one of sexual
selection.

Meanwhile, his pervasive idea of struggle for survival was understood by the public as justifying economic competition within and
between societies, although among fellow citizens the game was limited
by a few rules. Darwin's interpreter, Huxley, deplored having the
"scientific" duty to sanction society's "natural" elimination of the
poor—his consolation was that this process improved the breed. No
one but Marx was enough of a "survivalist" to preach direct, armed
struggle for the means of life.

It is clear that, as before, sociological speculations were closely
tied to the practical problems of the age. One of the men who influenced Darwin's biological thought was the Reverend Thomas Malthus

whose *Essay on the Principle of Population* (1798), in harmony with Ricardo's "classical" economics, preached Self-Denial or Doom. Population, said Malthus, grows faster than food. Hence there must be famine. Mercifully, war, disease, and other disasters help reduce the human pressure on the food supply, though not enough to prevent the misery that we see among the poor and that we dare not relieve, for fear of increasing the demand on a forever scarce subsistence. Malthus' first version of this theory had been amplified by massive historical research in 1803, and for nearly a century no prospect but that of scarcity increasing as a result of man's own productive and reproductive powers came to cheer the Darwinian sociologists.

Their sole comfort came from another, purely intellectual source—pride in the discovery of the evolutionary secret itself, bitter as it might be. No one put this more eloquently than the American evolutionist and historian John Fiske:

To have lived when this prodigious truth was advanced, debated, established, was a rare privilege in the centuries. The inspiration of seeing the old isolated mists dissolve and reveal the convergence of all branches of knowledge is something that can hardly be known to the men of a later generation, inheritors of what this age has won.[10]

And in his own work Fiske demonstrated the "convergence" of subject matters. His own was American history and in his popular lectures upon it he did not hesitate to declare:

The government of the United States is not the result of special creation, but of evolution . . . our American history does not begin with the Declaration of Independence, or even with the settlements of Jamestown and Plymouth; but it descends in unbroken continuity from the days when stout Arminius in the forests of northern Germany successfully defied the might of imperial Rome. . . .[11]

We catch here an echo of the "Germanicism" mentioned in our discussion of the European historians,[12] but there rings also the defiant

---

[10]Quoted in Richard Hofstadter, *Social Darwinism in American Thought,* rev. ed., Boston, 1955, 13.

[11]*American Political Ideas,* New York, 1885, 6–7.

[12]See above, p. 200.

antireligious note. This period of social philosophy is indeed rightly known as that of the warfare between science and theology; but it could also be regarded as the great race between the accumulation of facts, which would yield the ultimate laws, and the relentless march of those same laws, which were to starve mankind, extinguish the sun, and reduce the universe to a perfectly still and even distribution of material particles at zero temperature.

By the third quarter of the nineteenth century, the enthusiasm of discovery had cooled too and pessimism was beginning to set in; and by the 1890's, the interested observer was witnessing, side by side: recantations of the belief in positivist and other doctrines, a profound conviction of Western decadence and global doom, and also signs of hopeful thought in new sectors of the scientific horizon.

Decline and Renaissance of the Scientific Faith

The fiercest tyranny, which was the eternal fixity of the economic "laws," had already begun to be questioned. The pioneer in this regard had been John Stuart Mill, who expressed his dissent as early as the 1849 revision of his *Principles of Political Economy*. From outside the profession, Thomas Carlyle's diatribes had disturbed the public and also inspired Friedrich Engels' *Condition of the Working Classes in England in 1844*, which directly moved Marx to turn his mind to economics. Independently, Ruskin's onslaughts on political economy appeared and nearly wrecked the magazine that printed them. Yet for another dozen years none of this opposition could stem the current of Social Darwinism and positivism.

What finally turned the tide and gave a new direction to the social sciences was a combination of weariness with the old formulas, new knowledge from beyond the seas, and new phenomena examined by a new generation on home ground. Why the purely material and mechanical interpretation of the human mind grew boring is perhaps not hard to explain: it was dull work and it only occasionally led to important results, such as those of Helmholtz on sound and other sensations. Elsewhere in the psychological laboratories, students took endless readings on the power of the eye to discriminate among shades of blue, and of the hand between unequal weights. Reaction times to stimuli yielded Weber's and Fechner's Constants and a few others, but none of these explained the "mechanism" of the mind—if any. The younger men came to think that German psychophysics was, in the words of William James, a science for a country "whose natives could not be bored."

Similarly in anthropology, the measurement of skulls and correlation of the results with race or social class or political opinion brought only disputes, together with the multiplication of skull groups until the so-called cephalic index ceased to have clear meaning. By the turn of the century more than a hundred "races of man" had been "found" by physical methods, and the last devoted investigators felt obliged to take hundreds of measurements on any one skull.[13] It would be eons before all the facts were "in."

In some branches, moreover, early gains were being lost. Some of the philological "facts," such as the radical diversity between Aryan and Semitic languages, were now exploded and the reference to an aboriginal Aryan tongue was recognized as a fiction. At the same time, explorations outside Europe produced such a welter of facts and shifted the gaze of anthropologists to cultures so different from the European, and yet so inwardly consistent, that they could no longer be regarded as examples of arrested development along a line leading to the perfected or European type. To accept them as independent entities meant throwing over the single-line evolutionary scheme on which all the sciences had consciously been built. Likenesses and differences were endlessly puzzling—was there diffusion among these centers of culture or spontaneous and independent similarity? Africa was a new-found land full of enigmas, from the gorilla to the pygmy man, both "discovered" by Du Chaillu before 1865, and both requiring a new look at old classifications.

---

[13] The best legacy of physical anthropology was scientific criminology. It began with the dubious doctrines of Lombroso about a criminal type, but became a useful science with Bertillon's system of the *portrait parlé* for the identification of criminals and the technique of fingerprinting, first developed by Sir William Herschel in India in the 1890's. In our century all the resources of physical science have been brought to bear on detection under such masters as Hans Gross and Edmond Locard.

The combined discomfort and sense of hope was widespread enough in the 1890's to produce a general revolt. In evolution proper, the pioneer work of the monk Gregor Mendel on inherited traits was recognized after a delay of thirty years, and the science of genetics was born. This coincided with a temporary return to Lamarckism under De Vries, who insisted that evolution worked by jumps (mutations) rather than small changes due to the survival of adaptive features. Darwin's defender, Weismann, gave half the battle away by asserting that although natural selection did take place, it occurred not among struggling individuals, but within them, in the germ plasm. And even Huxley recanted his cosmic evolutionism in 1893, so as to make room for a social evolutionism that should include ethics: the poor need not go to the wall for the good of the rest.

A parallel deviation in economics followed the introduction by Wicksteed, Jevons, Marshall, and others of the psychological element of choice. Their theory of "marginal utility" showed that economic man was not a virtual automaton implementing an insatiable demand; he was a conscious being who might want one watch or two watches or even possibly a third, but for whom the fourth watch on the market had much less appeal, and the fifteenth virtually none. Economics—this new word for "political economy" did not get established until the 1890's—was thereby changed back into what it had been for Adam Smith: a moral science dealing with values. Wicksteed illustrated this aspect—and also his notion of marginal utility—by asking how high a cliff a man would jump from to save his mother-in-law, and how much family prayers should be shortened to enable a guest to catch his train.

If these are economic choices, then all of human life is economics. In the daily haggling for goods, "other things being equal," it should be possible to measure each increment of marginal utility in a given supply of any desired commodity by observing what happens, and to plot the movements of any market accordingly. There was logic therefore in the supplanting of "political economy" by "economics": the new science was substituting for the large abstractions of the polity others representing the domestic psychology of buyer and seller.

The rehumanization of psychology proper was taking place in the same decades, 1870–90. In the latter year William James brought out his epoch-making *Principles of Psychology,* which both summarized and disposed of the century's physical doctrines of the mind. From the old associationism of Locke, through the windy evolutionism of Spencer, to the latest German findings about visual perception, James extracts the particles of tested truth and clears the ground for his view, unchallenged to this day, that the mind is a "stream of consciousness" (the phrase is his) acted upon by emotion, by the desire for order, by the fulfillment of purpose, by the vagaries of words, and by other tendencies that preclude analogy with a machine.

From the Nineties to the Present

If James does not mention Freud in that work but in a later one, it is because Freud had not yet published the hypothesis that was to add a whole *terra incognita* to the realm of mind—the unconscious. But Freud himself was building upon earlier researches, notably those of Charcot at the Paris hospital for mental diseases. Whether modern life was producing new kinds of aberration or whether the modern scientific attitude was discerning them more accurately, the fact remains that a number of curious phenomena, ranging from hypnosis to double personality, were now challenging the researcher. His methods could no longer be those of the physics laboratory, while his terminology, like his search for laws, must follow the devious paths suggested by the strange behavior of a logical but "unconscious self" which influences another self that is conscious but illogical, "normal" but also crippled by its experience of society.

Because Freud was trained in the severest discipline of materialist medical science, he insisted all his life that his work was scientific; and if complete candor in facing facts and great genius in devising hypotheses constitute science, then he was a scientist of the first order. But if we use the yardstick of either the experimental or the classificatory physical (tangible) sciences, his system is the least "scientific" of the now reigning doctrines.[14] What is significant for the historian of

[14] See Edna Heidbrieder, *Seven Psychologies,* New York, 1933, 376–412; and Robert S. Woodworth and Mary R. Sheehan, *Contemporary Schools of Psychology,* 3rd ed., New York, 1964.

ideas is that, despite the lack of proofs, Freud's doctrine has exerted the strongest influence of any. It has revolutionized psychiatry, permeated common speech and literature, and implanted itself in some corner of every social science, including history.

This is in part due to its proffer of a widely applicable determinism at a time when more simple-minded ones are in disrepute. But it is also due to its broadening of our conception of motives through its notion of ambivalence and displacement and through its calm acceptance of sex, hostility, and the desire for annihilation. Psychoanalysis fuses with its clinical practices too many wise thoughts, new and traditional, to be safely neglected in our personal and scientific inquiries. In the writing of biography, for example, it was this enlarged view of unconscious motives, as well as of the sexual element in mental life, that enabled G. Wilson Knight to bring together and interpret the huge, angry, and conflicting evidence about Lord Byron's marriage. But it goes without saying that the vulgar or amateurish addition of psychoanalytic jargon to historical and critical writings represents no gain. In this respect, Freud is on a par with Newton, Hegel, Nietzsche, and all other thinkers whose ideas suffer misuse.

The conviction that modern industrial life was producing for man an unexampled environment led the sociologists at the turn of the century to revise their science. Like the new psychologists, they distrusted the old simplicity. But opinion differed about the right assumptions to be made within the general ones inherited from Comte. To some, the manifestations that were so characteristic of modern life suggested that the study of large and impersonal phenomena was the only proper one for sociology; the individual hardly counted except as a sample unit: "The determining cause of a social fact should be sought among the social facts preceding it, and not among the states of the individual consciousness."[15] Thus did Émile Durkheim, one of the founders of the new genre and the teacher of many noted workers, affirm his major premise. The impression was strong that society was not simply a group of individuals but something more, *sui generis,* and with "laws" of its own. Statistics, probability, and the continuity of populations encouraged researchers to study mass phenomena. For a

[15] *The Rules of Sociological Method* (1894), Glencoe, Ill., 1950, 107.

time, the "psychology of the crowd" was a popular subject matter and the names of Tarde, Le Bon, and Trotter, among others, were in high repute.[16]

But the individual was hard to down, existing as he does, patently and disturbingly, in every "sample unit," including the observer himself. Hence the American revitalizers of the science, E. A. Ross and Lester Ward, strove for a new and humanized sociology. Franklin H. Giddings did not hesitate to declare in 1899 that "at present . . . all serious work in sociology starts from psychological data, and proceeds by a combination of psychological with statistical and historical methods."[17] From this it would appear that sociology is less a distinct "science" than a coordinator of other deliverances. Thus Max Weber, Karl Mannheim, and Friedrich Meinecke, the leaders of the German school that flourished during the first half of the present century, would be hard to classify as sociologists, social psychologists, or cultural historians.[18] Since Durkheim, the prevailing tendency has been to combine strict assumptions about method with broad receptivity to ideas. Two popular devices, the questionnaire and the interview, permit the individual's "state of consciousness" to be recorded. But the resulting "fact" is then merged with others and subjected to "control" either by comparison with other samples or by juxtaposition with evidence drawn from statistics.

The prevalence of polls is, of course, an offshoot of this new, talkative sociology, though no guaranty exists that a given poll is a serious piece of sociological inquiry. Nor is it always clear whether a poll is more important as a mirror of public opinion or as an influence upon it. What is noteworthy is that sociology, like psychoanalysis, no longer rejects alliances with its sisters (including history) but acknowledges its debts and even seeks to incur more. Thus the prime mover of quantitative sociology in the United States feels free to ask himself and his colleagues:

[16] *The Crowd* by Gustave Le Bon has been republished in paperback, with an admiring introduction by Robert K. Merton (New York, 1960).

[17] "The Psychology of Society," *Science*, N.S., IX (Jan. 6, 1899), 16.

[18] On these writers, among others, see Carlo Antonini, *From History to Sociology*, trans. by H. V. White, Detroit, 1959.

Do the sociologists need more thorough historical knowledge? Would the economist be helped by a course in the psychology of the consumer? Would the people in public law be helped by more training in public opinion research? Should the anthropologist be better informed of the theory of economic growth? How much would all departments in our Faculty profit from a good course in the logic and philosophy of the social sciences?[19]

This indication of a return to the original unity of the vast subject matter once denoted as history—and which history does not need to recapture, since it has never lost it—can be discovered also in the third science that underwent renovation at the turn of the century: Anthropology. The man who founded it anew, Franz Boas, was, like Freud, trained in materialistic science: he was a physicist. But he shared the critical attitude of the 1890's toward the previous views of man's social and individual evolution, which he thought too rigid and insufficiently supported by facts. His desire was still to derive the "laws" of culture, but he thought anthropology needed a greater spread of empirical data. Physical measurement went but a little way toward distinguishing groups; the only genuine material was that derived from observation of, and even participation in, the alien culture. From Boas' day, therefore, Culture has been the indivisible unit, and the anthropologist has been a field worker devoting years of his life to a sort of protracted sociological interview. Hence the anecdote of the youth in a remote tribe who is asked about the composition of the native family and who answers: "Father, mother, child, and anthropologist."

The impact of this new anthropology on the Western mind has been incalculable.[20] It is no exaggeration to say that the twentieth-century mind is best represented by the anthropological attitude: it suits our extreme self-consciousness, which makes each of us look on himself

[19] Paul F. Lazarsfeld, intramural communication, Columbia University, Nov. 4, 1955.
[20] And apparently on native cultures too. One of the authors of this book once asked a doctoral candidate how he knew the ritual of an Indian dance that was no longer being performed. The student replied that he had learned the details from an Indian informant; but further questioning brought out the fact that this informant was also too young to have seen the dance, to which the rejoinder was: "Oh, Boas told his father!"

and his neighbors as might an outsider, an anthropologist. Again, the contrast between our complex institutions and other, simpler ones, continues to give us a much-needed vicarious pleasure. We long to be in Samoa. Finally, the very notion of "cultures" as consistent wholes that have each its reason and rightness supports both our "scientific" assumption that true knowledge reports on reality without taking sides, and our moral assumption that we should not judge (that is, condemn) in order not to be judged in return.

A cultural historian might also say that all three of the redefined ologies of the early 1900's expressed a desire in Western man to withdraw from the consciousness of the surrounding chaos—psychology diving into the preconscious, sociology retiring to the realm of depersonalized action, and anthropology dwelling in remote and calmer communities. Even a fourth and newest science, the mythology that Frazer's *Golden Bough* made famous and fertile for literature, seems like an escape from the welter of drab modern facts to the more poetic horrors of the primitive mind.

To point this out is neither to discredit nor to belittle these social sciences. Rather, it is to draw attention to the tone of their scientific ambition; for the impulse to science, the desire for "laws," is also the desire to escape the bewilderment of disconnected and troublesome facts. Only, History remains more bewildering than Physics. The question, therefore, thrusts itself upon us whether the concerted drive of the last two hundred years toward a science of man and society (which should simplify History) has brought us any nearer to "the laws."

Writing near the end of his career, Boas admitted that "the earlier hope of the discovery of a necessary sequence of cultural states which would hold good for all mankind has been dissipated. . . . Although the doctrine of unilinear evolution can no longer be maintained, it seems possible that laws exist that determine the development of a given culture in a definite direction." But, he concluded, "nothing can be predicted in regard to the detailed style of development, the duration of the trend and the new direction that action and thought may take after its determination."[21]

[21] "Anthropology," in *Encyclopaedia of the Social Sciences*, New York, 1930, II, 110.

The effect of accepting these limitations has been to make the present value of anthropology one of moral and intellectual broadening. The common man, like the historian, has learned many new names and facts, and with them has acquired new notions of how human beings behave; he has come to appreciate the importance of myth, tradition, and folkways, and he has perhaps gained in tolerance.

The same gross effect can be credited to the work of the sociologists. They have grappled valiantly with the question: "What is a social fact?" The confidence that psychology would supply the answer vanished with its own belief in quantitatively fixed instincts—the assumption that man innately possesses a certain religious propensity, a fixed sexual drive, a given amount of gregariousness, so that a study of the results in typical individuals, when multiplied by the mass, would yield quantitative accounts of "the society." As soon as sociologists recognized that many social facts appeared to be the consequence of the collective organization rather than the basis of it, they were driven back to description, buttressed by the question-and-answer technique. "One must admit," writes a master of this art, "that a large part of what is now called sociological theory consists of *general orientation toward data, suggesting types of variables which need somehow to be taken into account, rather than clear, verifiable statements of relationships between specified variables.*"[22]

In economics, this characteristic split of personality within the social sciences—one part working toward "laws," the other part honestly acknowledging success only in "general orientation"—is of immediate practical importance. "Institutional economics," as it is called, has the task of analyzing and explaining the numerous institutions by which we gain or lose our livelihood—the production system, the wage system, the tax structure, and so on. The number of variables is huge, the statistics overwhelming, and the ingenious mathematics to coordinate facts and figures are beyond the reach of an ordinary education. Yet economic decisions are in the public's hands. The position of economic adviser to the President of the United States is accordingly prepotent in the national life. The chairman of the Council of Economic Advisers

[22] Robert K. Merton, *Social Theory and Social Structure: Toward the Codification of Theory and Research,* Glencoe, Ill., 1949, 9.

is the chief social scientist of the nation. To discharge its duties the Council relies on the two branches of the science just referred to. On the one side, the studies that seek to isolate variables by the construction of what are called "models"—hypothetical rules such as "if A rises, B falls," an example that ignores all but two entities. And on the other side, the gross method of lumping together large groups of economic variables. This method, founded by Mitchell and Keynes, has given us the notions of "national income," "price level," "employment level," and the like. It is useful but is wanting in the degree of exactitude that would permit prediction and control.

In these conditions, the most thoughtful among social scientists today take a view of their science that differs profoundly from the creed of the materialist fathers. Kenneth Boulding willingly harks back to the notion of moral sciences differing from the physical by their nature—and not merely by their subject. Speaking of economics, his own field, he declares: "For all the attempts of our positivists to dehumanize the sciences of man, a moral science it remains." And he quotes Lionel Robbins of the London School of Economics: "It is not an exaggeration to say that, at the present day, one of the main dangers to civilization arises from the inability of minds trained in the natural sciences to perceive the difference between the economic and the technical."[23]

The Parting of the Ways

The clearest sign of divergence between the historian and the unregenerate social scientist—a divergence not simply of method and results but of fundamental interest—is the attraction felt by the social scientist for "models" over actuality. Model-building having proved useful in the study of nature, it understandably appeals to those social scientists who wish to turn their studies into a quantitative science. The model in both cases is a construct, expressed in equations, that gives the observer an opportunity to note and measure actions and

---

[23] Kenneth E. Boulding, "Is Economics Necessary?" *Scientific Monthly,* LXVIII (April 1949), 240.

deviations in the field; and, with the aid of computers, to "simulate" the consequences or implications of any assumption made about fixity or change in one or more of the component parts. There are several types of models (algorithmic, heuristic, and so on) depending on the data available at the start and the results desired at the end. In certain domains of collective life, such as budgeting for a large corporation, the use of models is clearly advantageous. If the model is of the right type and intelligently constructed, the computations based upon it are like so many chances of trying this or that policy, wholly without risk, and with logical answers furnished in fourteen seconds.[24] The numerical accuracy is of course high, and the conclusions have the clarity that attaches to man's dealings when he can choose between more and less in tangible things.

It is these very qualities that attract the social scientist who wants to predict and control human affairs "in the large"; and it is these very qualities that unfit the model and its workings for the student of history. He does not want to predict or control, and he wants to understand not in the large but in the small. For him the model is always much too simple. He is not deaf to the question "What common factors or patterns recur in political revolutions?" but his interest carries him much farther than types and recurrences. He wants to know what the French revolutions of 1848 were like in detail and how February of that year differed from June. He is struck by the fact that at the first outbreak the young poet Baudelaire saw in it a chance to assassinate his hated stepfather—a revelation that no computer will ever simulate or disclose. The historian, in short, wants to mold his mind and imagination on the contour of the real and actual as closely, as minutely as possible; he finds, so to speak, his understanding of man in the geodetic survey map of the township, not in the Mercator projection of whole continents. And since such is the nature of his interest—his passion, rather—and since it conflicts with no other man's, it is futile and foolish to urge upon him methods and outlooks alien to his own and destructive of his use.

These last words may seem superfluous in a pluralistic culture

[24] See the lucid description of "Building a Corporate Financial Model," by George W. Gershefski, *Harvard Business Review*, July–August 1969, 61–72.

that enjoys and enjoins free speech. Yet the need for such warnings remains, because the desire for finalities is so strong in the human mind, and because it is freshly stimulated by every advance in likely techniques. The computer obviously suggested to more than one social scientist the possibility of combining many more facts in many more ways, thereby getting closer to the multitudinous reality of social life. Attempts have been made, for example, to predict the "socio-psychological implications of Man in Space." This means in effect the implications of a few men for three billion, and one feels a letdown on hearing that one investigator found his data in 944 space jokes, which he interpreted as signs of the mental assimilation of new facts. His fellow scientists disagreed, on the basis of different data, as to the speed and quality of this assimilation, and a sympathetic critic of the enterprise had to remind them all that their work was speculation, not prediction. "It is risky," said Dael Wolfle in *Science,* "to make quantitative predictions without firm knowledge of present status, and quantitative information about current social conditions and trends is often much more a wish than a reality."[25]

This last point is always related to the power of gauging (or foreseeing by pure imagination) the relevant variables. When some years ago the federal government used computers to find out whether it should rent or buy computers, the variable left out was the rate of obsolescence for the current machines. The computer's answer was "Buy"; the government bought; and IBM shortly announced the new "360" system, which turned the purchase just concluded into an expensive misprediction.[26]

Sisters Under the Skin

In such criticisms and failures of "social science," one need not always see its efforts as "enterprises of methodical guessing," which is the name Bertrand Russell gives to the ologies. Rather, they are

[25] CLXIV (June 6, 1969), 1121.
[26] Irwin D. J. Bross, "Dunce Caps for Giant Brains," *New York Statistician,* XX, No. 4 (March–April 1969), 2.

often repositories of truth as it is given man to know it about himself.[27] The historian can speak here with authority, for he sees the rise and development of the social sciences in parallel with the natural sciences, and he makes the simple observation that at no time have any of them possessed the last word on any insistent problem. The very meaning of progress in knowledge is that the previous generation erred in many respects; and the very nature of inquiry is that what it matters most to know *now* has not found an answer or even received proper attention. This is but another way of saying that, like the historian, the scientist, natural or social, is conditioned in both the choice of his problems and the form of his hypotheses by the whole weight of the culture in which he works. To remove him from it might serve an ideal purpose of pure knowledge, but this might well be so pure that no one could grasp it or use it.

These considerations bring us back to the position of history among these daughter disciplines, which have come home to brood after asserting for a while their youthful independence. It is clear that they still belong in part to their nurturing mother—they are historical by origin and necessity and they can never be wholly something else. In the middle of the last century, Ernest Renan, the French philologist who was enamored of science and German scholarship, predicted that in a few decades there would be no need of art, literature, ethics, and philosophy. There would only be curious histories of these anti-quated pursuits, because by that time we would *know*.

Later, the social sciences were ready to banish history on the same ground, that the "laws" would deprive mere events of any interest: we are not interested in the life story of any particular pinch of uranium in the reactor but only in the equation describing its total behavior. But this may be because the uranium atom has no voice to protest with (unless that is what it is doing when it assists at our annihilation). As far as we can now see, the need for descriptive reports on human behavior will continue, and hence history will also be in demand. Its

[27] The current compendium of knowledge derived from the social sciences is Bernard Berelson and Gary A. Steiner, *Human Behavior: An Inventory of Scientific Findings,* New York, 1964. For library research, see also Carl M. White and Associates, *Sources of Information in the Social Sciences,* Totowa, N.J., 1964.

ways, as is clear from the historian's method of attaining truth, correspond to two realities that we are not likely to get rid of in a hurry—one
is the dramatic (constructive or storytelling) habit of thought; the other
is the diversity and—as we often say—the irony of life. The interest
that human beings take in history therefore springs from some of their
least changeable tendencies. As a modern historian puts it: "Historical
inquiry has its deepest impulse in the lust for life."[28]

This is not to say that the social sciences lack the same impulse.
Their method puts them very much in the midst of life, and one of
their best side effects in recent years has been to force historians out
of the library and into the open air, where they can gain a worldly
perspective on written records. For although it used to be said that
an historian should be a man with experience of affairs of state, the
professionalizing of historiography a century ago gave an edge, if not
a monopoly, to the researcher in archives.

Arguing to the same effect, a past president of the American
Historical Association, himself a distinguished craftsman, reminded his
fellows some time ago that they ought to keep enlarging their outlook
not merely by direct experience but by familiarity with the findings
in other branches of knowledge. He instanced psychoanalysis, demography, and the study of epidemics, and he wound up by urging a
look at geophysics and the cultivation of a cosmic outlook.[29] Such
exhortations are all to the good, even when their execution turns out
difficult in practice. A good many historians, especially the younger
ones, were ready to heed the message and conquer the difficulties.
Yet after nearly ten years, a symposium entitled *History* takes the view
that the discipline it deals with has reclaimed its former independence
and that its flirtation with the behavioral sciences is over,[30] although
at least one reviewer disagreed with the judgment about independence
regained.[31]

In further rejoinder it should be said again that history can absorb

[28] W. K. Hancock, *Country and Calling*, London, 1954, 213.
[29] William L. Langer, "The Next Assignment," *American Historical Review*,
LXIII (January 1958), 283–304.
[30] John Higham, Leonard Krieger, and Felix Gilbert, *History*, Englewood
Cliffs, N.J., 1965.
[34] American Historical Association *Newsletter* III, (June 1965), 3.

all kinds of knowledge—indeed it must. What differentiates it from the sciences, social and natural, is its mode. Social science has no interest in contemplating life as such, but only in its regularities if they can be charted. On these it erects hypotheses that it hopes to prove, conscious that in so doing it distorts life far more than history permits itself to do. Scientific theory

is always simpler than reality. Even when it seems terribly complex, it is still "simpliste" as compared to the range of factors operating as conditions, as means, or as ends, in any actual concrete situation. . . . It is a great temptation to the theorist to work from a few premises. . . . It makes it easier for him to reach definite and precise answers. . . .[32]

There can be no question, then, of social science displacing history as a mode of understanding reality, any more than of history producing theory in the scientific sense. There should accordingly be no conflict between the two. History and the social sciences interpenetrate and cannot afford to ignore or condemn one another. The very forms of modern culture require study to be many-sided; our institutions are, as we say, complexes, and our interest in them is not exhausted by one set of questions. As has been said of one establishment (now in peril):

The university lends itself to analysis by the historian as a significant participant in local and national history, by the economist as a labor market, by the anthropologist as the scene of a special culture, by the psychologist as a system of anxieties and motives, by the social psychologist as a pattern of attitudes and myths, and by the sociologist as an enormously complicated system of interaction.[33]

To repeat, history and social science are true sisters because the historian must again and again rely on the results of surveys, studies, and statistics gathered by his painstaking colleagues in the ologies; and because they in turn cannot breathe or move without adopting

[32] Jacob Viner, *International Trade and Economic Development,* Glencoe, Ill., 1952, 12.
[33] Private communication.

toward their material the attitude of history, without handling it by the methods of research originally devised by historians. This second point is sometimes questioned, but consider the testimony of a sociologist studying English character. After explaining that he started by assuming Aggression to be his central theme, he says:

. . . English gentleness would seem to be a comparatively new phenomenon. I am not a qualified historian but the evidence from novelists and from contemporary travellers visiting England seems to me to show beyond question that the English people of the 17th and 18th centuries were remarkably pugnacious and violent, callous. . . .

And our "scientist" goes on for half a dozen pages impersonating the social, legal, and literary historian.

Turning next to method, the writer concludes that:

. . . the one further assumption which was important in deciding what questions to include . . . lies at the basis of the belief that character can be studied and analyzed. Put very briefly, it can be called the historical concept of character formation. . . . The way in which . . . potentialities are realized depends on what happens to the infant after birth, the order in which these experiences occur, and the emotions and values of the society in which it is reared.[34]

These assumptions are those long familiar to the historian. He too has suspected that national manners change, and as biographer he has known and shown that character formation depends on life's experiences and the order in which they come. When modern sociologists upbraid him for not using more of their data, he is entitled to reply that he does use them and did so long before the word "sociology" was coined. Herodotus and Voltaire, Montesquieu and Gibbon are crammed with social observation. Macaulay's third chapter is a masterpiece of social history, of which the Lynds' *Middletown* is the brilliant descendant a century later. Hildreth and Henry Adams in their "political" histories made excellent use of social and psychological data; Michelet's history of France is a storehouse of accurate information on every department of social and individual 'life; and Fustel de Coulanges

---

[34] Geoffrey Gorer, *Exploring English Character,* New York, 1955, 13–16, 27.

gave the pattern of institutional sociology in his work on *The Ancient City*. There are thus two possible reasons why social scientists keep urging historians to modernize their technique: one is that social scientists are too busy to read history; the other is that they do not recognize their own materials when presented in a different pattern. Theirs is abstract and, so to speak, additive; the historian's, narrative and concrete. But there is as yet no proof that one or the other is more instructive and useful to mankind. The abstract may facilitate immediate action, say in slum clearance, but concreteness may move the minds that move the bricks.

Certainly the narrative system, which does not and should not exclude the other, is not without advantages. What *picture* of the subject, one might ask, is left by the sociologist's many tables and innumerable answers to questionnaires? How do we assemble them into an image of Divorce, Poverty, English Character? A social worker concerned with a single problem can certainly make use of the knowledge, but what of the merely inquiring reader? No doubt, we are all broken in to the terminology of the social sciences; we juggle with the three averages, mean, median, and mode; we speak knowingly of bell-shaped curves as we give or receive academic grades; we take aptitude and personality tests from the cradle to the tomb, and we are game when an agent of the late Dr. Kinsey rings the doorbell to put his pertinent or impertinent questions. But it is questionable whether all that we take in as social science produces the full measure of the effect to which it is entitled.

At any rate, it seems fair to say that the works of social science that have made the strongest mark on the modern mind have been those that combined description with enumeration and imparted the results with imaginative power. David Riesman's *The Lonely Crowd* (1950) springs at once to mind as an example. But it had great predecessors in such works as Freud's *Civilization and Its Discontents* (1930), Boas' *The Mind of Primitive Man* (1911), and the Lynds' *Middletown* (1929). And there has been a stream of notable successors, including particularly Gunnar Myrdal's *American Dilemma* (1944, 1962), Freyre's *The Masters and the Slaves* (1946, 1956), and Claude Lévi-Strauss's *World on the Wane* (1961). Less renowned but equally indispensable to the historian who does not want to remain a "know-nothing" in the midst of his notes are such works as Dollard's *Caste and Class in a Southern Town* (1937); Kardiner, Linton, West, and Du Bois' *The Psychological Frontiers of Society* (1945); West's *Plainville, USA* (1945); Caplow's *The Sociology of Work* (1954); De Grazia's *Of Time, Work, and Leisure* (1962); and Staffan B. Linder's *The Harried Leisure Class* (1970).

That writers who can only be called historians are not blind to the value of results obtained by the methods of social science is shown by such works as Brinton's *The Jacobins* (1930), already mentioned, George Mowry's *The California Progressives* (1951), and David J. Rothman's *Politics and Power: The United States Senate, 1869–1901* (1966). But precisely because the historical researcher, who has always been a psychologist and sociologist, is receptive to the deliverances of the social sciences, he must not take all the "results" indiscriminately. Rather he must learn to be critical about them as he is about all other data, and to this end he must learn to recognize the special failings and characteristic fallacies that beset the sister disciplines.

Some Points for Critical Reading

The first sisterly observation to make is whether the writer has been at the pains of stating his assumptions. Not all are as open as Geoffrey Gorer, and it is best to begin by drawing out implications yourself. The most usual one in hiding is that of the mobility of the subject matter. *After Divorce*[35] is an admirably thorough survey of an interesting and recurrent situation; but this recurrence does not make it permanent. The present-day responses of United States citizens are not the same as their parents' thirty years ago or their contemporaries in Saudi Arabia. You are not, therefore, learning about "human nature" but about your next-door neighbors.[36] The very idea of human nature is an assumption of social science, and to say that it forms

[35] By William J. Goode, New York, 1956. Its sixteen pages of preliminary discussion make every needful point except that of showing the limitations of contemporary surveys.

[36] The title of Dr. Kinsey's famous book *Sexual Behavior in the Human Male* is a striking instance of a hidden—and in this case false—assumption: the book is not about human males, but about men in the United States in the mid-twentieth century.

the subject of its reports is to beg the fundamental question. There may be nothing but "human culture," a highly mutable affair.

A second cause of uncertainty is that the vocabularies of the social sciences are still individual and subject to fashions. Though the practitioners have tried hard to establish a fixed nomenclature and terminology, they have so far only succeeded in producing a number of imitations of the language of science. Here for example is a definition of language itself by a scientific linguist:

A language is a structured system of arbitrary vocal sounds and sequences of sounds which is used, or can be used, in interpersonal communication by an aggregation of human beings, and which rather exhaustively catalogs the things, events, and processes in the human environment.[37]

This matter of language is of enormous importance to all disciplines, despite the popular belief that "the facts" will somehow force their way through the thickets of expression. An authority on the use of computers, who is discussing an expectation that failed, finds the cause of failure in an element too readily ignored.

What happened here? The answer is: people are fooled by their own languages. Let me stress that the rapidly proliferating mythology of the computer rarely involves deliberate deception. The first victims of the myth are the myth-makers. . . . The myths arise from, are sustained by, and are transmitted through the elaborate double-talk of computer jargons. . . . The meanings of words are reversed. Thus

[37] John B. Carroll, *The Study of Language: A Survey of Linguistics and Related Disciplines in America*, Cambridge, Mass., 1953, 10. The reader will notice how the definition fails, both by excess and by omission, to satisfy standards of either literary or scientific exactitude: "structured system" is tautological—a system has a structure or it is no system: "sequences of sounds" is implied in "system," for if there is more than one sound there must be a sequence; "is used, or can be used," is false precision, for what is used obviously can be; "interpersonal communication by an aggregation of human beings" follows the tautological precedents: human beings are persons and communication is "inter," between or among them. "Rather exhaustively" betrays the inability to measure, and "the human environment" is either tautological (if it means all that human beings are surrounded by) or inexact (if it means the human part of the surrounding).

"data," which ordinarily refers to reports of events in the world about us, often refers in computer jargons to output generated from random numbers! [This practice] has led to total confusion between what is hoped for . . . and what actually exists.[38]

Third, the chief inadequacy of social-scientific language stems from the absence of true units in the subject matter of the science. To be sure, the linguists who have followed Leonard Bloomfield maintain that the phoneme, the single elements of sound uttered in speech, is the first genuine unit in any social science, but the inability to define this "atom" suggests that the claim may be premature.[39] What follows is that in the several sciences each worker must each time redefine what he means by a family, a divorce, a crime; and as we know from experience, the complexity of life strains these classifications, with the result that the greatest vigilance does not always keep apples and oranges from being added together.

Fourth—and this is a further consequence of the previous point— the "measurement" so often referred to is not true measurement in the physical scientist's sense, but simple counting. The history of physical science shows that one begins to measure only when a defined portion of the material itself is used as a standard for measuring any sample. To impose a number system on nonhomogeneous material is not likely to lead to genuine quantitative results. For example, if there were such a thing as a unit quantity of public opinion, and we were able to watch it acting upon a known social resistance under controlled conditions, we could then measure its effects through the acceleration produced in the resisting "mass," and hence measure the opinion itself. But we have no way of defining or measuring any of these. Instead, what we now add together is *your* considered judgment with John's impatient reply and Dick's remarks under close questioning and Tom's dislike of the questioner and Jane's misconception of the question. Granted that all these may add up to five votes, they still do not constitute or reflect the force we posit as Public Opinion.[40]

[38] Bross, *op. cit.*, 1.

[39] See W. Freeman Twaddell, "On Defining the Phoneme," *Language* (Supplement), March 1935.

[40] See Carroll Mason Sparrow in Lindsay Rogers, *The Pollsters*, New York, 1949, 47–61.

Fifth, wherever the counting professes to correct the ordinary man's or the historian's generalizing from a single instance or from "mere observation," two cautions have to be kept in mind. One is that the "correction" may produce results that are in conflict with the known reality, and thus have to be corrected again in making particular judgments: the demographer, for instance, declares that the American family of today has 3.7 people. There is nothing wrong with this abstraction, which makes comparison possible over time and space, but it is no more "exact" than a direct judgment of particulars or qualities not amenable to quantification.

If the reply is that the observer is not interested in tangible *fact* but in general *truth* and that we must allow him his means of expression, we do so, but here the second caution applies. The physical sciences assume—rightly for their purpose—the complete uniformity of nature and its "laws," whereas the social sciences dare not make this assumption about "human nature"; its fixity is still to be demonstrated. Physical science can in its domain generalize from a very few instances; the subjects called "humanities," so named because they deal with man and his life, record variety, vagueness, an infinite play of nuance. The social sciences try to bridge the gap between the other two disciplines by reducing variety to regularity, but find it hard to do. A chemist uses a purified sample of a substance and argues after a few tests that under the same conditions all samples will behave alike. The sociologist can only sample mankind, which is hard to purify, and he seldom reaches the same approximation twice. He knows how inadequate his "instances" are, but is helpless.

Sixth, the results of social science being difficult to assess, it is important not to be misled by either tautology or empty abstraction. Reports of "findings" in psychology, sociology, and social psychology fill our periodicals and turn out to be but doubtful correlations. Once in a while, someone lays claim to the discovery of a genuine "law." One such made a stir some twenty years ago, purporting as it did to fulfill the conditions of a true equation. It stated that responses to stimuli, both physical and verbal, diminish with increasing distance from the point of stimulation. Thus if in a given society an aunt resides with or near the mother, and assists in giving care to the child, the latter will regard her as a mother; less so, or not so, if the aunt lives at a distance:

Here enters the principle of stimulus generalization. The term used for "mother" is here regarded as a response. This response will naturally generalize to other relatives as a function of the similarity of the stimuli associated with them in relation to the stimuli provided by the individual's own mother. In all cultures there are some similarities; aunts as well as mothers, for example, are females. . . .[41]

One wonders whether these successive results could not have been obtained by inspection; indeed, whether they are not deducible from clear definitions of the related terms. Yet their "discovery" is offered as a contribution to cultural anthropology.

The publicity readily given to surveys both pretentious and trivial raises a doubt about the effect of associating science with weak thought. We read in the newspaper that "Children Much Alike and Yet Each One Is Different,"[42] and "Noisy Girl Babies May Be Brighter,"[43] both reports coming from acknowledged authorities. These are only headlines, but since the reader addressed is also the subject—is man and society—it is not irrelevant to ask how this "knowledge" affects our culture. Anthropologists and other social scientists have taught us to ask that question.

A full answer would require a book, but surely pretentiousness is always bad. We did not need to be told, after the Orson Welles broadcast of 1938 that announced a landing of men from Mars in New Jersey: ". . . a highly consistent structuration of the external stimulus world may, at times, be experienced with sufficient intensity because of its personal implications to inhibit the operation of usually applicable internal structurations or standards of judgment."[44] All this says is: "A carefully designed hoax can be so frightening that you lose your head." If this were all that the laws of social science can tell us, we should make all the more effort to strengthen our techniques as observers and reporters of the real world.

The researcher who does historian's work can at least preserve his sense of truth by concentrating on the tangle of his own stubborn

[41] Clark L. Hull, "A Primary Social Science Law," *Scientific Monthly*, LXXI (October 1950), 225 and *passim*.

[42] *New York World-Telegram and Sun*, Nov. 6, 1956.

[43] *New York Times*, July 22, 1967.

[44] Hadley Cantril, *The Invasion from Mars*, Princeton, N.J., 1940, 196.

facts. Always aware of the value of evidence, including that of the social sciences; always ready to use numbers to count numerable things—whether as supports of his descriptions or interpretations of single events—he is also aware of his duty to make individual judgments and of his right to affirm, in the impetuous words of William Douglass, the eighteenth-century American: "As an Historian, every Thing is in my province."

PART III

Writing

11

Organizing: Paragraph,
Chapter, and Part

The Function of Form and of Forms

Everything that we have said in this book about historical reporting has urged or implied the importance of Form. In discussing language a few pages back, we were discussing an aspect of Form. Without
Form in every sense, the facts of the past, like the jumbled visions
of a sleeper in a dream, elude us. The attentive researcher soon discovers
that facts and ideas in disorder cannot be conveyed to another's mind
without loss and are hardly likely to carry meaning very long even
for the possessor. This is because the mind is so constituted that it
demands some degree of regularity and symmetry—witness the arrangement of toilet articles on top of a bureau. A shopwindow in
which the objects for sale had been thrown helter-skelter would not
only give no pleasure to the passer-by, but would make it hard for
him to notice anything in particular.

In one sense, of course, any grouping has form of some kind,
but when we speak of Form with approval we mean attractive and
suitable form. In works of the mind we are affected by the presence
or absence of Form, whether or not we bother to analyze its character

and effect. In writing, the role of Form is continuous, for in the act of *im*pressing something on the mind, Form also *ex*presses. For example, in the sentence you have just read, the formal contrast of the ideas "impress" and "express" is driven in, as well as brought out, by the echoing similarity of the two words and by the further device of italicizing their first syllables. The same thing could be said without the same effect: would it then be the same thing? True, when one discusses what a piece is trying to say one often distinguishes its "contents" from its "form," but this separation is unreal; it is a feat of imagination. Actually, we know the contents only through the form, though we may guess at what the contents would have been had the form been more clear-cut.

It is the duty of the reporter to make sure that the contents he is in fact delivering are precisely those he intended. Form and intention should fit like skin on flesh. When the form is blurred or inappropriate we feel the disparity—the deformity, rather—as we do when we discover that a richly veined marble is but a piece of wood painted to look like what it is not.

In written matter, the most frequent and visible failure of form is that which comes from wrong emphasis. Why take pains to distribute emphasis in the right places? Because the mind cannot give equal attention to every part; it must be guided to those parts—of a sentence or a book—that it should attend to for a correct understanding. On the printed page, a "little form" such as italics is a signpost directing the mind to look this way or that. A footnote is likewise a form, whose make-up and uses we shall describe farther on. The larger forms we are about to discuss have less definable ways of producing emphasis than italics or footnotes, but length, beginnings, interruptions, and internal arrangements are also pointers.

We shall also be concerned about right emphasis when we look at the form of sentences, in Chapter 13. Right now, the principle will be exemplified through the larger forms of the *part, chapter,* and *paragraph,* which are the main masses that impress the reader while expressing the truth. All direct the mind, and so does the shape of any passage taken at random, even though its form goes by no special name. If the form fits, it aids understanding, and hence is an aid to memory. Consider the difficulty of following and retaining the congeries of disjointed ideas in this nonparagraph quoted from what is perhaps the most learned work on the history of the English stage:

The great spectacles of [Elizabeth's] reign were liturgies, undertaken by her gallants, or by the nobles whose country houses she visited in the course of her annual progresses. The most famous of all, the "Princely Pleasure of Kenilworth" in 1575, was at the expense of Dudley, to whom the ancient royal castle had long been alienated. Gradually, no doubt, the financial stringency was relaxed. Camden notes a growing tendency to luxury about 1574; others trace the change to the coming of the Duke of Alençon in 1581. Elizabeth had found the way to evoke a national spirit, and at the same time to fill her coffers, by the encouragement of piratical enterprise, and the sumptuous entertainments prepared for the welcome of Monsieur were paid for out of the spoils brought back by Drake in the *Golden Hind.* The Alençon negotiations, whether seriously intended or not, represent Elizabeth's last dalliance with the idea of matrimony. They gave way to that historic part of unapproachable virginity, whereby an elderly Cynthia, without complete loss of dignity, was enabled to the end to maintain a sentimental claim upon the attentions, and the purses, of her youthful servants. The strenuous years, which led up to the final triumph over the Armada in 1588, spared but little room for revels and for progresses. They left Elizabeth an old woman. But with the removal of the strain, the spirit of gaiety awoke.[1]

The trouble with this passage, plainly, is that the facts and ideas have not been organized, but rather thrown pell-mell at the reader. The result is that although the separate bits of information are all obviously there, the full meaning is not. Ordinarily, the reader has not the time, and most often he has not the knowledge, to put everything in its place and restore the intended meaning for himself. The passage just quoted has a form, but it is a bad form. The right shaping of it is scarcely begun: what we are given is but the materials for a paragraph; the learned author has served up his notes raw. If the word "form" by itself has become a term of praise, it is partly because the world recognizes what labor goes into achieving it. It takes effort to put everything where it belongs, to make one thing follow upon another, to leave nothing essential out. Form is always the result of a struggle.

[1] E. K. Chambers, *History of the Elizabethan Stage,* Oxford, 1923, I, 5.

Since it is inspiriting to see a workman at grips with his material, the student should read in the letters and diaries of Macaulay what an amount of thinking and worrying, of doing and undoing, went into the composing of the *History of England*.[2] When the first part was out Macaulay reread his work and then the eighth book of Thucydides,

which, I am sorry to say, I found much better than mine. . . . On the whole he is the first of historians. What is good in him is better than anything that can be found elsewhere. But his dry parts are dreadfully dry; and his arrangement is bad. Mere chronological order is not the order for a complicated narrative.[3]

A year later, still fretting about arrangement, Macaulay notes:

To make the narrative flow along as it ought, every part naturally springing from that which precedes; to carry the reader backward and forward across St. George's Channel without distracting his attention, is not easy. Yet it may be done. I believe that this art of transition is as important, or nearly so, to history, as the art of narration.[4]

Nearly four years after this, when one might have assumed that long practice had brought facility, Macaulay is still fighting against the same odds as any other writer.

Chapter XIV will require a good deal of work. I toiled on it some hours, and now and then felt dispirited. But we must be resolute and work doggedly, as Johnson said. . . . Arrangement and transition are arts which I value much, but which I do not flatter myself that I have attained.[5]

And to conclude, a month later: "I worked hard at altering the arrangement of the first three chapters of the third volume. What labour

---

[2] In any edition of G. O. Trevelyan's *Life and Letters of Macaulay* the principal passages will be found under these dates: Dec. 18, 1838; Nov. 5, 1841, through July 1843; Dec. 19, 1845; and July 17, 1848 ff.

[3] Trevelyan, *op. cit.,* Diary, Nov. 29–Dec. 4, 1848.

[4] *Ibid.,* April 15, 1850.

[5] *Ibid.,* Diary, Jan. 1, 1854.

it is to make a tolerable book, and how little readers know how much trouble the ordering of the parts has cost the writer!"[6]

"The ordering of the parts"—that is the researcher's first problem, once he has acquired a body of material and is turning his thoughts to the work as it shall be when finished. Chronology, Macaulay tells us, is not the answer; its order will only produce chronicles, which are notoriously unreadable.

Now there is only one other kind of order, the *topical*. This is the order dictated by subject instead of time. And subjects, as we saw in Chapter 2, are characterized by unity. They are intelligible units suitable for description. Why hesitate, then? The reporter on historical events who wants to be read will adopt the topical order. Yes, but not without modification. The pure topical order, exhausting one topic and jumping to the next, will deprive a story of all coherence. A history is a recital of events that took place in Time, and this must never be forgotten. You will kill interest as surely by leaving out the time sequence as by breaking up the natural clusters of ideas. Nothing replaces the strong effect of beholding one mass of facts *after* another, as we can verify by recalling those movies of which we happened to see the second half first.

The two fundamental forms of organization may be contrasted by imagining a biography built on the one and then on the other plan:

CHRONOLOGICAL ORDER

X is born, goes to school, breaks his leg, learns to smoke, is expelled from college, studies law, meets Jane Smith, finds a five-dollar bill, is called a liar, eats lunch, gets into towering rage, marries Susan Black, is elected mayor, goes fishing, is thought a radical, plays the stock market, suffers from asthma, sues opponent for slander, reads in bed, loses senatorial race, employs bodyguard, is accused of treason, goes to Mayo Clinic, dies. Will probated, widow remarries, memoirs published.

The fault of the strict chronological order is that it mixes events great and small without due subordination, and that it combines

[6] *Ibid.*, Feb. 6, 1854.

incidents that occur only once with permanent truths about habits and tastes, character and belief: it is a parody of life. The mind asks for something better than this jumble and says: "One thing at a time," meaning that it wants one subject, one idea gone into thoroughly, even if the parts of it were separated by many years. Yet the purely topical treatment will not do either:

TOPICAL ORDER

1. Character:	in boyhood, youth, maturity, old age
2. Hobbies:	in boyhood, youth, maturity, old age
3. Health:	in boyhood, youth, maturity, old age
4. Income:	in boyhood, youth, maturity, old age
5. Friends:	in boyhood, youth, maturity, old age

Such a run up and down a man's lifespan is intolerable to contemplate, and while entailing an enormous amount of repetition, would not leave a clear portrait. The only way therefore is *to combine, in all but the briefest narratives, the topical and the chronological arrangements.* Doing so defines the reporter's task as well as his difficulty.

The Steps in Organizing

In the combined form, the chronology moves forward within each topic, giving an occasional backward or forward glance as needed. Each section of the work deals with a topic or one of its natural subdivisions at some length, and *completely as far as that subject goes.*

The full bearing of this last sentence is important to grasp. Suppose, to continue our biographical example, that X's character is referred to in twenty places but is extensively discussed in three, these places corresponding to youth, maturity, and old age. In each place, enough must be said to engage the reader's interest and to settle whatever questions X's character raises. Nothing is more annoying than to find a few facts in one spot, a judgment in another, then more details about the earlier events because a fresh incident brings them up, and elsewhere again a dispute with another writer about the previous judgment. Such scattering leaves a confused and often a contradictory impression, coupled with the surmise that the writer himself has not cleared his own mind and said his say.

A biographer who was also a poet, the late L. A. G. Strong, has given a vivid analogy for what has just been discussed. He described a famous vaudeville entertainer named the Great Wieland, whose act

consisted in spinning plates on a long trestle table. Starting with three or four, he would soon have a dozen spinning, and be obliged to run from one end of the table to the other, in order to give a reviving twist of the fingers to one that was on the point of collapse. . . . The number of plates grew and grew, and the audience would cry out with excitement. . . . I saw him several times, and he never let a single plate wobble to a stop.

Everyone who attempts to write an account of a complex period or undertaking sooner or later finds himself in the Great Wieland's position, though not always equipped with the same skill. The story has so many aspects, all of which have to be kept alive in the reader's mind. Concentrate on one and the others will fall. Keep to a strict chronological sequence, and you will fail to trace the growth of individual elements. Attend to the elements, and you will have to dodge about in time, running like Wieland from one century back into the one before to keep an interest alive.[7]

Quite evidently the combination of Topic and Time calls for the art of Transition. The forms of transition—words, sentences, paragraphs, sections—take the reader by the elbow, so to speak, and make him face in the right direction for the next topic. Transitions, in other words, are devices of emphasis. They belong to Form and to forms, whether they are small words like "hence," "but," "accordingly," "nevertheless," or long passages that sum up and forecast, in one pivoting movement of thought.

Macaulay's problem—every writer's problem—can now be seen in its fullness: to be effective a mass of words must have Form. That form must satisfy the opposite demands of Unity (one thing at a time) and Chronology (a series of things one after the other), while also holding the reader's interest through Coherence (ease in passing from one thing to another). Any good arrangement will meet these demands. To find the right arrangement there is no magic formula. The necessity to do so recurs with every piece of writing; it can only be solved by hard and intelligent work upon the given sets of facts.

[7] *The Rolling Road,* London, 1956, 82.

Let us therefore put ourselves back to that earlier stage where the researcher confronts the mass of notes he has taken. Its form, we hope, is not that of complete but of modified chaos. Thanks to system, the cards or slips or notebook entries are indexed so as to produce (we will imagine) six broad categories. To vary the example, we will this time drop biography and imagine a piece of business history:

1. The founding of the company
2. First success and next twenty years
3. The big lawsuit
4. Reorganization and expansion
5. Branching out into new fields
6. Research and charitable enterprises

Now for a simple test: are these matters equal in importance? If so, in the finished book their treatment should be of approximately equal length. How long would the longest of these parts be, at a guess? The stack of classified notes will give us some idea. Supposing numbers 4 and 5 to run an estimated fifty pages each, we see at once that the two largest of our six divisions must be thought of as parts and not chapters. A fifty-page chapter, though not impossible, is ordinarily too long. And our dealings now are with chapters; at least we want to settle on some headings to cover subdivisions of equal and *moderate* length—say twenty to twenty-five double-spaced typewritten pages— 6,000 to 7,500 words.

A chapter is not a set form like the fourteen-line sonnet, but it has some of the properties of a set form: it has unity and completeness, and for convenience it may be assumed to have the length just stated. The function of a chapter is to dispose of one topic comfortably and give the reader as much as he will take in at one sitting. Hence it is also the right length for an essay. Moreover, if this approximate wordage is adopted for one chapter, it will generally be possible to make the others roughly equal. Chapters of fifteen or of forty pages would probably be harder to keep even; one could not count on their being all as short or as long. Of course, one can—sometimes must—vary the length from chapter to chapter, but there is a marked advantage to having similar units to juggle with in the search for the right arrangement: the longer the chapter, the fewer the breaking-off points in the work and hence the fewer rearrangements that are possible. If the chapters are too brief, too many breaks occur and coherence gives way to choppiness.

With the goal of equal and rounded-off units in mind, the researcher turns back to his notes and finds, on matching them with his six divisions, that whereas numbers 1 and 2 ("The founding of the company" and "First success and next twenty years") each propose a single topic falling neatly into a pair of chapters, the next two ("The big lawsuit" and "Reorganization and expansion") are badly entangled. The company's reorganization was proposed before the lawsuit, and this in fact brought on the case. Besides, when expansion occurred it was the start of the next set of events ("Branching out into new fields"). In short, the middle of the projected work is one large snarl.

The only solution is for the researcher to think of one distinct subject that could be separated from the rest and see what this leaves. If it destroys all possibility of making a realignment that will fit chronology and topical unity, he has probably taken out too large a piece as his first morsel. He must try again—in his mind, of course—or with just a piece of scratch paper to jot down the natural chunks of material, until some pieces seem to go together to form clusters; he discovers these whenever things hang together more than they hang with neighboring matters. Going over his notes slowly and watching for clues will help, but remember there is no substitute for imagination—"How would it be if—?" To make the trial and error progress, he has to make successive tables of contents. He has to make up chapter headings that will have the same weight—not minding the wording—and recast them till the series sounds convincing. He may wind up with something like this:

1. Founding the company
2. Success and the first twenty years
3. Cracking at the seams
4. The big lawsuit
5. Reorganization: New management and new projects
6. Expansion through subsidiaries
7. The completed empire
8. Research and charitable enterprises
9. Present performance and outlook for the future

With nine units, the writer's previous estimate of 230 to 250 pages divides into chapters of about twenty-five, as desired.

Now take a look at the foreseeable character of each chapter from the point of view of narrative: 1 and 2 have forward motion from the inevitable "background" through the early struggles to the end of twenty years full of persons and incidents. Then comes a more static chapter, "Cracking at the seams," which is largely descriptive and which resolves itself into a new drama, "The big lawsuit."

After this there is description again, to make clear the reorganization; then the account moves ahead once more through the details of the markets and subsidiaries added one by one to constitute "Expansion." Next comes a picture of the firm at its high point; then perhaps a backtracking to the very beginning: old Mr. Bingham had always wanted to add a research unit but not until . . ., etc. The same for the outlays to education and the like. The story of these two side-enterprises keep the reader moving back and forth from beginning to end and afford an unconscious review of the ground he has covered since page 1. To leave him there would be inconclusive. Hence a short chapter to tie all the loose ends together and close on the idea of forward motion. To test the scheme, the writer must make sure that the several chapters add up to the story as a whole, with nothing left out and no overlapping of subjects, though with as many cross references as are necessary for internal clarity.

Composing by Ear or by Outline?

Having reached this point you are not at the end of your troubles, but you have something like a structure. It remains to allot your notes to each chapter, after which you begin with one chapter and try to construct *it*. The same considerations of chronology, topical unity, coherence, and transition apply throughout: the part, the chapter, and the paragraph should have comparable Form. But there is this difference: as you get nearer to the paragraph, you cannot (and should not try to) forecast your structure completely. A series of paragraphs each built to one pattern like the pieces of a prefabricated house would be tedious. Nor should a chapter be assembled according to a blueprint. These cautions raise the question of outlines.

Writers divide fairly evenly into those who find outlines useful or indispensable, and those to whom they are a nuisance. By all means use them if they do not cost you too much in time and spontaneity. But do not force yourself to make them up if this does not come easily, or if once drawn up the outline drags you back. Certainly the best order for the parts of a paper is the order that comes out of one's sense of the subject and seems dictated by it. To a writer who develops that sense from the mere growth of the data under his hand, the outline is bound to seem stiff and suspiciously logical. When the time comes to fill it out, the material runs away and the outline loses control over the writer's thoughts. Conscience then inspires vain efforts to patch up the outline while groping for new transitions where the writing got off the prearranged track.

For such a writer the better procedure is to use the outline not as a guide beforehand but as a verifier afterward. We may picture the sequence of events something like this: you have set aside all but one batch of organized notes. A run through them (yes, once again) suggests that they fall quite evidently into three subgroups—perhaps four or five, but three is normal because every subject and sub-subject has a beginning (exposition), a middle (complication), and an end (resolution or conclusion). At any rate you now have a small number of smaller piles of notes.[8] You take the first pile in order, shuffle its contents until a rough sequence is established not so much in the cards as in your mind. You put them to one side and start writing. Some people need to look at their notes while composing; others prefer to gaze on the subject with the inner eye of memory and imagination. In either case the mind must take part in the work. Composing does not consist in merely blowing up each note to full grammatical size and tacking it on to the next; it consists—at least if you want to be read with any pleasure—in thinking about the subject from A to Z just as you want your reader to think.

You start; your ideas pull one another out of the wordless dark into the articulate light—you are writing ahead. Your facts and ideas dovetail naturally, with only occasional effort, even when the words

[8] If the notes are not on cards or detached slips, the sorting is done by a further, more exact marginal indexing. This suits people who prefer not to handle or look at their notes while writing, but who arrange them mentally and simply refresh their memory now and again by consulting the notebook.

halt and have to be changed. Incomplete or rough, the sequence of expressions corresponds to the understanding you have gained by research and reflection. The frequent rereading of the notes has made you feel that you know the story by heart, that you were there and can recount it. The *story* flows despite your pen's stuttering. Suddenly, you run into a snag. It is probably one of two kinds. In the first kind, the course you are on obviously leads to the spot you see ahead, but at your feet there yawns a gap. How to get over? The answer lies in another question: Is it a fact that is wanting to connect the parts? If so it must be secured—later. Or is it an idea, a transition? If so, mark the spot by some conventional sign in the margin, an *X* or a wavy line, pick up the thread wherever you can, and keep going forward.

The lack of certain facts is important to discover at this stage, and the way of composing here recommended offers the advantage that by going mentally from next to next you discover the flaws as you would if you were a reader. If you merely sew your notes together as they occur in the bundles of your first mechanical classification, you will probably conceal the gaps, and the reader will discover them as we did in reading the book on the English stage quoted above. If what you lack is a deft transition, do not rack your brains. When you come to revise your first draft the right idea may pop into your head, or else you will quickly see what small rearrangements will bring the gaping edges together.

The lack of proper order, connection, or *composition* in the strict sense, is most glaring in the narration of physical events, where our daily experience supplies an immediate test. To remember and adapt the test to the recital of abstractions, examine this short fragment of fiction:

There was an office facing them, at the rear of the hall, and a man and woman were regarding them from a box window which opened above a ledge on which lay a register book. They were middle-aged folk: the man, a fleshy, round-faced, somewhat pompous-looking individual, who might at some time have been a butler; the woman, a tall, spare-figured, thin featured, sharp eyed person, who examined the newcomers with an enquiring gaze.[9]

[9] J. S. Fletcher, *The Middle Temple Murder,* New York, 1919, 36.

In reading fast one may not notice the double flaw in this description. Yet it is evident, if one attempts to visualize what happens (as any reader of a report is entitled to do), that in line 2 a man and a woman are looking at the newcomers as they enter. Immediately before, the newcomers were making a survey of the box window, ledge, register—all quite uninteresting compared with the two picturesque characters gazing at them. And when we reach the end of the words describing the woman of the pair, there she is "examining the newcomers with an enquiring gaze" as she was already doing six lines above. Either the first reference to the newcomers' being gazed at is premature—if they were advancing from a certain distance—or it should be omitted from the end, since we knew it before and cannot take it as the new fact it pretends to be.

The second kind of snag in writing comes when you discover that you have steered around in a circle. The natural linking of ideas, instead of propelling you forward, has brought you back to a point earlier in your story. It is in this predicament that a scratch outline, made on the spot, can be a straightener. Cast your eye back to your beginning, jotting down as you go the main and secondary ideas, using the same key word for each idea that belongs to one subject. It is necessary here to reduce each sentence to its simplest thought in order to classify it; otherwise you will not clear up the mess. Assigning symbols for ideas, then, you soon find where you got off the track by seeing where, let us say, ideas E, F, G, and H were followed by F again. This may have led you unconsciously to avoid a second G and H. You leaped ahead to K, but felt disquieted and, after a sentence or two, stopped to take stock.

The solution is scissors and paste. Cut out the intruding ideas but keep any good passage that you have written, though it is out of place (K), and set it aside. Cut back to the good original section (E F G H), see if there is anything valuable in the second reference to F, inserting it near the first if desirable; and throw away all the other false twistings and turnings. Write fresh matter to sew together any wounds created by this surgery and keep looking ahead until the place for K comes into sight. Remember that for these remedial purposes all subjects have not one but a dozen handles to grasp them by. Depending on which you seize and which you present to be seized next in turn, you produce logical flow or jerkiness.

Visualize a subject (*S*) with branches radiating from it, all of them relevant circumstances that you will have to mention. By taking

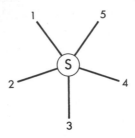

up each in turn you build up the unity of *S*. But there is along each branch a point where you get so far from the little round core that you cannot get back: the dotted line marks how far you can go without

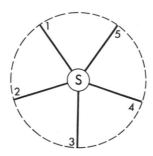

getting stranded. Always bear in mind that *S*, when completed, must throw out a link to another subject, *T*. If you go beyond the end of S_5 you will never come within reach of T_1. On the other hand, a

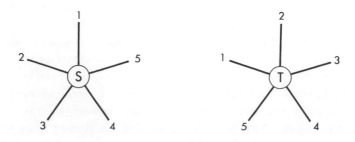

little ingenuity will tell you ahead of time that by keeping in sight the core of S and making the last of your journeys S_5 you can easily seize hold of T_1.

This obvious device will work between chapters as well as between sections of a chapter. There is always some topic that can come at the end of the chapter to relate it to the next, and there is also one that fits this arrangement by being the right beginning for the chapter following. This interlocking of ideas makes a tight book, yet it is not invariably necessary to fashion this kind of chain. Sometimes a new chapter will hark back to a much earlier topic in order to make clear the forthcoming facts, and this backward jump often provides variety in what would otherwise be a forced march at a relentless pace.

But no matter what is to be done at a given spot, it is indispensable to give the reader a clue. He will follow with docility for many paragraphs if the road is straight or gently winding. But if you want him to turn a corner you must firmly guide him: "We now turn back to those years when . . ."; or "From that day when he met his future wife"; or "Casting our minds ahead of the point we have reached"; or "Before we can understand the issue at stake, we must recall (or examine or describe)"; and so on. It is amazing what a reader will gladly absorb if he is occasionally told why, and given a hint of where the facts will take him.

There are, then, many exceptions to the rule of always going forward and they are inherent in topical treatment. We had a striking example of such an exception in the table of contents made up for the company history. In Chapter 8 of that hypothetical work the reader is to be brought back to the beginning twice. When this happens, the trip from the starting point forward should be speeded up in such a way that the necessary repetition is made to seem new. Otherwise the reader has the sinking feeling of going over the same ground laboriously and needlessly.

The most frequent cause of interference with forward motion and straight chronological order occurs, oddly enough, at the very start of the book or paper. The reason for this is that a subject always has two possible beginnings—the natural one, which research has discovered, and the conventional one, which is whatever the reader is assumed to know. This pair of beginnings must somehow be reduced to one by compromise between them or postponement of the less attractive. This process may be decisive. A writer whose work calls for sustained attention through many pages wants to grip the reader from the first word—"from the word 'Go' " is here appropriate—and interest him so completely that he will be compelled to continue reading. The first chapter of any book, the first page of any essay, the first paragraph of any review are therefore supreme tests of the art of composition. Where they break into the subject, what goes into them, how they insert themselves into the reader's stream of thought and stock of knowledge, and what they promise of future interest, are so many delicate questions asking for precise answers.

Movies use the flashback as one kind of answer, one that is as old as Homer's *Iliad.* In scholarship the device, when well handled, is fully justified. For instance in Lionel Trilling's authoritative *Matthew Arnold,* the logical beginning is Chapter 2, entitled "His Father and His England." But the effective beginning is the first chapter, mysteriously entitled "A," which opens with this beguiling sentence: "The secretary of old Lord Lansdowne, the liberal peer, was a singularly handsome young man, whose manners were Olympian and whose waistcoats were remarkable." After this one certainly wants to know more, which is not a feeling that arises of itself at the sight of any ordinary block of print.

Altering the logical order can also be used in reverse, as when one traces antecedents or surrounding conditions before venturing to open the subject proper. Either mode poses the problem of making a smooth transition when the normal order is resumed. Thus Macaulay's *History* begins with a statement of his purpose, which is to write the story of England from the accession of James II to recent times. For this he must give "the background," and we hear about Celtic Britain, the Norman Conquest, the Papacy, and a quantity of other familiar landmarks, followed by some of the main themes of the work, presented in their earliest historical forms, the whole moving forward in seven-league boots.

Chapter 2 is chronologically more unified and static: it surveys the political and religious history of the seventeenth century and ends with the death of Charles II. Chapter 3, famous as "Macaulay's Third Chapter," is panoramic. It is a wonderful bird's-eye view of social and cultural England in 1685. We are by then on the spot and almost at the time of the true opening. Chapter 4 catches up the end left dangling in 2 by *depicting* the death of Charles II, and with the words "that morning . . ." we are finally at the starting point announced some two hundred pages back.[10]

A good beginning is good not only for the reader but also for the writer. It is like a running start, or rather, like propulsion from a rifled barrel: it keeps one going in a straight line. Yet it often happens that the perfect beginning cannot be found by mere thought. You choose what you think good and start writing, but the thought wanders, the facts do not fall in naturally. In this situation, keep on for a time until a direction becomes clear. When you have finished six or eight pages, reread, and you will generally find that somewhere on page 2 or 3 is the true place to start. What went before was akin to the dog's walking round and round to beat down the grass before settling down.

The Short Piece and the Paragraph

We have been talking about books. The reader may object that he is not ready to compose on the large scale. Can he possibly shrink all this advice to the dimensions of a short paper and—equally useful— to the dimensions of a paragraph? The answer is Yes as regards the short piece. The more practiced he becomes in the composition of papers ranging from the three-page book review to the thirty-page report, the better he will be able to handle the chapter (which is the

---

[10] Macaulay worried about a proper beginning for a long time. "The great difficulty of a work of this kind," he wrote ten years before its publication, "is the beginning. How is it to be joined on to the preceding events? Where am I to commence it? I cannot plunge, slap dash, into the middle of events and characters. I cannot, on the other hand, write a history of the whole reign of James the Second as a preface to the history of William the Third. If I did, a history of Charles the Second would still be necessary as a preface to that of the reign of James the Second. I sympathise with the poor man who began the war of Troy *'gemino ab ovo'* [from the egg from which Helen was born]. But, after much consideration, I think I can manage, by the help of an introductory chapter or two, to glide imperceptibly into the full current of my narrative." [Diary in Trevelyan, *op. cit.,* Dec. 18, 1838.]

"working part" of the book), and the finer will his eye become in tracing the plan of the book itself.

The longish report (thirty pages) should be considered as a miniature book rather than an enlarged chapter. It has "chapters" and possibly "parts" of its own, though the chapters may be as short as five pages. For any of these subdivisions it is helpful to have headings, though they are not indispensable. What is essential is that the sections be separated, by numerals or by blank spaces. An unbroken stretch of thirty pages is hard to read, even in a novel, and very hard to compose, except by the virtuoso writer. The competent writer needs guidelines just as the reader needs breathing space.

As a sample of what such guidelines may be for writers in any of the shorter forms, here is a set of suggestions for the form of the book review. We will assume that it is written for a learned or literary periodical where the space allotted will usually not exceed 1,500 words—say the *American Historical Review* or the *Virginia Quarterly*.

The beginning, we know, is important. The first of your twelve paragraphs should present an idea of interest to the reader who will leaf through the magazine. If your first words are "This book . . ." he will not be able to distinguish your review from twenty others, and he will be entitled to conclude that you have not expended much thought on enlisting his attention. The opening statement takes the reader from where he presumably stands in point of knowledge and brings him to the book under review. The briefest possible description of its aim, scope, and place in the world therefore follows the baited opening sentence and completes the first paragraph.

The second classifies the book: what thesis, tendency, bias, does it uphold, suggest, evince? Paragraphs 3 to 5 go into the author's main contentions and discuss them. Do not repeat anything you said in the classificatory paragraph, but rather give detailed evidence of the grounds for your classification.

Paragraphs 6 and 7 may deal with additional or contrary points to be found in other authors or in your own research; but so far, these only amend or qualify what is acceptable in the new book. In 8 and 9 you deliver your chief objections and summarize shortcomings. If you have found errors, mention only the important ones—do not waste space on typographical or minor slips.

From errors you modulate into the broad field: how is our conception of it changed by the book? What further work is need to clear up doubtful points? Where have gaps been left that must be filled? You have now used up paragraphs 10 and 11 and you have one more in which to strike a balance of merits and faults, ending with some words about the author—*not* yourself or the subject.

For with book reviewing goes a moral obligation: you hold the author's fate in your hands as far as one group of readers is concerned. He and his work should, through you, be given the floor, have the last word. What you say in the review will, rightly or wrongly, be taken seriously. You are in honor bound to be scrupulously fair. Never use the author's admission against him, saying, "He entirely neglects the foreign implications," when it was he who warned you of this in the preface. Do not expect him to have written the book *you* have in mind, but the one *he* had. Recognize the amount of work that has gone into the product and be magnanimous: you may be severe on serious faults of interpretation and inference; but unless they are continual, forget the trifling errors in his text just as you concentrate on them in yours. Book reviewers are not infallible.

More than in the long work, essay, or article, it is in the paragraph that the writer's yearning for freedom can be indulged—up to a point. There is no formula for beginning or ending paragraphs that will not produce a dull, mechanical sound. The topic sentence, as its name indicates, comes early and announces the topic. But especially in reporting events, the topic sentence does not always live up to its promise of unifying the paragraph. It may and indeed will often be used, automatically, by good writers; but turning out such a sentence automatically, every time, is a mistake. Ask yourself, rather, what intertwined subjects the whole block of print will contain; what is the little core S and what are the branches it sends out as you employ your facts and use your ideas to make them cohere? In the paragraph as elsewhere this is a matter of linkage. The fault in the paragraph quoted at the beginning of this chapter is not the lack of a topic sentence: it has one; the fault is that the ensuing facts and ideas are not firmly linked but loosely associated.

Linking can be systematically practiced until it becomes habitual. In general—but only in general—the good writer makes the last thought in sentence A suggest the first thought in sentence B. At its most rigid this would give us the pattern: "Mr. Adams has written a book. The book is a history of the Jefferson and Madison administrations. Those administrations cover the years 1801–1817. Those years were notable for . . ." and so on. Perfect coherence but grisly reading. The coherence to aim at is that of a normally constituted mind, which likes variety in continuity. If on looking over your first draft you find that your mind as reader is not satisfied with your mind as writer, change the writing and make a mental note of the sort of jumpiness that ails you in composing. No man who writes attains adequate coherence thoughout his first draft. Everyone *must* revise, which means displace, add missing links, remove repetitions—in short, tinker. As we tinker, presumably, we improve and polish.

These various operations will in time become second nature, but at first the tendency when reading over one's prose is to find it perfectly lucid and forceful, not to say sublime. This is because the mind that has framed it keeps on supplying its deficiencies from special knowledge and the memory of what was meant. You must therefore lay aside your manuscript for several days and return to it as if it were written by someone else. And since this may not provoke sufficient self-criticism, you must examine each statement for its accuracy of form as well as relevancy of contents. Verifying fact has already been dealt with. Correct usage—little forms—will occupy us in the last chapter of this book, it being the last virtue required of our work before it is sent on its journey to printer and public.

12

Plain Words: The War on Jargon and Clichés

To Produce Sense, Weigh Your Words

To the general public "revise" is a noble word and "tinker" is a trivial one, but to the writer the difference between them is only the difference between the details of the hard work and the effect it achieves. The successful revision of a book in manuscript is made up of an appalling number of small, local alterations. Rewriting is nothing but able tinkering. Consequently it is impossible to convey to a nonwriter an abstract idea of where the alterations should come or how to make them. Only an apprenticeship under a vigilant critic will gradually teach a would-be writer how to find and correct all the blunders and obscurities that bespangle every first draft.

The image of tailoring that the word "alterations" suggests is an apt one to bear in mind. A first draft is clumsy, heavy, stiff—you must shorten something here, lengthen it there, move a button or a link forward or back, smooth out a wrinkle, make the garment fit. Only, in writing, the words are not solely the garment of the thought, they are its body as well; so that the pulling and adjusting of words has to go on until the thought you hoped to present and the thought

275

on paper coincide and displace the wrong thought or no-thought that accidentally got written down. This operation suggests what we can do to start our custom-tailoring: we must learn to see what does not fit. The rest depends on the apprentice's alertness and ingenuity.

The man who wants to write and be read must develop a new habit of attending to words—not just to important words and on occasions of formal writing, but to all words at all times. A student of painting does not think it outside his duty to attend at all times to shape and color, or a musician to sounds and rhythms. The writer must have for words the eye of a jewel expert, who knows the worth of his gems at a glance. The writer must recognize words and be able to juggle their multiple meanings with ease. When words form sentences, he must be as alive as a lover or a diplomat to the shades they convey. Psychologists who have tried to ascertain the mental traits of competent writers have concluded from their studies that "the effective writer is one who is sensitive to the overtones in what he is writing—that is, who is conscious of his audience and of the peculiar purposes of the individual communication."[1]

Any good writer could have told the experimenters as much. What their statement does is to define good writing and find its cause in the definition. But their conclusion is worth dwelling on because it restates with all the authority of "experiment" two fundamental points: the writer is *aware,* and whatever he writes has *a peculiar purpose.* It is out of these two necessities that the doctrine grew up of the *mot juste,* or "inevitable word" for a given spot. There is nothing frivolous or flossy about the demand for proper words in proper places; the only trouble with it is that the inevitable in this regard is something most of us are able to avoid with the greatest of ease. Take an example:

"Although this book differs from Harrisse's on Columbus, it is also important."

At least three words in this sentence are improper and darken understanding: "although," "differs," and "also." Taken together, "although" and "also" imply that a book which "differs" from a certain

[1] W. E. Coffman and J. Papachristou, "Experimental Objective Tests of Writing Ability for the Law School Admission Test," *Journal of Legal Education,* VII (1955), 390.

other book is unimportant. And "differs" by itself is an absurdity, since every work differs from every other. The writer may have meant something like this: "Although this book does not follow Harrisse's views on disputed points, it is not negligible," or "its interpretation is valuable." But more likely still, he had no such formulated idea. All he wanted to say was: "Here is a book; it opposes Harrisse's views; I think it important."

It is of course neither unusual nor criminal to write a first draft full of non-sense such as we have just quoted, or to begin with choppy and simple-minded remarks such as those that we substituted for the non-sense. The important thing is that in the second draft the writer—*you*—should have moved away from both these faults and produced a tenable statement. You discover what you really think by hacking away at your first spontaneous utterance. How to give your idea its definitive form is the subject of the next chapter. In this one we are concerned with the first step, which is to find out whether your original utterance is *un*tenable. This discovery comes from a close, unremitting scrutiny of words.

Be Strict About Signpost Words

The dictionary is the chief reference work on the researcher's shelf—or rather on his desk—to be used *more often* than is necessary, so as to make sure that the words he knows "perfectly well" are not in fact words that he knows *im*perfectly.[2] The chances are good, for example, that four out of five readers of this book do not truly know the meaning of "fruition." They doubtless think that it means "bearing fruit," "producing results." And in some contexts at least, they probably use with false or blurred meanings such words as: *connive, drastic, cohort, disinterested, deprecate, minimize, supposititious, perspective, evince,* and *decimate.*

[2] For writers, regardless of specialization, the desk dictionary that the authors of this book recommend is *Webster's New World,* published by the World Publishing Company. That dictionary is not to be confused in size or linguistic philosophy with the large *Webster's International,* Third Edition, which proffers a questionable view of language and its parts. For a good critique (among many others), see Robert P. Hudson, "Medical Writing and *Webster's Third,*" *Annals of Internal Medicine,* LXXI (August 1969), 435–38.

They probably make no distinction in their minds between *specific* and *particular, nomenclature* and *terminology, growth* and *development, component* and *constituent, mixture* and *compound, autonomy* and *independence, constant* and *continual*—in short, they find synonyms on every hand, whereas a glorious tradition has it that English can show but a single pair of exact synonyms, namely, "gorse" and "furze." Let this pleasant thought move you to reach for the dictionary again and again and learn there something to your advantage, which eventually means your reader's.

Unfortunately, some of the most important words you cannot, in a sense, look up. The small guiding and linking words that recur on every page are plain without definition. But do you sufficiently query their use in your prose? An "although," an "also," a "but," a "because" can overthrow your meaning while your attention flags. It might be supposed that anyone who writes English at all would know how to use "a" and "the" and avoid confusing them. But the analysis of ordinary words is so out of favor that the misuse of the definite and indefinite articles is continual. In a recent book appeared the sentence: "She then married the relative of the theatre manager." One might make a guessing game out of such statements: "How many relatives did the theatre manager have?" Again, one reads in a report about the rediscovery of the vanishing English diplomats, Burgess and MacLean: "Appearance of the two men was first announced at . . ." Such a unique event, surely, cries aloud for its defining *The:* THE appearance, the only one—and properly it should be reappearance.

Other lazy writers misuse "but," making it serve as an elegant variation of "and," or as a universal joint with no distinct meaning: "The company overextended its operations in hopes of stimulating its liquid position, but the disastrous end product was not hard to foresee." Why "but"? "But" marks an opposition, and in this sequence of ideas there is none. The word serves here merely to connect the last idea with each of the two dissimilar ones that precede. The first idea, which ends with "operations," requires "and" to tie it to the third, since there is no opposition between overextension and bad consequences; there *is* opposition between high hopes and bad results, which is only implied, and this inspired the misleading "but." The sentence wobbles at the joints and must be recast, the signal for alteration being given by the loose coupling.

The same, or worse, must be said of the myriad "howevers" that dot the printed page, usually at the head of the sentence. With some writers this mannerism says no more than that they are taking breath: ". . . escalation of the war. . . . Aahh—however, . . . much criticism was expressed at the time. . . . Aahh—however, . . . the enemy was winning. Aahh—however, . . ." The overuse of "however" is so flagrant that it prompts us to put the word on the List of Forbidden Words (see Figure 8), side by side with the tiresome "in terms of" about which something will be said in a moment. The hostile scrutiny recommended for *a, the, and, but, however* is to be applied to all other linking and organizing words. They are signals that guide the thought along its proper path and they must be kept accurate and strict. On this ground the doublings—*and/or, as to whether, if and when, unless and until*—are disallowed. They are needless, which is enough to condemn them, and they also betray the writer's ignorance or indecision. If you understand the meaning of *or*, you never want to write *and/or;* if you know how to use *whether*, you spare your readers the clumsiness of *as to whether;* if you grasp the force of *if*, you perceive that it includes *when.*

Picture All Images

When we pass from link words to nouns and verbs, the need is for concreteness and lucidity. You test your words by asking: Can this be touched or seen? If you write long strings of abstract nouns and use "have" or "are" and the passive voice instead of strong active verbs, your thought will be as hard to make out as an old faded photograph. Try reading this at a normal speed and then ask yourself what it says:

Whatever may be the considerations that have caused the President to delay giving to the people a clearer concept than they possess of the enemy's atomic threat and our ability to deal with it, surely an overriding reason why he should do this soon has now been supplied. That is the spate of conflicting and bewildering statements about the situation that recently have come from members of his own Administration and of Congress who may be presumed to have varying measures of inside information.[3]

[3] Arthur Krock, in the *New York Times*, Oct. 8, 1953.

Not only are these sentences long and lacking in euphony, but they lack concrete nouns and active verbs. The result is a general haze.

The tendency of a culture like ours, which is tinged with technology, is to seek out or invent the word that will sound most general, so as to "cover" with science-like authority all possible instances. That is how "contact" became a verb, how "mass media" replaced "popular press and broadcasting," how "communication(s)" turned into an academic subject. Excuses have been found for this substituting of tentlike notions for the names of particular things, but scientific portentousness is an evil just the same. Notice how "goals" have vanished under the tyranny of "objectives", how "use" is yielding to "utilization,"[4] how "visit" has come to seem poor and inadequate when we have the lovely "visitation" to play with. All this abstract and affected talk is intolerable in print.

Some writers, who justly fear overabstraction, try to avoid it by figurative language and the use of bright, "efficient" words that happen to be in vogue. In the business report quoted above, there occurred the phrase "stimulate its liquid position," and this was followed by the sentence: "The disastrous end product was not hard to foresee." These expressions are muddled and obscure by reason of two common faults. One is careless imagery, the other is jargon. The two often go together and their appearance in prose is always a symptom of verbal dry rot.

To the alert mind, all words convey an image—the representation more or less vivid of an act or a situation. When we say "Do you grasp my meaning?" the listener half pictures to himself a hand seizing something. When the answer is "No, I don't get you," the image is less vivid, yet it is clearly in the same plane: both remarks depict the taking hold of an object. In hasty speaking or writing one easily passes from image to image, saying perhaps: "It is difficult to grasp a meaning that is couched in florid language." The three images of "seizing," "lying on a bed," and "decorated with flowers" do not develop a single coherent image, and though the result is intelligible enough it is neither sharp nor strong.

Two words badly mated are often enough to produce incoherence, which—when noticed—will destroy meaning. What, in our example,

[4] And latterly to "usage," which in this sense is illiterate.

FIGURE 8   *Fifty Forbidden Words*

JARGON
basic
commitment
concept
context (figurative)
de-emphasize
essential(s)
(re-)evaluate(-tion)
initial (= first)
major
motivation
parameter

FEEBLE CONNECTIVES
however
in terms of
while (apart from time relations)
with (as a universal joint)

AFFECTATIONS
crisp
curious(ly)
dimension (figurative)
formulate (= say)
insightful
literally (figurative)
precisely
sensitive
state (= say)

ADVERTISERS' VERBS
accent

climax
contact
finalize
highlight
personalize
pinpoint
slant

JOURNALESE OR TEXTBOOKISH
approach (noun)
background
bitter
crucial
drastic
exciting
factors
fascinating
key (adjective)
meaningful
picture (= situation)
stimulating

ILLITERACIES
connive (= conspire)
[general] consensus [of opinion]
disinterested (= uninterested)
overly, thusly, illy (= over, thus, ill)
presently (= now)
too ("I don't know too much," "I don't feel too well.")

This list gives a choice of words that the self-critical writer will deny himself, at least for a time and as usually employed. They are, most of them, good words. But they have been spoiled by careless or excessive use until in their figurative or vogue sense they no longer mean much. For example: "Award Winner Is Described As Stylist of World-Wide Dimensions" (*New York Times,* Oct. 5, 1956). Forbidding oneself this kind of lazy and affected imagery will cause meaning to flow back into one's prose by introducing the other, direct and active, words that these stopgaps hide from view.

is "a liquid position"? Liquidity is a state of matter; position marks the place of a body in space: there is no coherence between them. The writer evidently combined the idea of being in a *good* position with the idea that it is good to have assets that are *liquid* (that is, taking any desired form, like a liquid). From this came "What is his position? —oh, it's liquid." But try the double image in different words: "How does he stand? —he stands liquid."

To this analysis, which may seem like quibbling but is not, one might object that "liquid position" is by now an accepted phrase of which everyone knows the meaning. The phrase, in other words, is a piece of jargon, possibly indispensable to businessmen. We shall take up this question in a moment. It is in any case a dubious image, made still more muddled by the preceding verb "stimulate." How does one "stimulate a liquid position"? A stimulus is a push, a jab, a "shot in the arm." In fact, one suspects that the writer's first thought was "give a shot in the arm to our liquid position,"[5] but the silliness of that vision somehow broke through to his mind's eye and led him to substitute the less vivid "stimulate" for "shot in the arm." In short, like the rest of us, the author was thinking in a series of loosely connected images, and made some slight effort to trim and adjust them. Only, he did not go far enough. He was afraid of "mixed metaphor," which has become a bugbear, though the fault almost always draws attention to itself, but he did not detect incoherent imagery, which so often passes unnoticed by both writer and reader. What then is the harm? The harm is that it *conceals all or part of the meaning.*

Consider the whole passage we have been examining; it is painfully general and indefinite: what did the company *do* when they "overextended operations"? How did they think this was going to help them? What *was* the disastrous result? Let us come down to earth and suppose some facts: the company opened ten new branch stores, hoping that the money would roll in and add to their cash on hand. But half

[5] This reduction to the absurd is not so farfetched as it seems. A Federal Reserve Bank vice-president declared: "In the month ahead efforts will undoubtedly be directed at preventing any further deterioration, if not in fact at rebuilding liquidity positions." (*New York Times,* Sept. 11, 1956.)

the stores failed and the firm sank deeper into debt. If this is what happened, why not say so? We can then see something and pass judgment upon it. The images raised hang together; they put us in the very presence of the overextension, the hope, the stimulus, the liquid position, and the "end product."

The merit of this rewording is not fanciful but practical. Given a chance to *see* all these things in clear words, a vigilant stockholder could have *fore*seen and said, "It can't be done. The installation of the new stores will eat up our profits for six months and the company needs cash in less than three. I move a vote of No Confidence in the Board of Directors." Somebody, one hopes, did ask and get answers on the concrete matters before the fatal policy was carried out. Of course, the modern appetite for verbiage being what it is, the likelihood is that some group of sleepy and trusting directors approved a hasty scheme expressed in generalities as incoherent as the one that occupies us. For images, if they are familiar enough and put together plausibly enough, will lull the half-attentive reader into swallowing any amount of nonsense.

Analyze, as a game with serious uses, the following sentences taken at random from the inexhaustible supply in one's daily reading matter:

On the offensive side, the Air Force foresees a lethally vital future for its intercontinental strategic missiles.[6]

But it was another [court] case that plummeted Carpenter to the pinnacle of the Wisconsin bar.[7]

While on the money side of our business a point worth noting is the trend which continues to develop in commercial banking with respect to deposit growth.[8]

And from student work:

[6] *New York Times,* March 16, 1955.
[7] E. B. Thompson, *Matthew Hale Carpenter: Webster of the West,* Madison, Wis., 1954, 40.
[8] Commercial Credit Company, Address to the Los Angeles Society of Financial Analysts, March 12, 1968.

In the West Coast of Africa, the British Colonial Office Project developed a pretty wealthy farmer.

The sister disciplines may not be the main highway on which the historian travels but they are side roads he cannot avoid.

The habitual maker of such visual monsters may from time to time catch himself at it and remove them. But in his ordinary state of mind he will continue to frame sentences made up of expressions like: "integrate the major material," "a context that lends perspective," "a background that ushers in the realization of," or "drafted with a loophole which is now in the hands of the secretary." The authors of these improbabilities were in a state of waking sleep, like the reporter who in describing the setting of an outdoor game wrote: "The birds filled the tree-tops with their morning song, making the air moist, cool, and pleasant."[9]

Decide Which Images Are Alive

The test of the images that occur to us and are put on paper is twofold: are they alive and are they compatible? Since most words have the power to raise images, it would be impossible to write if some of these images were not neutralized by a kind of remoteness, a deadness. For example, when a commercial firm is said to "open a branch" the image is dead and therefore acceptable. If our literal vision were aroused, the phrase would be absurd. "To stimulate conversation" is also a dead image, the two ideas of a push given and a man speaking produce no clash of images. But as we saw above, "stimulate" (or "rebuilding") and "liquid positions" do clash. On coming together the two expressions spring into life again and make us smile by their incongruity.

The cure for clashing images may follow several courses: (1) Drop one of the live images. Say: "improve the liquid position"; nobody now remembers the image that lies dead in the word "improve." (2)

[9] Quoted in William James, *Principles of Psychology,* New York, 1890, I, 263.

Cut out all imagery and "translate" into the concrete particulars that stood behind them, as we did above in supposing the facts of the case. (3) Use abstract general terms instead of concrete particulars, taking care to remain sharp and clear, for example: "The company took on more responsibilities in hopes of recovering strength, but this proved unavailing almost from the start."[10]

Jargon: Its Origin and Poisonous Properties

The foregoing examples show that the two straight roads to meaning are, on the one hand, simple particulars and, on the other, careful generality. The road of imagery, the third, is the winding and dangerous one. Nowadays everything a writer sees and hears tempts him to take it. Advertising pelts us with images to make commonplace objects alluring; business and professional men think to enliven their work by refreshing its vocabulary with new images, and statesmen and journalists try to influence our minds with slogans and catchwords based on images. All this is an indirect tribute to poetry, of course; meantime, the residue left in the writer's mind is jargon.

In the original meaning of the term, there is nothing wrong with jargon. All it means is the special tongue of a trade or art—what we now call technical terms—those of music or carpentry or sailing. Such terms are indispensable, there being usually no others to mean the same things; hence they must be accepted regardless of form or logic. When you discover that to a sailor the "mainsheet" is not a sail but a rope, there is nothing you can do about it. You learn his jargon and try to use it correctly.

But there is another kind of language called jargon, this time with a derogatory meaning, and which ought really to be called *pseudo-jargon*. This second kind is that which has gradually invaded business, the professions, government, and ordinary speech, until it now prevails over plain speaking. It is made up of terms and expressions that purport to be special and indispensable even though they are not technical

---

[10] Note that the "but" is here justified by the absence in the first clause of any hint that the company had overreached itself.

words. They are pretentious imitations of technicality. Two things prove their bastard origin—they are not definite and fixed in meaning and they can readily be dispensed with. They arise suddenly in some advertising, political, or academic circle, and they catch on, for no apparent reason but novelty and modishness.

In the sentence containing "liquid position," that piece of pseudo-jargon was accompanied by another: "end product." This latter term is preferred by all jargon lovers over the simple "product." Now it is conceivable that in some industries it may avoid confusion to distinguish between by-products and end products. But in ordinary speech no such need exists. "End product," "end result" are tiresome tautologies. The first was particularly uncalled-for above, where the meaning is actually "consequence." But perhaps we should be grateful that we do not as yet hear of the "end consequence," "end outcome," and "end upshot."

Other examples of pseudo-jargon are:

AREA for *subject*

CONCEPT for *notion, idea, conception*

CONTACT (verb) for *get in touch with, get hold of, meet*

CONTEXT and FRAME OF REFERENCE for *connection, relation, bearing*

DIRECTIVE for *orders, instructions*

EVALUATE for *assess, judge, gauge*

FOCUS for *deal with, treat, discuss*

HIGHLIGHT (verb) and also ACCENT and PINPOINT for *stress, insist upon, give attention to*

MINIMAL ESSENTIALS for *minimum or essentials*

MOTIVATION for *motive, reason, pretext*

MOTIVATED for *moved*

OBJECTIVE for *goal, aim, purpose, intention*

Certain adjectives, such as *basic* and *major,* are also dinned into our ears with a jargonlike "objective" as its "motivation." We are to sense something scientifically absolute about *basic,* something ultrabasic and supermajor; its jargonish tone and feeling will pervade a whole passage.

The writer who wants to present his ideas clearly and with force by eschewing jargon and sticking to plain words should first read Gowers' *Plain Words: Their ABC.* He will find there a list of the worst vogue words, with the reasons, special and general, why their use is reproved. He may then extend his awareness of meanings and pitfalls by mastering Follett's *Modern American Usage.*[11]

[11] Sir Ernest Gowers, *Plain Words: Their ABC,* New York, 1954; Wilson Follett, *Modern American Usage,* New York, 1966.

Some of the words and expressions discountenanced in these books or in these pages may pass out of use as quickly as they came in. That is not the point. The point is that at all times words and phrases are being launched that have the look and tone of jargon. Their long or short life on everybody's tongue has nothing to do with the permanent truth that no matter how mouth-filling and thought-saving for committee meetings, such words are fatal to good writing. One must therefore acquire a sensitiveness (the jargon user would say "an allergy") to new ones as they are made. Here is a specimen from academic writing, followed by the reasons why its growth should be cut short: "He footnotes this idea to Dr. Johnson." What is wrong with the new jargon-use of the verb "to footnote" with an indirect object?

In the first place, the combination is, to the best of our knowledge, unheard of. This is not by itself a sufficient argument to disallow it, but it is enough to give us pause. An author should remember that writing is a social act, which imposes the duty of self-restraint. We try to spell alike and ought to keep to common meanings and usages for the same reason—common understanding, communication. In the second place, this new usage has the characteristic tone of jargon, the air of the showoff drawing attention to himself: "See what I can do? I can footnote an idea to a man." In the third place—and this is the conclusive objection—the new usage renders doubtful and ambiguous whatever meaning was intended. We gather roughly that X made Dr. Johnson responsible for a certain idea.

Or did he? "Make responsible for" is sharp and clear, so that we could accept or deny this imputed responsibility. But what did occur? What are the facts? The reader is understandably impatient. Think of the many possibilities and the many words to impart them that were available to the jargoneer. He could say: "In a footnote, X *assigns to, ascribes to, attributes to, credits with, blames for, makes responsible for, foists upon, fathers upon, palms off on, charges with, accuses of, discovers in*... Dr. Johnson ... the idea in question." A slight rearrangement of name and noun would accommodate all these verbs, each of which carries a distinct meaning. The word chosen would not merely link Idea and Dr. Johnson, but would express the quality of the linkage as well as the opinion of the reporter. Instead of which, we have the vagueness and staleness of jargon surrounding the trivial fact that something took place in a footnote.

How to Live Without Jargon and Clichés

In the light of these objections the "effective writer"—to go back to the psychologists' phrase—will make a further resolve. He will train himself not only to be aware of jargon and of the words jargon displaces, but also to resist in his own mind the laziness implicit in all tricks of speech, all ready-made expressions that sound smart (or once did), all hackneyed tags and quotations, all seeming short cuts—for example the tacking on of "-wise" to some other word as a quick way to get nothing said: "The two nations got together trade-wise." (= started to trade? increased their trade? signed a trade agreement?) He will avoid the same trick with "-conscious" and "-minded," for example, "community-conscious" and "air-minded"; and will not pile up nouns without connectives as in "child sex education" and "population theory evidence." The lesson here is: to be heard and heeded you must do more than lay your ideas side by side like a babbling infant, you must *articulate* them.

Finally, and to the same end of saying what *you* mean, do not substitute semi-synonyms for the words that say something outright; avoid, for example, the widely prevalent use of "feel" for "think"— "Whitehead feels that Nature is a continuum." He does no such thing: he thinks, believes, argues, maintains, assumes, supposes, posits, postulates, imagines, demonstrates, proves—which of these is it? The same flabbiness occurs in "Karl Marx had the benefit of Engels' thinking." (= Engels' thought, views, opinions, knowledge, advice, etc.) There is no such thing as a man's "thinking" apart from the indefinite activity. Reflect on it and you will see that this usage is *not* a parallel to "I enjoyed the violinist's *playing,*" which is a sensible remark, but rather to: "I am going to write the story of Napoleon's living."

Jargon, clichés, and tricks of speech, as you can see, are not simply sets of words or faults of writing, but forms of escape. They denote a failure of courage, an emotional weakness, a shuffling refusal to be pinned down to a declaration. The cowardice comes out on paper like fingerprints at the site of the crime.

To remember the mood and the menace of jargon, remember its typical product, the all-purpose connective *in terms of.* A book review once commended a book as "the best in terms of the Church of

England." The enigma here is to find what "in terms of" signifies. Is it: the best book *about* the Church; the best *in the opinion of* the Church; or the best *for believers in* the Church? It is no small matter to take one interpretation rather than another. And the point is worth laboring because everyone meets such sentences every day without stopping to wonder what they really mean: "The general thinks in terms of army corps; the housewife plans her day in terms of dirty dishes; the child dreams in terms of electric trains." The trouble with the little phrase is that it fails to tell us how the action of the verb is related to its object. We want to know what *the terms* are.[12] We have to guess that perhaps the general thinks *on no less a scale* than that of army corps. The housekeeper plans her day *so as to allow time* for washing dishes. The child dreams that he *has been given* the promised train. But these "translations" are pure surmise. The meanings might just as easily be: "The general thinks that *he wants at least one* army corps." "The housewife makes her day *revolve around* dishwashing." "The child's dream *depicts his playing with trains.*"

And this does not exhaust the possibilities. What the guessing game shows is that the capable writer begins by being a searching reader, a questioner of texts, who uses his imagination to squeeze all the meaning out of what has been well said and to solve the riddles in what has been only half said. In this role the alert writer is identical with the trained researcher. Reading and writing are correlative acts of the mind; both engage the full resources of one's knowledge and attention upon the medium of words.

Omnibus Words, Dressing Gowns, and Circumlocutions

It would be a mistake to think that because they prevail, jargon and cliché are the only enemies of proper words. There are at least three other kinds of words that are equally harmful to the twin virtues

---

[12] The original use of the phrase in the physical sciences is logical and justified: there are terms. For example, one can measure force in terms of the acceleration imparted to a resistant mass, because the terms in which we express the acceleration—say, centimeters per second per second—are the terms in which we express the force.

of vocabulary as such—the virtues of *felicity* and *force*. All three kinds resemble jargon and cliché in being loose, empty, thought-saving kinds of words, but they differ in that they are perfectly good words, which *need* not be used loosely and mindlessly. They are damaging only when out of place.

Words of the first category are especially dear to the writer of histories and reports, because they seem to correspond to what he deals with: such words as *trend, factor, forces, situation, movement, condition, elements, circumstances*. As all-too-commonly used, they are blank cartridges—they merely make a noise. The way to restore their force is to use them for distinct purposes and *invariably* where they belong. A *trend* denotes a clear or measurable collective tendency. It expresses motion. There is a trend toward early marriage or building smaller houses. Don't say: "These new self-service elevators are a regular trend." Similarly, a factor is something that *makes*. Hence the absurdity of: "The gap was a factor he could not bridge."

Whenever possible, use the name of the thing you are concealing behind a loftier word. "The maritime elements were disaffected" —No! Come out with it: "The sailors were rebellious." If you are beset by the modern desire to have words completely "cover" the facts as "maritime elements" purports to do, find a truly descriptive phrase such as: "the sailors and their families"; or "their well-wishers"; or "those dependent on them"; or better still, "the seaboard population." As mentioned before, keep your eye on what your reader could go out and see or touch. Then you have him.

In this same first category of "omnibus" words are certain adjectives that writers of textbooks have made depressingly habitual. These books contain nothing but *bitter* attacks, *crushing* defeats, *shrewd* diplomats, and *ruthless* ambition. All such standard epithets deserve a rest. Attacks can be angry, vehement, violent, reckless, impetuous, sinister, unforgivable, and perhaps half a hundred other things. Let us have each a little different. They certainly were so in reality, and they would be more easily remembered when free of the label that makes them all alike.

The parroting habit also leads writers to clutter up their prose with a second kind of empty words. Gowers has happily named them "adverbial dressing gowns." He has in mind such pairs as *seriously* consider, *fully* recognize, *wholly* unjustifiable, *thoroughly* mistaken. He calls them dressing gowns because the writer is shying away from the naked word they wrap around. Try stripping the main word and see how your utterance gains in strength. To say "His act was unjustifiable" is far stronger than "His act was wholly unjustifiable." With the adverb you are straining to prove; you are frothing a little at the mouth; in the former you have judged, there is nothing to add.

The third category of encumbrances is the familiar one of long words and circumlocutions. No rule can be given about the length of words it is desirable to use. The length of the same word varies with the context (the literal use of *context* here is not jargon). For example, in the first sentence of this paragraph "circumlocution" seemed the shortest way to say what was meant. Elsewhere it might not be, as in "Refrain from circumlocution" for "Don't beat around the bush." The misfortune is that many people who in speaking would not ask anyone to "refrain" from anything feel it their duty to elevate their tone when they write letters, reports, reviews, and books. Oddly enough, the long dressy word comes first to their minds, perhaps from an association of ideas between the authority they desire for their writing and the tone of official pronouncements.

If that is what happens to you, translate back into the vernacular, either at once or in your second draft. Remember that the vernacular does not mean "slang" and need not imply colloquialism. The vernacular is the language of good speakers who are not watching their words but producing them easily and, on the whole, correctly. You cannot write as people speak, but you can write as people would be willing to speak if they were handed a part to read aloud. This is not the only way to write, but it is the best way to practice "translation" from jargon, clichés, empty words, and highfalutin.

When once you have the habit of translation in this sense you can adapt your diction to the occasion, for you will have at least mastered the instrument of vocabulary. Those who remember the dialogue of *Guys and Dolls* know that it is an artful mixture of slang, jargon, and highbrow bookishness. The effect is comic, yet one meets people who missed the virtuosity of it and who vaguely complain that the talk sounds "uneven," which shows that catching the drift is not the same as understanding words.

Idioms and Unwritten Laws

This last distinction is all-important for the would-be writer. He must not only recognize what is wrong with this or that word in his first draft; he must be able to summon up half a dozen in its place and choose among them. To his desk dictionary he may want to add a thesaurus. But he will spend long hours turning over pages if he has to rely on these books for inspiration instead of verification. His need is to be prompt and fertile in suggestion whenever he writes. The quality and speed of notetaking, as we saw in Chapter 2, also depend on one's verbal resources. There is thus every inducement to make words as such a subject of continual study. In this self-discipline, eye and ear, mind and memory, must equally participate. The eye notes spelling, aided by the ear, which also records idiom. The mind looks for distinctions between apparent synonyms, which the memory stores up and delivers again, with connotations.

Idiom is frequently "cast-iron," to use one of H. W. Fowler's terms. You *must* say "He acquiesced *in* the proposal," not *to*. If you slip here, it is probably because of "he agreed to," but note at the same time that "agree to" has a different meaning from "agree with," just like "compare to" and "compare with." A writer who compares himself to Shakespeare will be thought conceited, but if he compares himself with Shakespeare, he can emerge a modest, indeed, a chastened man. Idiom follows neither logic nor illogic; it simply is, and has to be learned. That is the price paid for being born to a rich and sinewy language.[13]

Connotations or overtones are still harder to learn, though many are second nature to most adults. Just as they know that one *rides* a horse and *drives* a car, so they know that one *celebrates* a wedding and *conducts* a funeral; one *reciprocates* a favor and *retaliates* an injury—not the other way round. Such usages may be regarded as halfway between

---

[13] Submitting to the fixity of idiom, good writers seldom tamper with common phrases that, superficially considered, seem to allow change. Write "past his prime," not "past his distinguished prime." Leave to the advertiser the privilege of saying "at its tastiest best"; and if you must qualify, do it outside the phrase, e.g., *not* "he put a reluctant stop," but "he reluctantly put a stop"—which has also the advantage of better logic.

idiom and right diction. A writer should not confuse "hard work" with "hard labor," "mitigate" with "militate," "fortuitous" with "fortunate." Whoever wants to command language must first master its traditions. But the subtler though no less strong customs of other words are often overlooked, with a resulting diminution of force. "Drastic," for instance, which has become so popular, implies an act that affects both the doer and the victim, though perhaps unequally. The shopkeeper who announces "Drastic cut in prices" is correct—the drastic act hurts him while wreaking havoc among the price tags. To use "drastic" as a mere synonym for "violent" or "thoroughgoing" is to waste a good overtone, which after a while will cease resounding and be lost for good. People will then ask, "How do you express the idea of injuring yourself so as to injure your enemy more?"

The present answers to such questions are nowhere written down in full. The facts about idiom and connotations are not easily found except in good writing—writing that is "effective" because it is "sensitive to overtones and the peculiar purpose" of the moment. Hence, let us say it again, he who writes must read—preferably pencil in hand. There is nothing childish in the practice of observing new words and turns of phrase; if the *Reader's Digest* can offer its public an occasional page for vocabulary-building, there is no affectation in doing the same at one's convenience.

If in addition one has the opportunity of reading the manuscripts of other writers, the effort helps in the correcting of one's own. Printed matter is like the words one has just set down—they both have a paralyzing effect on the critical instinct, whereas somebody else's manuscript prose looks wonderfully improvable.

By way of conclusion, scrutinize a pair of sentences from essays by advanced students and apply the principles laid down in this chapter. The first defines the German Customs Union that preceded the Empire:

1. "A basically geographical concept permeated with political overtones dependent on arbitrary historical and political boundaries of the included states."

A critical reader's comments would run: *basically* is both jargon and an adverbial dressing gown. *Concept* is jargon for *idea* or *conception.*

"Permeated *with*" is wrong; the idiom requires *by*. Moreover, the image is absurd: overtones cannot permeate a concept, and a geographical one at that. The rest is inoffensive but clumsy and vague.

2. "Memoirs must be studied for falsifications and for the author's own point of view, as well as sources, whether documentary or in the nature of narrative without official certification."

Comments: Memoirs are not *studied for* falsifications; they are examined or scanned. "Falsifications" is the wrong word, anyway—try "errors" or "falsehoods." The sentence limps badly, but that fault belongs to our next chapter. "Sources . . . in the nature of narrative" are nothing more than narratives. "Official certification" is jargon here for *official* by itself, which should go before "documents" in the rewritten: "as well as sources in the form of official documents or plain narratives."

The ease with which even trained eyes can overlook error and nonsense should make every writer at once endlessly cautious and forever modest. At least half a dozen men—colleagues, editors, and the author himself—must have gone over the preface of a valuable work on economics, which closes with these words: "Obviously, none of the people named above has the least responsibility for whatever may be found in this book. I alone am to blame."

What is the matter here—no jargon, no misfit among images, no false idioms? Nothing that is said is wrong, but something is left unsaid that turns the remark into a kind of joke. The intention was to tell the reader that for whatever *errors* he might find, he must blame the author, not the author's friends. As the words stand, the author "blames himself" for the entire contents of the book. The mistake is more amusing than grievous, and certainly not hard to forgive. If it is to be remembered at all, it should be for unwittingly revealing the spirit in which every writer must write and rewrite: "I alone am to blame."

13

Clear Sentences: Right Emphasis and Right Rhythm

Live Sentences for Living Thoughts

As everybody knows, meaning does not come from single words but from words put together in groups—phrases, clauses, sentences. A mysterious bond links these groups of words with our ideas, and this relation leads in turn to the miracle by which ideas pass from one mind to another. The reason for weighing words with care is to make sure that these units of speech correspond truly to one's inner vision; the reason for building sentences with care is to make sure that all the portions of our thought hang together correctly for truth and conveniently for understanding.

Everyone's mind, however eager it may be for information, opposes a certain resistance to the reception of somebody else's ideas. Before one can take in another's intent, the shape, connection, and tendency of one's own ideas have to yield to those same features in the other person's. Accordingly, the writer must somehow induce in that other the willingness to receive the foreign matter. He does so with the aid of a great many devices which, when regularly used, are called the qualities of his speech or writing.

These qualities go by such names as: Clarity, Order, Logic, Ease, Unity, Coherence, Rhythm, Force, Simplicity, Naturalness, Grace, Wit, and Movement. But these are not distinct things; they overlap and can reinforce or obscure one another, being but aspects of the single power called Style. Neither style nor any of its qualities can be aimed at separately. Nor are the pleasing characteristics of a writer's style laid on some preexisting surface the way sheathing and plaster are laid on the rough boards of a half-finished house. Rather, they are the by-product of an intense effort to make words work. By "making them work" we mean here reaching the mind of another and affecting it in such a way as to reproduce there *our* state of mind.

Since you cannot aim directly at style, clarity, precision, and all the rest, what can you do? You can remove the many possible obstacles to understanding, while preserving as much as you can of your spontaneous utterance. All attempts at reproducing a recognized style, whether Biblical, Lincolnesque, or "stark" for modernity, defeat themselves. You cannot be someone other than yourself. The qualities we have listed, and others you can name, should therefore be regarded as so many tests that you apply in the course of revision by self-questioning. You do not, while writing, say to yourself: "Now I am going to be clear, logical, coherent." You write a sentence and ask, as you go over it: "Can anyone else follow? Perhaps not. Then what is the matter? I see: this does not match that. And here—is this in any way absurd?" Clarity comes when others can follow; coherence when thoughts hang together; logic when their sequence is valid. You achieve these results by changing, cutting, transposing. You may ask: "Is there no way to write so as to avoid all this patching after-the-fact?" There is—and learning how is the subject of this chapter. But note at the outset that any helpful hints will only reduce the amount of re-writing to be done, never remove its necessity.

It is an interesting proof of what has just been said that no satisfactory definition of a sentence has ever been given: there is no specification to which you can build. Yet every educated person recognizes a sentence when he sees one. The mystery of its connection with a train of thought is the point of departure for our effort to make the sentence and the total thought coincide. To say this is to say that notions of correctness or proffers of approved models for sentences will be useless, and even paralyzing, unless they are taken with imagination. Whatever image you may have in mind when you see or hear the word "sentence," that image should not be of something rigid, static, and absolute; a sentence is above all functional, dynamic, and relative. A sentence, perfectly good when taken by itself, may be all wrong when it follows or precedes another. For the thought has to keep moving and its track must be smooth. If you need a structural image of The Sentence, think of it as an organism possessing a skeleton, muscles, and flesh.

Like a skeleton, a sentence is a piece of construction. Traditional grammar in fact speaks of related words as forming "a construction," and calls it awkward or harmonious, allowable or contrary to usage. But do not let the idea of a construction suggest a table or a house; to be sure, a sentence has to stand on its feet, but we liken it to a skeleton because a sentence, like the thought it carries, has to move. Motion is perhaps the fundamental quality of good writing. Motion is what makes writing correspond to thought, which is also a movement from one idea or vision to the next. A reader who knows nothing about the principles of writing may be incapable of analyzing what is wrong as he makes heavy weather through a book. But he feels very keenly whether his mind advances or sticks, goes straight or in circles, marches steadily forward or jerks two steps ahead and three back.

In order to move, the parts of the sentence skeleton must be properly jointed, articulated; the muscles and connective tissue must be strong and inserted at the right places; the burden of ideas must not be too great for the structure. And to cover all this machinery and make it pleasing, the surface must be reasonably varied and polished. Translating this into writers' terms, we say: clauses and phrases must fall into the right pattern of syntax, and the words must be chosen so that the tone and rhythm of the whole are appropriate. A telegraphic message may be exact and well knit, but it lacks grace and sounds unnatural. It moves but does not flow. One cannot imagine reading three hundred pages in telegraphic style. The words omitted in that style and which are restored in ordinary prose are no decoration or added charm; they are simply the rounded contour of the thought, reduced in the telegram to the bare bones.

The return of this image of the skeleton tells us that we have come full circle in our attempt to define at one and the same time what a sentence is and what it does. You may as a result be a little wiser about the virtues to aim at in writing. But you probably think, with reason, that what you need even more than a definition is direct advice, and for this we must look at examples. Yet, we repeat: if you want the examples to be serviceable beyond their immediate instruction, you should study them with the force of our definition behind them.

Five-Legged Sheep and Other Monsters

Let us begin with the schoolbook example: "The wind blew across the desert where the corpse lay and whistled." The sentence moves indeed, and the *information* it contains is not hard to find; but before we quite grasp it we laugh. And this alters the *meaning*, which was not intended to be jocular in the last three words. How to fix it? Our first impulse is to insert a comma after "lay." But reading the result gives an odd impression, as if "and whistled" was a dangling afterthought. Try it aloud and you will hear that a comma pause after "lay" makes "and whistled" sound not simply silly but a trifle puzzling. The only way the sentence sounds rhythmically satisfying is without the pause.

Clearly the diagnosis is that the meaning and the construction are at odds; bad rhythm gives the flaw away, the trouble being that the limb "and whistled" is attached to the wrong part of the body. Since the joke comes from the close link between the corpse and the whistling, we derive from this our first rule of sentence-making: *bring as close together as possible the parts that occur together in the world or go together in your mind.*

Now try to apply the rule to our sentence: "The wind blew across the desert and whistled where the corpse lay." No longer comic, but wrong again, because the new close-linking suggests that the whistling took place only near the corpse. In framing a sentence the need to link and connect implies the need to unlink and detach. Try again: "The wind blew and whistled across the desert where the corpse lay." At last we have the limbs correctly distributed—no front leg is hitched on to the hindquarters. Our sentence passes the test as far as avoiding absurdity and false suggestion goes.

But say it aloud once more and you will notice that it still sounds odd. It leaves the voice up in the air, and with the voice, the meaning. This is because the emphases are off beat. In an ordinary declarative sentence, the two spots of emphasis are the beginning and the end. Hence the two most important elements in the thought must occupy those spots. In our example the main elements obviously are: the whistling wind and the corpse. Whether the corpse lay or stood or leaned is a detail. The last idea sounding in our mind's ear must be "the corpse." Can this be managed? Let us see. "The wind blew and whistled across the desert where lay the corpse." A trifle better, but far from perfect. Why? Because modern English shies away from inversions. Idiomatic turns make a language what it is; to defy idiom is to lose force. In short, to sound natural we must stick to "where the corpse lay."

By this time we are sick and tired of wrestling with these twelve words and we conclude that they cannot be juggled into a proper shape. We are ready to scrap the sentence and go at the idea by a different route when a fresh form occurs to us. "The corpse lay in the desert, across which the wind blew and whistled." This is the best yet. The form is right and if the whole subject were only a little less dramatic we could let it stand. But there is a stiffness about "across which" that suits a description of scenery rather than of lonely death. This impression simply means that we have been made aware of Tone while trying to secure Right Emphasis, Right Linking, and Right Rhythm. These features of the sentence, we repeat, are not separable. On the contrary, a sentence is to be regarded as a compromise among their various demands.

If the Tone of "across which" is unsuitable, what *can* we do with the wretched corpse on our hands? Having twisted and turned it about, all that occurs is to abandon our second construction and try a third: "The corpse lay in the desert, and over it the wind blew and whistled."[1]

---

[1] The inveterate verifier is curious about the fact and he asks: *Does* the wind whistle when it blows across an unobstructed waste?

This is still disappointing: a compound sentence is too weak for this gruesome vision; it separates what eye and ear bring together to the mind. We have dismembered and reconstructed without success. What next?

The true solution lies in the so-called periodic sentence, whose form heightens suspense and generally favors rhythm: "Across the desert where the corpse lay, the wind blew and whistled." A peculiarity of the periodic sentence is that its suspensive opening phrase does not monopolize the emphasis we associate with beginnings. The second portion is still emphatic because the forepart rushes down toward it, so to speak, in an effort to complete its own meaning by finding a main subject and verb.

From our experience with a single bad sentence, we can now confirm our first rule of thumb and add to it others for similar use in framing and straightening sentences:

1. Right linking is the prime requisite. Begin by seeing to it that things related are not divided, and that things remote are not falsely joined.

2. Right emphasis comes next. It is what gives momentum to the thought, what makes the sentence move. It starts from a point of superior interest, travels through a valley of detail, and reaches a second point of high interest, which ends the journey by completing or advancing our understanding of the first.

3. When the emphases are right, the rhythm is likely to be right also, for our speaking habits naturally follow our habits of wording and of thought.[2]

4. At any point in the structure, the phrasing must be in keeping with the tenor of the whole. This is a matter partly of diction and partly of construction. The two together produce Tone.

---

[2]This does not mean that in speaking we usually place our words right for emphasis but that we sound them right, and hence the rhythm is natural. One says: "They *are* good—in *my* opinion." To convey the same meaning in print, one must write: "They are, in my opinion, good." Still judging the written word, explain the rather different meanings of: "In my opinion, they are good" and "They, in my opinion, are good."

To these four propositions there is an important negative corollary: Although a comma that is missing from a sound sentence should be put in, no putting in of commas will cure a defective sentence. When you are tempted to waste time in this effort, just remember "and whistled."

With these truths in mind, we can refine a little on the art of construction, though with no hope of exhausting the subject of improved sentence-building. We go back to the difficult art of linking. The desire to bring kindred things together often tempts the unwary to use phrases that can be read in two or more ways. Ambiguity sets the reader on the wrong track; he must back up and make a fresh start, or perhaps remain in doubt about the right fusion of ideas. When this happens too often, he is understandably aggrieved. Suppose he reads:

If there is lost motion in the rods and boxes in a boiler of steam generating capacity and a valve distributing power properly when the lever is hooked down, it develops into a pound that is annoying and detrimental to the machinery.

The reader's trouble begins at "steam generating capacity." Should this be "steam-generating," a hyphenated adjective modifying "capacity"? Or should it be "a boiler of steam, generating [power at] capacity"? Below, a similar hesitation arises at "valve distributing power." Doubt is settled by our knowledge that valves distribute power and not the other way round ("valve-distributing power" is nonsense.) But we have had to stop and figure this out. The second phrase exactly parallels the first—"steam-generating capacity"—and our retentive ear entices us to give their parallel forms a parallel meaning. Next we are stopped for a further instant at whatever "it" is that "develops into a pound." After talk of steam power, the word "pound" is ambiguous. We see at once that it is not a pound of pressure that is meant but a pound*ing*. Still, we have been jerked to a halt a third time. Finally, another, somewhat different, parallel between the two adjectives in the last part of the sentence tells us that this pounding is "annoying . . . to the machinery."

On the whole, this sentence intended for the instruction of engineers can tell us more about writing than about locomotives. And here is what it tells us: parallelism is so important a device in writing that its use must be kept pure. Do not give parallel forms to disparate ideas, and always carry out the parallels you start with. Do not ever suppose that variation is more elegant. Note the accumulation of horrors in:

When it came right down to it, he was no more able to spell out a conceptual pattern than, in the last analysis, he felt he could muster up the imagination to face such explosive problems of ethics as his sadly unhappy life had left him no room to size up with detachment.

At the words "he was no more able to," the writer has made a contract with the reader. Those words forecast a "than," to be followed by a second action parallel to the first. The contract here is broken. The "than" duly comes, but its proper adjunct is forgotten while the writer pursues his wandering thought down winding channels. Jargon and rank images ("spell out a pattern," "explosive problems," "room to size up") are mixed with clichés ("in the last analysis"), tautologies ("sadly unhappy"), and the redundancies that spoil the parallel—"he [felt he] could," and the words following "imagination." The cure is to give up the "no more than" construction and make two sentences, one about the conceptual patterns—whatever they may be—and one about the ethical problems of a sadly unhappy life without room.

An observation made in passing when we examined the sentence from the engineer's manual furnishes a second rule of good construction: *the antecedents of pronouns must always be unmistakable.* In the welter of rods, boxes, and valves no one can tell what "it" is that "develops into a pound." It cannot be the engine, which is not even mentioned. The motion, no doubt, develops into a pound, but the only motion mentioned is four lines above and it is *lost* motion. Technically, it is a kind of motion, but in syntax it does not exist. In any event, no less than six nouns in the singular precede "it," and two would be enough to create confusion. By rights, the last in order should be the true antecedent, but that happens to be "lever," which makes nonsense. The "it" is an orphaned relative with no references to show when questioned.

Modern Prose: Its Virtues and Vices

After so much wallowing in uncertainty we are eager for a good sentence. Here is one embodying a double parallel and making of it a dramatic image: "Too blind to avert danger, too cowardly to withstand it, the most ancient government of Europe made not an instant's resistance: the peasants of Underwald died upon their mountains, the holders of Venice clung to their lives."[3]

The modern reader who appreciates this sentence may say that in spite of its clarity, richness, and rhythmical excellence, it is alien to his mode of thought and hence beyond his power to imitate. We no longer enjoy these complex and balanced forms; they seem to us artificial. We prefer to write simply, as we speak—or so we like to believe. If the engineer's sentence above, and the biographer's right after, are fair samples of serious prose in our century, we are forced to admit that the elements of complexity are still with us, though unorganized. We are not so simple and straightforward as we pretend, and the truth is that we could not follow the advice of "write as we speak" even if we wanted to.

What prevents the written word from reproducing speech is that, in speaking, the voice, stress, facial expression, and gesture contribute a quantity of meaning that fills out the insufficiency of colloquial speech. Read the transcript of court testimony and you will see how difficult it is to understand. You have to guess how every remark was spoken, inflected, made clear by something other than words. In good writing the writer has to supply these elements which give point and direction to utterance. Hence the use of those transitional and qualifying words that are almost entirely absent from conversation.

And it is this necessity, of course, that leads to the other extreme. The writer may think as he would speak; but half-conscious of a lack, he fills out his spontaneous sentence with many words—to stop the gaps, to bottle up his meaning, which always threatens to fizz away.

[3] Marguerite, Lady Blessington, in her *Conversations of Lord Byron,* Philadelphia, 1836, 96, reports that Byron exclaimed about this passage from Hallam's *Middle Ages:* "This is the way to write history if it is wished to impress it on the memory."

Up to a point the effort succeeds. But superfluous words destroy explicitness. The fault of beginners and casual writers is that their sentences say the same thing twice over. Here is a brief example from a government publication:

The Council members will represent not only the interests of archivists and historians, but also those of political scientists, economists, genealogists, and teachers in the following areas: the expansion of the Federal archival program in Federal records centers and Presidential libraries; the use of archival resources for graduate studies; the increasing diversity in specialized and technical subjects documented by archives; and the best possible uses of limited financial resources.[4]

Part of the difficulty with this sentence is that it is not stripped down to its analyzable meaning; for example, the "Council" will represent all these complicated things, not its members; and again, what are "archival resources" but archives? And what do we make of the string of ideas beginning with "increasing diversity"? Every phrase is loaded with overlapping words and—this is the important point—the excess is not simply dropped by the reader. It stops his mind long enough to make him wonder whether some special nuance is meant or no. Since it is no, the effort has been wasted. Multiply this kind of fault through successive paragraphs and the reader bogs down.

From this we infer the generality that, all else being equal, *the ease with which thought can be gathered from words is in inverse ratio to their combined length.*

We did not say "to their number," for the length of the words themselves may be part of the impediment; and we did say "all else being equal," which means that occasions are frequent in which long words and long sentences are preferable. But a simple thought buried in a sentence stuffed with long words inevitably produces the effect commonly called "a mouthful." Like the mouth, the mind cannot wrap itself around it. The moral is: any sentence that grows on and on in a string of words ending in "-ity" or "-tion," hooked together with "of's" and "to's," must be whittled down to size with a hatchet.

---

[4] *Prologue: The Journal of the National Archives,* I (Spring 1969), 52.

Consider this, which purports to *make clearer* one of Shakespeare's plays:

The creation of character, indeed, is not to be regarded as the unique, or even principal, end of Shakespeare's dramatic creations, in which plot and motive, themselves handled with greater flexibility and insight, tend increasingly to find their proper context in a more ample artistic unity which embraces and illuminates them; but in the delineation of personality beyond the limits of convention his language first attained some sense of its full possibilities.

No mind, including the author's, can take in at one scoop the message of this clumsy compound. Therefore the critic had no excuse for offering it to the public, even if his mind does work on the rocket principle, shooting out fresh phrases at intervals as he proceeds where we cannot follow. He should make a first stop after "creations" and a second after "unity." Rereading this, the author would see that the portion beginning with "but" is so flabbily contrasted with what went before that he should ask himself what, in fact, he did have in mind.

Nor is sprawling his only sin against sense. He gives us an anthology of faults: (1) Awkward repetition: "creation" in line 1, "creations" in line 2. (2) Tautology: "themselves" in line 3, and the whole phrase beginning "find their proper context . . ." down to "embraces" ("context," "unity," and "embraces" say the same thing three times). (3) Illogic: how are we to interpret the comparison in "greater" and "more ample"? Than what? "Increasingly" suggests "as time went on," but we must guess this. (4) Pronouns adrift: "their" in line 4 and "them" in line 5 have two possible antecedents—"dramatic creations" on the one hand, and "plot and motive" on the other. (5) The vagueness of perpetual abstraction: what does it *mean* "to handle plot and motive with greater flexibility and insight"? "to find a proper context"? "to be embraced and illuminated by a more ample artistic unity"? "to delineate personality beyond the limits of convention"? And how in the name of heaven does a writer's *language* "attain some sense of its full possibilities"?

We see in this example what it means to be ponderous without being scholarly. The worst faults of "serious writing" are here conveniently grouped, the "noun plague" dominating them all. Not one plausible agent performs a recognizable act denoted by a strong verb. All is passive and diffuse and jargon-ridden.

As an antidote, let us turn to another writer on Shakespeare:

> Structurally, Tate has made few serious alterations. The most important is Bolingbroke's winning of the rabble. This is amusingly done and probably acted well enough. More serious is the "elevation" of Richard's character, a feat on which Tate plumes himself in the Preface. As a matter of fact, it spoils the play.[5]

Despite its choppiness, which might become tedious, and a lack of charm, which would preclude subtle thoughts, this passage at least answers the reader's prayer for simple and straightforward prose. What makes it such is the presence of what was absent in the former passage: plausible agents, recognizable acts, strong verbs. Of these last, there are still too few. A more searching writer would, for instance, have preferred: "Tate has altered but few structural parts . . ." Then the logic could be stricter: if "the most important" alteration is the one about Bolingbroke, how can the one about Richard be "more serious"? And to a good ear—pronouns and parallels again!—the sentence "This is amusingly done and probably acted well enough" sounds disjointed. The shift in voice calls for a second subject: "and *it* probably acted . . ."; for the passive "is done" will not go in harness with the active verb "acted."

Carpentry or Cabinetmaking?

All we have been saying is an extension of our original proposition that "good writing is an intense effort to make words work." The complaints and suggestions about the passages we have examined boil down to the demand that each word—noun, verb, adverb, or any other kind—should contribute something to the sense, and this with economy. If one word can do the work of two, use one. If you absolutely need a phrase, make it short. If the thought is complex and the sentence has

[5] Hazelton Spencer, *Shakespeare Improved,* Cambridge, Mass., 1927, 262.

to contain several clauses, see to it that each clause expends its energy where none will be wasted, that is, close to the idea it enlarges or qualifies.

A good rule to follow in order to achieve coherence with the least trouble is to stick to your subject, voice, or construction. Do not start with one idea or form and change it in mid-career. The writer above switched from a passive verb to an active and lost momentum. Another will write: "The topic one selects should be clear and precise and when one comes to look for the materials on it, it will be found that the subject itself serves as a guide to their selection." This is no doubt a faithful transcript of the way the thought arose in one mind, but its form is ill adapted to its penetrating another. In a second draft the writer should cling to his grammatical subject and see where it leads him: "The topic selected should be clear and precise—*so that* IT will guide the researcher—*when* HE comes to look for *his* materials." Twenty-three words in place of thirty-five, and a *continuous motion* instead of three hitches—from "the topic" to "when one comes" to an indefinite "it" and back to "the subject" again.

Only remain faithful to your subject and construction, making everything follow the one and fit into the other, and you will be surprised at the ease, speed, and clarity that you attain. All the thick connective tissue—or clanking chains, rather ("as regards," "as far as . . . is concerned," "in relation to," and the like)—will automatically fall away; associated ideas will be next to next; and your thought will be accessible to the reader who, by definition, is always on the run.[6]

For models of this kind of writing, study the advertising cards in any public vehicle. The ideas conveyed may be stupid, commonplace, or untrue; the words themselves may be flossy or jargonlike, but the construction is usually impeccable. One reason is that advertisers know they have only thirty seconds to make an impression. Another and a clinching reason is that they employ first-rate writing talents. When these are exerted in publicizing welfare agencies or, occasionally, political appeals, they produce classic utterances. What could be better than:

[6] Go back to Chapter 2 and follow once again the rewriting of sentences from the report on the Cutter vaccine (pp. 34–36).

"Eighteen million Californians need a fighting Senator with experience, ideas, and a heart."

Note how the attention is arrested, without fuss, by the opening phrase, which addresses every voter in the state, and how adroitly the emphases are managed: having started with our interesting selves we wind up with an appeal to the feelings. But "ideas" are not wholly forgotten, though "experience," as the chief political virtue, comes first in the series. Notice also the function of the single adjective "fighting." It is a strong word, but here it is more than that. Without it, the sentence might be a bare statement of need, suggesting no candidate to fill it. But with the epithet, it is clear that the declaration aims at someone, and behold! his picture is underneath it.

You may say that the ease, lucidity, and force of this bid for votes comes from the inherent simplicity of the idea. Not so. It is always easy to write a muddy sentence, and it would be surprising if the one we have been admiring had been struck off impromptu. The normal tendency is to join chunks of wordage each to each as they come and then tap them here and there with a hammer till they more or less resemble a structure.

Here are examples of two phases of composition—if indeed the first fragment can claim the name. The writer is a high-school teacher of English whose examination paper was first quoted in an article showing how illiterate are some of those who "educate" our young:

Hemingway works is the beginning of all modern American Literature. He doesn't write too much conversation in his books. Just enough to make the idea go across and his descriptions are brief with many adverbs.[7]

Now comes a hammered-down affair that is brisker and more literate but not much more satisfactory:

Thousands of years ago men first learned the secret of conducting water through crude pipes. ["Crude" is out of place here, since the secret sought was how to conduct water through pipes—which turned

---

[7] James D. Koerner, "Can Our Teachers Read and Write?" *Harper's Magazine*, CCIX (November 1954), 80.

out to be crude.] Long before the birth of Christ, the Chinese transported water through bamboo. [Christ is brought in for vividness, but the effect fails by making one wonder what His birth contributed to plumbing.] . . . and there is much evidence of the fine water supply system of the Romans. [By this point, the writer has given up, lost his grip on vividness, fact, and rhythm.][8]

The unpalatable truth is that since a really well-made sentence is not born, like the live body we compared it to, it can only be the result of much planning and fitting, of close measuring for balance, and of hidden jointing for solidity and smoothness—it is cabinetmaker's work, plus the living force that gives movement and stirs the inert frame into an animated whole.

The joiner's task calls for words that will bind the ideas together from end to end. But in a second draft, it is often desirable to omit some of the cross references. Where the reader's mind will take the jump alone, it is a waste to prod him. An example will show what is meant:

What course of procedure does this suggest? In spite of all the study on the broad topic of productivity, the sum total of knowledge useful to management is small. Government and economic research agencies should be encouraged to expand studies of productivity.[9]

This passage is clear and rapid because in the first sentence "this" refers adequately to the preceding paragraph and because in the second sentence the subject (productivity) is named again in a passing manner that allows our attention to dwell on the aspect of it that matters, namely, the *study* of productivity. The writer then omits a further reference after "the sum total of knowledge"—we know very well it is not knowledge at large, but knowledge about productivity. At the last gasp, however, the writer's art broke down: he repeated "studies of productivity" at an emphatic place, almost as if this were a new topic he was introducing. He might have said instead: "Government, etc., should be encouraged to enlarge this sum by extending [not 'expanding'] their researches."

[8] Steel Plate Fabricators' Association, *History of Steel Pipe*, Chicago, 1955, 3.
[9] First National Bank of Boston, *New England Letter*, July 31, 1956, 3.

When a writer falls back repeatedly on clumsy reference by means of "such information," "the above-mentioned," and insensitive repetitions of his subject in identical words, the paragraphs read like a lawyer's brief. Indeed, they cannot be read, but must be worked out, studied.

Now there is one place in any article or book where this sort of failure is fatal to the circulation of the work. That place is the beginning. To catch your reader, the hook must be baited with palatable stuff. A good writer will therefore toil over his opening sentence.

FIGURE 9   *Questions to Ask in Writing and Revising*

I   a. Has my paper (chapter) a single informing theme, with its proper developments, or is it merely a series of loosely connected ideas and images?

b. Does my beginning begin and does my conclusion conclude? (A beginning should not go back to the Flood, and a conclusion is not the same thing as a summing up.)

c. Is each of my paragraphs a division with a purpose; that is, does it organize a number of sentences into a treatment of one idea and its modifications?

d. Is each sentence contrived to stand on its own feet or is it thrown off balance by the load of qualifiers or the drag of afterthoughts?

e. Have I made proper use of transitional words and phrases to keep all my connections clear? For example, *nevertheless, moreover, even, still, of course* (in its use of minimizing the idea before), *to be sure, admittedly.* (The transitional word or phrase is usually better in the course of the sentence than at the beginning.)

II a. What is the *tone* of my piece? Is it too stiff and too formal, trying for the effect of authority? Is it perhaps too relaxed, too familiar, too facetious? Or is it, as it should be, simple, direct?

b. Are there any passages that I especially prize? If so, am I sure that, in my creative enthusiasm, I am not delighted with something "fancy"?

c. Have I been conscious of the reader and have I consulted his convenience? Or have I, on the contrary, been easy only on myself and used a "private" language?

Let his model be the one that opens Jane Austen's *Pride and Prejudice:* "It is a truth universally acknowledged that a single man in possession of a good fortune must be in want of a wife." This far from truthful proposition is an ideal opening, because it foretells in the smallest compass what we are about to be concerned with—marriage and money; and how we are to be concerned with them—in the spirit of irony.

Conclusions, too, are important, being the last word ringing in the reader's ear. They may be as difficult as beginnings if you have

---

   d. Could I, if called upon to do so, explain the exact meaning and function of every word I have used? For example, *subjective, objective, meaningful, realistic, impact, value.*

   e. Are my metaphors aids to the reader or merely ways for me to escape my own difficulty?

III a. Is it perfectly clear to which noun or noun-clause my pronouns refer? (The *slightest* ambiguity is fatal.)

   b. Have I tried to give an air of judicious reserve by repeating the words *somewhat, rather, perhaps,* and have I used for this purpose the illiterate "to an extent"? Or, conversely, have I overdone the emphatic with *very, invariably, tremendous, extraordinary,* and the like?

   c. Have I arbitrarily broken or altered the idiomatic links between certain words, particularly between verbs and their allied prepositions, committing such solecisms as: *disagree . . . to, equally . . . as, prefer . . . than?*

   d. Have I imported from sciences and disciplines in which I am interested a vocabulary out of place in civilized writing? What jargon and vogue words have slipped out by force of habit? Examples of jargon are: *integrate, area, parameter, frame of reference, methodology, in terms of, level, approach.*

   e. Have I preferred the familiar word to the far-fetched? the concrete to the abstract? the single to the circumlocution? the short to the long?

said a great deal and want to recall it in one, final, pregnant sentence. Here is a good example dealing with England's defeat of the Great Armada: "This triumph of sea power insured the survival of the Reformation in England and to a lesser extent in Germany, and helped maintain Holland's independence from Spain."

The Sound of the Sense

These two examples of opening and closing are models only to the extent that they combine a number of the qualities we spoke of earlier as desirable in all writing—clarity, balance, movement, force, and ease. Jane Austen's, it need hardly be pointed out, has grace and wit besides.

But the models further resemble each other in that they disclose a characteristic tone: we hear a voice and it is pleasing. Tone cannot be defined except negatively, when it is bad. Anyone can tell when a writer is talking down to him—that is the condescending tone. But there is also the pompous, the chattering, the precious, the chummy, the toplofty, the cynical and sneering, the vulgar out of the corner of the mouth—the varieties of bad tones are infinite, for they correspond to the mixtures of human emotions.

The curious thing is that a good writer will occasionally fall into a tone that he himself would reprove, yet will never notice the lapse. Either he is seduced by "language," as in preciosity or pedantry; or else he is betrayed by his feelings about the subject, as in cynicism or arrogance. These are reasons, not excuses. The reader is quick to notice what rings false and to resent it as a personal insult. Hence it behooves a writer to watch his tone. To do this he may have to put himself on guard against his most congenial adult attitudes. Until spoiled by sophistication, children who write are free of these. In consequence, a writer such as the nine-year-old author of *The Young Visiters*[10] has perfect tone. Pick up the book anywhere and no matter how difficult the subject, the tone suits:

[10] By Daisy Ashford, New York, 1919.

The Abbey was indeed thronged next day when Ethel and Bernard cantered up in a very fine carrage drawn by two prancing steeds who foamed a good deal. In the porch stood several clean altar boys who conducted the lucky pair up the aile while the organ pealed a merry blast. The mighty edifice was packed and seated in the front row was the Earl of Clincham looking very brisk as he was going to give Ethel away at the correct moment. Beside him sat Mr. Salteena all in black and looking bitterly sad and he ground his teeth as Ethel came marching up.[11]

What admirable control of rhythm and tone! The difficulty of exercising control has inspired a rule of thumb: If you are especially fond of a passage, strike it out. But this advice evidently goes too far, since "fondness" can express a sound judgment about a sentence well worked over. No. The only clue to bad tone is reading one's writing after an interval and responding to the text like an unprepared reader. Phrases will then begin to sound hollow, and they will be judged falsehoods or padding or irrelevance.

But many writers entertain something more than a negative ambition. They aim at a virtue beyond propriety of tone, and it is in this effort that some will overreach themselves and produce what is ironically stigmatized as "fine writing." The irony does not mean that writing cannot or should not be fine. Masterpieces of prose are there to prove that the quality is both desirable and achievable, and nobody would maintain that it comes to a writer without his trying. The objection is to the striving after a fineness that is affected or commonplace in cheap literature—fancy phrases.

If it were needed at this late date to prove that true fineness is at once the result of work and of a born writer's personality, a decisive example would be the famous ending of Lincoln's First Inaugural, for which his Secretary of State, William H. Seward, had proposed a first draft, as follows:

I close. We are not, we must not be, aliens or enemies, but fellow countrymen and brethren. Although passion has strained our bonds

[11] *Op. cit.*, 99.

of affection too hardly, they must not, I am sure they will not, be broken. The mystic chords which proceeding from so many battlefields and so many patriot graves, pass through all the hearts and hearths in this broad continent of ours, will yet again harmonize in their ancient music when breathed upon by the guardian angel of the nation.[12]

Lincoln worked it over four times and produced the well-known words:

I am loath to close. We are not enemies, but friends. We must not be enemies. Though passion may have strained it must not break our bonds of affection. The mystic chords of memory, stretching from every battlefield, and patriot grave, to every living heart and hearthstone, all over this broad land, will yet swell the chorus of the Union, when again touched, as surely they will be, by the better angels of our nature.[13]

Lincoln did not, in one sense, change a single idea of Seward's. But in another sense he changed them all. By a greater simplicity of vision, a truer feeling for the meaning of words, and a superior sensitivity to rhythm, he produced his own incomparable music, where Seward had merely lined up some appropriate propositions. Seward is (as we say) adequate, but he lacks the complete adequacy that thinks of everything and sets it in its proper place. Just compare Seward's "guardian angel," who is a cliché of the political platform and not a force, with Lincoln's "better angels of our nature," who stand here for conscience and generous impulse in each *living heart*. There was a chance of averting bloodshed by appealing to those forces, whereas Seward's plea was a dead letter before the ink was dry.

To sum up, the search for complete adequacy is, first and last, the only general rule for good writing. Try to find out what you mean—what you would go to the stake for—and put it down without frills or depreciatory gestures. Exhaust the means of literary expression, and you will produce sentences that parse and move and carry the ring of your voice. Keep your eye constantly on your subject—that portion

---

[12] *The Collected Works of Abraham Lincoln,* ed. Roy P. Basler, 9 vols., New Brunswick, N.J., 1953–55, IV, 261, n. 99.
[13] *Ibid.,* 277.

occupying your field of vision at the moment—and you will achieve, in addition to ease and lucidity, force. Contrary to common belief, this trinity of virtues does not mean that sentences must bark, or be cast in the same mold, or remain drearily declarative. Nor does keeping the subject ever in view mean that the writer's own personality vanishes. It mingles, rather, with every phrase he sets down, yet without interposing a thick mist of ego between the reader and the page.

Examine, by way of conclusion and summary of our suggestions, the following paragraph, taken from an English scholar's introduction to a volume of letters. Notice how much information is amassed and conveyed without being thrust at the reader; and respond also to the quiet working of a style in which no word is wasted and through which the native impulses of an urbane mind are revealed:

Saint Evremond admits that the company of his friends and their conversation were more important to him than his writings, which occupied his time only when there was nothing better to do. Like his contemporaries at the courts of Louis XIV and Charles II, he regarded literature as one of the necessary accomplishments of a person of quality, not as a means of earning money or reputation. And though posterity remembers him as a man of letters, he himself claimed to be remembered as a soldier first and afterwards as a courtier. For the fate of his compositions after they had left his pen he cared as little as tradition says he cared about his personal appearance in his old age. He wrote, as it has been said of another, for his own and for his friends' delight, and for the delight also, though he could not have foreseen it, of the pirate printers. They, of course, turned his carelessness to good account, and flourished on the proceeds of innumerable and horribly garbled impressions of his essays, exposed for sale on the bookstalls of London, Paris, and Amsterdam. Hitherto he has given no delight to the bibliographer, and I confess that I have profited little from an examination of a very large number of those unauthorized publications. At the same time my acquaintance with them, and with the one authentic edition of his collected works, has not altered my belief that a selection of his writings, even in translation, is worth reading, and therefore worth reprinting.[14]

[14] John Hayward, ed., *The Letters of Saint Evremond,* London, 1930, xiii.

14

The Arts of Quoting and Translating

Three Recurrent Tasks

Whether a researcher writes well or ill, he finds himself repeatedly quoting and citing. This is true regardless of his subject. And unless that subject is purely local, he also finds himself using sources in a foreign language, which perforce makes him a translator.

Quoting other writers and citing the places where their words are to be found are by now such common practices that it is pardonable to look upon the habit as natural, not to say instinctive. It is of course nothing of the kind, but a very sophisticated act, peculiar to a civilization that uses printed books, believes in evidence, and makes a point of assigning credit or blame in a detailed, verifiable way.[1]

Accordingly, the conventions of quoting and citing should be mastered by anyone whose work makes him a steady user of these devices. Citing is in fact so stylized and yet so adaptable to varying needs that we shall devote to it most of the next chapter. The present

---

[1] The vagaries of quoters and misquoters are studied and illustrated by Paul F. Boller, Jr., in his *Quotemanship: the Use and Abuse of Quotations for Polemical and Other Purposes,* Dallas, 1967.

one will deal with the two forms of quoting—in the original and in translation. They are capable of more skillful handling than is sometimes suspected, and a study of the technique will contribute to ease and efficiency if not to art.

The Philosophy of Quoting

The habit of quoting in nearly every kind of printed and spoken matter and the rules for doing it are quite recent developments in Western culture. Formerly, the practice was limited to scholars, and was taken as a sign of the unoriginal, timid, pedantic mind. Although Montaigne's *Essays* and Burton's *Anatomy of Melancholy* were admired for their abundance of quaint quotations, most writers preferred to appropriate the knowledge of others and to give it out again in their own words. [Emerson, by no means an unscholarly man, expressed a common feeling when he said: "I hate quotations. Tell me what you know."] And another scholarly New Englander, of our century, John Jay Chapman, pointed out that what the great quoters seize upon, they alter as they repeat it.[2]

The views of these two American writers should be kept in mind, not as a bar to quotation or as a license to quote inaccurately,[3] but as a reminder that *your* paper, *your* essay, *your* book should be primarily *your* work and *your* words.] What was said in Chapter 2 about taking notes through immediate assimilation and rewording holds good on the larger scale of the finished work. [If you have not made other people's knowledge your own by mixing it with your thoughts and your labor of recomposition, you are not a writer but a compiler; you have not written a report but done a scissors-and-paste job.]

And the chief defect of such an evasion of responsibility is that the piece will probably be tedious to read and lacking in force and

[2] *Lucian, Plato, and Greek Morals*, Boston, 1931, 3-4.
[3] But as H. W. Fowler says in his *Modern English Usage* under "Misquotation":
The misquoting of phrases that have survived on their own merits out of little-read authors . . . is a very venial offence; and indeed it is almost a pedantry to use the true form instead of so established a wrong one; it would be absurd to demand that no one should ever use a trite quotation without testing its verbal accuracy.

light. Many writers of master's essays and doctoral dissertations think that what is expected of them is a string of passages from other authors, tied together with: "on this point he said: ..." and "in reply, he stated: ..." These are varied with: "Six months later, Thomson declared: ..." and "Jennings thereupon differed as follows: ..." The effect is of an unbearable monotony. Every page looks like a bad club-sandwich—thin layers of dry bread barely enclosing large chunks of some heavy solid.

Unfit for handling, the sandwich falls apart, and the reason is easy to see: unless your words and your thought predominate in your work, you lose control of your "story." The six or eight people whom you quote in any given section had different purposes from yours when they wrote, and you cannot make a forward-moving whole out of their disjointed fragments. This fact of experience gives rise to the first principle of the art of quoting: *Quotations are illustrations, not proofs.* The proof of what you say is the whole body of facts and ideas to which you refer, that is, to which you *point.* From time to time you give a *sample* of this evidence to clinch your argument or to avail yourself of a characteristic or felicitous utterance. But it is not the length, depth, or weight of your quotations that convinces your reader.[4]

Two rules of thumb follow from the principle just enunciated: (1) Quotations must be kept short, and (2) they must as far as possible be merged into the text. The form of quoting that we have just used in introducing these two rules—stopping dead, a colon, and a new sentence—is convenient in books of instruction; it is awkward in writing that describes, argues, or narrates. Far better is the form that we use in the next line and that incorporates into your sentence "that portion of the author's original words which [you] could not have put more concisely" without losing accuracy.

Longer quotations than this cannot, of course, be inserted entire into your own sentence, but your words can lead to the brink of the other author's remarks and, *with or without an ushering verb, can make the two speakers produce one effect,* like singers in a duet. Consider a passage

[4] An apparent exception to this rule occurs when you try to prove a point by reproducing documents. The exception is only apparent, because documents that are longer than a couple of pages should be relegated to an appendix and only discussed or quoted from in the text.

from the biography of a famous English trial lawyer, in which the author wants to make use of an important letter:

He was bitterly disappointed when his old friend Clavell Salter was given the first vacancy. "I am told that S. is to be recommended," he wrote to Lord Edmund Talbot, "Well, he is a splendid chap and a great friend of mine of thirty years standing. I think he will tell you he owes much to me in the early days..." The letter is that of a bitterly disappointed man, and ends with a prophecy about his future, which came almost exactly true. "Well, I am fifty-nine; if my health lasts, I suppose I can enjoy another ten years hard work at the Bar." Within a few months of ten years after the date of the letter he died, almost in harness. Shortly after this disappointment he was approached as to the writing of his memoirs and he discussed the project and even wrote a few pages. "What will you call the book?" he was asked. "Better call it *The Story of a Failure*," he said sadly, and laid aside his pen.[5]

If instead of this running narrative and commentary, the biographer had used the lazy way of heralding each quoted remark with "he said" or one of its variants, we should have halted and started and halted and started at least four times. Notice that the method of Merged Quotation here recommended has the advantage of preventing the kind of repetition that *Punch* once picked up from the London *Times:*

Land at Freshwater, Isle of Wight, is being prepared as a rocket-motor testing site, the Ministry of Supply said yesterday. "This land is being prepared for the ground testing of rocket motors," a Ministry official explained.

"Clear now?" asked *Punch.*

Whole books have been composed on the system of repetition, especially in graduate schools. When the candidate has collected his material, he "writes it up" by the simple process of (1) announcing what the quotation implies, (2) giving the quotation, and (3) rehashing what has just been said. To the reader this is death in triplicate. To

[5] Edward Marjoribanks, *The Life of Sir Edward Marshall Hall,* with an Introduction by The Earl of Birkenhead, London, 1929, 377.

the author, who has to pay for the typing and possibly the printing, it is a great waste. Knowing how to quote might have reduced the bulk of paper and wordage by more than a third; for what we have called the merged quotation is usually docked of head and tail—only the body of it plays its part in *your* presentation.

A final caveat: a researcher must quote only what he has himself read (or heard), and he must weigh carefully his choice of source when variant texts present themselves. It is a shortcut but rarely an advantage to use another writer's quotation as one's own; the risks are not worth the time saved. Experienced editors of learned journals estimate that as many as 15 percent of all footnotes contain errors of one kind or another in the average article of even careful scholars. And the texts of quotations are probably no more accurate.

Misquotations can arise in an infinite number of ways. A newspaper report from London, for example, bears the headline: EDEN SAYS ROOSEVELT WAS RECKLESS. The article itself, reporting on the publication of Eden's memoirs, says that the writer has criticized President Roosevelt for "recklessness" in the conduct of foreign policy vis-à-vis the Soviet Union.[6] This is certainly plausible, even if the expression is rather bold for a former diplomat. But dare one quote him as having written it? No. Even though headline and text agree as to Eden's words, a little research—which means going to the book itself—shows both to be wrong: what Eden wrote was that Roosevelt's opinions of European affairs "were alarming in their cheerful *f*ecklessness."[7]

The Mechanics of Quotation

Certain forms must, as we said, always be observed in quoting. The modern quotatiousness that has made everybody aware of whose words are which, and that comes out in the announcer's " ... and I quote ... " or the casual speaker's "quote ... unquote"[8] has made

---

[6] *New York Times,* March 21, 1965.

[7] *The Reckoning: The Memoirs of Anthony Eden, Earl of Avon,* Boston, 1965, 433.

[8] There is no necessity for either of these verbal devices; they are affectation based on the formality of the written word. Moreover, "unquote" is nonsense probably born of confusion with "end quote." See Follett, *Modern American Usage,* "quote, unquote," 270–71.

us all slaves to a common reporting system. But its mechanics have a spiritual meaning: the system became universal because people saw the value of respecting a man's *ipsissima verba*, because they acquired some notion of the influence of context upon meaning, and finally because the recognition of rights in literary property made correct "crediting" necessary.

The most important conventions that rule the quoting of words in print have been exemplified in the last three pages, as well as earlier in this book. We can now set them down in a row, with a few relevant suggestions:

Merge   Update

(1) A quotation is introduced and closed by double quotation marks. A quotation within a quotation carries single quotation marks, and a third quotation, if required, brings double ones again.

(2) The omission of a word, phrase, or sentence is shown by three dots. If that omission follows the end of a sentence, the fourth dot that you will observe in some quoted material is actually the period at the end of the original sentence.

(3) If intelligibility requires the addition of a word or short phrase (seldom more), the added words should be enclosed in square brackets.[9] These words will generally be possessive adjectives—for example, [his], [your]—or the definite article [the], or a pair of words expanding a pronoun, such as an "it" in a quotation that would be unintelligible without an antecedent. One replaces this "it" with: [the document], or some such unmistakable substitute. One may also supply a word where ambiguity might result from the lack of a context: see the word [court] in the quotation on p. 283.

(4) The spelling, capitalization, and punctuation of the quoted passage must be faithfully reproduced unless (a) you modernize these features when quoting ancient texts, in which case you state your principles at some convenient point; or (b) you correct an obvious typographical or other error, in which case a footnote is required to draw attention to the change.

(5) An extension of the foregoing rule accounts for the familiar

---

[9] In legal scholarship, brackets are put around any capital letter that is supplied by the quoter when he changes the grammatical role of a word. This is rarely necessary in history-writing.

tag at the end of a quotation: [My italics.] It is perhaps a shade less obtrusive to use the phrase "Italics added"; in any case, a writer should not make a practice of sprinkling italics over other people's prose. If you choose your quotation with forethought and *set it with care* within your own remarks, it will generally not need the italicizing of words to make its point. If on rereading you think the force of the quotation somehow does not make itself felt, try cutting down the quoted words to those that actually contain the point. Then you will not have to underline them in order to make them stand out.

(6.) The quoting of titles and the like in the text is more properly called "citing" and this sometimes presents small problems. But note at the outset the second invariable rule of modern scholarship:[10] all book titles are printed in italics (underlined in typescript), and all essay titles are enclosed within double quotation marks.[11]

Apart from this convention, a question sometimes arises as to the wording of the title to be cited. Readers feel a certain awkwardness in reading: "This he achieved in his *When Knighthood Was in Flower.*" The remedy for this is simple: insert a cushion word or phrase, for example, "in his popular tale," or "in his next novel," or more flatly: "in his book, *When,* etc." In other words, when the title does not merge easily with your sentence, put in a noun with which the title shall be in apposition.

The penchant for merging is a by-product of the desire to write good sentences. This is so strong in good writers that they cut off the *A* and *The* of a title that they cite in running text: "Motley's *Rise of the Dutch Republic.*" This practice is sensible and long established, but if you follow it, take care that you do not subtly alter the author's intention. He may have been scrupulously exact in putting *A* in front of his subject to show that his conclusions are tentative; for instance: AN *Economic Interpretation of the Constitution* by Charles A. Beard. Conversely, an acknowledged master may at the end of his life bring out THE *Theory of the Cell,* that is, the complete and fully organized view of the subject, which fears no rivals for none exist.

---

[10] See Chapter 2, p. 28.

[11] Some periodicals devoted to book reviewing dislike the appearance of frequent italics in their pages and require book titles to be named within quotation marks. This practice does not lessen the importance of the rule or the unanimity with which it is observed in the world of research.

Except for these significant uses, the grammatical role of the definite and indefinite articles can be taken by other words: Samuel Smiles's *Life of George Stephenson, Railway Engineer.* We lose nothing by the omission, but watch again: we fall into gibberish if having properly elided a redundant article in one place we begin to use the decapitated title as if it were complete; do *not* write: "He then published *Life of George Stephenson,* etc."; any more than you would write: "Motley worked nine years on *Rise of the Dutch Republic."* The use of "a" and "the" in all contexts is a delicate measure of a writer's sensitivity to what he is talking about.

⑦ There should be firmer rules than there actually are about the *right* to quote. Legal doctrine is on this point indefinite, for all it says is that "fair use" is allowed. "Fair use" covers most scholarly and critical quoting, but it sets no clear limits to the amount that may be quoted without special permission. Hence the demand of most publishers that the author of a manuscript ask permission of the copyright holders for each of his quotations. But do you ask for six words? Obviously not. Some publishers allow passages of 250 to 500 words to be quoted without permission having to be asked. This latitude is sometimes stated on the copyright page: look there for the exact wordage granted free. Remember that an aggregate of, say, 300 words quoted by you here and there requires permission as if it were one long passage.

All American university presses allow one another's authors a thousand words on the "no permission needed" principle. For the rest, you must write and ask the publisher, giving the length, opening and closing words, and page references of the passage you want to quote, and also the name of your own publisher. Allow plenty of time before your publication date, for you may have to write to the author or to a third party—the owner of the copyright—to whom the publisher will refer you. Most British authors will express surprise at your wanting a written permission for what they do every day without let or hindrance. In this country it is otherwise, and one must be particularly careful about quoting words from popular songs as well as poetry.

"Credit" should naturally be given for every quotation, but there is no need to be overcome by gratitude: you are keeping an author's thought and fame alive when you quote and name him, and for this he owes you a debt. Some publishers will specify for your acknowledgment a formula of their own, occasionally quite long and in a style reminiscent of funerary inscriptions. They insist that its use is compulsory, but open a current book and you will see that thanks are given in a lump to all copyright owners on an acknowledgment page, or that each is named at the point where his material is used.

In citing and crediting authors, you must, as in all other phases of research and writing, use judgment. Many obvious quotations need no author's name. For instance, if you are so unadventurous that you find yourself quoting "To be or not to be," leave the author in decent obscurity. If you quote for a purely decorative purpose an anecdote that is going the rounds and that you found in your local newspaper, or a trifling news item from the same source, no reference is needed to the place and date (see the extract from *Punch* above). Remember, in other words, that quoting is for illustration and that citing is for possible verification. What is illustrative but unimportant (and in any case not likely to have been garbled or forged) will not need to be verified. It would therefore be pedantry to refer the reader to its source. Like Emerson, he wants you to tell him what you know.

Difficulties and Dangers of Translation Skip

When it so happens that what you want to tell your reader is the opinion of a foreign authority, your wish to quote carries with it the duty to translate. We will assume that you can read the language you intend to quote from. But this is the least of the prerequisites, even though the opinion is widespread that anyone who knows two languages can translate from the one into the other.[12] Nothing could

[12] An extreme yet frequent example is that of the person who, because he reads and understands a foreign language, thinks he can write it. Not long ago, an Italian publisher of scholarly books sent to his American patrons a magnificently printed and illustrated folder announcing a new edition of a medieval text. The description in "English" was all in this style:

Indispensable and basic to those who deal Dante's problems of Midiaeval Mysticism, *The Book of the Figures,* consisting in two volumes cloth bound and with superior cut gilt, reproduces the Reggian Codex and the other one, analogous, of Oxford, with very rich colour tables, which offer to the studious Enquirers a limpid Historical Document. . . . This new Edition will gain new consensus, especially out of Italy.

The fact that we can make out the drift of these remarks does not make them a translation of the original thought.

be further from the truth. The result of this fallacious belief is that readers and critics are forever complaining of the unreadable matter palmed off on them as translations, and that the principles of the art of translating are unsuspected or ignored by those most in need of them—authors, publishers, journalists, researchers, and students generally.

In a world whose inhabitants are more and more involved with one another across the frontiers of politics and language, it is obvious that translation is a daily necessity. Yet good translators being scarce, the world's work is hampered or spoiled by mistranslation. This leads on occasion to grave misunderstanding and does nothing to allay any preexisting friction. The problem at its simplest often occurs between the two branches of what we still think of as one language, namely English and American. According to Churchill, the word "table," in "tabling a motion," plunged an important war council into a "long and even acrimonious discussion," because the Americans took "table" to mean indefinite postponement, whereas the English understood it to mean "put down for subsequent discussion."[13] Again, the familiar words of science and technology, many of which are international, sometimes mislead through unexpected overlappings or false similarities, as when the French *éther* is made to stand for both "ether" and "ester."

Such misunderstandings define the first duty of the translator: he must thoroughly understand the meaning of the words in his original—not their general purport, but their precise meaning. The researcher in his guise of translator must once again be a critical reader of words, a haggler over shades of meaning. The shorter the passage to be translated the more important is this hairline exactitude, for the occasional errors in a long work tend to be corrected by the context, whereas a single quotation eight lines long affords the reader no such corrective.

The research scholar or technical expert in work of international scope, such as the far-flung foreign correspondent or the adviser to any of countless worldwide agencies, is therefore peculiarly vulnerable

---

[13] See G. V. Carey, *American into English: A Handbook for Translators,* London, 1953, 1 and 87; and Winston S. Churchill, *The Second World War,* London, 1950, III, 609.

in those parts of his work where in order to quote he must translate. At the worst, he commits a blunder and unknowingly misleads at the very moment when he is trying to inform. At the best, he launches no new error, but he imparts to every foreign writer or speaker a stiff, awkward tone, if not a downright silly and ludicrous one.

Let us suppose that sooner or later he does learn in one or more foreign tongues all the words in his special vocabulary; he is still far from fully equipped. For "what the original means" is not the same thing as "knowing the meaning of every word." It is words together that create meaning and give a particular statement its tone and force. Take a phrase that recurs in political declarations coming from France. A quite simple statement by a minister in office will begin with: *"Je sais bien que . . . ."* Now throughout the English and American press this will be translated as either "I know well that . . ." or "I well know that . . . ." Neither sounds quite right, for English or American speakers do not commonly say those words. What they *do* say that is vaguely connected with the original French is the somewhat accusing: "You know very well that [you gave away the secret]." In the first person singular the same expression conveys a different shade: "I know very well [what I did]"; which implies: "and it isn't what you think." But none of these phrases corresponds to the French. What then are those Frenchmen babbling about when they say *"Je sais bien que . . ."?* What is the force of *bien,* and how do we translate it? The answer is that *bien* here has nothing to do with the literal "well." It must be translated: "of course." What the original says is what we say when we begin with a concessive "Of course, I know [that this has already been tried, *but . . .*]."

Dictionaries and False Friends

The second rule of translation is that to ascertain the meaning of words as we are bidden by the first rule, we must go beyond the immediate dictionary meaning of the word to the significance of its role in the sentence. As an expert lexicographer puts it about *bien* in a handbook for translators, "it is only exceptionally that it should be translated 'well,' "[14] and he gives half a column of examples and equivalents.

What is true of all these troublesome little words in every language —*doch* in German, *più* in Italian, *más* in Spanish—is true in a different way of the connotations of abstract and important words. You cannot be sure that when you have the denotation firmly in mind you also have the right connotation. Worse, you will find that words coming from the same root have had different histories in two or more languages and have diverged completely. A dais in English is a platform; in French it is a canopy. A person described as *constipado* in Spanish merely has a cold. A *Friseur* in Germany will not curl or frizz your hair but will cut it.

A subtle and vexatious example of the same shifting of sense in diplomacy came to light at the League of Nations after the First World War. The French *contrôle* was frequently translated "control" until it appeared that in French the word means "supervise, pass upon, *have a voice in the control of,*" while in English it means "govern completely." Thus a French conductor who punches your ticket is a *contrôleur;* this is etymologically correct, since the root of the word is *contre-rôle,* a counter-roll or, as we now say, a checklist.[15]

To enforce the lesson by sticking to French, one may cite a few of the commonest words that have become traps for the heedless in the translation of legal and diplomatic documents, and most frequently in newspaper accounts: *admettre* does not always mean "admit," as in *"Le gouvernement ne peut pas admettre que . . ."* where the meaning is a softened "allow," "concede"—"The government will not grant that . . . ." Again, goods that are described as *en provenance des États-Unis* do not necessarily "originate" in the United States; they are merely being shipped from there. Once an Anglo-French committee was stumped by the description of a proposed course of action as *fastidieux.* It soon appeared that "fastidious" was nowhere near the meaning,

[14] J. G. Anderson, *Le Mot Juste: An Anglo-French Lexicon,* London, 1932, 44. A revised edition was brought out by L. C. Harmer in 1938.
[15] The French meaning occurs in English in the single phrase "control experiment," which is a check upon other work, with no idea of "control" in the ordinary sense.

which indeed could not be guessed by inspection, since it turns out to be "wearisome," "dull and fatiguing." Finally, there are tricky words such as *ressentir,* which as a verb means simply "feel" or "experience," with no notion of animus as in our "resent," but which as the noun *ressentiment* does carry the notion of anger or rancor, even more strongly than does "resentment." Such are the pitfalls of language.[16]

It follows that every translator needs all the help he can get from (1) dictionaries, (2) special lexicons and manuals for translators, (3) extensive reading in as many languages as possible, (4) a studious pursuit of etymology and word connections, and (5) the advice of educated native speakers of the language from which he is likely to translate.

Except for traveling light, a pocket dictionary is worthless. If you are going to translate correctly you need the best foreign-English dictionary in the particular language *and* a reliable all-foreign dictionary in that language. The best bilingual dictionaries of the modern tongues are those that (1) give long lists of equivalents whenever possible, (2) supplement these with examples of use in sentences, and (3) have been revised by scholars within the last quarter-century.

In addition to dictionaries you should try to own or to consult the special works referred to under 2 two paragraphs above, which attempt to explain the differences that lurk under similarity, the so-called "false friends" that suggest a meaning belied by the fact. Such books do not exist for all languages, but a few can be found, though they are not to be thought free from imperfections.[17] A steady reader in a foreign language will make up his own small-scale lexicon as he notices the endless oddities of foreigners' speech and his own.

---

[16] The consequences of missing the nuances or supplying gratuitous ones in the translating of diplomatic documents are patent. But the problem rarely comes to public attention as it did when the United States, through Ambassador Edwin O. Reischauer, formally persuaded the Japanese government to change its official translation of the word "containment," the well-known description of American policy toward world communism during the Cold War. The Japanese had long been using the word *fujikome,* which Reischauer, an outstanding student of the Japanese language, regarded as having a connotation of aggressiveness, calling up, as it does, the picture of a bulldozer at work. The Japanese Ministry of Foreign Affairs finally changed the translation to *sekitome,* a milder word meaning simply "to check" or "to dam." (*New York Times,* May 29, 1966.)

[17] See the short list in the section "For Further Reading" on pp. 400–01.

Literalism and Paraphrase

The successful reader in foreign languages will also be interested in everything he encounters that bears on translation. There is, for example, a lively little book by the late Monsignor Ronald Knox that deals with the difficulties and controversies he ran into when translating the Bible.[18] Now the Bible may be all Greek and Hebrew to you, but in these essays by Knox you come upon illuminating remarks that are applicable to translating to or from any language. For example:

> Among the many good things Mr. Belloc has done . . . is a little brochure . . . on Translation. The great principle he there lays down is that the business of a translator is not to ask "How shall I make this foreigner talk English?" but "What would an Englishman have said to express this?" For instance, he says, if you are faced with the French sentence, *"Il y avait dans cet homme je ne sais quoi de suffisance,"* you do not want to write "There was in this man I know not what of self-sufficiency"; you want to write, "There was a touch of complacency about him . . . ."
>
> Anybody who has really tackled the business of translation, at least where the classical languages are concerned, will tell you that the bother is not finding the equivalent for this or that word, it is finding how to turn the sentence. . . .
>
> The translator, let me suggest in passing, must never be frightened of the word "paraphrase"; it is a bogey of the half-educated. As I have already tried to point out, it is almost impossible to translate a *sentence* without paraphrasing; it is a paraphrase when you translate "Comment vous portez-vous?" by "How are you?"[19]

This last caution is worth expanding a little in order to banish once for all the fear that many writers and researchers have of being wrong when they depart from the word-by-word contents of their original. The term "paraphrase" frightens them because they know that a paraphrase from English verse to English prose entails a loss of meaning; you cannot paraphrase the soliloquies in *Hamlet* and say: "This is the equivalent of Shakespeare's meaning." It can only be a rough approximation. But in translating from a foreign language, what

[18] *On Englishing the Bible,* London, 1949.
[19] *Ibid.,* 4 and 12.

is loosely called paraphrasing is the only wording that deserves to be called a translation, no other being possible. To reinforce the Belloc example above, take the French expression: *"C'est une autre paire de manches."* The *only* possible translation of those words is: "That's a horse of another color." Plainly, none of the significant words has received its normal equivalent. The French says nothing about horses or their color; it talks of a pair of sleeves. But the horse is no "paraphrase" of the sleeves; it is their correct equivalent. To put into English each word separately is no feat to aim at;[20] the resulting sentence would be nonsense. Take it as an absolute rule that translation occurs not between words but between meanings. Father Knox gives the example of *en effet,* which he finds everybody translating "in effect" when the meaning is not in the least "in effect" but "sure enough"—no paraphrase, but an exact rendering of the force of the two French words.

What all these warning examples boil down to is this: *Accurate translating requires, in addition to a transfer of the full contents, a transfer of the full intention that goes with them.* This is of the utmost importance whenever a rhetorical device occurs in the original, such as irony, which conveys the opposite of what is actually said. When Thomas Nugent in the eighteenth century translated Montesquieu's *Spirit of Laws,* he completely missed the irony in a famous passage about Negro slavery; so completely, that he felt called upon to add a footnote of apology for the great author who, although enlightened, still defended slavery. The apology should have been addressed to the great author who was being thus misrepresented. Such blunders inspired the Italian proverb *"Traduttore, traditore"*—"A translator is a traitor."

The Act of Carrying Over, *or Translation*

The researcher is of course doing his best to be the very reverse of a traitor. His motto is Fidelity first and foremost. But for lack of

---

[20] For an enjoyable lesson on this point, and the humor to be drawn from willfully forgetting it, read in Mark Twain's "Private History of the 'Jumping Frog' Story" the portion that gives in English his impression of the French version of the tale.

good advice and a sound tradition, fidelity has been misconstrued into Literalism. Literalism dismisses responsibility toward the original with an implied shrug—"that's what it says!" There is no "it." There is a foreign mind, and there is yours, charged with the duty of reexpressing his thought. This second capacity depends upon your mastery of your own language. For unless you can discriminate between shades of meaning and turns of phrase in your native tongue, you will be blind and deaf to their counterparts in the text that is waiting to be transported into corresponding forms. If you cannot summon up half a dozen related expressions to render the spirit of the original, the letter of it will show through; you will be giving not a translation but a transliteration. At times, to be sure, you may want to tell your readers the exact word or phrase used by the author you are translating; this you do by reproducing it italicized in parentheses. But your prose should give his *thought*.

Supposing that you have made a sustained effort and that you have acquired the knack of producing for each sentence of your original a sentence that might have been written spontaneously in English, you still are only on the threshold of translating. You are doing good journeyman work, but you are not yet skillful, much less a master. You are headed for mastery only when you discern in the original the complete sum of the author's intentions and find a way to match those intentions one by one through comparable effects, distributed in the translation wherever they will fit.

A rough way to put this would be to say that a certain sentence in a foreign language contained, over and above its cargo of information, eleven additional points or features—an alliteration, a play on words, a rhythmical halt, an allusion to a famous poem, a colloquial turn, a long learned word where a short common one was expected, and so on. The able translator, noting these points, will try to give somewhere in his version the nearest form or effect his own language affords. Not until he has exhausted its resources—which really means *his* resources—will he consider the original sentence to have been carried over, that is, translated.

Some examples of successive attempts at this perfection of rendering will make the task and its method clear. Our first example will again be from the French, the language that, as translators agree, is among the leading European languages the most unlike English in the movement of its thought and the most deceptively like English in vocabulary. As such, it combines in the highest degree the two difficulties that must be met in every piece of translation. The following passage comes from a work which has been twice translated in our century, and which would benefit from a third effort that would retain the happy turns of the previous two. Here is the original:

Un des plus grands personnages de ce temps-là, un des hommes les plus marquants dans l'Église et dans l'État, nous a conté, ce soir (janvier 1822), chez Mme de M . . . , les dangers fort réels qu'il avait courus du temps de la Terreur.

"J'avais eu le malheur d'être au nombre des membres les plus marquants de l'Assemblée constituante: je me tins à Paris, cherchant à me cacher tant bien que mal, tant qu'il y eut quelque espoir de succès pour la bonne cause. Enfin, les dangers augmentant et les étrangers ne faisant rien d'énergique pour nous, je me déterminai à partir, mais il fallait partir sans passeport."[21]

In 1915 this was translated as follows:

One of the most important persons of our age, one of the most prominent men in the Church and in the State, related to us this evening (January, 1822), at Madame de M——'s, the very real dangers he had gone through under the Terror.

"I had the misfortune to be one of the most prominent members of the Constituent Assembly. I stayed in Paris, trying to hide myself as best I could, so long as there was any hope of success for the good cause. At last, as the danger grew greater and greater, while the foreigner made no energetic move in our favour, I decided to leave—only I had to leave without a passport."[22]

A dozen years later an anonymous version, said to have been done under the supervision of the well-known translator, C. K. Scott-Moncrieff, appeared in New York and has since been reprinted in a popular series. It is on the whole less accurate than the first. Our passage comes out in this form:

[21] Stendhal [Henri Beyle], *De l'Amour*, "Fragments Divers," CLXVI.
[22] Translation by Philip and Cecil N. Sidney Woolf, London and New York, 1915, 329.

One of the most illustrious persons of his time, and one of the foremost men in both Church and State affairs, told us this evening (January 1822), at Madame M's house, some of the very real dangers he had run at the time of the Terror.

"I had had the misfortune to be one of the most prominent members of the Constituent Assembly: I remained in Paris, trying to hide myself as best I might, so long as there was any hope of success for the good cause. At last, as the dangers were increasing and other countries were making no effort to help us, I decided to leave, but I had no passport."[23]

The meaning of the original is simple and the text presents no grammatical difficulty; the reader of the English "understands" it, as he thinks, through and through. Nevertheless some points are in doubt, since at those points the meaning has struck two pairs of translators rather differently. Quite apart from the resulting hesitation, the reader may feel that he would like to know what the "good cause" is which both translate literally. Could closer attention to nuance achieve greater fidelity? Let us try, adding explanatory comments and signposts as we go:

One of the greatest figures [*not* "persons" and *not* "illustrious"] of this age ["his age" would conflict with what follows], *who is* [needed for the sentence to sound English] among the foremost men *in Church and State* [English idiom], told us at Madame de M's this evening (January 1822) [the natural English order for Place and Time is to put the shorter modifier first] *about* the very real dangers to which he had been exposed [one *runs* a risk but not a danger] during the Terror.

"I had [the pluperfect is literal but throws us off] the misfortune of being *among the foremost* [phrase repeated from above, as in the original] members of the *National Assembly* [the more familiar name in English, little used in French]. I *hung on* in Paris [= the true force of the original], trying to hide [*not* 'hide myself,' which suggests children playing] *in one way or another* [*not* 'as best I could,' which goes without saying], so long as there was any hope of success for *our cause* [that is, the 'good cause' was naturally his own, but it is also that of the people he is addressing]. At last, the danger increasing [singular, since he is not counting but gauging] while the foreign powers [not 'countries,'

[23] Translation by H. B. V., New York, 1927; Black and Gold Edition, New York, 1947, 341.

which is weak, nor 'the foreigner,' which is vague] *were taking no strong action* in our behalf, I *made up my mind* ['decided' gives no sense of a gradual resolution] to leave—only, [comma essential; otherwise the sentence means 'no one but I'] I had to leave without a passport." [Here as elsewhere the second translator omits a whole idea.]

Now if a dozen simple lines are capable of improvement by the application of a little critical thought, it is easy to imagine how much attention long and complex passages require. Our shelves are full of works in "famous" translations that yet contain page after page of gibberish—the gibberish that comes of a too-easy literalism. For examples of this fatal fault, one has only to leaf through the two volumes of Henry Reeve's "famous" translation of Tocqueville's *Democracy in America.* Here is the beginning of Chapter 2:

A man has come into the world; his early years are spent without notice in the pleasures and activities of childhood. As he grows up, the world receives him when his manhood begins, and he enters into contact with his fellows. He is then studied for the first time, and it is imagined that the germ of the vices and the virtues of his maturer years is then formed.[24]

The Necessity of Knowing English

This innocent nonsense should be enough to dispel the illusion that French is an "easy" language, to which almost anything vaguely intelligible is a good enough equivalent. No language is easy; all translation is hard. But both grow easier with practice and become an interesting challenge to the person who is, to begin with, eager to express his own thoughts with lucidity. For translation *is* writing your own thoughts. True, you have just borrowed them from another mind; you have overheard, so to speak, a secret spoken by a foreign agent. Your concentration upon it makes you aware of its effect as a whole and in parts—this depends on your knowledge of the foreign

---

[24] Alexis de Tocqueville, *Democracy in America,* the Henry Reeve Text, as revised by Francis Bowen, now further corrected and edited by Phillips Bradley, New York, 1945, I, 26.

tongue. And the total awareness inspires you to reproduce somehow every one of the effects—this depends on your knowledge of your own tongue. It follows that one can translate faithfully only from a language one knows like a native into a language one knows like a practiced writer.

An example from the German, again comparing two translations, will show what the second requirement means. Goethe tells in his autobiography how in his eighth year he and his family were much excited by the outbreak of the Seven Years' War and the ensuing partisanship for or against Frederick the Great:

Und so war ich denn auch preussisch oder, um richtiger zu reden, Fritzisch gesinnt: denn was ging uns Preussen an? Es war die Persoenlichkeit des grossen Koenigs, die auf alle Gemueter wirkte. Ich freute mich mit dem Vater unserer Siege, schrieb sehr gern die Siegslieder ab, und fast noch lieber die Spottlieder auf die Gegenpartei, so platt die Reime auch sein mochten.[25]

The "standard" translation, originally by John Oxenford (pseudonym), reads as follows:

So it was that my sympathies were on the side of Prussia, or more accurately, of Fritz; what, after all, was Prussia to us? It was the personality of the great King that impressed everyone. I rejoiced with my father in our conquests, willingly copied the songs of victory, and perhaps yet more willingly the lampoons directed against the other side, poor as the rhymes might be.[26]

The three people who had a hand in this did not satisfy at least one modern reader, who produced a new version during the Second World War. The passage occurs there in this form:

And so my views were Prussian, or, to speak more correctly, those of Frederick, for what did we care about Prussia? It was the personality of the great King which moved all hearts; I rejoiced with my father over our victories, most readily copied out the songs of triumph and

---

[25] Goethe, *Dichtung und Wahrheit,* Bk. II, paragraph 4.
[26] *Poetry and Truth,* a revised translation based on that of John Oxenford and A. S. W. Morrison, revised by Minna Steele Smith, London, 1913, I, 35.

almost more readily the lampoons against the other party, however poor the rhymes might be.[27]

In this pair of renderings almost the only part that seems assured is: "It was the personality of the great King." As for the rest, in either version, the least that can be said is that it does not come up to the jauntiness of the original. Here we have the old poet looking back on the first enthusiasm of his childhood, recalling a distant hero worship, half-political, half-poetical; how shall we express it when he has done it so well in the simplest, clearest German? We can only try—and very likely fail:

And so here I was, a regular Prussian, or more exactly a Fritz man: for what was Prussia to us? It was the personality of the great King that swayed all minds. With my father I gloried in our victories. I eagerly made copies of the triumphal songs, and still more eagerly, perhaps, of the jeering songs against the other side, no matter how feeble their rimes.

So much for the goals of fullness and felicity. A peculiar danger the researcher must guard against when he has been plunged for some time in foreign sources is the inability to distinguish between the idiom he understands "like a native" and his own. This failing overcomes even the best translators and produces those odd passages we encounter in scholarly and other books. For example, a writer on French political parties will speak of "the militants" who attended a meeting, meaning "the rank-and-file"; or again, a student of Italian culture will write "The Illuminism" instead of "The Enlightenment"; just as a reporter on contemporary German life may slip into the habit of piling up adjectives in front of his nouns ("an easy-to-suspect assertion") without noticing that in coining such expressions he is Germanizing at variance with the genius of the English language.

The safeguard against this excessive adaptability of the mind is to translate in three steps: (1) a rough draft, quickly made with the original at hand; (2) a second draft, some days later, with the original out of sight: if you find a strange combination of English words, a

---

[27] R. O. Moon, *Goethe's Autobiography*, Washington, D.C., 1949, 34.

twisted idiom, replace it by what the sense and the language require; (3) a third and possibly final draft, for which you consult the original, phrase by phrase, to make sure that *all the ideas and implications have found a place somewhere in your version.* Then, perhaps, you have a piece of prose that may pass for a translation.[28]

[28] The mechanical problems of translating coinage and weights and measures, and of transliterating Russian, Chinese, and other proper names, are so special and varied that they cannot be taken up in a book dealing with fundamentals. Generally, teachers, editors, or publishers will have a set form to suggest or impose. Failing this, you will find a number of guides on these several problems.

15

The Rules of Citing:
Footnotes and Bibliography

Types and Functions of Footnotes

Some years ago a joint biography of Benedict Arnold and Major André was issued with an announcement to the purchaser: "Source references available on request from the publishers, in a pamphlet designed to be affixed to the book."[1] By mailing a postcard to the publishers, one received a booklet of twenty-five pages, a package of footnotes. Passing over the question of where the library reader of the book will seek its documentation when the booklet is mislaid or out of print, we turn at once to the larger question: What are footnotes for? Are they a standard accessory of every good work outside fiction or are they optional for both the writer and the reader? From the answers to these questions we shall learn whether it is indeed proper to deny footnotes to the reader when he wants them and put him to the trouble of asking for them by mail.

Footnotes are of two kinds. The first explains an assertion in the body of your work and is therefore reading matter. This kind of

[1] James T. Flexner, *The Traitor and the Spy,* New York, 1953.

338

footnote is used when the elucidation or elaboration of remarks in the text itself would break the thread of the story, or otherwise divert the attention of the reader. Such comments and sidelights are sometimes so numerous and full that they take more space than the statements they supplement. This abuse should be avoided, for, as one facetious objector pointed out, "it is quite a chore to keep focussing up and down the page, especially if you have old eyes or a touch of astigmatism."[2] Yet it would be wrong to outlaw this form of running commentary. When skillfully used it serves to fill out the narrative with details that would clog the main story but that greatly enrich the understanding of leisurely and reflective readers.[3] There is no warrant for the maxim "if it's important, put it in the text; if it's not, leave it out altogether." The danger to avoid is that of writing, in a succession of long footnotes, a separate book or article running parallel to the first. This was the evil that made one reviewer say that he was so enthralled by reading the small print at the bottom he found it hard to remember the couple of regular lines at the top of the page.

The form of the explanatory footnote is simple: it consists of declarative sentences, usually in a more conversational tone than the rest of the book, like a stage aside. For example, in the main text of *The Age of the Great Depression,* Dixon Wecter wrote that a new magazine named *Ballyhoo* "rocketed to a two-million circulation largely by debunking the specious salesmanship of the twenties."[4] To this neutral report of fact he added the footnote: "Its creator was a disillusioned Manhattan editor and artist, Norman Anthony, but the name which *Ballyhoo* made famous was that of a fictional high-powered advertising man, one Elmer Zilch. In a chapter called 'Jackpot!' Anthony gave the history of this magazine in *How to Grow Old Disgracefully* (N.Y., 1946)."

This note, plainly, is to give diverting information that seemed to the author too detailed to find room in a paragraph surveying the

---

[2] Frank Sullivan, "A Garland of Ibids for Van Wyck Brooks," *New Yorker,* April 19, 1941, 15.

[3] See, for example, Lawrence A. Cremin, *The Transformation of the School,* New York, 1961.

[4] Vol. XIII of *The History of American Life,* New York, 1927–48, 15.

years 1929–31. The author in effect is saying that he knows more about the subject under discussion than he can relate at the pace and on the scale of his main discourse, but if you will step outside, he will extend his remarks.

Although in such works as textbooks footnotes may be unwanted, they cannot arbitrarily be ruled out even there. You may, for instance, want to give comprehensible equivalents for foreign coinage or land measures, or supply the original words of quotations translated in your text, or furnish evidence on a subject tangential to the theme of your chapter or book, such as a four-line "identification" of a little-known character whose name is mentioned in passing. If in any kind of work your footnote is important but in danger of becoming too long, metamorphose it into an appendix, where you can take all the space you require and more adequately serve both yourself and your reader. This is what James G. Randall did in his *Lincoln the President*[5] with his illuminating information on Lincoln's relationship with Ann Rutledge.

The second kind of footnote is the source reference; it records the origin of, or the authority for, the remark in the text. Footnotes of this type are used for both direct and indirect quotation. They form the main part of the "apparatus" that is said to distinguish a "work of scholarship" from a "popular work." They give us confidence in the book that displays them by announcing to the world that the "report" is open to anyone's verification. They declare in their way that the author is intellectually honest: he acknowledges his debts; and that he is democratically unassuming: the first comer can challenge him.

The form of this kind of footnote demands special attention. Though its arrangement and abbreviations may puzzle the inexperienced reader, to the informed it is a shorthand intelligible at a glance. Most readers are aware from their own observation that no method has been universally agreed upon for writing reference footnotes. Often the publisher or editor to whom you submit your work will propose or require the style used by the firm. If he does not, you will find it convenient to follow one of two widely used systems: that codified by a group of learned societies and published by the Modern Language

[5] New York, 4 vols., 1946–52.

Association;[6] or that described in the University of Chicago manual,[7] which has found wide acceptance among writers and researchers. It is useful to add that an inexpensive, paperbound digest of the Chicago rules has been published by Kate L. Turabian.[8]

Whatever the style—and the variations from one publisher to the next are slight—the principle underlying all the forms is the same. It is implicit in the purpose of the reference footnote, which is to refer you to sources. The note must be so framed that the reader can tell unfailingly the type of source cited—a manuscript or a printed article, a newspaper or a book, a letter or a conversation. These distinctions are important, for in estimating evidence sources are weighed, not counted. Each kind of source impresses the reader in a different way. For example, a magazine article is generally written with more care than a newspaper column but probably with less than a book. Other things being equal, such as authorship and place of publication, the article will be judged on this comparative rating. Similarly, a conversation may, depending on how it was recorded, prove to be less convincing than a manuscript.

Form and Forms in Footnote-Writing

All these varieties of source are indicated by the typographical form of the note. If a manuscript is being cited the footnote will begin with the abbreviation "MS" (or "MSS" to show the plural):

MS Diary of Edmund Ruffin, February 17, 1857.

If the manuscript has a title it is cited in quotation marks without the label "MS":

"Big Me," William Herndon's autobiography.

A magazine article is always cited in quotation marks followed by the title of the magazine in italics:

[6] *The MLA Style Sheet,* ed. William R. Parker, rev. ed., New York, 1967.
[7] *A Manual of Style,* 12th ed., Chicago, 1969.
[8] *A Manual for Writers of Term Papers, Theses, and Dissertations,* 3rd ed., Chicago, 1967.

Mrs. Kermit Roosevelt, "F.D.R., Lady Churchill, and the Brussels Sprouts," *Harper's Magazine,* CCXIII (August 1956), 62–64.

As we have seen (p. 322), an absolute rule in modern research is that *any printed source referred to in a footnote appears in italics* (in typescript, underlining is the equivalent of italics).

Apart from manuscripts, which are cited as we have just shown, the use of quotation marks around a title in roman type indicates that here is a *portion* of the source that follows—a printed source, since *its* title is italicized.[9] Thus it comes about that we cite articles in magazines as we do. Note that chapter and book bear the same typographical relation as article and periodical.

Because footnotes are for convenience, the most important datum generally appears first. Most often it is the author's name that greets the reader:

Theodore H. White, *The Making of the President: 1968,* New York, 1969.

The title of the work may come first if it is deemed more important than either the author or the editor. This is true, for instance, of encyclopedias, dictionaries, anthologies, annuals, and the like:

The United States in World Affairs: 1967, ed. Richard P. Stebbins, New York, 1968.

Sometimes the name of the editor of a work, rather than the author, should come first. This is especially to be observed when two or more collections of a man's writings are being used and must be quickly distinguishable:

Worthington C. Ford, ed., *The Writings of George Washington,* 14 vols., New York, 1889–93.

John C. Fitzpatrick, ed., *The Writings of George Washington,* 39 vols., Washington, D.C., 1931–44.

[9] In learning these conventions, be sure not to confuse "printed" with "published." Many printed works found in libraries were never published, but were circulated privately.

Since the use to which the notes will be put by the reader is practical—either to verify an assertion in the source or to seek more information from it—footnotes should never be used as ornamentation or ballast for your text. The quality and extent of your scholarship are not measured by the number of notes or by their elaborateness. Though printed outside the narrative, they are a part of your presentation, and their handling should show this. For example, it is now common practice, when you name an author and his book in the text, to use the "split footnote," which merely completes at the bottom of the page the information given above. Footnote 5 of this chapter illustrates the split footnote. Instead of repeating "James G. Randall" and *Lincoln the President,* it merely adds where and when the book was published and the number of volumes. Although this form is relatively new in scholarly writing, it is in keeping with the same desire to conserve space, time, and words that prompted the making of conventions in the first place.

The smaller "forms" and the rules to be followed within a footnote will become second nature as you follow the instructions of a style sheet throughout your manuscript. But be sure that you know the exact meaning of the signs and abbreviations from the first time you set them down. Remember, for instance, that a colon or semicolon or, more rarely, a comma separates a title from its subtitle:

> Eugene P. Trani, *The Treaty of Portsmouth: An Adventure in American Diplomacy,* Lexington, Ky., 1969;

that you cite the volume number of a magazine in Roman numerals (you must learn to read and write them quickly and correctly):

> *Notes and Queries,* 9th Series, VIII (July–December 1901), 97–98;

that you cite the name of a newspaper in italics but not the city, which is not considered part of the title:

> St. Louis *Post-Dispatch,* June 3, 1970.

Sometimes, it is true, you will find:

> *New York Times,* Jan. 21, 1968

in order to avoid confusion with *The Times* of London. Likewise, the state is given in parentheses when the town is obscure:

Thibodaux (La.) Minerva, March 1, 1856.

Remember that you cite in brackets the name of an anonymous or pseudonymous author when you wish to supply it:

> "Strix" [Peter Fleming], *My Aunt's Rhinoceros and Other Reflections,* London, 1956;

that you may omit the date and place of publication, and certainly the publisher's name, when you plan to furnish them in your bibliography:

Gustavus Myers, History of Bigotry in the United States, 18;

that, thanks to uniform scholarly texts, the citation of the ancient authors can be given in condensed fashion, by name (and work if more than one is extant), followed by two numbers—those of the "book" (chapter) and "chapter" (paragraph):

Herodotus, 3. 14.[10]

Every one of these footnotes will be understood at sight by any well-read person. More difficult—but just as rational—are the footnotes that refer to books cited earlier in the same piece of writing. Certain Latin words, abbreviated or in full, indicate these connections.[11] Such repeating symbols, being in a foreign tongue, are often but not always italicized. The abbreviating is done not to puzzle the layman, but (again) to save space. The resulting fragments have become an international shorthand, like musical notation or typographers' marks, and they are pronounced as written: "e.g." is *ee gee;* "op. cit." is *opp sit;* and so on.

The most commonly used is *ibid.,* which is the abbreviation of *ibidem,* meaning "in the same place." That "place" is, *and can only be,*

---

[10] In citing poets the second set of numbers indicates the lines: Lucretius, II, 121.

[11] Recent codifiers of scholarly usage tend to prefer repeating the short title to any use of the Latin abbreviations, and indeed there are indications that the whole apparatus is being simplified as well as Anglicized. But since thousands of books use the older systems dating back as far as the seventeenth century, it behooves the researcher to learn the classic symbols and usages.

the book cited in the footnote *immediately preceding*. For example:

> [2] Hajo Holborn, *A History of Modern Germany, 1840–1945,* New York, 1969, 795.
> [3] *Ibid.,* 675.

If the next footnote, number 4, then refers to a different book, and footnote 5 harks back once more to Holborn's volume, you must write "Holborn, *op. cit.,*" short for *opere citato,* and meaning "in the work cited." What we have, then, is this:

> [2] Hajo Holborn, *A History of Modern Germany, 1840–1945,* New York, 1969, 795.
> [3] *Ibid.,* 675.
> [4] George F. Kennan, *Memoirs, 1925–1950,* Boston, 1967, 130.
> [5] Holborn, *op. cit.,* 799.

The perfect clarity of this arrangement will not be affected by the fact that a page may be turned between notes 2 and 3, and several pages between notes 3 and 5. But you must guard against using *op. cit.* when you cite more than one book by the same author. Each citation must unmistakably tell the reader which is meant. Suppose that you switch back and forth between Beard's *An Economic Interpretation of the Constitution of the United States* and his *Economic Origins of Jeffersonian Democracy.* These long titles will clutter your page or text if you refer to them each time in full. The remedy is to use a "short title." In this way you make clear in which Beard volume the reference given as "6" is to be found:

> Beard, *Economic Interpretation,* 6;

and later:

> Beard, *Economic Origins,* 302.

Occasionally it is necessary to tell the reader that in a certain work he will find almost anywhere, and not on one page rather than another, the attitude or opinion in question. This signal is given by the word *passim,* meaning "here and there:"

> [1] For the development of the ante-bellum political cleavage, see Allan Nevins, *Ordeal of the Union,* New York, 1945, II, *passim.*

It hardly needs to be pointed out that if one is going to cite at all, one must use *all* these symbols and abbreviations correctly.[12] Wrongly or vaguely used they will mislead as surely as they will perform their complicated task neatly when used with precision. Moreover, you should learn the meaning of those that are obsolescent, such as "cf." for the "see" as it occurs in our last example, or *supra* (above) and *infra* (below).[13] Learn all the current forms by heart and treat them as technical terms. Go to the trouble of finding out that "e.g." stands for *exempli gratia* and means "for example." It says something quite different from "i.e.," which stands for *id est* and means "that is." The one offers a random illustration; the other states an identity. To sprinkle these letters about interchangeably is comparable to what a doctor would do if he thought that "grain" and "gram" were "pretty much the same thing." No one can hope to become a professional who does not first master the minutiae.

Footnoting: When, Where, and How Much?

Though the modern writer is never entirely free from the necessity of accounting for his words through footnotes, it is not he who determines the number and fullness of these notes, but the subject in hand and the audience whose attention he hopes to hold. To the extent that footnotes communicate a part of his meaning and attest his reliability, they are as important as any other part of his writing. Hence an author should develop his judgment about when and what to footnote.

All quotations that are more than passing phrases require a footnote. So do all novel or startling assertions and all distinct elements in a demonstration or argument. Beyond this, a good rule is to write a note whenever you think an alert person might feel curiosity about the source of your remarks. Do not document notorious facts, such as the date of Columbus' discovery of America or that Edward VIII abdicated the British throne in 1936. Do not write as if the reader

[12] The commonest are listed in Figure 10.
[13] It is well to use English equivalents, but do not imitate the writer in whose book one continually reads "See me above"; "See me below."

FIGURE 10   *Common Abbreviations*

A.D. in the year of our Lord (preceding the date)

anon. anonymous

B.C. before Christ (following the date)

bk. book

c., ca. about

cap. capital letter

cf. compare

ch., chap. chapter

ed. editor, edition, edited, edited by

e.g. for example

et al. and others

etc. and so forth

et seq. and the following

f., ff. and the following page(s)

fl. flourished (of persons)

ibid. in the same place

id., idem the same as before

i.e. that is

infra below

ital. italics

l., ll. line(s)

l.c. lower-case letter

loc. cit. in the place cited

MS, MSS manuscript(s)

n. note, footnote

N.B. please note

n.d. no date

N.S. New Series; New Style (of dating, since 1752)

op. cit. in the work cited

O.S. Old Style (of dating, before 1752)

p., pp. page(s)

passim here and there

q.v. which (or whom) see

rev. revised, revised by, revision

rom. roman letter or type

sc. to wit, namely

sic thus (to show that an obvious error is an exact reproduction of the original)

supra above

tr. translation, translator, translated (by)

v., vide see

v., vol. volume

viz. namely

Some abbreviations used in books may be readily understood from the context, but a writer has to know their exact meaning before he can use them accurately. A correct understanding, of footnotes particularly, requires one to distinguish between one term or symbol and another, just as the ability to read Roman numerals at sight is necessary for the quick and errorless hunting down of references.

were convinced that you are a liar. The reader is, on the contrary, a trusting beast—at least until you shock or betray him.

He will feel betrayed when he catches you repeatedly in error, and shocked when you go against his preconceptions. A new subject consequently requires many more footnotes than a familiar one. For example, when Walter P. Webb wrote *The Great Plains*,[14] he was attempting to show a correlation between the development of the Plains and technological improvements. He had to give, as we say, "chapter and verse," that is, footnotes, for a quantity of things such as arms manufacturing and barbed-wire design. His materials and the pattern he wove out of them were both original. Writers on the same subject since Webb have been able to do with fewer footnotes, for the simple and sufficient reason that they can now cite Webb.

These two phases of scholarship on one and the same subject illustrate an important point: in certain circumstances, *anything* may be a source—an ad in a newspaper, an old theatre program, a throwaway in a political campaign. But once scholarship has begun to work upon such materials, the published results *must* be used and cited among others of the former kind.

Similarly with great books. You should now cite by preference the scholarly edition of Thoreau's *Works,* not the casual reprints of *Walden* that you can buy at the newsstand. This is both for the convenience of the reader (who is better able to go straight to the standard edition in a library than to lay his hands on that same cheap reprint) and for the advantage you yourself will derive from the textual perfection or critical elucidations of the *Works.* But observe that if you cite, as you may,

Hazlitt, Works, VI, 114

you should not only make sure that the reader knows whose edition you are citing, but also consult the reader's possible interest in knowing *which* work is being referred to. Much may hang on this and you should not skimp but write in full:

Hazlitt, Table Talk, Works (Waller and Glover), VI, 114

[14] Boston, 1931.

This is but one of the questions that the character of the reader should play a part in deciding. Fortunate is the author who knows in advance who his reader will be. A man writing a history of Italian fascism, for example, will plan his work (including his footnotes and bibliography) in one way if he addresses his peers and in another if he is producing a work of popularization. If the former, he will assume that his readers know the outlines of Mussolini's life, are acquainted with the theory of the corporate state, and remember the outcome of the war in Ethiopia. He will mention and even discuss these things but he will not *explain* them as to an entirely uninformed reader; the footnotes will therefore bear almost wholly on new or disputed points. The writer for the so-called popular audience, however, will have to give sketches of figures like Il Duce, Matteotti, and Badoglio, and may even have to retrace the origins of the word "facism" itself. His footnotes will be of the commenting and amplifying kind, and will refer to sources only by way of suggesting additional readings. Logically, the scholar should write fewer footnotes than the popularizer; but usually the proportion is reversed and scholarship is hedged about with footnotes to a degree that often frightens off the overmodest reader.

This excess is a legacy from the 1870's and 1880's, when historians sought to become "scientific" and preferred being thought forbidding to being thought "literary." Now better judgment prevails. Footnotes are necessary but need not be obsessive. As was said earlier, they have wormed their way into popular writing and become familiar to all who can read. In books, the footnote is coming back into its own by recapturing the bottom of the page after a time of exile at the back of the book. Most trade publishers now accept without a murmur footnotes that are footnotes instead of backnotes.

Still, circumstances occur in which the "backnote" is called for. Sometimes the commenting notes are printed at the foot of the page and the reference notes at the back. Sometimes, both mingle at the back. In either case, it is essential to make it as easy as possible for the reader to find quickly the remarks that he should read right after the superior number ([23]) in the text. For this purpose, one thing is indispensable: the section of notes at the back should not indicate merely "Chapter 4," "Chapter 6," before each group of twenty or thirty numbered notes. The reader has no idea in what numbered chapter he is. Repeat, therefore, the chapter heading, for he does know that he is reading the part entitled "Rolling Down to Rio." Better still, use that heading at the top of each page of notes belonging to that chapter (in which case it is called a "running head").

Another aid to the reader in finding his way through backnotes is to provide either page numbers or catch phrases or both. The page number indicates that on page 293 of the text there is a word marked with an asterisk (*) or dagger (†) or superior number ([23]). Since you have just been reading that page, you turn to the back until you find "P. 293" along the left-hand margin. The catch phrases serve to distinguish one note from another on the same page:

> P. 293. *ran a temperature.* Though the doctor who was called in diagnosed typhoid fever, it was actually diphtheria. MS Rollins Papers, Item 261.
> —— "Pop Goes the Weasel." This was apparently the extent of his musical repertory. See *Memoirs of a Dizzy Life,* 602 ff.

In essays, articles, or reports, the foot-and-back principle of dividing explanatory from reference footnotes is seldom used, though if the piece is over fifteen or twenty pages in length there is no reason not to separate the two kinds. The notes in a shorter paper will obviously be so few that it would be a nuisance to leaf back and forth.

The one exception to these allowable choices is the scientific or technical paper, in which it is customary to do without explanatory footnotes and to cite all references at the end. These citations (particularly in physics, chemistry, and mathematics) are brief, giving only last name and initials, the journal title, often abbreviated, and the volume and page numbers in bare figures. In the text itself you will commonly find something like (Bohr, 1949), which means: "The statement just made rests on the article of that year which I cite in my bibliography below."

Bibliographies: Varieties and Forms

"Bibliography" is a rather loose term for research workers to be using, but there is no other that is as readily understood to mean "information about books." The first image in your mind is perhaps of a list of titles, grouped together at the end of a chapter or volume, after the text and before the index. This is the commonest meaning of the word.[15]

Since a bibliography in this sense cites a number of books, it may be looked upon as a collection of footnotes separated from their text and shorn of particular page references. In fact some writers make up their bibliographies—or at least fill them out—by picking up titles out of their own footnotes. Even when padding is not the aim, it remains true that bibliographies contain much the same information as reference notes, but arranged in a different way for a different purpose. The points of difference will strike the eye if the two forms are juxtaposed:

> Howard Haycraft, *Murder for Pleasure: The Life and Times of the Detective Story,* New York, 1941, 139.
>
> Haycraft, Howard,[16] *Murder for Pleasure: The Life and Times of the Detective Story,* New York, Appleton-Century, 1941/1969.

The first is a footnote; the second a bibliographical entry. In the second, the last name begins, so that the eye can quickly find it in its alphabetical place; the publisher is given as a help to finding or buying the book; and there is no page number of course. Some writers give the total number of pages (and the publisher's name), but this, though sometimes helpful, is not compulsory.

What then determines the amount of information to be given and the arrangement of the collection of titles? As before, as always, it is the particular use that the particular bibliography will most likely serve. The function of bibliographies is often misunderstood; to some writers and readers it is a device to cause wonder. One is supposed to think, "Good Heavens! Did he read all that?" But the real reason

[15] We saw in Chapter 4 that volumes containing lists of books organized by subject and flanked by criticism were also "bibliographies." But there are still other bibliographies, which consist of detailed descriptions and collations of rare or famous books, or which list and describe an author's complete works in all their printed forms. These bibliographies help to identify editions, establish dates, prove authorship, and the like.

[16] In giving the author's full name in the bibliography, avoid excess of zeal, especially with French names. See above, p. 85.

for a bibliography is to enable others to learn from it. Short or long, a bibliography should be drawn up to second the intention of the article or book it supplements. Three general kinds exist for you to choose from.

The first and most frequently used in books read by the general public is a single list arranged alphabetically by authors' names. This type is a catchall for whatever has the slightest bearing on any part of the subject—articles, handbooks, interpretative works, newspapers, encyclopedias—everything. Too often this parade of print is a useless ritual. The writer indiscriminately shows off not only the books he has steadily used but also those he has casually looked into. Such a list gives the appearance but not the substance of learning.

Far preferable in this first class or type is the "select bibliography." This will help anyone working on your subject, because it excludes the worthless works and records only the valuable. One defect, however, in the "select bibliography" is that a student who independently comes upon a book that is relevant but unlisted does not know whether it has been rejected as bad or simply overlooked. Despite this disadvantage the researcher treasures the select bibliographies as embodying a deliberate and presumably thoughtful choice; with its aid he is one step ahead of the card catalogue.

Bibliographies of the second type are arranged according to the materials used, and may be called "classified bibliographies." Sometimes the division is simply between primary and secondary sources.[17] Sometimes it is only between manuscript and printed materials, or between books and periodicals. The subdivisions depend on the author's intention in writing the book and upon the variety of sources he has used. Keith Sward's *The Legend of Henry Ford*[18] contains a bibliography broken down into: Books, Magazine and Newspaper Articles, Public Documents, and Legal and Quasi-Legal Actions—a division that fits the needs of most readers. The last category was dictated by the contents of the biography, which narrates numerous and important patent suits.

Biographies almost always raise special problems because their subjects, so to speak, force the biographer's hand. He must follow where

[17] See Chapter 5, p. 112, note 17.
[18] New York, 1948.

they lead. But to this guidance the author must add his own imagination. The subject of a biography has to be resurrected, and this requires the creation of a distinctive pattern. When C. Vann Woodward composed *Tom Watson, Agrarian Rebel*,[19] he was dealing with a Populist leader from Georgia whose career was full of puzzling paradoxes. The bibliography is worthy of the subject and fits it because its categories match the substance and significance of the life. These are the divisions:

1. Collections of Private Papers and Manuscripts
2. Newspapers and Journals
3. Writings and Publications of Thomas E. Watson
4. Newspapers and Periodicals Edited by Watson
5. Autobiographies, Memoirs, Reminiscences, and Published Correspondence
6. Biographies and Biographical Articles
7. Controversial and Political Writings of Contemporaries
8. Special Studies, Monographs, and Articles
9. Unpublished Monographs

In category 3 Woodward lists his entries by alphabetical order of titles. If Watson is remembered at all it is as a politician rather than as an author, yet the list is complete, so as to record in one place the man's unmemorable writings.

Compare that arrangement with the one in the life of Admiral Mahan.[20] The writings here are listed not alphabetically but in the chronological order of publication between 1879 and 1931. Again, book and bibliography match, for this study of Mahan is a history of the development of a man's opinions about the role of sea power in the course of empire.

The third type of bibliography is the critical, which may take the form of an essay. This type is best suited to a large subject on which a whole library of books and articles is available. The critical remarks about each book mentioned enable future students to have the considered opinion of a scholar who has examined the literature, made a judicious selection from it, and balanced the virtues of various books into a comprehensive annotated reading list. It is usually convenient to divide this kind of bibliography by chapter. If the comments

[19] New York, 1938.
[20] William E. Livezey, *Mahan on Sea Power*, Norman, Okla., 1947, 301–11.

are appended to each book in an alphabetical list, they should be brief and in the literal sense "telling." There is little use in writing: "A thorough scholarly treatment, generally considered definitive." Say rather: "The only book that deals with all aspects of the subject with equal thoroughness and accuracy. Criticism has disputed but a few details."

Of late years the essay form of critical bibliography has sometimes been used as a substitute for footnotes, and has turned into a chatty interlude. This often masks a lack of critical judgment. Here is a sample:

> For Roosevelt's mannerisms while watching a movie see "The President," by Henry F. Pringle, the *New Yorker,* June 16, 1934, and "Roosevelt," an article by Geoffrey T. Hellman in *Life,* January 20, 1941. The quotation concerning lovely ladies is from *This Is My Story,* p. 319. That he never took women on cruises is in Tully, p. 3. Missy Le Hand's role in the appointment of Homer Cummings is mentioned in Edward J. Flynn, p. 126. See *This I Remember,* p. 49, and *My Boy Franklin,* p. 22, for details on Roosevelt's attitude toward money. The quotation about the six-dollar pair of trousers is from *Letters,* Vol. I, p. 303. . . .[21]

A bibliographical essay may be made readable but must be informative *and* critical. Note how simple and direct is the discussion of books in Richard Hofstadter, *The American Political Tradition and the Men Who Made It:*[22]

> There is no satisfactory biography of Roscoe Conkling, but Donald Barr Chidsey: *The Gentleman from New York* (New Haven, 1935) is helpful, and the older eulogistic work by Alfred R. Conkling: *The Life and Times of Roscoe Conkling* (New York, 1889) has significant material. David Saville Muzzey's sympathetic *James G. Blaine* (New York, 1934) is the best study of the Plumed Knight; Charles Edward Russell's *Blaine of Maine* (New York, 1931) is more critical. . . .

Hofstadter's bibliography is arranged by chapter, and within each

[21] John Gunther, *Roosevelt in Retrospect,* New York, 1950, 388.
[22] New York, 1948, 365.

chapter by subjects, in the order in which they are covered in the text. The value of this organization and these judgments is clear to anyone who has found and used such a bibliography in a moment of need. Academic scholars will often turn to their colleagues for this sort of help, informally given, when venturing into unknown territory. Thus a specialist in nineteenth-century English literature working on Dickens' London might call upon a colleague in British history to ask what is the best book on the English Factory Acts. In a printed work, the critical bibliography makes of the author a colleague of the reader.

But the limitations of the device should be known before one chooses it. It is especially suited to biographical subjects where dozens of works have already appeared about every facet of a man's life and work. It is not suited to a subject on which the facts must be dug out of a quantity of scattered books and articles not readily found in libraries, or out of family papers and other manuscripts. Take for example the instructive work by Jeannette Mirsky and Allan Nevins, *The World of Eli Whitney*.[23] The printed sources on which it draws range from a history of Connecticut dated 1840 to a study of cotton processing published in 1944. Again and again these authors consulted only a page or so in one of a miscellaneous group of books: they were seeking or verifying but a single fact and had no need to read the work entire. A critical bibliography could not have been written after this type of research without a great waste of time and talent. And had it been done it would have been of use only to a person writing on *exactly* the same subject. Such a person should not exist.

The type of bibliography you elect to draw up for your work is therefore not something you can decide about before you are well past the midpoint of your research. You are called upon to decide so many questions in the writing of any piece of work that it should come as a relief to know that the form of your bibliography will be virtually dictated by your subject and to a lesser extent by your audience.

[23] New York, 1952.

Taken together, footnotes and bibliography signalize our relation to the fragments of the written record that we have dredged up out of the sea of books, made our own, and reshaped again in answer to our fresh questions. Footnotes and bibliography anchor our writing in tradition and connect our living thought with the corpus of past scholarship, without which at this late date there is no new scholarship.

16

Revising for Printer and Public

Errors and Their Ways

to revise, means to rev isit, notin order to see thee sights again
but to tidy thme up

The sentence you have just read stands in obvious need of grooming. Its grammatical form will pass, but its graphic form is faulty
and annoying. It does not pass; it stops you; the meaning is dimmed
because letters are transposed, words are run together, and the punctuation is at odds with sense and syntax. The work of grooming, of
making presentable what you have to present is revision in the second
degree. The first has brought your words and sentences to a high point
of clarity, ease, and force.[1] Now you have a typescript that we hope
will not be so liberally dotted with visual blemishes as the opening
sentence of this chapter. But no matter how careful your typing or
your typist, there will be such errors and you must scrub your manuscript clean. This is equivalent to washing your face and combing
your hair before appearing in public. It is but common courtesy, for

[1] See Chapters 2, 6, 12, and 13.

357

a succession of small specks creates a large hindrance to your reader's concentration and pleasure.

But you cannot be sure, at this stage of final revision, that all the errors will be small and, like transposed letters and misplaced commas, readily detected. Before you send your report to the board, your thesis to the department, your article to the editor, your book to the publisher, you must make one last cast for the important errors of fact and sense that have persistently hid from you as you pursued more visible game. Blunders, illogicalities, Irish bulls, contradictions between one page and the next, probably still lurk in the passages you think you have completely verified and polished. How can you unblind yourself to them?

To the knowing reader, any error in your text is an error, grave or slight; that is all there is to it. But to you who have committed it, the cause is important and will help you to spot it while there is yet time. Errors, you will find on reflection, are of several kinds, distinct in origin, and worth regarding theoretically in hopes of reducing their number. By becoming aware of the sort of misstep that your particular mind and hands are likely to make, you can often outwit them. Few people go in for every kind of mistake. It is elementary, of course, that you look over your citations to confirm titles, dates, and other figures, and over your quotations for the correct wording, punctuation, and the like. Few things are harder than to copy a long passage with absolute fidelity, and the more intelligent and quick of perception you are, the more likely you will be to make a slip. Your only hope is to use your quick perceptions to *verify* what your leaping eye or hand has misdone.

Similarly, you will have been prompt to note errors in any of your printed sources, and you will make a blacklist of books that may be valuable but are full of small errors.[2] Each borrowing from such books must be verified, in doing which you will often uncover a trail of error leading back to the original sin, trustingly copied through a dozen books.

This kind of error is annoying and sometimes damaging, but it is not at once comic and infuriating, like the Blunder. A blunder may

[2] See Albert Jay Nock's wise remarks on this subject in the Bibliographical Note to his *Jefferson*, Washington, D.C., 1926, 333.

be defined as a whopper, a lulu of such magnitude as to make the reader laugh, or howl—hence, a howler. The blunder, too, is due to misplaced quickness of mind rather than to ignorance. All blunders, as a student of the genre has remarked,[3] presuppose some knowledge, which has unfortunately been hooked up the wrong way. For example, when Victor Hugo in exile was beginning to learn English and also writing a novel laid in the British Isles, he had occasion to refer to the Firth of Forth. This he felt impelled to translate for his French readers as *le premier des quatre*—"the first of the four." It is clear that if he had known no English whatever he would have been incapable of producing this jewel.

The remedy is never to trust your first intuition of meanings, explanations, allusions, and references without letting the intuition cool and considering it from all sides, preferably with the aid of reference works. Put yourself in the place of a total ignoramus, and go over what you have written as if every portion of it was hard to understand and of doubtful meaning. *Apply this test especially to what you "know as well as your own name."* For example, you are convinced that the saying "God tempers the wind to the shorn lamb" is from the Bible and since it is so well known, you will not bother with an exact reference but will simply introduce it with "in the Biblical phrase . . . ." The misfortune is that the saying is not from the Bible at all, but was coined by Laurence Sterne.[4] In other words, what we have long mis-known wears for us an air of certainty that leads to blundering.

More mysterious is the occurrence of blind spots that prevent our seeing the blunders that we could detect at sight in the works of another. Some years ago, for instance, a biography of Haydn appeared with a portrait of the composer bearing the caption: "Haydn in his Eightieth Decade." One can see how the confusion of ideas came about, but when one thinks of the number of times these ridicu-

---

[3] H. B. Wheatley, *Literary Blunders*, London, 1893, 2. Every researcher should know Sigmund Freud's illuminating observations on the psychology of errors in his *Psychopathology of Everyday Life*. For a condensed account, see his *General Introduction to Psycho-Analysis*, New York, 1920 (reprinted, Garden City, 1952), 25–71.

[4] In "Maria," *A Sentimental Journey Through France and Italy* (first published 1768), paraphrased from Henri Estienne, *Prémices* (1594).

lous words were read by author, editor, printer, proofreader, and publisher's helpers before issuing in print, one is struck with wonder. And yet an experienced author will *not* wonder. There is about the texts that one is producing a sort of glare that blinds one to their obvious blemishes at the very time when one is toiling to perfect them. This resembles the facility with which we can say "Tuesday" for "Thursday" when we are most eager to make an appointment.

An error sometimes reveals far more than its physical magnitude or innocence would suggest, and knowing this will put you on your guard. Suppose, for instance, that the book before you refers to "Governor Alfred E. Smith of Kansas." A howler, yes, you may say, but after all, governors are legion; a slip of the pen is quickly made—and it is only one word wrong. On the contrary: much more than that is wrong: to locate Al Smith in Kansas means that the author lacks any kind of mental image of the man. The figure to him is a name, not a body with a distinct aura. The writer has apparently not taken in Smith's career, let alone reflected on it, hence is all at sea and not merely off his course. The error *resembles* that of making Alexander Hamilton's birthplace Jamaica instead of Nevis—an "intelligent" error of association between two British islands of the West Indies; whereas the "slip" about Al Smith is actually as grievous a misstep as citing a book one has not read.

We must be charitable when we criticize one another's productions, because error is inevitable. But the erring one should draw on that charity as rarely as possible. Rather, he should convince the reader that—as Sydney Smith put it—his errors have come "not in consequence of neglect but in spite of attention."[5] A writer who is invariably wrong in naming details and none too exact about the pivotal fact in his reasonings is like a friend who spills his glass or chokes on a crumb at every meal: it is not a crime but it becomes an unmitigated nuisance.

The Craft of Revision: Maxims and Pointers

As your experience grows you will find that revising is pleasurable, even though its purpose is the discovery of your own failings. The

[5] Letter to Francis Jeffrey, August 1802, in *Selected Writings,* ed. W. H. Auden, New York, 1956, 195.

ultimate effort is the stage that some artists find peculiarly satisfying: the "fixing" of a pastel or the final polishing of a precious gem or the casting of a piece of sculpture. It is exhilarating and exhausting and you should be prepared for both sensations.

The first thing needful is that you should allow enough time for thoroughness at a deliberate, not a hurried, pace. What "enough time" is will depend on the length of your article, thesis, or book, and on your own habits of work. But the penalty of frantic, last-minute patching is no secret from anyone—a low mark, whether it be given by a professor, an employer, or the public. Many a gifted piece of writing has been lost in the flood of print because it was hastily revised and hence bore the marks of an imperfection at once pitiable and insulting.

If your work is a book, you should revise it chapter by chapter. If it is an article, part by part. This division of the task compels you to see the work in its small rather than in its large aspects. Even if you are submitting your report to a restricted private audience, conduct your revision as if you were giving the script its last review before it goes to the printer. This will make you as attentive as he, who is trained to set type in any language, familiar or not. He therefore sees, not paragraphs or sentences or words; he sees only single letters. So should you. His instructions always are to "follow copy," that is, reproduce what is there, not what ought to be there. You, of course, must "follow copy" in a second sense, scanning not only single letters but also sentences, consistency—indeed, everything.

For although you have long since passed the rewriting stage, you cannot avoid rereading yourself as one interested in the meaning. You will seize any chance to improve your diction or syntax or transitions. Like a cabinetmaker who uses ever finer grains of sandpaper until he has achieved a glasslike smoothness, a reviser usually makes no radical changes; he only rubs and writes and rubs again. More than once, probably, you have been from the outset dissatisfied with a word. It stands there plaguing you still, because you could not think of the right substitute: all the synonyms are equally wrong. But now you must make a move: *stet* or—what? Your move is usually no more dramatic than a line through the dubious word and its replacement with the least undesirable alternative.

Once in a while you cannot avoid making sizable changes. You suddenly read your words in a new light and discover that you have conveyed an entirely erroneous impression, or seemingly contradicted yourself, or left ambiguous what you are very sure about—all this due to "not seeing" and now caught by reseeing or revision. Take as a subject for a last-minute perception of ambiguity: "She had outlived her ambition without realizing it." This seemed to the writer entirely correct even after innumerable readings. Suddenly the ambiguity caused by the two meanings of realize[6] became so clear the wonder was, how could it have been tolerated for so long? The meaning required a change to: "She had outlived her ambition without achieving it."

Painstaking writers, whose work looks effortless in its precision and right proportioning, keep revising to the end. Even if your form is set in all particulars, the appearance of a new edition of an old work may necessitate a change in your text at the last minute. It is a good rule never to consider your revision complete until the presses have started to roll.

When you go over a typescript that will be read by strangers in that form and not in print, you will naturally be on the lookout for missing punctuation and misplaced capitals, figures or letters transposed, italics omitted, and the like. But see to it also that the words you have used are correctly spelled. Spelling is one of the decencies of civilized communication. No doubt there are reasons, physical and psychological, for misspellings, but a reason is not an excuse. This is especially true if you are fond of treacherous words such as "corollary" and "supersede" and "apophthegm"; the least you can do is to learn to spell them. It is like paying for what you use instead of stealing and spoiling it. As to the commoner words, such as "receive," "benefited," "indispensable," and "consensus," it should be a matter of pride with you not to exhibit your work pockmarked with infantile errors. If you are adult in years yet still in doubt about any of these spellings, go after it and settle it once for all.

And while you are about the task of making your text fully presentable, a polished mirror of your mind, see to it that neither

---

[6] "Realize" in the sense of "recognize," "acknowledge," "become conscious of" deserves a place on the list of forbidden words. Almost every sentence where it occurs in that sense would be improved by its replacement.

you nor your typist has made the annoying mistake of mixing the Roman and Arabic figures for 1. Volume Two of a work should be typed as II or 2, never as 11. Likewise, most typewriters have a zero; do not use the *O*, large or small. Again, leave a space after the comma or period before beginning the next word or sentence. Lastly, do not join by a hyphen what you mean to separate by a dash. The dash consists of two hyphens close together. Without the use of conventions such as these, the lump of words is unreadable; in any case, the misuse of letters, figures, and spaces is unprofessional. Reread the opening sentence of this chapter and imagine ten pages in that form, which is what some writers complacently proffer to their instructors or associates. Trivial departures from convention? Yes, but they stop your reader and make him think of your incompetence instead of your ideas.

In revising, it is always helpful to have the assistance of someone who will be, like you, attentive to details, and who, because of friendship for you or dedication to your subject, is willing to devote his energies to assisting you. You will require this Jonathan to aid you in collating quotations (that is, comparing them word for word and point for point with the originals) or in verifying against the sources the statistics used in your tables. He should read aloud words or figures to you with a clear enunciation, so as to enable you to follow them easily in the printed copy and make corrections. It is estimated that error occurs in 10 percent of all quotations and tables that are not verified by collation. If nothing else moves you, reflect that your reviewers will catch some of the errors you have missed and that the unfavorable comments may give the impression of a uniformly careless execution even if your work is 90 percent accurate and reliable.

The Craft of Revision: The Professional Touch

In making changes and corrections you must write legibly, otherwise your reader or editor will not notice them quickly or follow your meaning smoothly. If you must insert a word or phrase, be sure that the point of insertion is clearly shown by a caret,[7] and that the added

[7] For the caret and other conventional signs, see Figure 11.

words are not only neatly written but also conveniently placed for the eye, between the lines, which have been double-spaced for this very purpose. Do not sprawl over the margins or in any way attract the eye to five manuscript words out of a whole typed page.

Some inserts are longer, amounting to a paragraph or more. If so, they should be typed and pasted where they belong. This is the rule for any manuscript submitted to a publisher or going ultimately to a printer. For a typist who will produce clean copy, you can simply staple your typed slips to the left-hand margin, using two staples and letting the free end cover a part of your text. Mark the slip "insert" (or "insert A" if more are to come), and at the right point of the text put a caret and write the word "insert" and A (or B, C, etc.) with a circle around them. If you have to attach more than two inserts, cut and paste to make the page manageable: a manuscript with little flags flying all over it is liable to tearing, misplacing of parts, and broken reading.

If inserts and additions lengthen the text beyond the limits of the original page, go on to a fresh one. All you have to do is number the runover sheet the same as the original with the letter *a* added. If more than one page is needed, use *b, c,* and so on. Do not worry if, say, page 10a is only half-filled. Draw a vertical line from below the middle of the last line of text to the bottom of the sheet. The printer will "run in" page 11 to fill the space, for like Nature he abhors a vacuum.

Your lesser corrections, we have said, should be interlined, *above* the line to which they belong, never below. The margins are reserved for instructions to the printer, who will apply them to the word or words marked with the appropriate signs (caret, slash, underlining, dots, etc.) on the same level as the marginal comment ("cap.," "l.c.," "tr.," and the like). Do *not* draw guidelines from the error in the center of your text to the comment in the margin. Always see your copy as it will look to a stranger who does not know your words by heart, yet must make out your meaning rapidly. Remember he is probably earning his living, not playing a puzzle game.

The minor virtue that you must adopt as a reviser is consistency. Every time you make the same sort of correction, indicate it in identical fashion. This is the only way you can conduct proper discourse with editor and printer. The convenience of not writing out instructions over and over again is the reason for the proofreader's, that is, the typesetter's, marks, which have become so widely accepted as to constitute an international sign language. A few may be mentioned as examples of a shorthand you should master for your advantage and others':

1. When you must change a whole word, draw a horizontal line through it. When it is only a letter you are altering, draw a vertical line through it. The vertical should project on each side in order to be clear; not so the horizontal.

2. When you have crossed out a word, and regret your decision to do so, you restore it by writing the word "stet" in the margin and putting a series of dots under the word. *Stet* is a Latin word meaning "let it stand."

3. Bear in mind that your editor expects your typescript to be marked up. An altogether clean one suggests that you have not taken the trouble to proofread your work. This is slacking, for there are never too many pairs of eyes engaged in hunting down "typos."

4. If your handwriting is uncertain, use print letters, shaping and spacing them carefully. Never try to patch up a typewritten word by writing over its constituent letters. Cross it out and put its replacement just above it.

The reviser's awareness of the way error begets error makes him take as his golden rule: "Leave nothing to chance or to the guesses of editor and printer." Whoever the reader may be, never leave him in doubt about your meaning. If you are being edited before printing, revisions by several hands will have decorated your copy with a quantity of pencil marks, some full of purpose and meaning, others random and mysterious. It is usually the punctuation that suffers from the handling, both because people differ about it and because the marks are small and indistinct. One thing you can do to forestall confusion is to put a circle around a period, thus: ⊙; and a caret over or under other common marks: ⌃, ⌄, ⌁, ⌄, ⌀, ⌄, and so on.

One of the most frequent of last-minute changes is in the paragraphing. Even the best of writers will discover that a sentence that seemed like an appropriate ending to a paragraph now strikes him as an excellent topic sentence for the next. If you change your mind about the right place to break the paragraph and decide to have none where one now exists, write "No ⁋" in the blank space in front of the indention and also draw a "running line" from the word that closes the previous paragraph. Here is a set of markings for such a change of mind:

....If we think of the colonies as

advance outposts of the European powers,

we have an idea of how Europeans looked

upon them. Thus they represented their

sovereigns' strength and prestige.

no ⁋ The rivalry of European countries

was reflected in the history of the

colonies overseas. ⁋ Nothing illustrates

this fact better than the story of

English-Dutch relations in America.

no ⁋ Holland occupied little territory

but she was located at the mouth of the

Rhine. Like a watchdog, she sat

astride the trade routes that led out

of Germany....

If in typing, two words have been run together, draw a vertical line between them; otherwise you risk confusion or, even worse, misunderstanding through miscorrection. Suppose, for example, that your copy contains this sentence:

`He greeted the crowd withoutstretched arms.`

There is a chance that your editor may absent-mindedly divide the words after "without"; for the work of editing tends to concentrate the mind on visual detail at the expense of meaning and such a blunder can remain unseen through several readings. You save yourself the resulting absurdity by marking your copy in this way:

`He greeted the crowd with#outstretched`

`arms.`

Conversely, the pieces of a word must sometimes be brought together. Here is the way:

`The author's chief qualification was in sight.`

Another recurrent problem of revision is that of changing the capitalization. You have, let us say, cut a long sentence into smaller pieces and, like a cut earthworm, each segment now has a life of its own. To show a change from a small (or lower-case) letter to a capital (or upper-case), draw three small lines under the letter:

`It was a blueprint for an elaborate`

Cap/ `feudal society, and at the top of the`

`pyramid of government was the landed`

`aristocracy.`

To reduce a capital to a small letter, draw a slanting line (slash) through it:

Life was harsh on the range, The

cowboy was a lonely figure.

The most common kind of alteration is the transposing of letters, words, or larger units. If two letters have been reversed they can be put right as follows:

Psecial

If two words are in the wrong order, do this:

Praz, Mario, Machiavelli in Inghilterra,

Rome, 1943.

When a whole paragraph has to be moved to a new place, the simplest way is to circle it completely and draw a line from it up or down the margin to the caret that shows the point of insert. In a grafting operation of this kind, make certain that the broken edges will fit when brought together. The connecting words must be as appropriate as they were before the surgery. Sometimes the mood and voice of the verbs have to be changed. Sometimes you must find synonyms for words because the same ones are now repeated too near each other for euphony.

Occasionally there is need to remove a paragraph from one part of a chapter to a distant one. You have a choice of methods. One is to use the same device as that which serves on a single page: circle the paragraph that is to be moved to page 22 and write next to it: "Tr. to p. 22." (If more than one transposition is to be made, letter them all consecutively beginning with *A*.) Then mark page 22 with a caret to show where the traveling paragraph belongs and in the margin write: "Tr. from p. 8."

The alternative is to retype the paragraph and make of it an insert on page 22, crossing it out altogether on page 8. This is preferable when the gap is greater than the one between the page numbers just cited, for instance in a large book in which a portion of page 8 is removed to page 300. At the printer's the manuscript may be split up among several typesetters, or the early portion may be returned to the author with his first galley proofs, or be in some way hard of access when page 300 suddenly calls for the presence of page 8.

When your revising is finished to your satisfaction, go through the manuscript to make sure that the pages are arranged and numbered consecutively, including charts, graphs, and other illustrations. You have, of course, made an exact duplicate copy of your work showing every correction or instruction, even those made at the last minute before you turn in the original. If this main copy goes astray or is damaged, you can replace it immediately. Few of us could take calmly what happened to Carlyle when he entrusted the manuscript of the first volume of *The French Revolution* to John Stuart Mill, whose housemaid used it to light the fire. This was before the days of typewriters and carbon copies and copying machines, and Carlyle had to start afresh from his notes—an act of fortitude one shudders to think of.

After your editor has brought to your text the suggestions that occur to him, he sends back the altered copy for your approval.[8] Editors' creative instincts can be useful to you in improving the form and phraseology of your work. It is clear, however, that an editor can sometimes become so possessive about your text that his suggestions begin to do violence to your meaning and intent. Do not let him write his book over your name, and on no account let him dispatch your work to the printer with his changes unexamined by you. He is in good faith when he says they are "only minor," but you may not think them so, and the time and expense of discovering and changing them in proof should not be an added burden on you.

In general—and this applies to friends or colleagues who help you by reading your manuscript ahead of publication—the criticisms and

[8]At a book publisher's a manuscript is usually edited by two people in two different ways: the editor goes over it for sense, organization, and literary style; the copyeditor goes over it for spelling, grammatical niceties, and consistency of form.

suggestions you receive must be interpreted in the light of *your* purpose, *your* plan, *your* style. This caution will make little difference in mechanical corrections; it applies to larger matters. Almost always, the word or passage that is questioned needs to have something done to it—it shows where the intelligent reader stumbled or jibbed. But this does not mean that what *he* suggests as an improvement is what you should accept as the right thing.

The Handle to a Writer's Works

It may come as a surprise that one of the very last acts of revision before printing is the putting of a title to the piece. Yet the common experience is that the title is written last more often than not. You may have thought of your report, article, or book in some descriptive phrase that fitted it very well. You have used this formula in telling your friends what you were working on, and again the phrase fitted the form of your spoken sentence. But the description was never a title. By itself it was unsayable. We know, for example, that Thackeray called his first great novel *Pen and Pencil Sketches of English Society*. The reason was that he had illustrated the book himself and that his earlier literary work had consisted of character sketches. Under that cumbrous rubric the work we now know as *Vanity Fair* had little chance of catching the eye or capturing the imagination of publisher or public. It lacked a handle.

When the piece offered to view is science or scholarship, the duty to provide a convenient handle to pick it up and hold it by is just as great. And baptizing the work once the chapters and parts have been named is always a ticklish business. The difficulty of titling is due to the fact that modern titles are not descriptions but tags. Publishing usage is not likely to permit one to write simply *A History of the United States*. Perhaps the label has been seen too often. So it must become *The Land of the Free*, supplemented by an explanation in smaller type, "A History of the United States." Within this allusive style there are fashions, and these it is well not to follow if one wants to avoid embarrassment a dozen years later, when the fashion has faded. At one time the titles of even serious biographies tended toward the flowery: *Poor Splendid Wings,*[9] *So Fell the Angels,*[10] and the like. Allusiveness continues to attract the author and publisher who want their joint product to stand out from the mass of printed books, but it should be held in check by common sense. *The Better Half* no doubt suggests its subject, disclosed in its subtitle, "The Emancipation of the American Woman," but it is a question whether *Fearful Symmetry,* even with the explanatory words "A Study of William Blake," does not go too far toward coyness and the nod of the knowing.[11]

A title should indicate what realm of thought or action the work treats of, and possibly also what contribution or assertion it makes. *Born Under Saturn* fails on both counts and is rather hackneyed besides.[12]

Such considerations need not keep a title from legitimately arousing curiosity. Marjorie Nicolson's *Newton Demands the Muse* does this admirably, and with economy and dignity. It tells us at once that science and poetry jointly form the subject, while the alluring image it raises is more vivid and true to the reality of the past than any pair of abstractions. When a title that is short enough to be easily remembered proves too general to fit the book closely, a subtitle performs that adjustment. Thus *The Flowers of Friendship* absolutely requires "Letters Written to Gertrude Stein." Simplicity, in titles as elsewhere, is a great virtue, and as elsewhere it is found only by hard work and self-control. The last thing one wants from a title is a glimpse of the author taking a pose.

The titles of chapters can be fuller, more descriptive than those of a book. A certain harmony among the names of chapters is a pleasing and useful thing, just as an artificial attempt to suggest drama or "revelations" is futile and displeasing. Remember that readers browse before buying and judge the unknown by its outward features. Sometimes an excellent book is as it were mislabeled by its injudicious chapter titles. For example, Stewart H. Holbrook's sound and valuable

[9] A critical study of Pre-Raphaelitism by Frances Winwar, Boston, 1933.

[10] An account of Salmon P. Chase and his daughter Kate by Thomas and Marva Belden, Boston, 1956.

[11] The study of Blake is by the distinguished critic Northrop Frye; the study of American women is by Andrew Sinclair.

[12] Two excellent works hide under this designation—one a biography of William Hazlitt by Catherine Maclean and the other a study of the character and conduct of artists by Rudolf and Margaret Wittkower.

Story of the American Railroads[13] fails to represent itself justly to the roving eye because its chapter headings lack harmony and attempt sensationalism. The first five are acceptable:

1. Panorama
2. The Prophets
3. Primeval Railroading
4. Railroad Fever
5. "The Work of the Age"

But then we fall on:

6. Forgotten Genius [which is a short digression about one man]
7. The Pennsy and the Central [which sounds as if out of chronological order in a book of thirty-seven chapters].

From then on the sense of progression and tone is broken by such headings as "War Comes to a 'Neutral' Line," "Locating the Route," "Out in the Wild and Woolly," "Up in the Cold and Icy," "The Carriers are Harassed," "Through the Dark Ages—and After," "The Fast Mail," "Spotters," "The Little Fellers," "News Butchers," and—unexpectedly sedate for the last one—"The Railroad in the Drama." After the colloquialism of the middle chapters, one's sense of fitness wants for that last topic something like "The Footplate and the Footlights"—a deplorable parallel, but at least one in keeping with the prevailing mood.

One test of the harmony we speak of is length. If you start out terse and dramatic with: 1. "Hope"; 2. "Effort"; 3. "Power"; you cannot very well continue with: 4. "There's Many a Slip Twixt the Cup and the Lip." In fact, it is best to avoid the monotony of a striking device repeated: make the harmony arise from tone and what the novelists call the "point of view." This often means naming your chapters in the same voice, form, or construction. For example, if you have: 1. "The Outbreak of Revolution," and continue "The . . . of . . ." through 4. "The Rise of the Consulate and Empire," you ought not to switch to 5. "Napoleon Falls"; you have bound yourself to: "The Fall of Napoleon."

[13] New York, 1947.

Essay titles differ somewhat from chapter titles in that they do alone the work of catching and holding the glancing eye. But like chapter titles, they may be a little more explicit than book titles unaided by subtitles. This usually means deciding what the first impression is that you want to create on your reader's mind. The idea must be important yet not give the point away; it must be arresting without being an impudent nudge. An excellent example of just the right mixture is the title of an essay by Meyer Schapiro on Lewis Mumford's *The Culture of Cities.* It is called "Looking Forward to Looking Backward."[14]

The chance for such felicity is rare. Usually, one has to fall back on the simply declarative with "in," "and," "on," or the possessive case, as links between ideas: "Machiavelli's Politics," "The Education of Engineers in Russia," or "T. E. Lawrence on Leaders in the Middle East." The trouble with these titles is that they do not enable the reader to keep the memory of one such essay clear from another on the same theme. They do not state or evoke enough, what they say is not distinctive, they are not *telling.* A sharp, clear message is needed, even if the article is not the first to treat that subject. If Lionel Trilling, for example, had written "A Poet's Letters" or "Keats and His Letters," his memorable essay would be much less easily brought to mind than under its actual title: "The Poet as Hero: Keats in His Letters." Note how strongly affirmative this is, for all its quietness, and how vivid is the substitution of "*in* his letters" for the ubiquitous "and."

The lesson is plain: Keep revolving ideas for your title from the moment you begin writing. Make lists of possible ones, and if you are lucky the ideal phrase will flash on you before it is time to part with your manuscript.

Revision at a Distance: The Printer and You

At last you are going to be published—that is, if your essay or dissertation is workmanlike in form and mature and original in contents.

---

[14] *The Partisan Reader,* New York, 1946, 310.

Publishing, of course, means a fresh set of problems, but most of them are mechanical; and unless yours is an unusual case you will never see those who query you and ask for your last revises.[15] Though the typesetters of your text may be several, to you they will be "the printer"— an anonymous, collective function and dignity like "the firm" or "the house."

Before many weeks have passed the printer will send you evidence that he has not been idle: galley proofs. These are long sheets of paper on which your work has been printed. A galley (so named from the tray in which the type is held) will contain the equivalent of two or three pages of text. As you reread your words for perhaps the twentieth time, you will not escape the feeling that they are familiar, and yet they will seem new. This is partly because they now look clean, black, and definitive, partly because your old landmarks have vanished. You associated a certain phrase with the top of page 8, and a certain paragraph looked long and sprawling. Now the phrase is lost somewhere and the paragraph has shrunk to a modest size. This is a pleasant discovery you should take advantage of: it allows you to read your text again with a fresh eye.

It may happen that you will come upon an egregious blunder even at this stage, but you must restrain yourself from wanting to redo whole passages under the inspiration of your own words. The changes you make in galleys are charged to you unless they are "printer's errors." At the rate of seventy-five cents a line (1969), they can be an expensive indulgence, especially since substituting a single word for another sometimes necessitates resetting an entire paragraph. The experienced author has learned to limit his desire for change and, if change is unavoidable, to draft the alterations in such a way that they will affect but one line of type (or slug) at a time. Experience also teaches that one may change one's mind about a correction a few minutes after making it, or the next morning, before the galleys have gone back to the printer. This dictates the rule: *correct all galley and page proofs in erasable pencil.*

---

[15] When the printer's proofreader is in doubt, he will "query" ("?" or "Qy" in margin) and suggest what seems to him right. When you have answered and he has made the change, the proof sent is a "revise."

To communicate with the printer you use the same traditional signs referred to before. Study the list given in Figure 11 and make the symbols a part of your technical equipment like the alphabet and the multiplication table. When you correct galleys, it is convenient to use a red pencil for the printer's errors and one in another color for changes that depart from copy. This will make it easier to fix responsibility for costs later on. Always mark your changes in the margin next to the line being altered—the left for corrections nearest that side, the right for the other half of the line. The printer will be more surely guided thus, and will avoid compounding the original mistake.

If you can manage it, correct your proofs with the help of another person who "holds copy," that is, reads your manuscript aloud while you enter the corrections on galleys. Have him spell the proper names and read out every punctuation mark, paragraph break, and all deviations from ordinary roman type, such as capitals, italics, and boldface. If you can arrange to read the proof a second time, preferably with a different person holding the copy, you will catch more errors than you now suppose possible. In this kind of collating you must try to see your work in its smallest portions and temporarily lose sight of its meaning. It is like scrutinizing a halftone picture in the morning paper so closely that you see only dots, instead of the different shadings that the eye puts together to make a likeness. In reading galleys all words are equally important.

The printer's marginal queries will draw your attention to some peculiarity in the text, some error in spelling, some ambiguity in your instructions, or some other equally cogent problem. Never let these queries go unanswered.[16]

---

[16] The printer may sometimes seek your help in solving a layout problem, such as three successive lines ending in a hyphen or three lines containing an identical word at beginning or end. Again, it is a tradition, apparently as old as printing itself, that the "typographical widow" must be killed at all costs. The widow is defined as less than a full line of type that ends a paragraph and begins a new page. You may be asked to oblige by adding a phrase or two to your text. See Karl Brown, "The Typographical Widow: Who is she? What is she?" *New York Public Library Bulletin,* LII (January 1948), 3–25, and the sequel "The Typographical Widow: Who is she? What is she? Encore," *op. cit.* (September 1948), 458–66.

FIGURE 11 *The Proofreader's Marks and Their Use*

INSTRUCTION TO THE PRINTER	INDICATION IN THE MARGIN	INDICATION IN THE TEXT	THE CORRECTED TEXT
Take out letter, letters, or words.	*ℛ*	He marked the proopf.	He marked the proof.
Insert space.	#	He marked theproof.	He marked the proof.
Insert letter.	*ℎ*	He maked the proof.	He marked the proof.
Set in lower-case type.	*lc*	He Marked the proof.	He marked the proof.
Reset in italic type.	*ital*	He marked the proof.	He marked the *proof*.
Reset in roman (regular) type.	*rom*	He marked *the* proof.	He marked the proof.
Reset in boldface type.	*bf*	He marked the proof.	He **marked** the proof.
Insert period.	⊙	He marked the proof	He marked the proof.
Transpose letters or words.	*tr*	He the proof marked.	He marked the proof.
Let it stand as it is.	*stet*	He marked the proof.	He marked the proof.
Insert hyphen.	/=/	He made the proofmark.	He made the proof-mark.
Equalize spacing.	*eq.#*	He marked the proof.	He marked the proof.
Insert comma.	⤳	Yes he marked the proof.	Yes, he marked the proof.
Insert apostrophe.	⤳	He marked the boys proof.	He marked the boy's proof.
Enclose in quotation marks.	❝ ❞	He marked it proof.	He marked it "proof."
Use a capital letter.	*cap*	he marked the proof.	He marked the proof.
Use small capitals.	*sc*	He marked the proof.	He marked the PROOF.
Push down space.	⊥	He marked the proof.	He marked the proof.
Close up space.	⌒	He ma rked the proof.	He marked the proof.
Insert inferior figure.	$\widehat{2}$	Sulphuric acid is HSO_4.	Sulphuric acid is H_2SO_4.
Insert superior figure.	$\backslash 2$	$a^2 + b^2 = c$	$a^2 + b^2 = c^2$
Spell out.	*spell out*	He marked the 2nd proof.	He marked the second proof.
Start a new paragraph.	¶	reading. The reader marked.	reading. The reader marked
No paragraph; run in.	*no ¶*	marked. The proof was read	marked. The proof was read
Printer's query to author.	?	The proof read by	The proof was read by

Let me begin by reminding you that the possession of the true thoughts means everywhere the possession of invaluable instruments of action; and that our duty to gain truth, so far from being a black command out of the blue, or a "stunt self imposed by our intellect, can account for itself by excellent practical reasons.

—James William

Let me begin by reminding you of the fact that
the possession of true thoughts means everywhere
the possession of invaluable instruments of action;
and that our duty to gain truth, so far from being a
blank command from out of the blue, or a "stunt"
self-imposed by our intellect, can account for itself
by excellent practical reasons.

—William James

After galley proofs only one chance of revising remains—the reading of page proofs. These proofs result from dividing the corrected galleys into page size and running off a new set of long sheets; two or three of the future pages appear on each sheet, with page numbers at the appropriate places. Changes, except of the most minor sort, are now very costly, virtually prohibitive. You read page proofs only to make certain that in correcting the galleys the printer has not committed new errors in the lines he has reset. Even if you have absolute faith in your editor's ability and willingness to correct page proofs for you, you must also do it yourself.

The author's last duty before launching his work is the preparation of an index. Some few kinds of books do not call for them, such as the collection of literary essays, the casual anthology, and of course fiction generally. But all works for study and consultation need an index. By it their usefulness to the public is greatly increased, particularly if the index is well made.

Many a writer who is wanting in patience and energy will turn the tedious task over to a professional index-maker—or to his spouse. This is a mistake unless the author is a bad bungler; for however competent the spouse or the professional may be, the author has a special understanding of the book and its contribution to knowledge, which only he can accurately reflect in the index. The index is the book reduced to its essential themes and topics. Indexing these so that the reader can penetrate the work and find his way through it easily and with dispatch is a technical task that the beginner can learn by following step by step the instructions in Martha Wheeler's manual.[17]

The general principles are simple enough: with the page proof in hand, you take slips or cards of convenient size—3 × 5 will do—and you write on each the name or word that you consider sufficiently important to index. These are known as "entries." They are followed by the number of the page or pages on which the reader will find these topics treated. Subentries may be made in order to break up a large subject or indicate the aspect of it that is dealt with or referred to on a given page. The slips or cards are alphabetized as you go along, to facilitate the adding of later page numbers. When complete, the set of cards is either sent as it is to the printer, or pasted on sheets, or transcribed in typewritten pages like the remainder of your copy.

The degree of detail in an index varies not with your inclination but with your subject matter. A biography, for example, must contain, besides the names of persons and places, entries for the principal activities of the subject's life. But a collection of edited letters needs an even finer sorting of topics, because in the biography the table of contents leads to the data a researcher would seek, whereas the letters can in most cases be arranged only chronologically, and this tells us nothing about their contents. Since the editor cannot predict all the uses to which his work may be put, the index must by its completeness anticipate everyone's questions. *The New Letters of Abigail Adams: 1788–1801,*[18] for instance, contains entries for "Bathing machine," "Bleeding and blistering," "Conechigo waggons," "Lyons: cloaks from," "Measles," "Newspapers: malice of," "Theophilanthropy," "Wine cellar: at Quincy."

To whatever kind your book may belong, make your index such as to prevent the reader's saying that he could not find again a choice

---

[17] *Indexing,* 5th ed., Albany, 1957.
[18] Ed. Stewart Mitchell, Boston, 1947.

passage he came across in its lively pages. At the least, an index will guide the reader to the proper names mentioned in the book. At the most, it will provide a clue to every single item of interest, from a total eclipse of the sun to a passing anecdote.[19] By the care of its preparation, the index shows the author's pride in his work and his regard for other researchers. Both it and they deserve better than to be slighted at his hands.

It may be that after all the pains you and others have taken to make your work an example of perfect printing, you will open your first author's copy and immediately fall upon a grievous typographical error. This will make you indignant for a day or so, while you imagine that every reader sees nothing but that ridiculously misspelled word. Console yourself, if you can, with the thought that in the five centuries of printing few works have been letter perfect. And before Gutenberg, it was the copyists who provided the absurdities, one at a time, by hand.

[19] In this regard, the indexes that Samuel Butler prepared for his works are models. One finds, for example, in *Evolution, Old and New,* "Day, Portrait of Mr." and also "Portrait, of Mr. Day." Indexes often tempt their makers to mild eccentricities and even jokes. In a work on economics privately printed in the 1890's, one finds under "Price": "of this book and where to obtain it." For other curiosities of indexing see H. B. Wheatley, *How to Make an Index,* London, 1902.

Afterword:
A Discipline for Work

You have now reached the end of a long course of advice, exhortation, and instruction. It may seem to you that you have been told too many things to be able to apply all of them at once to your research and writing; you have been made self-conscious about unsuspected traps, and this has damped your carefree mood. Or again, you may think that you have been told some useful things, but not the ones that you needed for your project in hand. If either of these impressions is yours at the moment, your reading has not been in vain. You have been shaken out of your normal ways and made to reflect on your powers and responsibilities. The only alarming symptom at this point would be the feeling that now you know all there is to know and can apply it forthwith.

Such a belief would be dangerous for two reasons: first, because this book has given you but the principles of research and writing, with some illustrations; which means that you still have to make the transfer and adaptation of the rules and suggestions to your work and your needs; and second, because no new knowledge can ever be grasped and made use of in one sweep of the mind. Time is needed to assimilate it by the formation of new habits. Time is also needed to go back to one or another topic in order to refresh your memory about what was actually said. In a word, now that you have finished reading or studying this book, you should begin to use it as a mentor at your elbow and as a work of reference on your desk.

This suggestion brings up a matter we have not yet discussed, one that is generally taken for granted, though perhaps without warrant—the matter of when and how to work. Some hints were given in Chapter 2 about the division of tasks in research, and we may repeat it here: you should keep your clearest stretches of time for the uninterrupted study of your main sources. Verifying dates, hunting down references, and, generally, all broken-field running should be reserved for occasions when you have a shorter time at your disposal or when you are feeling less alert or energetic than usual. Your best mind should go to what takes thought.

The same principle applies to writing, with variations and additions. Faced with the need to write, most people (including practiced writers) experience a strong and strange impulse to put off beginning. They would do anything rather than confront that blank sheet of paper. They start inventing pretexts for doing something else: they need to look up another source, they have not sufficiently mulled over the organization of the paper, they want to steep themselves in their notes once more. Or—what is really cowardly—there is some shopping that cannot wait, or again, the typewriter keys need a thorough cleaning. Let it be said once for all: *there is no cure for this desire to escape.* It will recur as long as you live. But there are palliatives, and some of them are good enough to turn the struggle virtually into a game.

The palliative principle is that a regular force must be used to overcome a recurrent inertia: if you can arrange to write regularly, never missing your date with yourself, no matter whether you are in the mood or not, you have won half the battle. You do not have to be pleased with what you do, nor expect a set amount to be done by the end of the session, but *some* writing you must do on the morning or afternoon or evening that is kept sacred for the purpose. The writer's problem is the inverse of the reformed drunkard's. The latter must *never* touch a drop; the former must *always* do his stint. Skip but one writing period and you need the strength of Samson to get started again.

It goes without saying that these writing periods must be close enough together to create a rhythm of work, and that they must be chosen with an eye to the greatest convenience in your present mode of life. For example, if you possibly can, set aside one free morning or day for writing. The longer the free period, the better. A time with no fixed obligation at the end is preferable to one that will draw your eye to the clock halfway through, and so on. Similarly with the place. Do not try to write at home if you can hear your roommate's hi-fi tapes or the domestic symphony of kitchen and nursery noises; conversely, do not attempt to write in an office where the phone and your associates will interrupt every ten minutes.

In making your arrangements, consider that a likely cause of the distaste for beginning is that writing is for all of us an act of self-exposure. Writing requires that we create some order in our thoughts and project it outside, where everybody can see it. The instinct of self-protection, of shyness, combines with the sense of our mental confusion or uncertainty to make us postpone the trial of strength. Hence the desirability of being alone and uninterrupted. In silence our thoughts can settle into their proper shapes; they will be exclusively the thoughts bearing on our topic, and as soon as a few of them are down on paper they will draw out the rest. The momentum will increase until, after a time, the bulk of work done will set up a desire to keep adding to it. The hour or day set aside for writing will be waited for, and the work will truly be *in progress*.

Since the problem is best seen as one of inertia and momentum, other rules of thumb suggest themselves as corollaries:

1. Do not wait until you have gathered all your material before starting to write. Nothing adds to inertia like a mass of notes, the earliest of which recede in the mists of foregone time. On the contrary, begin drafting your ideas as soon as some portion of the topic appears to hang together in your mind.

2. Do not be afraid of writing down something that you think may have to be changed. Paper is not granite, and in a first draft you are not carving eternal words in stone. Rather, you are creating substance to be molded and remolded in successive drafts.

3. Do not hesitate to write up in any order those sections of your total work that seem to have grown ripe in your mind. There is a moment in any stretch of research when all the details come together in natural cohesion, despite small gaps and doubts. Learn to recognize that moment and seize it by composing in harmony with your inward feeling of unity. Never mind whether the portions that come out are consecutive.

4. Once you start writing, keep going. Resist the temptation to get up and verify a fact. Leave it blank. The same holds true for the word or phrase that refuses to come to mind. It will arise much more easily on revision, and the economy in time *and momentum* is incalculable.

5. When you get stuck in the middle of a stretch of writing, reread your last two or three pages and see if continuity of thought will not propel you past dead center. Many writers begin the day's work by reading over the previous day's accumulation. But there are other ways of beginning, such as writing one or two letters, transcribing or expanding a few notes, making an entry in a diary, and the like. The common feature of such a wind-up or running start is that the chosen act is one of *writing* and that it is brief—a *few* notes or lines before tackling the main task.

6. Since the right openings for chapters or sections are difficult, special attention must be paid to them. As you collect your materials, be on the watch for ideas or facts or even words that would make a good beginning.[1] Remember that in any extended work you begin many times, not only at each new chapter, but often at each subsection. Supposing that writing a twenty-page chapter takes you three sessions, you may find it helpful to break off in the middle of, and not at, a subdivision. In this way you take up the story in midstream, instead of having to begin the day *and* the section together. Some writers make a point of breaking off the day's work just before they completely run down and while they still see ideas ahead. They scribble two or three final words to call these up at once on resuming work.

7. It will often happen that the opening paragraph of the whole piece (or of any of its parts) will on rereading seem quite alien to

[1] See again Chapter 13, pp. 310–11.

what follows. This calls for a pair of scissors. What has happened is that the first paragraph was simply the warming-up, and the true beginning was set down in the second. From this common experience you should infer that a slow sluggish start on Saturday morning is no reason for discouragement. You are priming the pump, choking the car, and the splutter is of no consequence.

8. A writer should as soon as possible become aware of his peculiarities and preferences regarding the mechanics of composing. He should know whether he likes the pen or the typewriter, what size and color of paper he prefers, which physical arrangement of his notes and books pleases him best, even what kind of clothes and which posture he likes to assume for work. In all these matters he is entitled to complete self-indulgence provided he remains faithful to his choices. This is consistent with our underlying principle: indulge yourself so that you will have no excuse for putting off the task; and stick to your choice, so that the very presence of your favorite implements will confirm the habits of the good workman.

When the first draft is done the back of the job is broken. It is then a pleasure—or it should be one—to carve, cut, add, and polish until what you say corresponds reasonably well to what you know. The span of time and other conditions of revising are less rigorous than those of first drafting. If your manuscript has passed into typed form, you can use a spare half-hour to proofread it and mark the rough spots with little x's or wavy lines in the margin. You can be thinking about substitutions and additions until the next free hour when you can Revise with a big R, as against typographical revising with a small one—respectively the big operations described in Chapters 2, 12, and 13, and the lesser mentioned in Chapter 16.

Ideally, a report should be in progress in its entirety long before it is finished. The earlier parts will be well advanced while the last ones are still in the rough, the research for them not yet finished. Research will in fact continue to the end, which is, in the case of a book, indexing in page proof. But the revision at one time of different parts in different stages of perfecting is an excellent way of seeing one's construction as a whole and in detail. Each critical observation supplies hints to be carried out in other parts, and this evens out the advantages of experience gathered on the way. Follow this suggestion and your work will not seem, like so many, better done in proportion as it approaches the end.

But it is a little premature to speak here of the end. Despite what was said at the outset of this section about having completed a sizable course with us, the reader is only at the beginning of real work. Whatever his enterprise—short report or extended monograph—let him take his courage in both hands and, by the application of his best mind, bring order and meaning out of the welter of facts. With the best will in the world, his work will not be free from error—so much it is safe to predict. But that part of it which is sound, clear, readily grasped and remembered will be a contribution, no matter how limited its scope, to that order among ideas which we call knowledge. For as Francis Bacon wisely observed in his *New Method,* "truth will sooner come out from error than from confusion."[2]

_____
[2] *Novum Organum,* Bk. II, XX.

For Further Reading

The list of books that follows is not a bibliography in the sense of a repertory comprising the works cited in the text or consulted in its preparation. Only a few such books are listed here. Instead, we have documented the three parts of our work by pointing to the articles, texts, and reference books that our readers may turn to in the pursuit of their particular aims, or for the additional elucidation of our principles.

We saw, first, that all research was to a greater or lesser degree historian's work—hence the books about historians and historiography. We showed at many points that comprehension and expression were correlative acts of the researcher's mind—hence the books on language and writing. Finally, we maintained that there exist leads to the literature and the facts of all branches of knowledge—hence the bibliographies grouped under appropriate headings.

The following checklist cannot, of course, be complete; but by the time the reader has begun to make use of these books, which supplement the precepts in our text, he will be able to find his way alone.

The student whose work requires that he attend to successive editions and dates of publication will notice that during the past fifteen years the large output of reprints, in paperback and other forms, has introduced a bibliographical chaos unequaled since the eighteenth century. Here are a few of its features: paperback reprints do not always give the book's "printing history" or the source of the text; such reprints are rarely listed in reliable, comprehensive, bibliographical guides; the same work often flits from one "reprint house" to another within a very few years; at times, the title of the work is changed without notice to the reader—and by this means the work of a dead author is sometimes offered to the public ostensibly as a new work, posthumous in a peculiar sense.

Given these conditions, it is extremely difficult to ascertain which is the latest edition of an important work. And for works by authors still living it is hard to decide whether to refer a reader to the paperback (or small hardbound reprint edition) that is in print today but may be unfindable tomorrow. For libraries do not invariably keep or catalogue paperbacks, yet these may embody revisions of the original edition, dated perhaps only two years earlier. To sort out the facts about even a handful of contemporary books would be a life's work. In giving below a list of useful new books and reprinted classics, we have spent only a reasonable—that is, a small—amount of time in tracing the fortunes of valuable works through the reproductive mill.

I. On the Historian's Work

Method

Altick, Richard D., *The Art of Literary Research*. New York, Norton, 1963.

Cantor, Norman F., and Schneider, Richard I., *How to Study History*. New York, Crowell, 1967.

Carter, Clarence E., *Historical Editing*. Bulletin No. 7, Washington, D.C., National Archives, 1952.

Clark, G. Kitson, *Guide for Research Students Working on Historical Subjects,* 2nd ed. New York, Cambridge University Press, 1968.

Daniels, Robert V., *Studying History: How and Why*. Englewood Cliffs, N.J., Prentice-Hall, 1966.

Dow, Earle W., *Principles of a Note-System for Historical Studies.* New York, Century, 1924.

Garraghan, Gilbert J., and Delanglez, Jean, eds., *A Guide to Historical Method.* New York, Fordham University Press, 1946.

Gottschalk, Louis, *Understanding History: A Primer of Historical Method,* 2nd ed. New York, Knopf, 1969.

Gray, Wood, and others, *Historian's Handbook,* 2nd ed. Boston, Houghton Mifflin, 1964.

Gustavson, Carl, *A Preface to History.* New York, McGraw-Hill, 1955.

Hancock, W. K., *Attempting History.* Canberra, Australian National University Press, 1969.

———, "Inquiring and Narration," in *Country and Calling.* London, Faber and Faber, 1954.

Hockett, Homer C., *The Critical Method in Historical Research and Writing.* New York, Macmillan, 1955.

Kent, Sherman, with the assistance of James T. Schleifer, *Writing History,* 2nd ed. New York, Appleton, 1967.

Morison, Samuel Eliot, "The Experiences and Principles of an Historian," in *Vistas of History.* New York, Knopf, 1964.

Perkins, Dexter, ed., *The Education of Historians in the United States.* New York, McGraw-Hill, 1962.

Renier, G. J., *History: Its Purpose and Method.* Boston, Beacon Press, 1950.

Schellenberg, T. R., *The Management of Archives.* New York, Columbia University Press, 1965.

Social Science Research Council, *Theory and Practice in Historical Study: A Report of the Committee on Historiography.* Bulletin No. 54, New York, Social Science Research Council, 1946.

———, *The Use of Personal Documents in History, Anthropology, and Sociology.* Bulletin No. 53, New York, Social Science Research Council, 1945.

Vincent, John Martin, *Historical Research.* New York, Holt, 1911. [Reprinted, New York, Peter Smith, 1929.]

Fact-Finding and Verification

Altick, Richard D., *The Scholar Adventurers*. New York, Free Press, 1966.

Benét, William Rose, *The Reader's Encyclopedia*, 2nd ed. New York, Crowell, 1965.

Clark's Famous 250-year Perpetual Calendar, Covering the Years 1753-2002. Richmond, Va., Dietz, 1943.

Fadiman, Clifton, and Van Doren, Charles, eds., *The American Treasury 1455-1955*. New York, Harper, 1955.

Hadas, Moses, *Ancilla to Classical Reading*. New York, Columbia University Press, 1966.

Heywood, Valentine, *British Titles, The Use and Misuse of Titles of Peers and Commoners, With Some Historical Notes*, 2nd ed. London, A. and C. Black, 1953.

Jones, H. G., *The Records of a Nation: Their Management, Preservation, and Use*. New York, Atheneum, 1969.

Langer, William L., ed., *An Encyclopedia of World History*, 4th rev. ed. Boston, Houghton Mifflin, 1968.

Mayer, Alfred, *Annals of European Civilization 1501-1900*, Foreword by G. P. Gooch. London, Cassell, 1949.

Morris, Richard B., ed., *Encyclopedia of American History*, rev. ed. New York, Harper, 1970.

————, ed., *The Harper Encyclopedia of Modern History*. New York, Harper, 1970.

Shepherd, William R., *Historical Atlas*, 9th ed. New York, Barnes & Noble, 1964.

Winks, Robin W., ed., *The Historian as Detective: Essays on Evidence*. New York, Harper, 1969.

Truth and Causation

Bloch, Marc, *The Historian's Craft*. New York, Vintage Books, 1964.

Carr, Edward Hallett, *What Is History?* New York, Knopf, 1962.

Dunning, William A., *Truth in History and Other Essays*. Port Washington, N.Y., Kennikat Press, 1965.

Einstein, Lewis, *Historical Change.* Cambridge, The University Press, 1946.

George, H. B., *Historical Evidence.* Oxford, Clarendon Press, 1909.

Gottschalk, Louis, ed., *Generalization in the Writing of History.* Chicago, The University of Chicago Press, 1963.

Nagel, Ernest, "Some Issues in the Logic of Historical Analysis." *Scientific Monthly,* LXXIV (March 1952), 162–70.

Randall, John Herman, Jr., *Nature and Historical Experience.* New York, Columbia University Press, 1958.

Schuyler, Robert Livingston, "Indeterminism in Physics and History." *Social Studies,* XXVII (December 1936), 507–16.

Smith, John E., "Time, Times, and the 'Right Time'?, Chronos and Kairos." *Monist,* LIII (January 1969), 1ff.

Thomson, David, *The Aims of History.* London, Thames and Hudson, 1969.

Weiss, Paul, *History, Written and Lived.* Carbondale, Southern Illinois University Press, 1962.

Schools of Thought

Berlin, Isaiah, *Historical Inevitability.* New York, Oxford University Press, 1955.

Cohen, Morris R., "American Ideas on History," in Felix S. Cohen, ed., *American Thought.* Glencoe, Ill., Free Press, 1954, 48–65.

Fitzsimons, Matthew A., Pundt, Alfred G., and Nowell, Charles E., *The Development of Historiography.* Harrisburg, Pa., Stackpole, 1954.

Flint, Robert, *Historical Philosophy in France and French Belgium and Switzerland.* New York, Scribner, 1894.

Fueter, Eduard, *Geschichte der Neueren Historiographie.* Munich, Oldenbourg, 1911. [3rd ed., 1936.]

Fussner, F. Smith, *The Historical Revolution: English Historical Writing and Thought, 1580–1640.* New York, Columbia University Press, 1962.

Geyl, Pieter, *Debates with Historians.* Cleveland, World, 1964.

Harrison, Frederic, "The History Schools: An Oxford Dialogue," in *The Meaning of History, and Other Historical Pieces.* New York, Macmillan, 1894.

Higham, John, Krieger, Leonard, and Gilbert, Felix, *History.* Englewood Cliffs, N.J., Prentice-Hall, 1965.

Löwith, Karl, *Meaning in History: The Theological Implications of the Philosophy of History.* Chicago, The University of Chicago Press, 1957.

Lukacs, John, *Historical Consciousness.* New York, Harper, 1968.

Muller, Herbert J., *The Uses of the Past: Profiles of Former Societies.* New York, Oxford University Press, 1957.

Nevins, Allan, *The Gateway to History,* rev. ed. Garden City, N.Y., Anchor Books, 1962.

Nisbet, Robert A., *Social Change and History.* New York, Oxford University Press, 1969.

Nugent, Walter T. K., *Creative History.* Philadelphia, Lippincott, 1967.

Plumb, J. H., *The Death of the Past.* Boston, Houghton Mifflin, 1970.

Robinson, James Harvey, *The New History: Essays Illustrating the Modern Historical Outlook,* with a new introd. by Harvey Wish. New York, Free Press, 1965.

Salmon, Lucy Maynard, *Why Is History Rewritten?* Introd. by Edward P. Cheney. New York, Oxford University Press, 1929.

Seligman, Edwin R. A., *The Economic Interpretation of History,* 2nd ed. New York, Columbia University Press, 1961.

Sellar, W. C., and Yeatman, R. J., *1066 and All That.* New York, Dutton, 1954.

Shafer, Boyd C., ed., *Historical Study in the West* [France, Great Britain, West Germany, the United States]. New York, Appleton, 1968.

Smith, Page, *The Historian and History.* New York, Knopf, 1964.

Stern, Fritz, ed., *The Varieties of History: From Voltaire to the Present.* New York, Meridian, 1956.

Strayer, Joseph R., ed., *The Interpretation of History.* Princeton, N.J., Princeton University Press, 1943. [Reprinted, New York, Peter Smith, 1950.]

Toynbee, Arnold J., *A Study of History,* Abridgments of Volumes I–VI, VII–X, by D. C. Somervell. New York, Oxford University Press, 1947 and 1957.

Trevelyan, George Macaulay, *Clio, A Muse and Other Essays*. Freeport, N.Y., Books for Libraries Press, 1968.

Von Mises, Ludwig, *Theory and History*. New Haven, Conn., Yale University Press, 1957.

Walsh, W. H., *An Introduction to Philosophy of History*, 3rd ed. London, Hutchinson, 1967.

Woodward, C. Vann, "Clio with Soul." *Journal of American History*, LVI (June 1969), 5–20.

The Great Historians

Antoni, Carlo, *From History to Sociology*, trans. by Hayden V. White. Detroit, Wayne State University Press, 1959.

Barzun, Jacques, "Gobineau," Chap. IV of *Race: A Study in Superstition*, rev. ed. New York, Harper, 1964.

Beale, Howard K., ed., *Charles A. Beard: An Appraisal*. Lexington, University of Kentucky Press, 1954.

Belloc, Hilaire, "Ten Pages of Taine." *International Quarterly*, XII (1905–06), 255–65.

Black, J. B., *The Art of History: A Study of Four Great Historians of the 18th Century*. New York, Russell & Russell, 1965.

Burckhardt, Jacob, *Judgments on History and Historians*. Boston, Beacon Press, 1958.

Bury, J. B., *The Ancient Greek Historians*. New York, Dover, 1958.

Engel-Janosi, Friedrich, *Four Studies in French Romantic Historical Writing*. Baltimore, Johns Hopkins Press, 1955.

Gay, Peter, *A Loss of Mastery: Puritan Historians in Colonial America*. Berkeley, University of California Press, 1966.

Gooch, G. P., *History and Historians in the Nineteenth Century*. Boston, Beacon Press, 1965.

Hofstadter, Richard, *The Progressive Historians: Turner, Beard, Parrington*. New York, Knopf, 1968.

Hutchinson, William T., ed., *The Marcus W. Jernegan Essays in American Historiography*. New York, Antiquarian Press, 1961.

Jameson, J. Franklin, *The History of Historical Writing in America.* New York, Antiquarian Press, 1961.

Kraus, Michael, *The Writing of American History.* Norman, University of Oklahoma Press, 1953.

Maitland, Frederic William: Selections from His Writings, ed. with an introd. by Robert Livingston Schuyler. Berkeley, University of California Press, 1960.

Mathew, David, *Lord Acton and His Times.* University, Ala., University of Alabama Press, 1969.

Momigliano, Arnaldo, "A Hundred Years After Ranke." *Diogenes,* VII (Summer 1954), 52–58.

Peardon, Thomas P., *The Transition in English Historical Writing, 1760–1830.* New York, Columbia University Press, 1933.

Schmitt, Bernadotte E., ed., *Some Historians of Modern Europe.* Port Washington, N.Y., Kennikat Press, 1966.

Sélincourt, Aubrey de, *The World of Herodotus.* Boston, Little, Brown, 1962.

Shotwell, James T., *The Story of Ancient History.* New York, Columbia University Press, 1961.

Thompson, James Westfall, and Holm, Bernard J., *A History of Historical Writing,* 2 vols. Gloucester, Mass., Peter Smith, 1967.

Toynbee, Arnold J., ed., *Greek Historical Thought from Homer to the Age of Heraclius.* New York, New American Library, 1964.

Vico, Giambattista, *The Autobiography,* trans. with an introd. by Max Harold Fisch and Thomas Goddard Bergin. Ithaca, N.Y., Cornell University Press, 1944.

Von Laue, Theodore H., *Leopold Ranke: The Formative Years.* Princeton, N.J., Princeton University Press, 1950.

Wilde, Oscar, "The Rise of Historical Criticism," in *The Complete Works.* New York, Doubleday, Page, 1923, X, 69–182.

Wish, Harvey, *The American Historian.* New York, Oxford University Press, 1960.

The Sister Disciplines

Barzun, Jacques, *Darwin, Marx, Wagner,* 2nd ed. Garden City, N.Y., Anchor Books, 1957.

———, *Race: A Study in Superstition,* rev. ed. New York, Harper, 1964.

Berelson, Bernard, *Human Behavior.* New York, Harcourt, 1967.

Bernstein, Jeremy, *The Analytical Engine: Computers, Past, Present, and Future.* New York, Random House, 1964.

Childe, V. Gordon, *Piecing Together the Past: Methods and Theories of Archaeology.* New York, Praeger, 1956.

Deuel, Leo, ed., *The Treasures of Time.* Cleveland, World, 1961.

Gross, Edward, "Social Science Techniques: A Problem of Power and Responsibility." *Scientific Monthly,* LXXXIII (November 1956), 242–47.

Hull, Clark L., "A Primary Social Science Law." *Scientific Monthly,* LXXI (October 1950), 221–28.

Hyman, Herbert H., Cobb, William J., and others, *Interviewing in Social Research.* Chicago, The University of Chicago Press, 1954.

Jouvenel, Bertrand de, *The Art of Conjecture,* trans. by Nikita Lary. London, Weidenfeld and Nicolson, 1967.

Krug, Mark M., *History and the Social Sciences.* Waltham, Mass., Blaisdell, 1967.

Langer, William L., "The Next Assignment." *American Historical Review,* LXIII (January 1958), 283–304.

Lazarsfeld, Paul F., "The Obligations of the 1950 Pollster to the 1984 Historian." *Public Opinion Quarterly,* XIV (Winter 1950–51), 617–38.

McIver, Robert M., *Social Causation.* New York, Harper, 1964.

Reuter, Edward B., *Handbook of Sociology.* New York, Dryden, 1941.

Salvemini, Gaetano, *Historian and Scientist: An Essay on the Nature of History and the Social Sciences.* Cambridge, Mass., Harvard University Press, 1939.

Sills, David L., ed., *International Encyclopedia of the Social Sciences,* 17 vols. New York, Macmillan and the Free Press, 1968.

Simon, Julian L., *Basic Research Methods in Social Science*. New York, Random House, 1968.

Social Science Research Council, *The Social Sciences in Historical Study: A Report of the Committee on Historiography*. Bulletin No. 64, New York, Social Science Research Council, 1954.

Sorokin, Pitirim A., *Fads and Foibles in Modern Sociology and Related Sciences*. Chicago, Regnery, 1956.

Spahr, Walter E., and Swenson, Rinehart J., *Methods and Status of Scientific Research with Particular Application to the Social Sciences*. New York, Harper, 1930.

Teggart, Frederick J., *Prolegomena to History: The Relation of History to Literature, Philosophy, and Science*. Berkeley, University of California Press, 1916.

Thorndike, Lynn, "A Historical Sketch of the Relationship Between History and Science." *Scientific Monthly*, XXVI (April 1928), 342–45.

———, "The Scientific Presentation of History." *Popular Science Monthly*, LXXVI (February 1910), 170–81.

Vendryès, Joseph, *Language: A Linguistic Introduction to History*. New York, Barnes & Noble, 1951.

Woolley, Sir Leonard, *Digging Up the Past*, 2nd ed. Baltimore, Penguin Books, 1961.

Young, Pauline, *Scientific Social Surveys and Research*, 4th ed. Englewood Cliffs, N.J., Prentice-Hall, 1966.

II. On Writing and Composition

Diction and Style

Allbutt, Sir T. Clifford, *Notes on the Composition of Scientific Papers*, 3rd ed. London, Macmillan, 1925.

[Anon.] *Titles and Forms of Address: A Guide to Their Correct Use*, 12th ed. London, A. and C. Black, 1964.

Blanshard, Brand, *On Philosophical Style*. Bloomington, Indiana University Press, 1954.

Crouch, William G., and Zetler, Robert L., *A Guide to Technical Writing*, 2nd ed. New York, Ronald Press, 1954.

Emberger, Meta Riley, and Hall, Marian Ross, *Scientific Writing*. New York, Harcourt, 1955.

Follett, Wilson, *Modern American Usage*. New York, Hill and Wang, 1966.

Fowler, H. W. and F. G., *The Concise Oxford Dictionary of Current English*, 4th rev. ed. Oxford, Clarendon Press, 1951.

————, *The King's English*, 3rd ed. Oxford, Clarendon Press, 1934.

Gowers, Sir Ernest, *The Complete Plain Words*. Baltimore, Penguin Books, 1964.

Graves, Robert, and Hodge, Alan, *The Reader Over Your Shoulder*. New York, Macmillan, 1943.

Herbert, A. P., *What a Word!* London, Methuen, 1959.

Hull, Helen, ed., *The Writer's Book*. New York, Barnes & Noble, 1956.

Johnson, Ellen, *The Research Report: A Guide for the Beginner*. New York, Ronald Press, 1951.

Lucas, F. L., *Style*, 2nd ed. London, Cassell, 1955.

Marks, Robert W., *The New Physics and Chemistry Dictionary and Handbook*. New York, Bantam Books, 1967.

Quiller-Couch, Sir Arthur, *On the Art of Writing*. New York, Putnam, 1943.

Sears, Donald A., *Harbrace Guide to the Library and the Research Paper*. New York, Harcourt, 1956.

Strunk, William, Jr., and White, E. B., *The Elements of Style*. New York, Macmillan, 1959.

Trelease, Sam F., *The Scientific Paper: How to Prepare It, How to Write It*, 2nd ed. Baltimore, Williams & Wilkins, 1951.

Weil, Benjamin H., ed., *The Technical Report: Its Preparation and Processing, and Use in Industry and Government*. New York, Reinhold, 1954.

Williams, C. B., and Griffin, E. Glenn, *Effective Business Communication*, 3rd ed. New York, Ronald Press, 1966.

Williams, C. B., and Stevenson, A. H., *A Research Manual for College Studies and Papers*, rev. ed. New York, Harper, 1951.

Forms

American Standard Abbreviations for Scientific and Engineering Terms. New York, The American Society of Mechanical Engineers, 1941.

Author's Guide. Englewood Cliffs, N.J., Prentice-Hall, 1962.

Bernstein, Theodore M., and Garst, Robert E., *Headlines and Deadlines: A Manual for Copy Editors*. New York, Columbia University Press, 1963.

Campbell, William G., *Form and Style in Thesis Writing*. Boston, Houghton Mifflin, 1954.

Carey, Gordon V., *Making an Index*. Cambridge, The University Press, 1951.

―――, *Mind the Stop: A Brief Guide to Punctuation with a Note on Proof-correction*. Cambridge, The University Press, 1939.

Chaundy, T. W., Barrett, P. R., and Batey, Charles, *The Printing of Mathematics: Aids for Authors and Editors and Rules for Compositors and Readers at the University Press, Oxford*. London, Oxford University Press, 1954.

Collins, F. Howard, *Authors' and Printers' Dictionary*, 10th ed. London, Oxford University Press, 1956.

Collison, Robert Lewis, *Indexes and Indexing*. New York, De Graff, 1953.

Gay, Robert M., *Stops: A Handbook of Punctuation*. Middlebury, Vt., Middlebury College Press, 1941.

Harlow, H. F., "Fundamental Principles for Preparing Psychology Journal Articles." *Journal of Comparative Physiological Psychology*, LV (December 1962), 893–96.

Jarrett, James, *Printing Style for Authors, Compositors, and Readers*. London, Allen and Unwin, 1960.

Kaplan, Benjamin, *An Unhurried View of Copyright*. New York, Columbia University Press, 1967.

Labaree, Leonard W., ed., *The Papers of Benjamin Franklin*. New Haven,

Conn., Yale University Press, 1959, I, xxxiv–xlvii [canons of document editing].

Long, Ralph B., *The Sentence and Its Parts: A Grammar of Contemporary English.* Chicago, The University of Chicago Press, 1961.

Modern Language Association of America, *The MLA Style Sheet,* rev. ed., comp. by William R. Parker. New York, 1959.

The New York Times Style Book for Writers and Editors, ed. and rev. by Lewis Jordan. New York, McGraw-Hill, 1962.

Southgate, M. Therese, "Advice to Authors: Guide to the Preparation of Manuscripts submitted to the *Journal of the American Medical Association . . ." Journal of the American Medical Association,* CXC (October 5, 1964), 113–36. [Available as a separate publication.]

Style Manual for Biological Journals, 2nd ed., prepared by Committee on Form and Style of the Conference of Biological Editors. Washington, D.C., American Institute of Biological Sciences, 1964.

Style Manual for Guidance in the Preparation of Papers for Journals Published by the American Institute of Physics, 2nd ed. New York, American Institute of Physics, 1967.

Suggestions on How to Organize, Present, and Illustrate a Technical Paper. Bulletin No. 8, Washington, D.C., American Chemical Society, 1961.

Summey, George, *American Punctuation.* New York, Ronald Press, 1949.

Turabian, Kate L., *A Manual for Writers of Term Papers, Theses, and Dissertations,* 3rd ed. Chicago, The University of Chicago Press, 1967.

United States Government Printing Office Style Manual. Washington, D.C., Government Printing Office, 1967.

Weil, Benjamin H., *Technical Editing.* New York, Reinhold, 1958.

————, and others, "Technical Abstracting Fundamentals," presented before the American Documentation Institute, December 15, 1962. [Mimeographed copy in School of Library Service Library, Columbia University.]

Wheeler, Martha Thorne, *Indexing: Principles, Rules, and Examples,* 5th ed. Albany, New York State Library, University of the State of New York, 1957.

Translation

Anderson, J. G., *Le Mot Juste: An Anglo-French Lexicon* (1932). Rev. ed. by L. C. Harmer, New York, Dutton, 1938.

Arrowsmith, William, and Shattuck, Roger, *The Craft and Context of Translation*. Garden City, N.Y., Anchor Books, 1964.

Barzun, Jacques, "Food for the N.R.F., or What Will You Have?" *Partisan Review*, XX (November–December 1953), 660–74.

Bissell, Clifford H., *Prepositions in French and English*. New York, Richard R. Smith, 1947.

Brower, Reuben A., ed., *On Translation*. Cambridge, Mass., Harvard University Press, 1959.

Carey, Gordon V., *American into English: A Handbook for Translators*. London, Heinemann, 1953.

Chevalley, Abel and Marguerite, *Concise Oxford French Dictionary*, introd. and *passim*. New York, Oxford University Press, 1950.

Farrell, R. B., *Dictionary of German Synonyms*, reprinted with corrections. Cambridge, The University Press, 1962.

Flood, W. E., and West, Michael, *An Elementary Scientific and Technical Dictionary*, 3rd ed. London, Longmans, Green, 1962.

Grebe, Paul, *Der Grosse Duden: Fremdwörterbuch*, rev. ed. Mannheim, Bibliographisches Institut, 1960.

Kastner, L. E., and Marks, J., *A Glossary of Colloquial and Popular French*. New York, Dutton, 1929.

Knox, Ronald A., *On Englishing the Bible*. London, Burns Oates, 1949. [The American edition is *The Trials of a Translator*, New York, Sheed & Ward, 1949.]

Koessler, M., and Derocquigny, J., *Les Faux Amis: les pièges du vocabulaire anglais*. Paris, Vuibert, 1949.

Levieux, Michel and Eleanor, *Cassell's Beyond the Dictionary in French*. New York, Funk & Wagnalls, 1967.

Lewisohn, Ludwig, *German Style: An Introduction to the Study of German Prose*. New York, Holt, 1910.

Matthias, Theodor, *Der Grosse Duden: Rechtschreibung der deutschen Sprache*, 10th ed. Leipzig, Bibliographisches Institut, 1929.

Mawson, C. O. Sylvester, *Dictionary of Foreign Terms*. New York, Bantam Books, 1961.

Newmark, Maxim, *Dictionary of Science and Technology in English, French, German, Spanish . . . with Conversion Tables and Technical Abbreviations*. New York, Philosophical Library, 1943.

North, Eric M., ed., *The Book of a Thousand Tongues*. New York, published for the American Bible Society by Harper, 1938. [Revision in progress.]

Postgate, J. P., *Translation and Translations: Theory and Practice*. London, Bell, 1922.

Savory, Theodore, *The Art of Translation*. London, Cape, 1957.

Smith, W. J., *A Dictionary of Musical Terms in Four Languages*. London, Hutchinson, 1961.

Tytler, Alexander Fraser, *Essay on the Principles of Translation* (1791). New York, Dutton, 1907.

Von Ostermann, Georg, *Manual of Foreign Languages*, 4th ed. New York, Central Book Company, 1952.

III. Guides and Bibliographies

General

Besterman, Theodore, *A World Bibliography of Bibliographies*, 4th ed., 5 vols. Geneva, Societas Bibliographica, 1965–66.

Shores, Louis, *Basic Reference Sources*. Chicago, American Library Association, 1954.

Winchell, Constance M., *Guide to Reference Books*, 8th ed. Chicago, American Library Association, 1967.

Special

AERONAUTICS

Dennis, W. K., *An Aeronautical Reference Library*. New York, Special Libraries Association, 1943.

AGRICULTURE

Blanchard, Joy Richard, and Ostvold, Harold, *Literature of Agricultural Research.* Berkeley, University of California Press, 1958.

BIOLOGICAL SCIENCES

Altsheler, Brent, *Natural History Index-Guide,* 2nd ed. New York, Wilson, 1940.

Kerker, Ann E., and Schmidt, Esther M., *Literature Sources in the Biological Sciences.* Lafayette, Ind., Purdue University Library, 1961.

Smith, Roger Cletus, *Guide to the Literature of the Zoölogical Sciences,* rev. ed. Minneapolis, Burgess, 1955.

BUSINESS

Cowan, Edwin T., Jr., *Sources of Business Information,* rev. ed. Berkeley, University of California Press, 1964.

Manley, Marian Catherine, *Business Information: How to Find and Use It.* New York, Harper, 1955.

Wasserman, Paul, *Information for Administrators: A Guide to Publications and Services for Management in Business and Government.* Ithaca, N.Y., Cornell University Press, 1956.

CHEMISTRY

American Chemical Society, Division of Chemical Literature, *Searching the Chemical Literature,* rev. ed. Washington, D.C., 1961.

Bottle, R. T., *Use of the Chemical Literature.* London, Butterworth, 1962.

Crane, E. J., and Patterson, A. M., *A Guide to the Literature of Chemistry,* 2nd ed. New York, Wiley, 1957.

Dyson, George Malcolm, *A Short Guide to Chemical Literature.* London, Longmans, Green, 1951.

Mellon, Melvin Guy, *Chemical Publications: Their Nature and Use,* 4th ed. New York, McGraw-Hill, 1965.

[See also Engineering and Metallurgy]

EDUCATION

Alexander, Carter, and Burke, Arvil J., *How to Locate Educational Infor-*

mation and Data: An Aid to Quick Utilization of the Literature of Education, 4th ed. New York, Bureau of Publications, Teachers College, Columbia University, 1958.

Good, Carter V., and Scates, Douglas E., *Methods of Research: Educational, Psychological, Sociological.* New York, Appleton, 1954.

ENGINEERING AND METALLURGY

Barnes, Ralph M., and Englert, Norma A., *Bibliography of Industrial Engineering and Management Literature,* 5th ed. Dubuque, Iowa, Brown, 1946.

Dalton, Blanche H., *Sources of Engineering Information.* Berkeley, University of California Press, 1948.

Holmstrom, J. E., *Records and Research in Engineering and Industrial Science,* 3rd ed. London, Chapman & Hall, 1956.

Kabe, Kenneth Albert, *Chemical Engineering Reports: How to Search the Literature and Prepare a Report,* 4th ed. New York, Interscience, 1957.

Milek, John T., *Guide to Foreign Sources of Metallurgical Literature.* Pittsburgh, Rimbach, 1951.

Topia, Elizabeth W., *Guide to Metallurgical Information.* New York, Special Libraries Association, 1961.

[See also Mathematics]

FASHION

Laver, James, *Literature of Fashion.* New York, Macmillan, 1948.

FINE ARTS

Chamberlin, Mary Wills, *Guide to Art Reference Books.* Chicago, American Library Association, 1959.

McColvin, Eric R., *Painting: A Guide to the Best Books.* London, Grafton, 1934.

GENEALOGY AND HERALDRY

Clark, Hugh, *An Introduction to Heraldry,* 18th ed., rev. by J. R. Planché. London, Bell and Daldy, 1873.

Doane, Gilbert Harry, *Searching for Your Ancestors: The How and Why of Genealogy,* 3rd ed. Minneapolis, University of Minnesota Press, 1960.

GEOGRAPHY

Wright, John Kirtland, and Platt, Elizabeth T., *Aids to Geographical Research: Bibliographies, Periodicals, Atlases, Gazetteers, and Other Reference Books,* 2nd ed. New York, pub. for the American Geographical Society by Columbia University Press, 1947.

GEOLOGY

Mason, Brian, *The Literature of Geology.* New York, American Museum of Natural History, 1953.

Pearl, Richard M., *Guide to Geologic Literature.* New York, McGraw-Hill, 1951.

Smith, Roger Cletus, *Guide to the Literature of the Geological Sciences,* 6th ed. Minneapolis, Burgess, 1962.

GOVERNMENT PUBLICATIONS

Hauser, Philip M., and Leonard, William R., eds., *Government Statistics for Business Use,* 2nd ed. New York, Wiley, 1956.

Leidy, W. Philip, *A Popular Guide to Government Publications,* 3rd ed. New York, Columbia University Press, 1968.

Schmeckebier, Laurence F., and Easlin, Roy B., *Government Publications and Their Use,* rev. ed. Washington, D.C., The Brookings Institution, 1961.

HISTORY

American Historical Association, *Guide to Historical Literature.* New York, Macmillan, 1961.

Bemis, Samuel Flagg, and Griffin, Grace Gardner, *Guide to the Diplomatic History of the United States, 1775–1921.* Washington, D.C., Government Printing Office, 1935. [Reprinted, Gloucester, Mass., Peter Smith, 1959.]

Carman, H. J., and Thompson, A. W., *A Guide to the Principal Sources for American Civilization (1800–1900) in the City of New York: Printed Materials.* New York, Columbia University Press, 1962.

Dutcher, George Matthew, and others, eds., *A Guide to Historical Literature.* New York, Macmillan, 1931. [Reprinted, New York, Peter Smith, 1949.]

Goldentree Bibliographies in American History, Arthur S. Link, gen. ed. New York, Appleton, 1969– . [Twenty-five pamphlets by various hands; two published.]

Greene, E. B., and Morris, R. B., *A Guide to the Principal Sources for Early American History (1600–1800) in the City of New York,* 2nd ed. New York, Columbia University Press, 1953.

Handlin, Oscar, and others, eds., *Harvard Guide to American History.* Cambridge, Mass., Belknap Press of Harvard University Press, 1954.

Hewitt, Arthur R., *Guide to Commonwealth Studies in London.* London, pub. for the Institute of Commonwealth Studies by Athlone Press of London University Press, 1957.

Morley, Charles, *Guide to Research in Russian History.* Syracuse, N.Y., Syracuse University Press, 1951.

Thomas, Daniel H., and Case, Lynn M., *Guide to the Diplomatic Archives of Western Europe.* Philadelphia, University of Pennsylvania Press, 1959.

Webb, Herschel, *Research in Japanese Sources: A Guide.* New York, Columbia University Press, 1965.

LAW

Berman, Harold J., *The Nature and Functions of Law: An Introduction for Students of the Arts and Sciences.* Brooklyn, Foundation Press, 1958.

Price, Miles Oscar, and Bitner, Harry, *Effective Legal Research: A Practical Manual of Law Books and Their Use.* New York, Prentice-Hall, 1953.

Roalfe, William R., *How to Find the Law,* 5th ed. St. Paul, Minn., West, 1957.

LITERATURE

Altick, Richard David, and Wright, Andrew, *Selective Bibliography for the Study of English and American Literature,* 2nd ed. New York, Macmillan, 1963.

Bond, Donald Frederick, *A Reference Guide to English Studies.* Chicago, The University of Chicago Press, 1962.

Kennedy, Arthur Garfield, and Sands, Donald B., *A Concise Bibliog-*

raphy for Students of English, 4th ed. Stanford, Stanford University Press, 1960.

Palfrey, Thomas Rossman, Fucilla, Joseph Guerin, and Holbrook, William Cottar, *A Bibliographical Guide to the Romance Languages and Literature,* 5th ed. Evanston, Ill., Chandler, 1963.

Sanders, Chauncey, *An Introduction to Research in English Literary History,* with a chapter on research in folklore by Stith Thompson. New York, Macmillan, 1952.

Taylor, Archer, and Mosher, Fredric J., *The Bibliographical History of Anonyma and Pseudonyma.* Chicago, The University of Chicago Press, 1951.

MATHEMATICS

Parke, Nathan Grier, *Guide to the Literature of Mathematics and Physics Including Related Works on Engineering Science,* 2nd rev. ed. New York, Dover, 1958.

MEDICINE

Medical Library Association, *Handbook of Medical Library Practice, with a Bibliography of the Reference Works and Histories in Medicine and the Allied Sciences,* 2nd ed., Janet Doe [and] Mary Louise Marshall, eds. Chicago, American Library Association, 1956.

Morton, Leslie Taylor, *How to Use a Medical Library,* 4th ed. London, Heinemann, 1964.

MUSIC

Duckles, Vincent Harris, *Music Reference and Research Materials: An Annotated Bibliography.* London [New York], Free Press, 1964.

Haydon, Glen, *Introduction to Musicology: A Survey of the Fields, Systematic and Historical, of Musical Knowledge and Research.* New York, Prentice-Hall, 1941. [Reprinted, Chapel Hill, University of North Carolina Press, 1959.]

McColvin, Lionel R., and Reeves, Harold, *Music Libraries,* 2 vols. London, Grafton, 1937–38.

PHYSICS

Whitford, Robert H., *Physics Literature: A Reference Manual.* Washington, D.C., Scarecrow Press, 1954.

[See also Mathematics]

POLITICAL AND SOCIAL SCIENCE

Burchfield, Laverne, *Student's Guide to Materials in Political Science.* New York, Holt, 1935.

White, Carl M., and Associates, *Sources of Information in the Social Sciences: A Guide to the Literature.* Totowa, N.J., Bedminster Press, 1964.

PSYCHOLOGY

Daniel, Robert Strongman, and Louttit, Chauncey McKinley, *Professional Problems in Psychology.* New York, Prentice-Hall, 1953.

[See also Education]

SOCIOLOGY

[See Education; Political and Social Science; Psychology]

TYPOGRAPHY AND ALLIED ARTS

Bigmore, Edward C., and Wyman, Charles, *A Bibliography of Printing,* 3 vols. London, Quaritch, 1880–86. [Reprinted, New York, Philip C. Duschnes, 1945, 2 vols.]

Glaister, Geoffrey Ashall, *An Encyclopedia of the Book.* Cleveland, World, 1960.

Grannis, Chandler B., ed., *What Happens in Book Publishing,* 2nd ed. New York, Columbia University Press, 1967.

Ulrich, Carolyn F., and Küp, Karl, *Books and Printing: A Selected List of Periodicals, 1800–1942.* New York, The New York Public Library, 1943.

Index

Abbreviation(s): in notetaking, 31; U.F.O., 68; in library catalogue, 75; A.L.S., 77 and *n.*; in citing, 344 ff.; Latin and English, 344–45, 347 *n.*; list of common, 347 (fig.); uniform use of, 347

Accuracy: in research, defined, 58–59; not of detail alone, 60; cumulative effect of, 114–15; in stating ideas, 131 ff.; in quoting, 358

Actium, defeat at, 169

Acton, John E. Dalberg-: on power, 141–42; on Macaulay, 181 and *n.*

Adams, Abigail, 378

Adams, Henry, as social historian, 244

Adams, James Truslow, 91

Adams, John Quincy, 14; and Monroe Doctrine, 131

Adenauer, Konrad, 12 (fig.)

Advertising: champions fact, 7–8; and common phrases, 292 *n.*; good writing in, 307

Affidavit, as written evidence, 147

Age of Louis XIV, The, 198

Agricultural History, 73

Alexander I, of Russia, 182

Alexander the Great, 12 (fig.), 20, 189

Allbutt, T. Clifford, on notetaking, 27 and *n.*

Alphabet: importance of, 24 and *n.*; basis of order, 65, 68; in reference books, 75–76

American Bibliography, 90 *n.*

American Historical Association, 77, 242

American History, Harvard Guide to, 92 *n.*

American History, Writings on, 92 *n.*

American Library Association, 75

American Revolution, 81–82

Anatomy of Melancholy, The, 317

Ancient City, The, 245

Anderson, Frank Maloy, in quest of "Public Man," 120–28, 126 *n.*, 150

Anderson, J. G., quoted, 326–27

André, Major John, biography of, 338

Anecdotes: in cartoons, 12 (fig.); verifying, 93, 106 ff., 140; large number of, 124; as records, 148 (fig.)

Anglo-Saxonism, 199

Annals, Chinese, 47; as sources, 148 (fig.)

Anne, Queen of England, 144

Anniversaries, and sense of past, 11

Anthony, Norman, 339

Anthony, Susan B., 213

Anthropology, 16, 218 ff., 223; in Montesquieu, 219, 244; explorers' work, 220; J. F. Blumenbach on, 220; measurement of types, 223; physical, 230; cultural, 235–36, 250; F. Boas reforms, 235; wide influence today, 237; and the university, 243; a "law" of, 249

Anthroposociology, 223

Appendices, 69; use of, 128, 318 *n.*, 340

Appletons' Cyclopaedia of American Biography, 84

Aquinas, Saint Thomas, 95, 116

Archeology: and history, 13, 218; assessment of finds, 150, 172 *n.*; origins, 221

Architecture, embodies history, 11, 221

Archives, national, 50 and *n.*, 209, 304; microphotography for, 66 *n.*;

408

European, 205 *n.*; research in, 242
Armada, the Great, 257, 312
Arminius, 228
Arnold, Benedict, biography of, 338
Arnold, Matthew, 94; L. Trilling on, 270
Arrangement: essential, 19, 33; original, 25; of words, 39; of ideas, 40; in great historians, 258; requires work, 258; must concentrate attention, 260; steps in, 260–64; by reshuffling, 263–64; suggested by experience, 266; of facts, 385
Art: as history, 9, 46, 74 and *n.*; as historical record, 102 *n.*, 148; Greek, 134–35
Artifacts: coins, 115; as relics, 148 (fig.); early study of, 218, 221
Aryan tongue, 230
Ashford, Daisy, quoted, 313
Atkinson, Alex, 36 *n.*
Atlases, 78 (fig.)
Augustine, Saint, historical system of, 56, 116, 187, 193 (fig.)
Austen, Jane, quoted, 311
Authenticity: defined, 102 *n.*; of documents, 102, 110–11, 124–28, 149 and *n.*, 156; of anecdotes, 106 ff.
Authorship, establishing, 109–11, 119 ff.
Average, three kinds of, 245

Babylon, 221
Backnotes: their use, 349–50; catch phrases in, 350
Bacon, Francis, quoted, 385
Badoglio, Pietro, 349
Bagehot, Walter: love letters of, 73; on social evolution, 226–27
Bailey, Thomas A., quoted, 182 *n.*
Baldridge, Letitia, 101 *n.*
Balzac, Honoré de, 79
Bancroft, George: historian of democratic America, 206 ff.; funeral honors, 207 *n.*
Barbarossa, Frederick, 51
Baron, Salo W., 221 *n.*
Baroque, 176
Barrow, W. J., on library books, 66
Bartlett's Familiar Quotations, 94
Barzun, Jacques, 19 *n.*, 104 *n.*, 113 *n.*
Bateson, F. W., quoted, 154
Bathtub hoax, 109 and *n.*
Baudelaire, 239
Bayle, Pierre: his *Dictionary,* 57; on history, 185

Beard, Charles A.: economic causes in work, 71–72; ideas in work, 215; cited, 322, 345
Beginning: serves emphasis, 256; or exposition, 265; natural and obvious, 269–70; of book review, 271–72; false, 271; how to find, 271; of paragraph, 273; opening sentence, 310–12
Behavorial sciences, 45 *n.*, 242; *see also* Social sciences
Belief, quality of, 143
Belloc, Hilaire: *Paris* (cited), 73; on translation, 329–30
Ben Hur, 71
Benedictines (St. Maur), 199
Bengesco, Georges: cited, 78 (fig.); quoted, 127
Beowulf, 199
Berlioz, Hector, 105; manuscript letters of, 113–14, 113 *n.*; *Rákóczy March,* 114
"Bernhard Hühne," 84
Bernhardt, Sarah, 52
Bertillon, Alphonse, 230 *n.*
Bias: in folk history, 51; unavoidable, 51; how to check, 60; cultural, 81; in history writing, 137, 174 ff.; causes of, 150; in daily life, 151; not subjectivity, 165; ubiquitous, 165; sources of, and correctives, 179–86; self-awareness about, 180; extreme form of interest, 180, 186; test of harm in, 181–82; in judging historical writing, 182; not offset by scorn, 184; political, in European history, 204
Bible, 78 (fig.), 90, 193 (fig.), 296; translated, 329
Bibliography: as device, 5; in science, 23; preparing, 27–28; how gathered, 32; in periodicals, 75; types of, 75, 76, 78 (fig.), 79; supplements card catalogue, 76; of indexed newspapers, 88–90; and verification, 90, 127; United States, 90 *n.*; computer and, 96 and *n.*; drudgery of, 315; lists, 350–55; purpose of, 350–51 and *n.*; relation of, to footnotes, 351; as collation, 351 *n.*; alphabetical by author, 351–52; classified, 352; select, 352; critical, 353–54, 355; in essay form, 353–54; passage from essay type, 354; not a substitute for footnotes, 354; suitability of, 355

409

410

Carnegie, Andrew, 214
Carpenter, Matthew Hale, 283
Carrel, Armand, 200
Carroll, John B., quoted, 247 and *n.*
Carson, Rachel, 20
Carter, Howard, 221
Casey Jones, 210
Castiglione, Count of, 160
Catalogue, *see* Card catalogue
Causation, *see* Causes
Cause(s): Hume on, 168; meaning of, 168–69; ramifications of, 168, 172; and conditions, 169; psychological, 169; incommensurable, 170 and *n.*; as controlled states, 172; single, 187, 201–02
Ceram, C. W., 70 (fig.)
Chaddock, Robert E., 73 *n.*
Chambers, E. K., quoted, 257
Chapman, John Jay, on quotations, 317
Chapters: how formed, 32, 256, 271–72, 310 (fig.); defined, 262; length of, 262; headings for, 263–64, 372; varying role of, 264; composed from notes, 265, 383; transitions in and between, 269; importance of first, 270
Charcot, Jean Martin, and Freud, 232
Charles II, of England, 270–71, 315
Chase, Salmon P.: and coinage, 115–16; biography of, 371 and *n.*
Chateaubriand, François-René de, 85 and *n.*
Chaucer, 199
Chemical Abstracts, 78 (fig.)
Chemistry: soil, 73; history of, 134; and general formulas, 135; formulas in, 171–72; part of Comtian system, 224; assumes uniformity, 249
Cherry tree legend, 17 *n.*
Chidsey, Donald Barr, 354
China: history in, 46–47; Japan's war against, 162; Republic, 208
Chopin, Frédéric, 140
Christendom, 187–88
Christianity: spread of, 172; Gibbon against, 180; and orthodox history, 187; and scope of history, 198; in Guizot's history, 200
Chronicles, 148 (fig.); in Middle Ages, 56, 117, 118; and legend, 117; not wholly factual, 132; lack of form in, 177
Chronology: sense of, 116; in various

eras, 118; itself needs pattern, 176, 258 ff.; supplies order, 176; combined with topical order, 260; form must respect, 261
Churchill, Winston, 13, 288, 325
Ciano, Count Galeazzo, 112 *n.*, 160
Citation, 338–56; in writing, 316; of titles, 322; purpose of, 323–24; for verification, 340; of manuscript, 341; of magazine article, 341–42; from collected works, 342, 348; of newspapers, 343; of periodicals, 343; Roman numerals in, 343; of ancient authors, 344; pseudonyms and anonyms, 344; in scientific papers, 350; of foreign authors, 351 *n.*
Civil rights, 53
Civil Service, reform of, 130–31
Civil War, American: 70; paper money in, 115; Secession winter of, 120, 125; historians of, 161; European counterparts, 208; and national unification, 208; a binding experience, 212; divides American history, 212; semi-religious role, 212
Civilization and Its Discontents, 245
Classification, *see* Form; Pattern
Cleopatra: arts of, 135; Pascal about, 169
Cleveland, Grover, 14
Cliché, *see* Jargon
Clio, A Muse, 57 *n.*
Coffman, W. E., quoted, 276
Coherence, defined, 19–20, 33, 40, 274; form must show, 261; depends on length, 263
Coins: motto on U.S., 115; as records, 148 (fig.); *see also* Numismatics
Cold War, 182, 328 *n.*
Coleridge, Samuel Taylor, 155
Collation, 103–06, 110–14; effect of, 114; in final revision, 363; in proofreading, 376–77
Collingwood, R. G., 144
Columbia Broadcasting System, Inc., 6–7
Columbus, Christopher, 119, 347
Comédie Humaine, La, 79
Commager, Henry Steele, 78 (fig.)
Common sense, and historical method, 151 ff., 157
Communism, 182–83
Communist Manifesto, The, 15

80; historical, 81–82, 142; steady use of, 277; recommended, 277 *n.*, 292; insufficient for translating, 326; special, for translating, 327–28

Dictionary of American Biography, 80; supplements, 210

Dictionary of National Biography, 80, 84

Dilettanti, English Society of, 221
Dilthey, Wilhelm, 144
Diplomatics, defined, 150; *see also* Dates
Divine right, *see* Monarchy
Documents: do or do not lie, 50–51; not sole historical source, 51; genuine and authentic, 102 and *n.*, 124; analyzed for ideas, 142; "planted," 147 *n.*; how examined, 149; questioned, 150; in context, 156; collecting, in modern times, 199; *Monumenta Germaniae Historica*, 199; national, 199; publication of, 199; "Rolls Series," 199; "Calendars of State Papers," 199; on Henry Ford, 205; on John D. Rockefeller, 205; quoting, 318 *n.*; translation of diplomatic, 327–28, 328 *n.*
Dollard, John, 246
Donald, David, on Charles Sumner, 122 *n.*
Douglas, Stephen A.: Chicago speech, 106 ff.; biography of, 108–09; at Lincoln's inauguration, 120–21, 125; and Public Man, 122, 125–26
Douglass, William, on historian's work, 251
Dow, E. W., on notetaking, 26 *n.*
Drake, Francis, 257
Du Bois, Cora, 246
Du Chaillu, Paul, his discoveries, 230
Dulles, John Foster, on Russia, 182
Dunning, William A., on truth in history, 161
Du Pont de Nemours, E. I., 221
Durkheim, Emile: on sociology, 233; his influence, 234

East Side, West Side, as title, 67
Economics, 10, 16, 72, 218; history of, 15; in Marx's system, 190; founders of, 221–22; classified, 223 *n.*; laws disputed, 229; marginal utility theory, 231; a moral science, 231,

238; a new name, 231; varieties of modern, 237; K. Boulding on, 238; L. Robbins on, 238; J. Viner on, 243; and the university, 243; government research in, 309
Eden, Anthony, quoted, 320
Editing: self-, 39; and scholarship, 71; documents, 104; letters, 112–13; fallible, 294, 359–60; sets style for translated matter, 336–37; sets style for footnotes, 340–41; of complete works, 342; instructions for, 365 ff.; copy- 369 and *n.*; limit of usefulness of, 369; literary, 369 and *n.*; and proofreading, 378–79
Editions, meaning in research, 71–72
Editor, *see* Editing; Publisher
Edward VII, 87
Edward VIII, 347; marriage of, 202
Egypt, hieroglyphics deciphered, 222
Eisenhower, Dwight D., 116 *n.*; reader of Thucydides, 52; military decision, 167
Eliot, George, 73
Elizabeth I, of England, 11; plays given for, 257
Elizabeth II, of England, 11
Elizabethan stage, Chambers on, 257, 266
Emancipation Proclamation, 53
Emerson, Ralph Waldo, on quotations, 317, 324
Emphasis: element of form, 256; in sentences, 299 ff.
Encyclopedia Britannica: microfiche collection, 66 *n.*; editions of, 80
Encyclopedias, 77, 87; types of, 78 (fig.); revision of, 80–81, 80 *n.*; when to use, 80–81; foreign, 81 and *n.*; national, 81; religious, 81
Engels, Friedrich: influenced by events, 190; inspired by Carlyle, 229
Engineering, 301–02
England: sea power, 141; and trade, 141; Hume's history of, 198; origins of modern, 199
English Revolution (1688), Carrel on, 200
Epidemics, 34, 74, 242
Erasmus, Desiderius, 54
Errors: ubiquitous, 100, 103–04, 104 *n.*, 109; in dates, 105, 119; typographical, 272, 321; in quotations, 321–22, 363; effect of, on reader, 348; in final draft, 357–60;

413

Errors (*cont.*):
kinds of, 358–59; steps to remove, 359; what they show, 360; S. Smith on, 360; after publication, 379; Bacon on, 385; turned to account, 385

Essay on the Manners and Customs of Nations, 57, 198

Essay on the Principle of Population, An, 22

Eternal Recurrence: Nietzsche on, 143; Shakespeare on, 193

Ethnology, 223

Evans, Arthur, 221

Evidence: for probability, 108–09; circumstantial, 110–11; new, 112; mute, examples of, 146–47; verbal, examples of, 146–47; oral and written, 146–47, 147 *n.*; types of, 146–48, 148 (fig.); intentional and unpremeditated, 147; manuscript and printed, 147; private and public, 147; self-revealing, 149; supporting hypotheses, 152–54; science used in judging, 156; contradictory, 157–59; supernatural, 161; basis of objective judgments, 165; in pattern making, 179; in Spengler, 195; in Toynbee, 195

Evolution: stimulus to historiography, 57; date of idea, 132–33; Saint-Simon and, 187–88; Comte and, 188; Marx and biological, 190; Buffon on, 220; Erasmus Darwin on, 220; Lamarck on, 220, 226; as organizing principle, 222; social, 226; Bagehot on social, 226; Spencer on social, 226; in society, 226–27; De Vries on, 231; Huxley on, 231; Weismann on, 231

Evolution, Old and New, 220 *n.*; 379 *n.*

Eyewitnesses: unreliability of, 15; and public events, 65, 125, 159; daily life, 99; and truth, 105, 152, 159, 160 and *n.*; merits of, 149; number of, 150; reliability of, 160 ff.; infallible, do not exist, 161; competence of, 166–67

Fact(s): as fetish, 13, 49; in research, 16, 74; basis of history writing, 49; curiosity about, 58; as stubborn obstacle, 60; finding single, 91–93, 158; books of, 94; computers and, 95–98; verification of, 109; pure and mixed, 129; conventional, 129, 145; ideas clinging to, 129, 131, 133; ideas as, 132; sources of, 148 (fig.); repeating and nonrepeating, 170; historian selects, 173; not self-arranging, 175; given order by chronology, 176; seen through ideas, 176; like and unlike, 178; random when found, 192; arbitrary classification of, 195; and language, 247–48; natural grouping of, 263; missing during composition, 266; chaos to be ordered, 385

Fallacies: in first drafts, 40; through words, 139; reductive, 140–41, 144, 201; debunking, 144; vulgar, 144, 183; reductive, in Spengler, 195; reductive, in Toynbee, 195

Farley, James A., recollections of, 162, 165

Fascism, 349

Faÿ, Bernard, 204 *n.*

Fechner, Gustav Theodor, 230

Federalist Papers, The, 95

Feminism, 195, 213

Ferdinand I, of Austria, 15, 16

Fernando Po, rainfall in, 63, 65

Ferry, Jules, 73

Field work, 23 *n.*, 64

Fifteen Decisive Battles of the World, 174

Fillmore, Millard, 109 and *n.*

Films, as records, 148 and (fig.)

First World War, 116, 194, 202

Fiske, John: on Darwinism, 228; on American history, 228–29

Fitzpatrick, John C., 342

Fleming, Peter, 344

Fletcher, J. S., quoted, 266

Flexner, James T., quoted, 338

Flying saucers, 68

Flynn, Edward J., 354

Follett, Wilson, 85 *n.*, 286, 320 *n.*

Footnotes: in scholarship, 5, 128; in literary criticism, 17–18; a form, 256; in jargon phrase, 287; errors in, 320; purpose of, 338; explanatory, 338 ff.; source reference, 338, 340; length of, 339; in textbooks, 340; style of, indicative, 341; author's name in, 342; editor's name in, 342; italics in, 342; titles and subtitles in, 342, 343; "split," 343; economy in, 343 ff.; when to use, 346–48; on disputed points, 349;

Gregory I, Pope, 215
Gregory VII, Pope, 215
Grimm, Jacob, 222
Gross, Hans, 230 n.
Grove's Dictionary of Music and Musicians, 105
Guide to Reference Books, 77, 94
Guiteau, Charles, 130 and n., 144
Guizot, François, 199–200
Gulliver's Travels, 144
Gunther, John, quoted, 354
Gutenberg, Johann, 379
Guys and Dolls, 291

Hahn, Otto, quoted, 8
Hall, Edward Marshall, quoted, 319
Hallam, Henry, quoted, 303 and n.
Hamilton, Alexander: as author, 17; doubtful quotation, 93; and history writing, 209; in duel, 214; birthplace of, 360
Hamlet, 329–30
Hammurabi, 174
Hancock, W. K., 51 n.; on phases of research, 184; on Risorgimento, 184; quoted, 242
Hand, Judge Learned: on history, 53–54; on imponderables, 169
Handwriting, and authorship, 120
Harding, Warren G., papers destroyed, 74 and n.
Harnack, Adolph von, on Macaulay, 181 n.
Harrison, Benjamin, 71
Harrison, William Henry, 14
Haycraft, Howard, 351
Haydn, Johann Michael, 105–06
Haydn, Joseph: date of birth, 104–06; blunder concerning, 359
Hayter, Alethea, 15 n.
Hayward, John, quoted, 315
Hazlitt, William, 348
Heaton, Herbert, on importance of failure, 209 n.
Hegel, G. W. F., 233; dialectic in, 186, 190; on Reformation, 188; as system-maker, 189 ff., 193 (fig.); as influence on Marx, 190; general influence of, 194–95; lectures on history, 199–200; and law of human behavior, 223–24
Heidbrieder, Edna, 232 n.
Hejira, 130 n.
Helleiner, K. F., 191 n.
Hellman, Geoffrey T., 354
Helmholtz, Hermann, 229

Hemingway, Ernest, 308
Henry VIII, marriages of, 202
Herculaneum, 221
Herndon, William, 341
Herodotus, 149 n., 244; "Father of History," 47–48; Longinus on, 49; his style, 50; his moralism, 56; a social scientist, 218; and biology, 218 n.; how to cite, 315
Hero(es) : in Carlyle, 189; people as the, 198; Cromwell as, 202; Daniel Boone as, 209; urban man as, 209; Davy Crockett and Johnny Appleseed as, 210; Lincoln and Lee as, 212
Herschel, Sir William, and fingerprinting, 230 n.
Higham, John, 45 n., 242 n.
Hildreth, Richard, as social historian, 244
Historian(s) : of hobbies, 8; as generalist, 15, 18, 77, 173; as biographer, 16; as literary critic, 16–17; many-sided tasks of, 16; as researcher, 16; scientific, 16, 49, 55, 57, 171, 207–08, 349; scale of enterprise of, 17; Chinese symbol for, 47, 49 n.; desire to influence events, 53; decries present-mindedness, 53; diverse aims of, 54; as Christian apologist, 56; states assumptions, 60–61; uses imagination, 61–62; must give proof, 101–02; raises and settles doubts, 107; and skepticism, 128; intellectual pose of, 144; not improviser, 154; enlarges the past, 162; as "single competent witness," 167; sees man as unity, 172–73; judges pragmatically, 173; gives form to events, 176; measures time, 176; Woodrow Wilson on, 184; systematic, 187 ff.; of progress, 190, 192 (fig.); American and European compared, 196–216; in Europe, 196–205; in America, 205–11; as evolutionist, 227; differs from social scientist, 238 ff., 243–44; his motives, 242; uses social sciences, 243–45; W. Douglass on, 251; Macaulay as social, 270–71; literary, 349
Historical and Critical Dictionary, 57
Historiography: in China, 46, 49 n.; in Greece, 47–48; defined, 49, 50 and n.; as detective work, 54;

416

U.S. government documents, 92 n.; computers and, 96; role of, and form, 377; how to prepare, 377–78; suitability of, 378–79
Index Translationum, 75
India, lack of history of, 46
Indian, American, 212 n.
Individual, in history, 139, 234
Industrial Revolution, 183, 190; H. Heaton on, 209 n.; R. B. Morris on, 209 n.; in American history, 211–12; and statistics, 225
Information storage and retrieval, MEDLARS, 96 n.
Inscriptions, 148 (fig.); deciphering, 170
Institutions, as relics, 148 (fig.)
Interest: in history writing, 133; through partisanship, 150; as source of objective judgment, 167, 183; dictates selection, 175; distinguished from bias, 180; cannot be eliminated, 184–85; ends in bias, 187
Interviewing, 64; in sociology, 234
Italics: a form, 256; in translation, 330; in footnotes, 342
Italy: a royal marriage in, 160–61; W. K. Hancock on history of, 184; unification of, 201

Jackson, Andrew, 14, 73 n.; and labor movement, 82; A. Kendall and, 123 n.; Bancroft supports, 207
Jacobins, 98; club membership, 178 and n.; Brinton on, 246
Jacobites, 202
James II, of England, 270
James, Henry: biography of, 61; speech habits of, 166–67
James, William: on history, 10; and pragmatism, 172 n.; quoted, 230, 284, 377 (fig.); on psychology, 232
Japan: "opening" of, 68; war on China, 162–63
Jargon: examples of, 137, 281 (fig.), 285 ff.; "subjective" and "objective," 165; avoidance of, 280; modern currency of, 284, 302, 306; defined, 285; Gowers on, 286; and pseudo-jargon, 286; ostentatious, 287; and S. Johnson, 287; from science, 311 (fig.)
Jefferson, Thomas, 14, 81 n., 112, 214, 345, 358 n.; birth date of,

130, 144; as President, 132; and history writing, 209
Jesus Christ, 117, 309
Jevons, William Stanley, 231
Joan of Arc, 13, 86
Johnny Appleseed, 210
Johnson, Lyndon B., on Lincoln, 53
Johnson, Samuel, 258, 287
Johnson, Thomas H., 91
Jones, John Luther (Casey), 210
Jordan, Elizabeth, 167
Judgment: grounds for, 155; nature of critical, 155, 159; in history writing, 172–73

Kansas-Nebraska Bill, 106–07
Kardiner, Abram, 246
Keats, Charles, 84 n.
Keats, John, 140, 373
Kendall, Amos: named as Public Man, 123; characteristics of, 123–24; in "Kitchen Cabinet," 123 n.; not Public Man, 124
Kendall, J. E., 124
Kendall, Paul Murray, 156 n.
Kennan, George F., 345
Kennedy, John F.: assassination of, 14, 151–53, 160 n.; as reader, 52
Keynes, John Maynard, 238
Kinsey, Alfred C., 245, 246 n.
Knight, G. Wilson, 233
Knox, Ronald, on translation, 329
Koerner, James D., quoted, 308
Konkle, Burton Alva, 91
Krieger, Leonard, 45 n., 242 n.
Krock, Arthur, quoted, 279

La Bruyère, J. F. de, 104
Laboratory work, 23 n.
Lamarck, Jean-Baptiste (Monnet), 220; on evolution, 226; and De Vries, 231
Lamartine, Alphonse de, on history, 53
Landor, Walter Savage, 140
Langer, William L., 91
Language: embodies history, 11, 255, 277 n.; as relic, 148 (fig.); and facts, 247–48; English and American, 325; French deceptively like English, 327, 332; see also Linguistics; Translation; Writing
Law, Roman, study of, 170
Lawrence, T. E., 373; on documents, 50–51
Layard, Austen H., 3, 221
Lazarsfeld, Paul F., on training sociologists, 235

Le Bon, Gustave, 234
Le Sage, Alain-René, 206 n.
League of Nations, documents relating to, 139
Lee, Robert E., 212
Lefebvre, Georges, quoted, 97
Legends: visual, 12 (fig.); their investigation, 116–19
Lenin, N., 212
Letters: autograph, signed, 77 and n.; editing, 104, 112–15, 378; written for posterity, 147 n.; as relics, 148 (fig.); as records, 157–59
Letters of Junius, 14
Lévi-Strauss, Claude, 245
Lévy, Michel, 114
Liberalism, 16, 181, 183; in partisan history, 198
Libraries: contents of, 5; research in, 23 and n.; catalogue cards in, 23–24, 64–65, 67–74, 70 (fig.); puzzles in, 60; as repositories of facts, 64 ff.; kinds of, 64–65; use of, 64 ff.; reference section in, 65; rate of growth of, 65–66; "microfiche," 66–67; "ultra-microbook" and, 66–67, 66 n.; topical classification in, 69 and n.; open shelves in, 70; call numbers in, 72; book classification in, 72–73; and interlibrary loans, 89; repositories of controversies, 129; research in Europe's, 197, 204; see also Library of Congress
Library of Congress: standard card system of, 64 and n., 65, 72; contents of cards, 70 (fig.); printed catalogue, 75, 90; as repository, 90
Life magazine, 8, 64
Lincoln, Abraham, 12 (fig.), 91, 106, 120, 296; assassination of, 13, 160 n.; L. B. Johnson on, 53; inauguration anecdote, 121; attending opera, 122; and Public Man, 122; quotable remarks of, 125; on Declaration of Independence, 133; as national hero, 212; first inaugural address, 313–14; and Ann Rutledge, 340
Lincoln Memorial, book on, 59
Linder, Staffan B., 246
Linton, Ralph, 245
Literalism: in quoting, 141–42; in translating, 329 ff.
Literature: critic of, as historian, 16–18; as history, 45 and n., 46;

as relic, 148 (fig.); English, 199; displaced by science, 241
Linguistics, 218; and history, 192; rise of, 222–23; Aryan tongue, 223; language defined, 247 and n.; and tradition, 293
Lives (Plutarch), 52
Livy, in tradition of Herodotus, 56
Locard, Edmond, 230 n.
Locke, John, psychology of, 219, 232
Loesser, Arthur, 74
Logic: in research, 59; in reasoning, 139; in writing, 292 n., 296, 305
Lokken, Roy N., 126 n.
Loliée, Frédéric, 160 n.
Lombard Street, 73
Lombroso, Cesare, 230 n.
Lonely Crowd, The, 245
Longinus, praises Herodotus, 49
Look magazine, 8
Louis XIV, 315; Spengler on, 195; Voltaire on, 198
Lowe, David G., 66 n.
Luce, Clare Boothe, her illness, 100–01, 101 n.
Lucian, Plato, and Greek Morals, 317
Lucretius, 192 (fig.)
Lusitania, last cargo of, 77
Luther, Martin: in Hegel, 189–90; as hero, 202
Lybyer, A. H., 119
Lyell, Charles, 222
Lynd, R. S. and H. M., as historians, 244–45

Macaulay, Thomas Babington: on composition, 175; on Thucydides, 175, 180; as "Whig historian," 181; and History of England, 181, 270, 271 n.; appraised, 181 n.; view of England, 183; as social historian, 244; on form, 258 ff.
Machiavelli, Niccolò, 338, 373
MacLean, Donald Duart, 278
McMaster, John Bach, on American uniqueness, 208
Macmillan, Harold, 52
McNeill, William H., 195 n.
Magazines: and research, 8; as sources, 121
Magnalia Christi Americana, 205
Mahan, Alfred T., 353
Malone, Dumas, on Jefferson's letters, 112
Malthus, Thomas, 22, 192 (fig.); in-

Monumenta Germaniae Historica, 199
Moon, R. O., 335–36
Morris, Gouverneur, 94
Morris, Richard B., 91; on bankruptcy records, 209 *n.*
Morrison, A. S. W., 335 *n.*
Morse, S. F. B., 123
Mortimer, Raymond, quoted, 154
Motives: historical, 130; psychological, 130; insight into, 138
Motley, John Lothrop, 211, 323
Mowry, George, 246
Mumford, Lewis, 373
Murray, J. A. H., 81
Music: social history of, 74; and musicology, 114; and nationalism, 114
Musicology, as history, 9
Musset, Alfred de, 140
Mussolini, Benito, 112 *n.*, 204 *n.*, 349
Muzzey, David Saville, 354
Myers, Gustavus, 344
Myrdal, Gunnar, 245
Myth(s), 108 and *n.*, 109, 117–19, 236, 247

Nagel, Ernest, 171 *n.*
Names: and seeking identities, 85–86, 85 *n.*; English, 86 *n.*; verification of, 102 and *n.*, 103, 104
Napoleon I, 12 (fig.), 15, 105, 288; in Hegel, 189; in Egypt, 220, 222
Napoleon III, 15
Narrative, as historical form, 176–77
National Trust for Historic Preservation, 10
National Union Catalog, 75, 90 and *n.*
Nationalism, 15; in history, 51; and music, 114; as a faith, 197; in historiography, 197 ff.; growth of, 198; in American history, 207
Natural rights, system of ideas, 133
Nebuchadnezzar, 52
Negro in American History, The, 212 *n.*
Nevins, Allan, 345 *n.*, 355
New Christianity, 224
New Deal, the, 212
New Freedom, The, 214
Newspapers, 151, 157; and sense of past, 11; indexes to, 84, 87; in research, 87 and *n.*; as reference source, 89–90; on computers, 95;

and reductionism, 141 and *n.*; colonial, 206 *n.*; how to cite, 343
Newton Demands the Muse, 371
Newton, Isaac, 88 and *n.*, 219, 233
Nicolson, Marjorie, 371
Nietzsche, Friedrich, 192 (fig.), 233; his ideas, 132; on Eternal Recurrence, 143
Nineveh, 3 *n.*, 221
Nixon, Richard M., 11, 84–85
Nock, Albert Jay, 358 *n.*
Notebook, users of, 26 and *n.*, 27
Notetaking, 23; methods of, 25–32; practice of eminent historians, 26 and *n.*; E. W. Dow on, 26 *n.*; discipline in, 28; requires thought, 28–29; mechanical, 29 *n.*; by paraphrasing, 29–30; sample of, 29 ff.; abbreviations in, 31; indexing, 31–32; selectivity in, 31; symbols for clarity, 31; on reference works, 79; and classification, 88; from newspapers, 88; value of system, 262; arrangement after, 264 ff.; results subdivided, 265
Novel (form): resembles history, 9; English and Continental, 15; length, 20–21; factuality, 48
Novum Organum, 385 *n.*
Nowell-Smith, S., 167
Nugent, Thomas, 330
Numismatics, 24, 311, 337 *n*; and history, 115; coins as records, 148 (fig.), 149

Objective: meaning of, 164–65; not synonymous with "true," 165; examinations, 165 *n.*
Oman, Charles, 26 *n.*
Optimism, in history writing, 191
Oral History Center, 147 *n.*
Order, *see* Arrangement
Origin of Species, The, 132–33, 226
Origins, determination of, 210
Orosius, 56
Orwin, C. S., 51
Osborn, A. S. and A. D., 150 *n.*
Outline: not compulsory, 265; for verifying order, 265; to find flaw, 266–67
Oxenford, John, 335
Oxford English Dictionary on Historical Principles, 18, 81

Page, Evelyn, 126 *n.*
Pagination, of manuscript, 368–69

423

Salter, Clavell, 319
Samoa, symbol of primitive, 236
Savigny, Friedrich, 222
Scammon, Richard M., 92
Schapiro, Meyer, 373
Schliemann, Heinrich, excavates Troy, 221
Science, 37; and history, 55, 147, 170–71, 207–08, 218; in periodicals, 76 n.; computers and, 97–98; applied to documents, 156; impermanent, 173; order not automatic, 175; in modern world, 183; of man, 217, 220; its two meanings, 217; applied to Marxism, 223–24, 223 n.; as positive knowledge, 224; studies society, 224; combats theology, 229; and society, 236, 240; mental risks of, 238; history of, 241; international vocabulary of, 325–26; footnotes in, 350; papers on, 350; and poetry as subject, 371
Scott, Walter, teaches Europe history, 57
Scott-Moncrieff, C. K., translator of Stendhal, 332
Sculpture: as history, 9; writing resembles, 23; as record, 148 (fig.)
Sea Around Us, The, 20, 22
Sears, Paul B., on ancient irrigation, 13
Second World War, 6, 11, 48, 53, 84, 167, 214
Selection, *see* Pattern
Self-awareness: in research, 60; in dealing with ideas, 133; in controlling bias, 180; measurement of, 183; for good writing, 276; in revising, 359
Sellar, W. C., 51
Sentences: faulty, 34–36, 39; topic, 273; euphony in, 279–80; overabstraction in, 279–80; rhythm in, 294, 299–300, 308–09, 312, 313; characteristics of, 295 ff.; relation of, to words, 296–97; undefinable, 296–98; must move, 297; contents *vs.* meaning, 298; first rule governing, 298–99; emphatic places in, 299–300; tone of, 299–300; periodic, 300; rules of thumb for, 300, 306–08; linkage in, 301; parallel construction in, 301 ff.; 306; when to omit, 303–04; cobbled, 307–08; speed, 307, 309; antece-

dents of pronouns, 311 (fig.); many tones possible, 312 ff.; embodying quotation, 318–19; turning foreign into English, 331; final revision of, 361
Seward, William H.: and Public Man, 122, 125; and Lincoln's first inaugural address, 313–14
Sex: and evolution, 227; acclimated by Freud, 233; in Kinsey's work, 246 n.
Shafer, Burr, 12 (fig.)
Shakespeare, William, 86, 117, 156, 211, 292, 329; sonnet quoted, 192; criticism of, quoted, 305
Shaw, George Bernard, 49
Shelley, Harriet, 137–38
Shelley, Percy Bysshe, 137–38
Sicily, invasion of, 167
Sinclair, John, coins term "statistical," 225 n.
Sister disciplines, *see* Social sciences
Skepticism: in verifying, 106 ff.; value of, 128; against history, 160, 161; misplaced, 163 and n., 184; and evidence, 153–54
Smiles, Samuel, 323
Smith, Adam, 222, 231
Smith, Alfred E., 360
Smith, Denis Mack, on Garibaldi, 29
Smith, Captain John, 205
Smith, Minna Steele, 335 n.
Smith, Sydney, on errors, 360
Social sciences, 72, 218 ff., 236, 241 n.; in European history, 204; origins of, 219; history and, 242–43; examples, 244; *see also* under their several names
Socialism: Utopian, 15, 110–11; in partisan history, 197; and race, 223; Christian, 224; *see also* Marx, Karl
Socinianism, 198
Sociology, 16, 218 ff., 224; in Montesquieu, 219; Durkheim on, 233; impetus to, from Hegel, 223; "laws" of, 233; proper study of, 233; Franklin H. Giddings on, 234; method of, 234; and other disciplines, 234; E. A. Ross on, 234; Lester Ward on, 234; P. Lazarsfeld on, 235 and n.; and the university, 235, 243; R. K. Merton on, 237; modern theory of, 237; historical method in, 243–44; in numerous historians, 244–45; critique

428

A	0
B	1
C	2
D	3
E	4
F	5
G	6
H	7
I	8
J	9

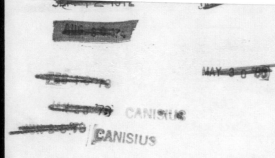